Brezhnev and the Decline of the Soviet Union

Leonid Brezhnev was leader of the Soviet Union from 1964 to 1982, a longer period than any other Soviet leader apart from Stalin. During Brezhnev's time Soviet power seemed at its height and increasing: space missions, rising living standards at home, a strong foreign policy reach into all parts of the world including south-east Asia, South Asia, Africa and the Middle East, the equal of the United States as a nuclear power. Yet, as this book, which provides a comprehensive overview and reassessment of Brezhnev's life, early political career and career as leader, shows, the seeds of Soviet decline were sown in Brezhnev's time: huge over-commitment of resources to the Soviet industrial-military complex and to massively expensive foreign policy overstretch, a consequent failure to deliver on citizens' rising expectations in other areas of the economy, and an over-confident ignoring of dissidents and their demands. The book will be of great interest to Russian specialists, and also to scholars of international relations and world history.

Thomas Crump was Lecturer in Anthropology at the University of Amsterdam 1972–1994 and is the author of twelve books.

D1568490

Routledge Studies in the History of Russia and Eastern Europe

Brezhnev and the Decline of the Soviet Union

Thomas Crump

 Routledge
Taylor & Francis Group

LONDON AND NEW YORK

First published 2014
by Routledge
2 Park Square, Milton Park, Abingdon, Oxfordshire OX14 4RN

and by Routledge
711 Third Avenue, New York, NY 10017

First issued in paperback 2016

Routledge is an imprint of the Taylor & Francis Group, an informa business

British Library Cataloguing in Publication Data
A catalogue record for this book is available from the British Library

Library of Congress Cataloging in Publication Data
Crump, Thomas, author.
  Brezhnev and the decline of the Soviet Union / Thomas Crump.
     pages; cm. — (Routledge studies in the history of Russia and Eastern
     Europe ; 17)
  1. Brezhnev, Leonid Il'ich, 1906–1982.   2. Soviet Union—Politics and
  government—1953–1985.   3. Soviet Union—Foreign
  relations—1953–1975.   4. Soviet Union—Foreign
  relations—1975–1985.   I. Title.   II. Series: Routledge studies in the
  history of Russia and Eastern Europe ; 17.
  DK275.B7C78 2013
  947.085'3—dc23
                                                            2013015812

ISBN 13: 978-1-138-68734-9 (pbk)
ISBN 13: 978-0-415-69073-7 (hbk)

Typeset in Times New Roman
by RefineCatch Limited, Bungay, Suffolk

Contents

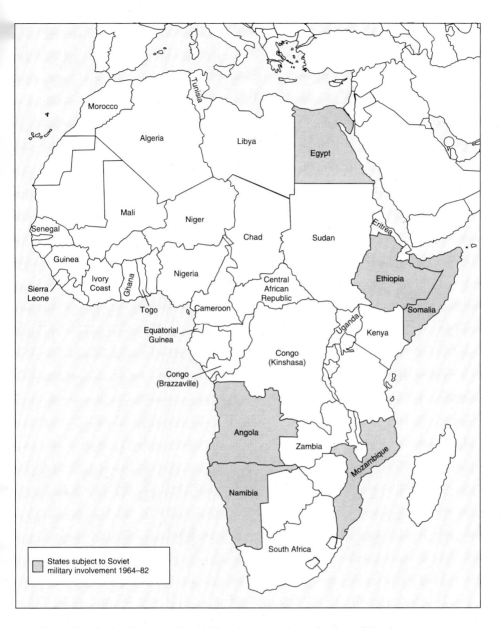

Map of the Soviet Union and its neighbouring countries at the time of Brezhnev

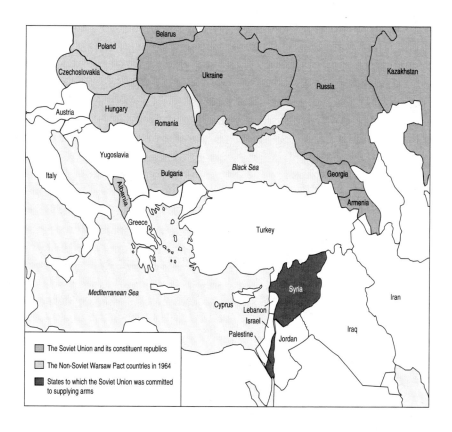

The Soviet Union and its constituent republics

The Non-Soviet Warsaw Pact countries in 1964

States to which the Soviet Union was committed to supplying arms

Foreword

By The Rt Hon Lord David Owen,
Uk Foreign Secretary (1977–1979)
during Brezhnev's tenure

The fascination of this book is that while focused on Leonid Brezhnev's life from 1906–1982 it is set in the complex history of Russia as it developed into the Soviet Union. As someone who as Foreign Secretary met him when President in the Kremlin in the autumn of 1977, I can attest – despite his then ill health – to his personal significance in that history. His is a life more than usually representative of the era in which he lived. He was grounded in industry, agriculture, the Communist Party and in the Army from being surprise-attacked in the Ukraine in 1941.

I have decided in this (Foreword/Review) to bring out from the historical opening chapters those crucial steps which brought Brezhnev to prominence. I do this, unusually, because they are not well known and in my view hold the key to analysing his later successes and failures.

His first job was in the foundry where his father worked as a Russian who had arrived in Kamenskoye on the River Dnepr in the Ukraine part of Imperial Russia. An assiduous student, Leonid went to the Management Technical School in Kursk after which, in 1926, he became an agricultural surveyor. In 1927 he was sent to Bielorus and later Sverdlovsk. In 1929, at the first opportunity, he joined Konsomol the party's youth and in 1931 became a full member.

Nikita Khruschev arrived in the Ukraine as General Secretary of the Party in 1938 and recalled in 1963 that he had appointed the young Brezhnev as provincial secretary at Dnepropetrovsk. When the Great Patriotic War, as it is still referred to today in Russia, was started by Hitler, attacking without any warning on 22 June 1941, the Germans made rapid progress and the Ukrainian capital, Kiev, fell on 16 September. Nikita Khrushchev, the Party boss in the Ukraine, escaped to Moscow.

Brezhnev was responsible for evacuating heavy machinery, skilled workers and getting in all-important harvests. Besides which he arranged to evacuate his wife, children and family. He then became a political commissar in the Soviet 18th Army on the fourth Ukrainian Front retreating in the face of the Germans along the Black Sea to the port of Novorossiisk which fell on 6 September. Here he was awarded the First Order of the Red Banner. He was promoted to Major-General on 2 November 1944. He fought as a military commander, not a politician, in Czechoslovakia, a country he grew to love and which later, in 1956, posed a fundamental challenge to his leadership.

Brezhnev was at the victory parade in Moscow on 8 May 1945 and, more significantly thereafter, at Stalin's victory banquet. He now had another expertise – the military – to add to industry, farming and the Party. As First Secretary of the Party in Zaporozhye after the war, a manufacturing city for aluminium and ferro-alloys with the large Lenin Denpr Hydropower station, he had a huge task. He and Khrushchev, back in charge of the Ukraine, had to bring in equipment from all over the Soviet Union to restore the ruins of battle and the 40% of assets and wealth that had been lost during the war. From 1950 to 1952 he became First Secretary of the Moldavian Communist Party and impressed Stalin. He also had additional responsibilities in both the Soviet Army and Navy. He became an alternate member of the Presidium, a new body of 25 created by Stalin to replace the Politburo.

By the time of Stalin's death in 1953 Brezhnev had risen fast and Khrushchev was recognised as his 'krysha' or roof. In the coup against Beria organised by Khrushchev and Malenkov in July 1953 it was a special detachment from the armed forces led by Marshal Zhukov with, interestingly, Brezhnev alongside him that took Beria into custody, with the standard presidium bodyguard provided by the NKVD not reacting. On 18 December Beria was sentenced to death and shot.

In February 1954 Brezhnev was appointed second secretary to the party in Kozakhstan and promoted First Secretary in August to manage Khrushchev's virgin lands policy, an anathema to Malenkov and Molotov.

On 25 February Khrushchev made in secret his famous, four-hour speech, denouncing almost every action during Stalin's rule. A speech that Mikhail Gorbachev later recalled was a huge political risk. When Malenkov, Molotov and Kaganovitch tried to oust Khrushchev in June 1957, the Party's Central Committee was mobilised against the presidium and Marshal Zhukov was key in identifying the three as complicit with Stalin while exempting Khrushchev. Malenkov went away to be the manager of a hydro-electric plant in Kazakhstan. Meanwhile Brezhnev was brought back to Moscow from having delivered, or appeared to have done so, four successful harvests to be Deputy Chairman of the Central Committee of the CPSU. He was never again away from the centre of power for 25 years. He was part of the Moscow 'nomenklatura'.

As the leading academician A.A.Arzumanyan who had worked with Brezhnev in the war years said "You don't need to teach this man anything as far as the struggle for positioning and power is concerned." He was popular, approachable, always helping to promote and decorate colleagues and, unlike Khrushchev, he never threatened the nomenklatura.

Brezhnev was appointed Chairman of the CPSU in 1960 and already Khrushchev's hypomanic personality was making it hard for colleagues to work with him. On his 70th birthday on 17 April 1964 he found shortcomings in all the potential candidates to succeed him and even Brezhnev was "not suited." In July his abusive behaviour and lack of control at a plenum of the Central Committee was the writing on the wall. By October Brezhnev emerged seamlessly as the new 'vozhd' or leader with the help of Mikhail Suslov and together, with men like Kosygin and Podgorny, the future was set. Podgorny became Head of State, but for reasons of *realpolitik* never challenged Brezhnev. Kosygin remained Chairman of the Council of Ministers until his death in December 1980 but his power declined steadily through the 1970s. Initially Kosygin concentrated on economic reform started by Khrushchev while Brezhnev focused on trade with the West and exports. Trade doubled with West Germany over the years before Ostpolitik. Andropov, as head of the KGB, was consistently supported by Brezhnev and succeeded him when Brezhnev died in 1982.

In Chapter 5 on nuclear weapon and Chapter 6 on dissidence and human rights there is much food for thought. Particularly in building understanding of the importance to the West of the Helsinki Final Act in 1975 covered in Chapter 9. Chapter 7 covers the Brezhnev Doctrine which he stated on 3 August 1968 in the Slovak capital of Bratislava. "Each Communist Party is free to apply the principles of Marxism-Leninism and socialism in its own country, but it is not free to deviate from these principles if it is to remain a Communist party ... The weakening of any of the links in the world system of socialism directly affects all socialist countries, and they cannot look indifferently upon this." Ostpolitik is also covered in this Chapter.

Chapter 8 is on US Presidents and the nuclear arms race; Chapter 9 on the mixed blessings brought by Brezhnev's new German friendships and the aftermath of Helsinki. Chapter 10 covers Brezhnev's blind spots, Africa and the Middle East. Chapter 11, South and Central Asia and is subtitled the challenge that Brezhnev could not ignore. As far as Afghanistan is concerned I believe it was possible to have refused pressure from the military to start a three day airlift on 24 December 1979 of Soviet forces to the Bagram airbase outside Kabul. The actual decision was taken two weeks earlier at a meeting of the Politburo with Brezhnev, a sick man, in the chair. Chapter 12 covers the confrontation with China and in the final Chapter 13 the 'why's and wherefore's' about the fall of the Soviet State.

As so often in this book the author, with astuteness and historical perspective, asks all the right questions. To me, perhaps because I am at heart a doctor of medicine and have written about *In Sickness and in Power* I believe the answer lies, above all, in the ill health of the country's leader, Brezhnev. He was dependent towards the end increasingly on tranquilizers and was not fit to govern in 1977 when I met him. His was a record of economic stagnation or 'zastoi.' Had he been replaced then by Andropov, the reformists, who were predominantly in the KGB, might have had an effect. Andropov's health only deteriorated later in office and he was responsible for one of the most important changes, the unprecedented emigration of Jewish people. But the 'ifs of history' are legion.

The ideology of Soviet Communism was fundamentally flawed and it was always going to crack. It eventually did so in 1989 with the fall of the Berlin Wall, a Brezhnev legacy from Khrushchev and itself rooted in Stalinism.

July 2013

Preface

This book, focussed on the Soviet leader Leonid Brezhnev (1906–1982), is my third study of the historical legacy of a head of state, presented in the light of the circumstances underlying his rise to that position, as well as what he did once he attained it. In the case of Abraham Lincoln, the title of my book, *Abraham Lincoln's World* (Continuum 2009), makes this explicit; in that of the Showa Emperor of Japan (misleadingly still known to many as Hirohito), my title, *The Death of an Emperor* (Constable 1990, OUP 1991), defines the occasion that led to my book – and any number of others – being written, but tells little about its contents. In the case of these two books, my main qualification as an author was to be found in the time spent, the places visited, and the people encountered in, on one side, the United States, and on the other, Japan. I know both countries from one end to the other. This was critical because neither Lincoln nor the Showa Emperor had any essential concern beyond that for the future of his own country. At the same time neither was much concerned with his own public image: the welfare of the people they served counted for far more. This is not how Brezhnev will be remembered, as became abundantly clear to me in writing this book.

I never came to know the Soviet Union as well as I know the United States or Japan – or for that matter quite a number of other countries worldwide. Brezhnev, however, in complete contrast to Lincoln and the Showa Emperor, was a man who wanted to be a major actor on the world stage – and to a considerable extent succeeded in being so. A man of extreme vanity, he lived for the headlines, which in a newspaper like *Pravda* were almost written, when occasion required, at his dictation. He had the pretension not only to make history, but to write it; his three volumes of autobiography were of no use to me, however, since their story ends some ten years before he succeeded Khrushchev as First Secretary of the Soviet Communist Party. Published in the mid-1970s, when Brezhnev was at the height of his power, they were immediately taken up in the Russian literature syllabus of Soviet high schools, along with Tolstoy and Dostoyevsky. Although required reading, both teachers and pupils saw them – in the words of one man who was a schoolboy at that time – as 'ghost-written bull-shit'. (This was also what US President Ronald Reagan later thought of Brezhnev's letters, although 'crud' was the word he used).

In my relatively short time in the Soviet Union I did once actually see Brezhnev, but only as one of the dignitaries standing on the roof of Lenin's tomb on the occasion of the annual May Day Parade in Moscow's Red Square. Outside Moscow I also visited St Petersburg (still known as Leningrad), Kiev, Dneprodzerzhinsk (Brezhnev's birth-place), Dnepropetrovsk, Odessa and Zaporozhye; I also travelled a fair distance by bus and train, while flying across the whole of Russia quite a number of times on the way to the Far East – often in near perfect weather – provided a good insight to its vastness, and indeed desolation. My informal contacts were surprisingly wide-ranging, including a breeder of race-horses, an orthodox nun, a KGB *rezident*, a Ghanaian student at the Patrice Lumumba University, bus-drivers, hotel concierges and any number of schoolboys – you name it. Such contacts, too numerous to mention, were generally much easier in East Europe outside the Soviet Union, where I visited almost every country – some more than once – in Brezhnev's time.

It also helped me enormously that I knew African countries such as Egypt, Ethiopia, Mozambique, Senegal and Somalia, in which Brezhnev was all too ready to see the Soviet Union involved, although he never visited any of them. The same is true of Israel (where my knowledge of Russian was surprisingly helpful in making contacts) and above all the Far East, where my understanding of such countries – critical, if not fatal, for Soviet foreign policy – as China and Korea, may be judged from my own book, *Asia-Pacific* (Hambledon-Continuum 2007).

As for my written sources, the bibliography and end-notes tell all that need be known, but I would like to note here how readable and informative are books written by major actors such as Henry Kissinger, Anatoly Dobrynin, Andrei Sakharov and, last but not least, Mikhail Gorbachev, who, too late in the day, had the vision, which, if it had been shared by Brezhnev, might just have arrested the decline which is the theme of this book. I doubt it, however: the system itself was simply too dysfunctional.

The events leading up to World War II and defined by the overwhelming ambition of Adolf Hitler, leading Nazi Germany on a path of almost unimaginable destruction, made me politically conscious at a very young age, and by the end of World War II, this meant coming to terms with Joseph Stalin's plans for a new world order. Although I began my own informal study of Russian – at the age of 14 – even before the war ended, I had to wait another five years odd before I actually saw any real Russians – not in the Soviet Union, but as a young British officer in Vienna in the days of the four-power post-war administration of the city, as was memorably portrayed in the film of Grahame Greene's *The Third Man*. Soviet soldiers, not particularly obtrusive, were then part of the scene: contact was impossible, even though, in civilian clothes, visits to their part of the city, were possible. My first actual visit to the Soviet Union had to wait until Khrushchev's day, more than ten years after my time in Austria. As the years passed I began to meet more and more people, of varying backgrounds, who, on the basis of their own experience, were able to tell me things about the Soviet

Union and its East European satellites which I would not have learnt otherwise. From this process, which after more than 60 years still continues, there are a number of names that I should like to mention in gratitude for the help they've given me: Dr Anna Alexandrova, Ms Svitlana Antipova, Ms Kateryna Bardadym, Prof. A.S. Besicovitch FRS, Mr Semyen Bykh, Ms Katya Cholerton (née Batushkova), Dr Richard Davy, Prof. Aleksandr Dvukhzhylov, Prof. Ernest Gellner FBA, Prof. Shlomo Goitein, Dr M.H. Khan, Adm. T.K. Khan, Ms Oleksandra Kozorog, Prof. Valentina Kravchenko, Prof. Stanislav Kulchytsky, Dr Olga Marshenko, Prof. Vojtech Mastny, Prof. Ruslan Medzhitov, Prof. Seweryn Ozdowski, M. Andrzej Potocki, Ms Jiřína Rybáčková, Mr Charles Smith, Mr Valentin Spirodonov, Mr Coen Stork, Mr Rogier van Tooren, Ms Olena Vlasenko, Ms Ella Voroshenko, Prof. Eric Wolf and Ms Cécile Yahuda.

Of these the oldest was born in 1891, the youngest in 1977; coming from Czechoslovakia, England, Ghana, Israel, the Netherlands, Pakistan, Poland, Russia and Ukraine, their number includes diplomats, journalists, museum curators, professors, senior service officers, students and teachers: common to almost all of them is the experience of involvement in the affairs of the Soviet Union, particularly in the days of Brezhnev. One or two have been friends for sixty odd years; others I know only by correspondence. Inevitably a number of those who helped me did not live to see the end of the Soviet Union, let alone the publication of this book. Lord Owen is a case apart: as UK Foreign Secretary during the last two years (1977–1979) of L.J. Callaghan's Labour Government he was constantly involved in Soviet affairs while Brezhnev was still at the height of his powers. I am most grateful to him for writing a foreword to this book (which contains an excellent summary of what I am trying to achieve). I doubt if any of all those who helped me would agree with all I say. I alone as author must answer for any errors and omissions; all I can say is that I have done my best to avoid them, and present an original and informative interpretation of what Vaclav Havel referred to as 'the gloomy grey ocean of the Brezhnev Soviet bloc'.

Finally, my daughter, Laurien – a professional historian teaching at the University of Utrecht – supported me during the whole time I was working on this book: I trust she will forgive me for not taking into account all her criticisms. We are not only of different generations, but also of different professions: as an anthropologist rather than an historian my starting point is that of an observer of people, places and everyday life. As I discovered when working as a 'chercheur scientifique' at the Maison des Sciences de l'Homme in Paris in the mid-1970s – in the days when Fernand Braudel was at its head – this is also true of many top-ranking historians of our day, so I need make no apologies.

Part I

Introduction

1   The Ukrainian crucible

The Brezhnev family at home

'The past is never dead. It's not even past' – William Faulkner

Kamenskoye, at the beginning of the twentieth century, was a growing industrial town on the right bank of the River Dnepr. Although its location, in the *oblast* of Yekaterinoslav, meant that it was part of Imperial Russia, the fact that the *oblast* was also part of Ukraine was critical in determining the character of the lives of those who lived there. For one thing, the majority were not Ukrainians, but Russians, recent arrivals who had come to the region to work in the new heavy industry born out of the Russian industrial revolution. One such Russian was Ilya Yakovlevich Brezhnev, who had arrived, with his newly married wife, Natalya, early in 1906. When they left home in the small Russian village of Brezhnevo, Natalya was already pregnant, and their first son, Leonid Ilyich, was born on 19 December 1906.[1]

In their early years in Kamenskoye Ilya worked as an unskilled labourer in a local iron foundry, but, while Leonid, his brother and sister, were still children, Ilya was promoted to become a rolling-mill operator. Kamenskoye was an urban sprawl, where – beyond the industrial centre with its vast foundries – modest wooden houses, known as 'izba', spread out along unmade-up roads, both along the Dnepr, and inland. Typical houses had their own plot of land, with space for kitchen gardens, orchards, and small enclosures for domestic livestock. In summer the street scene was colourful and animated. The trees would first be in blossom before bearing fruit, sunflowers would be in bloom, geese and other domestic fowl, to say nothing of the odd pig, would wander across the roads, where otherwise almost all traffic would be horse-drawn. In season, berries and mushrooms could be harvested from local commons and woodlands – where it was also possible to trap hares and wild-fowl (Kravchenko 1946: 10) – while fish were abundant in the great river, half a mile wide, and never far away. Above all peasant markets supplied the food – wheat, potatoes, meat and dairy products – essential for an urban population.

In winter the land was deep in snow, and the river frozen. A house was kept warm by a tiled wood-burning stove (Matthews 2009: 26),[2] livestock were sheltered in an outhouse, and there was also a store for food preserved for the winter to ensure a diet of bread, potatoes, cabbage and apples, supplemented by cheese, salted fish and different types of pork-sausage.[3] Drink, as also in the summer, was tea or beer according to the time of day, and this being Russia there was almost certain to be a bottle of homemade vodka (Brezhneva 1995: 5) kept in some dark corner of a house lit by oil lamps.

The foundry where Ilya worked – and where his sons would be employed – had to be built on a scale far larger than any house simply to contain the vast machinery needed for its operations: these, in turn, involved high levels of noise, heat, dust and fumes, for in Imperial Russia little was done to ensure the health and safety of the work-force.[4] Even so, the Brezhnev family enjoyed health and prosperity at a level notably higher than that of the rural population. Ethnic Russians were literate, and their children went to school. There was little contact between them and the country Ukrainians, who had not only their own language, but their own deviant version of the orthodox faith. Their agriculture – based largely on the cultivation of wheat – remained primitive, with little use of machinery, or other inputs such as artificial fertilizers; although essential both to the economy of Imperial Russia, and its export trade, it came nowhere close to realizing the productive potential of 'the breadbasket of Europe'.[5]

If a boy such as Leonid Brezhnev was to have anything like a wide historical perspective, he would have to take into account, on one side, the *longue durée* of a people who had been attached to the same land in Ukraine for centuries, and on the other, the relatively short history (lasting only a generation or two) of the urban Russian population. In the course of 1917, when Brezhnev was ten years old, the collapse of Imperial Russia in February – a result of continuous setbacks in the war against the so-called 'Central Powers' of Germany and Austria – and the success of Lenin's Bolshevik revolution in October,[6] marked the beginning of a turbulent four-year period (1917–1921) in which the interests of the urban Russians were pitched against those of the much more numerous rural Ukrainians. Inevitably the events of these four years shaped the lives not only of the Brezhnev family, but of almost the whole population of Ukraine. Critically for the future of Russia, the Brezhnev family – and not least, Leonid, the older son – came out as winners at a time when losers were much more numerous. In these four years, Leonid, who, in 1915, aged eight, had passed into secondary school,[7] began to find his direction in life. To understand how this happened, the historical background, first of Ukraine, and then of its urban Russian population, provides the key.

The long history of Ukraine

Ukraine is a vast area of land, very roughly rectangular, extending for 1316 km along its east-west axis (between 22° and 40° E.) and for nearly 893 km along its north-south axis (between 45° and 52° N.),[8] so that its total area is 603,700 square kilometres.[9] Situated between the much the same latitudes as France, in area Ukraine is some 9 per cent greater, while its population is some 16 per cent smaller:[10] being at the other end of Europe, its climate is continental, with warmer summers and much colder winters – as the invading German army, in World War II, discovered to its own cost at the end of 1941.

The topography of Ukraine is remarkably uniform. The characteristic landscape is defined by apparently endless steppe, with occasional woodlands scattered across it. From almost any high point, such as the top of the highest buildings in cities such as Kiev, Kharkov or Dnepropetrovsk, the overwhelming impression on any viewer is of arable farmland, cultivated in cereals, such as wheat or barley, and in certain western regions, sugar beet. The long Dnepr river, as it flows south to the Black Sea, divides Ukraine, with its capital Kiev, located on the west bank. Down river, this is also the location of other large towns, such as Dnepropetrovsk and Zaporozhye – and also Dneprodzerzhinsk (as Kamenskoye has been known since 1934), the home town of Leonid Brezhnev. The Dnepr is remarkably wide, with its rate of flow, and depth, varying considerably according to the season – with the peak occurring in the early summer as the winter snows melt in the vast catchment areas.

The great mass of the traditional population, consisting mainly of peasant cultivators, inhabiting hundreds of small, run-down villages, and speaking Ukrainian as their mother tongue, were subordinate, in one way or another, to other ethnic minorities: just which of these counted in any one village community depended largely on whether it was located on the left (East) or right (West) bank of the Dnepr. On the left bank, the landowners, with their countless serfs (only emancipated in 1861) tended to be Russian, on the right bank, Polish. Significantly also this division reflected the boundaries of the Pale of Settlement – which determined where Jews might live in Imperial Russia – so that most were to be found, on the right bank, where they were as numerous as in Poland itself.

For much of the seventeenth and early eighteenth centuries, the right bank of the Dnepr defined Poland's eastern frontier, although Kiev, and the area immediately surrounding it, always belonged to Imperial Russia. This was agreed between Imperial Russia and the Kingdom of Poland in January 1667 (Subtelny 1988: 146]. The southern parts of Ukraine, including the whole of the Black Sea coast, then belonged to Turkey. In the course of the eighteenth century, Turkey, after a succession of defeats in battle, lost to Imperial Russia all its land in Ukraine, a process that ended in 1783, with Catherine the Great formally declaring the incorporation of the Crimea. The result was that 'the steppe, which for millennia had been a source of danger for the sedentary populations that ringed it, [was] at last . . . made accessible to the peasant's plow' (ibid.: 176). For Russia and the Ukraine, that was only half the story: with Turkey no longer an obstacle to settling southern Ukraine, Russia was free to develop the northern coast of the Black Sea: in 1789, only seven years after the Turks had ceded their small fortress of Khadzhibei, the Empress Catherine the Great decreed that the city of Odessa be founded on the same site. This was sound policy, and within some 80 years proved to be even more so, when, with steamships already plying the Black Sea, the Russian railways (in 1866) reached Odessa: before the end of the nineteenth century it became the fourth largest city in Imperial Russia.

Poland

Imperial Russia, in the course of the eighteenth century combined with Austria and Prussia to eliminate the kingdom of Poland as an independent state. The process started in 1709 when the Russian emperor, Peter the Great, having won a decisive battle with Poland, incorporated all Ukraine into the Russian empire, taking 'the English subjugation of Ireland to be a fitting model' (Subtelny 1988: 165) for his rule. Two hundred years later, in 1914, Lenin, still in exile in Switzerland, noted that '[Ukraine] has become for Russia what Ireland was for England: exploited in the extreme and receiving nothing in return' (ibid: 269]. This is more or less true. Peter the Great forced Ukraine to export wheat via Russian ports such as Riga and St Petersburg,[11] at the same time not only forbidding export to Poland, but also – with a view to encouraging industry in Russia – subjecting imports from Poland to high excise duties (ibid.: 180). Although, in 1785, Catherine the Great granted a Charter of Nobility, providing for the Ukrainian *starshyna* to be incorporated in to the Russian *dvorianstvo*,[12] this only helped a small privileged minority. The broad mass of Ukrainian peasants were looked down upon by Russians in much the same way as the indigenous population of Ireland was looked down upon by the English: in both cases, the men of the soil were seen as too helpless to look after their own interests – while at the same time their unskilled labour could be exploited by the gentry and nobility.

Gaining the whole of Ukraine was not enough to satisfy imperial Russia under Catherine the Great. Poland, subject to a succession of weak governments was also up for grabs: as Catherine's contemporary, the Prussian Emperor, Frederick the Great, had observed, Poland should be 'eaten like an artichoke, leaf by leaf' (Lukowski 1999: 17).[13] While, Catherine and Frederick had no difficulty in agreeing to the piecemeal annexation of Poland, they considered it prudent to allow Austria to participate, so reassuring the Empress Marie Theresien that Russia had no plans to expand into the Balkans – which Vienna saw as a back-yard won from the Turks in the 1680s. In the event Austria jumped the gun, early in 1772, by annexing a small strip of Poland in the Carpathian mountains. As a result, neither Russia nor Prussia had any inhibitions about proceeding with their own plans, and in 1772, three bilateral treaties, signed by the representatives of Russia, Prussia and Austria, provided for the partition of a substantial part of Poland:[14] Russia advanced its frontiers to include almost the whole of the headwaters of the Dnepr, Prussia acquired the western part of Polish Prussia, and Austria, Galicia (which geographically was part of Ukraine).

Poland survived this first partition, but only at the cost of losing much of its population – which did, however, become more homogeneous, with a mainly Polish-speaking population adhering to the Roman Catholic Church. King Stanisław Augustus tried hard to come to terms with the new line-up, a task made more difficult by the tide of events in the world at large, with first the American victory over Britain in the war of independence (1776–1781), and second, the fall of the *ancien régime* in France (1789–1792). The prospect of Warsaw becoming a centre for revolutionary thought, if not action, was not a welcome one for the autocratic governments that were still intent on eating up Poland 'leaf by leaf'. Defiantly, the 'Great Sejm' (1788–1792) (as the Polish parliament was known) produced a new written constitution,[15] while at the same time approving the creation of a new 100,000-man army. True to form, conservative opponents among the nobility joined together to ask Catherine the Great to help overthrow the new constitution. Although the Poles, with a brilliant general, Tadeusz Kościuszko, commanding its army, fought hard for their independence, a decisive defeat by the Russians at Maciejowice in 1795, meant the end of independent Poland; a third and final partition divided what was left of the country between Russia and Prussia – and also Austria. Ukraine was indisputably part of Imperial Russia, with its territory extending further to the west than ever before. Prussia had become a significant European power, and Austria had added yet two more provinces to its empire.

The nineteenth century saw the emigration of hundreds of thousands of Poles and Ukrainians to the United States and Canada. In particular, Kościuszko's service in the War of American Independence meant that his cause, at home in Poland, was not forgotten, nor the injustices suffered by his people forgiven. This helped ensure that by the end of World War I, with the United States as one of the Allied Powers, the cause of Polish independence would be on their agenda for post-war Europe; after all, the three great powers which had partitioned the country in 1795 had all been defeated in the war.

Jews and the Pale of Settlement

This, however, is running ahead. It is time to look at one particular aspect of Poland and Ukraine, as they were during the centuries that preceded World War I: this was the presence of Europe's, if not the world's, largest Jewish population.[16] As early as the fourteenth century, King Casimir of Poland, with a view to strengthening his own hand against the nobility, encouraged Jewish immigration from the Holy Roman Empire, particularly to his capital, Kraków (Lukowski and Zawadzki 2001: 28). From the beginning Jews were only welcome, if at all, in towns, where by the seventeenth century – numbering more than 200,000 – they were the fastest expanding group (ibid.: 54). They were also more secure than anywhere else in Europe (Löwe 1993: 14).

As, in the course of time, Poland came to incorporate the whole of Ukraine west of the Dnepr, Jews became increasingly dominant in Ukrainian commerce. Allowed only to live in towns, they began to establish their own self-contained communities, known as 'shtetls'. Even in the towns which also had an indigenous Polish or Ukrainian population Jews had in the 'kahal' their own institution of local self-government (ibid.: 15). In any case Jews, among themselves, spoke their own language, Yiddish, and maintained their own religious institutions, such as notably the *yeshiva*, a college devoted to the study of their sacred texts.

At the same time the great landowners in the countryside blocked the growth of towns (Levine 1991: 253), regarding them as potential havens for fugitive serfs or as sites for markets beyond their control (ibid.: 259). Worse still, it was Jewish merchants and pedlars, who provided the vast army of serfs with access to a market economy – essential for earning the money for meeting fixed costs, such as rent and tithes, and buying such commodities as salt, wax, nails and cloth, and most critically, for the role of the Jews, beer and vodka (ibid.: 255). The leading gentry, intent on strengthening their own economic position, if necessary at the cost of the serfs, encouraged the growth of 'private' towns on their estates, and by ruling to ban Jews from the crafts of the 'old' towns outside the feudal domain, left many of them with little alternative but to seek their living in these 'new' towns; 'shtetls' were often the only alternative and there was a limit, both social and economic, to the number that could be founded (Löwe 1993: 86).

That Jews had to come to terms with the need to find a niche in a feudal society, also meant that the landowning nobility had to find a way of accommo-dating them. Their solution was to grant the Jews a monopoly of the local sale of alcohol – an institution known as the *'propinacja'* (Levine 1991: 251) combined with the right to collect, on a commission basis, rents, tolls and taxes. Although for Jews there was often little alternative to accepting this role – particularly in the 'new' towns – they were also at the same time traders and craftsmen, if on a very modest scale. Although, from the seventeenth century onward Poland, having been marginal in wars of religion, flourished as the 'breadbasket' of Europe (ibid.: 254), steadily deteriorating terms of trade for wheat in Poland's export market (ibid.: 257) meant that the *propinacja* had an additional advantage for large estates: distilling grain for local consumption became an increasingly profit-able alternative –[17] so much so that on one of the largest noble estates, that of the powerful Czartoryski family, it accounted for some 40 per cent of the harvest (Löwe 1993: 16).[18]

The results of the *propinacja* were disastrous for every class involved in it – which in the predominately agricultural economy of Poland meant substantially the whole population. Inevitably the peasants, particularly in Ukraine, who had been degraded into becoming a servile labour force blamed the Jews. If the Chmielnicki massacres of the mid-seventeenth century (Levine 1991:159) were the first major uprising directed against the Jews, they were by no means the last: pogroms occurred intermittently until the early twentieth century, with that in Odessa in 1905 attracting worldwide attention and condemnation. The lower levels of the landowning classes also resented the perceived economic advantage bestowed upon Jews by their role in the *propinacja*. At the end of the day, how-ever, the biggest losers were the noble families that had originated the institution. The whole system was designed to ensure the most inefficient and unproductive use of a vast extent of Europe's richest agricultural land; it is no wonder that Hitler coveted it, nor that, finally, he invaded the Soviet Union in 1941 to acquire it as *lebensraum* for German settlers. Critically, in the eighteenth and nineteenth centuries the great landowners also paid a price for their disastrous and short-sighted management of their estates: by 1914 they had lost half their land, with much of the rest mortgaged – ironically, in some cases, to Jewish bankers (Löwe 1993: 5). It is not for nothing that in Germany *Pölnische Wirtschaft* – or 'Polish economy' – connotes 'chaos'.

For Imperial Russia the final partition of Poland in 1795 did not mean that new land was 'made accessible to the peasant's plow'. The land gained from Poland had been ploughed by peasants for centuries. Even so, something had to be done about the Jews, who had otherwise scarcely a foothold in the Russian Empire. The solution was to define the so-called 'Pale of Settlement', which meant drawing a line across the map defining a vast area,[19] west of the line, open to Jewish settlement. Because this area coincided more or less with the land lost to Russia by Poland, there need not be, at least in principle, any change in the status of Jews.

In principle not in practice: rural Jews, except for those involved in the *propinacja*, were required to move to cities (Löwe 1993: 28). If, at first sight, hardly a radical reform – given how few Jews there were in this category – it did recognize the economic success attained by Jews in Western Europe during the earlier years of the eighteenth century – and as a mere matter of history, their families could only have come from Poland (or its 'Commonwealth' partner, Lithuania).

From the end of the eighteenth century Jews in Russia were only too conscious of the new prospects opening up for them – as witness, even in the first half of the nineteenth century, the many who emigrated to the new world, along with Poles, Ukrainians and any number of others no longer subjects of the Russian Empire. Part of the problem, from a Russian perspective, was assimilation.[20] Jews – among the best educated of all Russian subjects – could hardly be absorbed into an illiterate peasantry (Löwe 1993: 39), but to find a place in literate urban society they would have to learn Russian, a policy facilitated, if not encouraged, by new laws enacted during the reigns of the first two nineteenth century Tsars, Alexander I (1805–1825) and Nicholas I (1825–1855); the underlying motive was not so much to advance the interests of Jews, but to win their support in counteracting Polish unrest. With the death of Nicholas I in 1855, the way was open to the 'Great Reforms' of his successor, Alexander II, in the middle years of the nineteenth century. These were a reaction both to the Polish uprising of 1863, and to the imagined threat of a worldwide kahal, intended to mobilize expatriate Jewish populations to fight against Russia (ibid.: 48). The result was the emergence of a new class of liberal and secular Jews, permitted to live outside the pale. Because all those who had graduated from either gimnaziya[21] or universities belonged to this class, quotas were imposed on cities with substantial Jewish populations.[22] Even so, the rate of Jewish enrolment in both institutions was at four times the national average, which was, in any case, extremely low.[23] Alexander II's overriding principle, that Jews could be assimilated 'as far as their moral status allows'(ibid.: 40), meant that they could become lawyers and judges, who, together with other 'helpful Jews' – pharmacists, obstetricians and some 'guild' artisans, as well as the graduates – could live anywhere (ibid.: 41).

In the second half of the nineteenth century, when Imperial economic policy – largely for reasons of defence – was to catch up with Western Europe by investing in industry, the construction of railways across the vast expanse of Russia had the highest priority. Given the empire's critical shortage of capital, management and advanced technology, these key factors in production had to be sought outside: only unskilled labour, an essential factor in nineteenth century railway-building was abundant, with demand being largely satisfied by displaced serfs – emancipated across the whole empire (including Ukraine) by Alexander II in 1861 – and prisoners (Crump 2007b: 234). As for capital, however, and management know-how, the railway boom was a gift to foreign investors and Jews. Indeed one of the most valuable concessions went to the French Péreire brothers, who were also Jewish.[24] Having only built two of the four lines listed in the concession within the agreed time limit, the Péreire brothers pulled out at an enormous profit to themselves. The most successful scam, however, was that of Lev Poliakov, who having started his working life as a Jewish plasterer in Kiev (in the heart of Ukraine), made a fortune out of the concession for the Kozlov-Voronezh railway: it was no coincidence that when Count Tolstoy, the minister who had granted the concession, died, his estate included shares in Poliakov's company worth half a million roubles. It was not for nothing that one common argument used by the many opponents of modernization was that 'railways help the Jews' (Löwe 1993: 69). Inevitably their anomalous status encouraged corruption at every level, and not only in the railways.

To the extent that it was, by force of circumstance, accepted if not encouraged in nineteenth-century Russia, Jewish upward mobility, both social and economic, led inevitably to a growing number of relatively prosperous, Russian-speaking Jews. These were attracted not only to the cities outside the Pale, but also to the new cities within it, where the permitted quota – up to 10 per cent – was higher. Of these much the most important was the port city of Odessa, where by the end of the century Jews – constituting a third of the population[25] – had become dominant in the wholesale export trade in grain, which was still the mainstay of Ukraine's economy.[26] Indeed, in Imperial Russia, as much as later in the Soviet Union, the export of grain, at almost any cost, was seen as essential.[27] If the case of Odessa exemplifies how enterprising Jews were attracted to new centres of economic growth, the same was true, to a lesser degree, of the coal and steel towns of Ukraine, such as Kamenskoye, home to the Brezhnev family – or, for that matter, Yuzovka, where a rural family, the Khrushchevs, in 1907, came to work in the local coal mines. Because, in these towns, the perceived success of Jews in business was attributed to their exploitation of other resident communities (Klier 1992: 20) – not necessarily native Russian-speaking – they were all too often the scene of the pogroms that occurred in times of stress.

Historically, the result of the internal Jewish diaspora proved to be most signifi-cant outside Ukraine, particularly in present-day Russia. There are two reasons for this. First, the privileged status allowed to a minority of Jews strongly favoured the most enterprising, best educated and, often enough, most unscrupulous among them, so that in any city with a Jewish community its members were likely to share these attributes, with inevitable consequences for their place in society: no wonder then that this was often resented. Second, the conquest and occupation of the whole of Ukraine by German forces following Hitler's invasion of the Soviet Union in June 1941 meant that some 90 per cent of all Soviet Jews died in the holocaust (Snyder 2010: 342). The result, after the defeat of Nazi Germany in 1945, was that such Jews as did survive were to be found in those parts of the Soviet Union that were never overrun by the Germans. Particularly after the recognition of the new state of Israel by the United Nations in 1948, they came to constitute a well-educated, articulate, Russian-speaking community. What is more, being only too conscious of the fact that they had a home, not only in the Soviet Union, but outside it, they were seen as potentially subversive – as they had also been in the days of the Tsars. As shown in Chapter 9, this was something that Brezhnev had to come to terms with during his years as first secretary of the CPSU (Communist Party of the Soviet Union): the point to be made in this chapter is that in the small world of a clever, ambitious boy growing up in Kamenskoye, before, during and after World War I, Jews played a conspicuous and significant part.[28]

The industrial revolution

The industrial revolution came late to Imperial Russia, and when it did, its progress would have been impossible without considerable foreign investment – not only financial, but also in men and materials. In particular, the vast expansion of the railway network in the second half of the nineteenth century – strategically essential if Imperial Russia was to remain a great power on equal terms with Britain, France and Germany – depended upon the supply of iron and steel on an unprecedented scale. The need for modern armaments, also for strategic reasons, added very substantially to the demand. Critically, Imperial policy dictated that both railways and armaments were subject to state control. Significantly this meant that many of those entrusted to carry out this policy, such as Count Kleinmichel in the case of railways, were descendants of the Germans invited by Peter the Great to administer Imperial Russia at the beginning of the eighteenth century.[29]

As elsewhere, both in Europe and North America, the success of the Russian industrial revolution depended on finding abundant reserves or coal on one side, and iron ore on the other. Right in the centre of Ukraine, an area, defined, on the eastern side, by the coal seams of the basin on the Don river, known simply as 'Donbas', and on the western, by the iron ore in the land surrounding the town of Kryvyi Rih,[30] satisfied these criteria. The Dnepr separated these two areas so that, almost inevitably, much of Ukraine's new iron and steel based industry was located along the river.[31] The new railways, which, together with the armament industry, were the main users of steel – both for rails and rolling stock – ensured the transport of both coal and iron to the new foundries, such as those of Brezhnev's home town, Kamenskoye. Much of the Ukrainian countryside was transformed, so that '. . . it was not uncommon to see some of the biggest, most modern factories, mines and steel mills in Europe amidst villages where peasants still harnessed themselves to the plow and eked out a living from the land as they had for centuries' (Subtelny 1988: 265).

Once again, such transformation of the industrial landscape would have been impossible without foreign investment. This opened the door to new enterprise in the country's iron and steel industry, so that in 1870 the Welshman, John Hughes, sailed to the Ukraine with eight shiploads of equipment and around a hundred specialist ironworkers and miners. There his New Russia Company built a metallurgical plant and rail producing factory. For the work-force Hughes built a company town, Yuzovka – named after himself – complete with amenities, such as, on one side, an Anglican church for the British expatriates, and a Russian Orthodox church for men locally recruited.

At a time when some 87 per cent of all Russia's coal came from Donbas,[32] that needed for Hughes' New Russia Company was mined almost within the city limits, with a Russian work-force, recruited from far and wide, labouring in abysmal conditions at the pit-face, and consigned, outside the pits, to the lowest level of Yuzovka's working class society. The Russian steel-workers, on the other hand, ranked much higher, as did, to an even greater degree, the families belonging to the privileged and well-endowed British expatriate community (Taubman 2003: 31). Local Jews found their own niche as traders and craftsmen, attracting – as all too often happened – envy and mistrust as the reward for their contribution to the local micro-economy. After John Hughes' death in 1890, Yuzovka continued to flourish, and in the three years 1914–1917 that Russia was at war with Germany, the factories of the New Russia Company were major producers of artillery shells. This is significant, for Ukraine was home to only 15 per cent of Russian manufacturing, while, with its vast reserves of coal and iron, it counted for 70 per cent of all extractive industry (Subtelny 1988: 167).

The way mining and industry in Ukraine relied for the most part on Russian labour reflects a consistent government policy of encouraging emigration out of the Russian heartland – a policy later taken over by Stalin, who enforced it with appalling disregard for human rights. In the late nineteenth century this was what brought the Brezhnevs to Kamenskoye, and, a generation later, in 1908, the Khrushchevs (including 14-year old Nikita Sergeyevich) to Yuzovka.[33] Moreover, in the final days of Imperial Russia, with transport over both land and sea powered by steam, migration was not confined within the boundaries of the empire. This was particularly true of Ukraine so that Canada ended up with more than a million residents of Ukrainian descent, with the US not far behind. The result was that Ukraine acquired a considerable and independent *supporters' club* on the other side of the Atlantic. During his term of office as First Secretary of the CPSU this was a factor that Brezhnev found difficult to come to terms with, although this problem was almost nothing compared with that posed by the well-organized American Jewish community – many of whom also had Ukrainian ancestry.

If the picture, presented above, of the world of the young Brezhnev disregards the indigenous Ukrainian-speaking rural population, the reason is that this would have made relatively little impact upon him, or others like him. Although, for local residents, the great expanse of rich black soil would begin almost as soon as they left the built up area, this vast territory was effectively a 'no-go-zone'. Although Russians living in a town like Kamenskoye had little to seek in the surrounding countryside, the way of life of the millions of peasants living in wooden houses in countless villages, accessible only by rutted dirt roads – almost impassable during the spring thaw – was a factor that could not be left out of account in any overall plan to rationalize the Russian economy.

Rural Ukraine

Although in Imperial Russia there was never such a plan, life in the countryside in the half-century leading up to World War I was not entirely free from change. Events in the world at large, such as recounted above, did change peasant life. The most significant of these was the emancipation of serfs, throughout the empire, by Tsar Alexander II, in 1861. Critically this came at a time when former feudal estates could no longer survive as viable units in the world economy. Throughout the nineteenth century, large landowners, by force of circumstance, were selling, or at least mortgaging their properties, to the point that by 1914 they had lost more than half of their land (Löwe 1993: 5). At the same time agricultural labourers were leaving their ancestral villages to work in the new industrial and mining centres – such as Kamenskoye and Yuzovka. In spite of the abolition of serfdom, those who remained were ill-equipped to realize anything close to the full potential of their land. Forced to accept a transport infrastructure quite unsuited to modern times, and with means to farm efficiently far beyond their reach,[34] villagers had to survive on at best a small margin of production above subsistence level – liable to be lost entirely in a poor season. None the less in such dire straits some did better than others: in particular, there emerged a class of 'kulaks', consisting of peasants who had managed to acquire their own land – often helped by loans from local Jewish traders – from disintegrating local estates, to become dominant in their home villages. Where *kulaks* constituted 15 to 20 per cent of a village population, another 30 per cent were 'seredniaki', with the remainder seen as 'bidniaki' – a word derived from the Ukrainian *bidny*, meaning 'poor' (Subtelny 1988: 263). In villages organized in this way there was no clear-cut distinction between the classes, whose emergence, in any case, was historically very recent. Becoming a *kulak* was hardly the first step on a rags-to-riches road to wealth: even if rich from a local perspective, a *kulak's* income would be less than half an average city worker's wage (Yekelchyk 2007: 108]. At all events the dividing line between *kulaks* and the rest of a village population was by no means clear-cut. In a society intent on identifying a class of exploiters *kulaks* could fill the bill, but Jews, as classic aliens, were still more likely to be cast in this role. Moreover, in the last half of the nineteenth century, the emigration of some two million Ukrainians to the newly acquired Russian Far East (Subtelny 1988: 262), was an equally important factor in defining the structure of what remained of Ukrainian rural society.[35] In any case its defining characteristic, as in much of the rest of Imperial Russia, was always poverty, coupled with illiteracy, alcoholism and superstition. As the twentieth century dawned, this was hardly a base upon which to build a prosperous agricultural economy – even if it comprised some of the richest agricultural land in the world. Where, geophysically, rural Ukraine lacked nothing, socially and economically it was nowhere.

If the picture portrayed so far in this chapter is that of a rural society, destined to subsist at only the lowest levels of culture and education, this is more or less correct. At the beginning of the twentieth century Ukrainians were seen as no more than 'little Russians', and their language as just one of many Russian dialects. It was only in the 1830s that a small group of scholars in Kharkiv began to identify themselves as 'Ukrainians'. The imperial government reacted by making life for such people steadily more difficult, to the point that with the Ems *ukase* of 1876, Tsar Alexander II banned the publication and importation of all books in Ukrainian, together with the use of the language on the stage (Subtelny 1988: 44). At the same time, in Kyiv, the historic capital of Ukraine, the only Ukrainian language newspaper, the *Kieveskii Telegraf*, was shut down, together with the local branch of the Imperial Geographical Society after it had been accused, on little evidence, of being a front for Austrian subversion. Not surprisingly, many leading figures in Russia's popular revolutionary movements – such as that of the *narodniki,* active in the late nineteenth century – were ethnic Ukrainians. It did not help their cause that they were associated with the group that assassinated Tsar Alexander II in 1881. Indeed, this event was a major factor in blocking any worthwhile reform under his successors, Alexander III (1881–1894) and Nicholas II (1894–1917). All in all it is not surprising that when, in the course of 1917 (the eleventh year of Leonid Brezhnev's life), the established order was turned upside down, many of those in the Ukraine, even if they were ethnic Russians, contemplated a totally new society. This would only emerge, in any definitive form, in 1921. In the meantime Ukraine would enjoy – in the event hardly the right word – four years as an independent republic, with any number of different forces each fighting its own corner. This is the world in which Brezhnev completed his education, and decided – if the official records are to be believed – on the course that would define his future, and that of the country in which he was born.

World War I and Ukrainian independence

When Imperial Russia, allied with France, Britain and a number of lesser states, entered into World War I in August 1914, its industrial economy was at its peak. For families like that of the Brezhnevs in Kamenskoye this had meant several years of a steady, if modest rise in their standard of living. All this came to an end with Russia's entry into war. Millions were conscripted for military service, while industry – deprived of much of its labour – was committed to the manufacture of armaments on an unprecedented scale.[36] Worse still, in two years the tide of war had turned against Russia, and that a time when its allies were also achieving little success – whether against Germany on the western front, Austria in northern Italy or Turkey in Asia Minor.

With mutinies in the army, strikes in mining and industry, food riots on the streets (Abramovitch 1962: 12) and shortages of almost everything, the strain upon Russia was much greater, and by the end of February 1917, the state – no longer able to maintain law and order in St Petersburg – began to fall apart. Thousands of soldiers and civilians came on to the streets to demonstrate against Tsar Nicholas II, who at that time was at the army's general headquarters on the front line. A telegram he sent ordering the dissolution of the State Duma was ignored. Instead a provisional committee organized at the Tauride Palace, with the popular Alexander Kerensky[37] as its effective head, took over the government of Russia. At the same time the palace became home to a new 'Soviet', or council with both worker and soldier deputies claiming, with considerable justice, to represent the broad popular masses. The basic model derived from the councils of factory workers that emerged in 1905 to play a major part in the ultimately unsuccessful series of uprisings triggered by the massacre of hundreds protesting in front of the Winter Palace on 22 January, an event known to history as 'Bloody Sunday'. The prototype for the original 1917 Soviet was the short-lived *Saint Petersburg Soviet of Workers' Deputies*, a largely *Menshevik* group.[38] Set up by Leon Trotsky following a strike by railway workers on 8 October 1905, it organized a general strike, extending to 200 factories, in Saint Petersburg and Moscow. The scene was set for a power-struggle whose outcome would dominate both Russian and world politics almost to the end of the twentieth century.

Following the fall of the imperial government in February, the Tsar Nicholas II abdicated and the name of the capital city was changed to Petrograd.[39] Critically for the future of Russia, Kerensky's government continued the war against the Central Powers.

While all this was happening, Vladimir Ulyanov (1870–1924) – a dedicated revolutionary lawyer known to history simply as Lenin – was running the underground Social Democratic Party from Geneva, where he had lived in exile since 1907. There, as leader of the dominant Bolshevik wing of the party he had no purpose in life but to establish in Russia a revolutionary government organized according to the principles of the German political philosopher, Karl Marx, whose works he had studied intensively over a period of nearly 30 years.[40] Lenin's subversive and revolutionary activities in Switzerland were known to the German government, and when the Russian government collapsed in February 1917, a plan was conceived in Berlin for the return of Lenin to Russia. Travelling first across Germany in a sealed train, he finally reached Finland. There, after a brief stay, he took the train to Petrograd, where his arrival at the Finland Station on 16 April – a signal event in Soviet history – was greeted by local supporters of his revolutionary cause. The history of Russia's local 'soviets'[41] during the summer of 1917 hardly needs re-telling: what counts is how, in a few days at the end of October, they combined to overthrow the Kerensky government. The remarkable success of Lenin's Bolshevik revolution was achieved mainly in the large cities of historic Russia: critically this meant Moscow as well as Petrograd. Victory, however, was far from complete. Vast areas were still contested by rival forces, many with outside support, and among them was almost the whole of Ukraine. With the outbreak of civil war in many different and widely separated areas, Lenin's Bolsheviks had a hard fight ahead of them if they were ever to achieve their final goal of a Soviet state extending across the whole of Imperial Russia. What happened in the four years following their initial success in the October revolution of 1917 was critical for the long-term survival, if not success, of the Communist regime established after the last stronghold to hold out against them, in Georgia, was overrun in 1921.

Immediately following the October revolution, Lenin, knowing well that warweariness was the main reason for its success (Abramovitch 1962: 132), published the Congress of Soviets' '*Decree on Peace*', urging all the belligerent powers to negotiate for peace. This was a signal to the world that Russia was ready to accept a separate peace, a prospect which, while alarming its western allies (by this time including the United States), presented to its enemies, the Central Powers, a taste of victory. The situation was even more difficult for Russia as a result of Ukraine having declared independence under a new government, known as the 'Rada',[42] in Kiev, its capital city. This had originally been organized in March 1917, as a democratic forum of three political parties, of which the largest, that of the Social Revolutionaries, proclaimed Marxist principles as the basis for realizing national independence. This aim was not negotiable with the Kerensky government – or at least not until its planned All-Russia Constituent Assembly had been convened – so while Petrograd wanted, for the time being, no more than a modus vivendi (Reshetar 1952: 70), nationalists in Kiev were calling for a Ukrainian People's Republic (ibid.: 81) – mistakenly assuming that this was in accordance with Lenin's principle of recognizing the rights of ethnic minorities. In the event, once the Bolsheviks were in power, Joseph Stalin, appointed by Lenin as Commissar for Nationalities, demanded that Ukraine should repudiate the writ of the Rada, and instead convene a congress of workers, peasants and soldiers to recognize that of Petrograd. To leave no doubt about where he stood, Stalin, in a *Pravda* article, accused the Rada of siding with landowners and capitalists (ibid.: 96). The Rada, in an appeal for support by Britain and France asked for their representation at Kiev, at consular level, to be upgraded by the appointment of ambassadors. This request would, however, only be considered if Ukraine was committed to continue the war against the Central Powers. Although this was clearly asking too much, Noulens, the French Ambassador in Petrograd did point out to Trotsky, the Commissar for Foreign Affairs, that a decree by his government of 11 November 1917, did allow Ukraine to become an independent state. Stalin, however, was not to be held back, and set up a rival Rada, subservient to Petrograd and representing the pro-Bolshevik Soviets in Ukraine, at the same time as Soviet troops were fighting to prevent its separation from Russia. With Red Guards in East-Central Ukraine seizing Chernihiv, Poltava, Kharkiv and Yekaterinoslav Stalin had considerable local success (ibid.: 109); this extended to the home town of the 11-year-old Leonid Brezhnev in Kamenskoye – as he and his family could hardly have failed to notice. When the Red Guards went on to capture Kiev, the Rada had no choice but to seek a separate peace from the Central Powers at Brest-Litovsk, where armistice negotiations with Russia had been underway since 20 November 1917, with a ceasefire agreed for 4 December. None the less, on 26 December the Rada accepted an invitation to send its own delegates to Brest-Litovsk 'for the purpose of controlling and influencing the acts of the Bolsheviks' (ibid.: 102). Trotsky, after failing to have two of his nominees included in the delegation, harangued the Ukrainian delegates, to be humiliated in turn by their refusing to recognize the *Soviet Council of People's Commissars*, on the ground that no Don Cossack or Crimean Tartar,[43] nor anyone from Moldavia or Siberia was included in it. While all this was happening in Brest-Litovsk, almost the whole of Ukraine was lost to the Bolsheviks. In desperation, the Rada delegates, having learnt of the fall of Kiev, signed a separate peace treaty with Germany (Abramovitch 1962: 137) and Austria (Reshetar 1952: 115) on 9 February. Then, on 3 March, Trotsky, back in Brest-Litovsk, was forced to recognize Ukrainian independence and agree to the withdrawal of all Bolshevik troops, who, by this time, occupied almost the entire country (ibid.: 116) – a humiliation that would not soon be forgotten. Worse still, the next day he had to agree a new protocol moving the Polish frontier east so that effectively the key region of East Galicia, with Lvov as its largest city, became part of Austria. The Rada was rewarded with diplomatic recognition by Germany, Austria, Turkey and Bulgaria, but at a heavy price. German and Austrian troops first occupied Ukraine, and then, worse still, forced the Rada to surrender its power to a new dictator, Lieutenant-General Paul Skoropadsky, who with German support had staged a successful *coup d'état*. On 28 April, a meeting of large landowners recognized the general as 'Hetman', reviving an ancient title for the Ukrainian sovereign from the days before the 1667 Treaty of Andrusovo effectively partitioned Ukraine between Russia and Poland.[44] This had to be the end of any prospect of a Marxist state, such as was envisaged by the Rada in its early days. Instead, as in old times, landowners together with some more prosperous peasants were left to call the shots. While the position of the latter, as landowners, was protected, the rights of poorer peasants to land that they had claimed under the Rada were annulled (ibid.: 175–176). The rationale behind this policy was to make agriculture more efficient, which was essential if Ukraine was to meet its obligation to the Central Powers – agreed at Brest-Litovsk – to set aside 35 per cent of the grain harvest, together with livestock, potatoes, eggs, sugar and dairy produce to meet the costs of the occupation (ibid.: 177). The industrial and mining economy fared no better: the fall, by two thirds, of coal production in the Donbas meant a critical loss to industry, leading to high unemployment in the eastern provinces of Yekaterinoslav,[45] Kharkiv and Kherson. With strikes on the railways brutally suppressed, saboteurs blowing up munitions stores, the writ of the Hetman meant a reign of terror. In any case the depredations of the Russian Bolsheviks – when they were contesting the territory of Ukraine with the Rada in the days before Brest-Litovsk – meant that once the treaty had forced their departure, Ukraine was in no position to meet the demands of the Central Powers (ibid.: 179). Significantly, for the latter, one justification for tying up some 500,000 soldiers in their occupation of Ukraine was that it was essential for preventing it falling into Bolshevik hands. Much more important, however, was the way Ukrainian agricultural production was needed to prevent major famine in Central Europe.

Civil war in Russia: 1918–1921

It was not only the Central Powers, and their Ukrainian vassal-state, that stood in the way of the Bolsheviks: by the summer of 1918, Anton Denikin – who had been one of the Tsar's more successful generals – commanded a substantial volunteer army of soldiers, including many officers, whose reluctance to submit to Lenin's new government was sufficient incentive to take up arms against it. In the winter of 1917–1918 this army, led by another Tsarist general, Kornilov, had formed along the river Don in an area where 'Don Cossacks', with their own general, Kaledin, were already contesting the Bolshevik takeover. This was reason enough for the western Allies – concerned by the way the Bolsheviks were negotiating a separate peace with the Central Powers (Abramovitch 1962: 169) – to support the Cossacks. Kornilov, however, judging that Kaledin's forces would be of little use in battle, led his forces on the epic 'frozen march' south to the Kuban region of the northern Caucasus. Kaledin, in despair, committed suicide, and Kornilov, after fighting a number of battles against Bolshevik forces, was himself killed in action. It was then that Denikin took over the command of the 'White' – as opposed to 'Red' – Army, to continue fighting Bolsheviks for another two years.

In this Denikin was not alone. The Imperial Russian Army had formed a special legion out of Czech prisoners of war captured while fighting for the Austrian empire, of which, together with any number of other ethnic minorities, they had long been reluctant subjects – so much so that they were only too eager to join the western allies in the war against the Central Powers. Following Brest-Litovsk, the French government successfully negotiated with Moscow for the Czechs, as private citizens, to leave Russia via the Trans-Siberian railway. After a first contingent, numbering some 10,000, had safely reached Vladivostok, Trotsky, in Moscow, sent a telegram to every station along the line ordering the Czechs to be disarmed and interned. The senior Czech officer, General Cecek, reacted by mobilizing his soldiers, who at Penza – a sort of halfway station – had commandeered a large store of arms and ammunition, to become a fighting force so effective that within a short time it controlled the whole line of rail in Siberia, including Vladivostok. In the Volga region, the Czechs linked up with the White forces (who had also agreed an alliance with the Don Cossacks) to form a People's Army. Lenin reacted to the unprecedented crisis for his government by declaring 'the Socialist Fatherland' in danger (Abramovitch 1962: 174). Deploying every available resource it was not until October that he won back the lost ground. Even so, the forces opposing him, now commanded by the Tsarist Vice-Admiral Kolchak, were still able to hold out in Siberia, where a British force under General Knox – which had arrived via Vladivostok, was there to lend support.

Allied forces from Britain, France, the United States and Japan had landed in Vladivostok as early as August. Behind this operation was the fear, on the part of the British and French, that as a result of Brest-Litovsk Germany and Austria would be able to mobilize prisoners of war in Siberia to open a new front against Russia (Abramovitch 1962: 178); because this concern was not shared by the American President, Woodrow Wilson, the operation was delayed. Washington finally agreed to intervention on 6 July 1918, fearing that otherwise the Japanese would act on their own and seize Russian territory.[46] Subsequent Japanese operations on the Asian mainland, from the 1920s onwards, were to show that Wilson's concern was well-founded; the Allied intervention in August 1918 frustrated Japan's ambitions for the time being.[47] The result, therefore, in the autumn of 1918, was that the Red Army was left defending the Soviet Union on two fronts, one, in the east, where it faced Kolchak, and the other in the south, where it faced Denikin. What is more its ambition to regain Ukraine was still unfulfilled. Here, however, the Red Army was helped by Denikin's refusal to help Ukraine, for which he had two reasons: first, that it was effectively ruled by the Central Powers, and second, that he too could not countenance its loss to Russia.

By this time everything was once more up for grabs, because the Allies were on the way to defeating the Central Powers, which one by one, ending with Germany, had all surrendered by the final armistice of 11 November 1918. What then did this mean for Russia, and more particularly Ukraine? Lenin and the other Soviet leaders, having pulled Russia out of the war a year earlier, were excluded from the peace negotiations held at Versailles in 1919, and could only advance Soviet policy, which included the incorporation of Ukraine, by force of arms – which is more or less what happened during the critical three years of 1919, 1920 and 1921.

From an Allied perspective, what counted in international politics at the end of World War I was that the four great continental empires in Europe, Austria, Germany, Russia and Turkey had all been defeated, to the point that their ruling houses were all eliminated – in the case of the Austrian Habsburgs after ruling for more than 600 years. In Russia, the Romanov dynasty had ended with the murder of Tsar Nicholas II, together with his wife and five children, on 17 July 1918, an event orchestrated by Lenin and calculated to alienate the outside world. The consequences of the imperial cataclysm varied drastically among the four lost empires. Turkey, after 1918, was a state confined to its ethnic, mainly Turkish-speaking heartland in Asia Minor, retaining next to nothing of its former possession in Europe or the Arabic-speaking world. Critically for both Russia, and the western allies, the Black Sea, and access to it through the Bosporus, became open to shipping. Austria, suffered a comparable fate, with the separate components of its empire entering the international stage as sovereign states. This conclusion, fundamental to the Treaty of Versailles, was to be seen in the emergence of Albania, Bulgaria, Czechoslovakia, Hungary, Poland, Romaina and Yugoslavia on the map of Europe – and significantly every single one of them would play its own distinctive part in the policies of Leonid Brezhnev, some 45 years later, after he had become first secretary of the CPSU.[48]

In 1918 and 1919, however, one of these new states, Poland, would count for more than any of the others, and that for one main reason: a very substantial part of its territory had, until 1917, been part of Imperial Russia. The question to be answered by events occurring from 1918 to 1920 was just how great the part incorporated in the newly resurrected Poland would be. It would be decided by a war bitterly fought between Poland and the new Soviet Russia in the course of 1920, following an initial Polish offensive launched on 25 April. At first the war went well for the Poles, to the point that they even entered Kiev in May; the tide, however, soon turned when the Red Army, supported by a number of Polish communists such as Felix Dzerzhinsky,[49] proved to be an unexpectedly effective fighting force – so much so that by mid-summer Lenin, with his army close to Warsaw, was contemplating the possibility of bringing the proletarian revolution into the heart of Europe (Lukowski and Zawadzki 2001: 200). By autumn the tide had turned once more, with, in September, a decisive Polish victory on the River Niemen. Lenin then decided to call it a day, so that by the Treaty of Riga of 18 March 1921, he accepted a western frontier for Soviet Russia far to the east of the so-called 'Curzon Line'[50] that had represented the original proposal by the Allied Powers at Versailles. Already in 1920, Soviet Russia – much against Lenin's will – had been forced to sign peace treaties recognizing the independence of the three Baltic states, Estonia, Latvia and Lithuania.[51]

Needless to say the opposition of the Allied Powers was decisive for Lenin's failure to secure the historic boundaries of Imperial Russia. There were two reasons for the Allied policy: first was the continuing mistrust of Lenin derived from his deliberate agreement to a separate peace with the Central Powers, and second, the fear of proletarian revolution, orchestrated by Moscow, in post-war Europe – where communist parties had become extremely active in the political void following the defeat of the Central Powers. Such fear was also justified by one essential principle of Marxism-Leninism, which was that the first successful communist revolution, at national level, was no more than the opening stage on the road to revolution worldwide. In the event the success of the October revolution in Russia was followed, in March 1919, by a communist revolution in Hungary, led by Bela Kun: this, however, collapsed for want of popular support in October. Significantly, also, Soviet Russia did nothing to help Kun, although urged to do so by some Ukrainian Party members.[52] On the other hand Lenin (following a precedent set by Karl Marx) did set up the Third Communist International in 1914, committed to world revolution and led by Russia from headquarters in Moscow. This, the so-called 'comintern', had its inaugural meeting in Moscow in 1919, and a second, attended by delegates from 37 countries, in 1920 (Bullock 1991: 108). This, and the meetings held in later years, provided a forum for revolutionaries, such as Zhou Enlai from China and Ho Chi Minh from Indochina, to discuss their own – ultimately successful – plans for Marxist revolution at home. Stalin, however, never thought much of the comintern, and dissolved it in 1943, in the middle of World War II (ibid.: 873). It had, however, been strongly supported by his foreign minister, Maxim Litvinov, between the wars, and often enjoyed a high profile, internationally, as at the time of the Spanish Civil War (1936–1939).

British and French forces in Russia: 1918–1920

Allied support for Poland was far from being the only instance of actions direct-ed to achieving the collapse of Soviet Russia. As early as December 1917, France and Britain had reacted to Lenin's successful revolution in Russia by agreeing spheres of action within the country where they would seek to contain, if not reverse it. France would be responsible for the Black Sea coast and its hinterland, with troops based on Sevastopol, Odessa, Kherson and Mikolaiv, while Britain would take care of the Caucasus, Armenia, Georgia and Kazakhstan (Reshetar 1952: 234). They also supported Kolchak in Siberia with a small military detachment (Fleming 1963: 104), at the same time supplying his forces along the railway from Vladivostok.

A year later, in November 1918, almost immediately after the defeat of the Central Powers, the two countries combined to take over the strategically important railway from Batum to Baku. Later in the same month, at a week long conference at Jassy in Romaina, representatives of various Russian forces fighting the Red Army asked for military support from France and Britain, contemplating a force of 150,000 troops: this the two allies would only grant on condition that Russian factions agreed on unification – a condition unlikely to be satisfied seeing that each had it own agenda, often incompatible with that of the others. Paris ordered the French General Borius, in the Ukraine, to 'faire cause commune avec les patriots russes', leaving him to work out just what this should mean in practice: his answer was to limit his support to Russian volunteers (such as those serving under Denikin) and deny it to Ukrainian forces, who were tainted by their having collaborated with the Central Powers before the final surrender in the autumn of 1918. Given that the alternative was collaborating with the Soviet forces, who at various times had already occupied almost all of Ukraine, this left the new nation, such as it was, with nowhere to turn for help. The result was that at the beginning of 1919 Ukraine was defending itself against the Red Army in the north, Poland in the West and France in the south. The French were particularly culpable, since the German administration of Ukraine in the summer of 1918 had largely been orchestrated by Emil Henno, their egregious vice-consul in Kiev, while, when the crunch came later in the year their forces never confronted the Red Army – the threat that they were supposed to contain. French soldiers, who thought they had just won a war, had no heart for a new one, and indeed, when, at the beginning of the operation, General Dorius had said 'voici une enterprise qui, certes, tournera mal' (Fleming 1963: 247), he was doing little more that making a self-fulfilling prophecy – allowing, at the same time, Chicherin, Lenin's Foreign Commissar in Moscow to blame the parlous situation in Ukraine on 'Anglo-French and American imperialism' (ibid.: 240). With the Red Army occupying Kiev on 4 February 1919, the local Soviet Foreign Commissar immediate protested against French support for a 'small government of capitalists, landowners and officers', set up to collaborate with a revived imperialist Russia (ibid.: 243). In any case the French simply pulled out on 3 April, leaving a country beset by strikes, and temporarily home both to tens of thousands of White Russian volunteers and even greater numbers of uprooted urban Ukrainians (ibid.: 249). The British held out for another few months, but by the end of the year they too were gone (Fleming 1963: 218), leaving Kolchak to the mercies of the Red forces: this meant execution on the banks of a frozen river, just before dawn on 7 February 1920 (ibid.: 217).

At the same time, in the Ukrainian countryside, anarchy at the centre meant that there was no government able – or even willing – to satisfy the peasants' demand for the return of their own land, and when, later, the Soviet regime was equally reluctant to act, it was widely believed that this was because many of the new Bolshevik commissars were Jews. There was certainly some truth in this, if only because Soviet Russia was perceived – particularly by educated Russian-speaking Jews – as supporting the cause of economic justice in a way likely to lead to their emancipation. It was not for nothing that leading Bolsheviks such as Trotsky, Zinoviev, Maisky and Litvinov were Jewish, but in the final days before Ukraine was definitively incorporated into the Soviet Union this was no help to Jews who lived there: some 3,000 died in pogroms (Reshetar 1952: 255). One critical result, favourable to Moscow, was the alienation of foreign support for a nation where a leading politician could say to the Jews, 'know that you are a people disliked by all nations and you are acting disgracefully among a Christian people' (ibid.: 254).

In 1919 not only Ukraine, but much of Russia, was a political kaleidoscope – with chaos and extortion ruling at every administrative level – in which individual survival depended on allegiance to local holders of power. In a time of shifting alliances, such loyalty at one stage could be fatal at another – and this was true at every level of society. Particularly in Ukraine this meant that a politician's main concern was often his own survival, best realized by finding a safe haven abroad (Reshetar 1952: 266). If representing his country diplomatically was the best means to this end, it was still fraught. Ukraine was denied representation at Versailles, where the peacemakers scarcely came to grips with the Russian problem, preferring to allow Poland to call the shots at every critical stage.

In retrospect Ukrainian independence, whatever the colour of its government, never had a chance in the critical years, 1917–1921. Within Ukraine any number of factors – geographical, social, economic, ethnic, religious – militated against any sort of effective unification. At the same time the cause of Ukrainian independence only attracted foreign support to the extent that it might block the expansion of Soviet Russia: with Poland – following the Treaty of Riga – incorporating a considerable part of western Ukraine, the final allied decision to pull out in Russia was merely a question of *realpolitik*. The price paid was that the Red Army, in spite of its defeat in Poland, was able to defeat all those opposed to it in the old Imperial Russia. The Cheka, Lenin's secret police, killed thousands to consolidate the new Soviet Russia (Snyder 2010: 10). In these dire circumstances what did life add up to in the Ukraine, first during the years (1917–1921) of its bitterly contested independence, and then, after 1921, during the long years of incorporation into the Soviet Union?

Every day life in Kamenskoye

In answering this question the focus will be on Kamenskoye – home to the Brezhnev family – and, derivatively, on the other industrial and mining centres along the middle reaches of the Dnepr river and in the Donbas. As in almost every other part of Ukraine the tide of war swept back and forth over the whole area, which was plundered in turn by 'reds', 'whites' and a variety of freebooters. The result was destitution, anarchy, starvation and lawlessness on an unprecedented scale (Kravchenko 1946: 24f). City dwellers, where they could do so, returned to the country villages where their families had originated (Kenez 1999: 45). As money gave way to barter – with household goods being traded for salt, sugar, sunflower-seed oil and salt pork – death was everywhere, with dreaded typhus as its main agent (Matthews 2009: 22). The horrors of everyday life were such as to be reported far beyond Russia, to the point that food relief, supplied by Herbert Hoover's *American Relief Administration*,[53] finally came from America. By this time it was already very late in the day, and in any case the greater part of the help given went to the Volga region rather than Ukraine (Kravchenko 1946: 33). In principle, power, even at local level, derived from Lenin's Bolshevik regime in Moscow, with Sovnarkom,[54] the Council of People's Commissars, the central authority established almost immediately after the 1917 October revolution. In practice, it was not until 1921 that this was undisputed at places like Kamenskoye, a process completed through the agency of the notorious Cheka – the 'extraordinary commission' headed by the Lenin's ruthless Polish henchman, Felix Dzerzhinski (Bullock 1991: 66), whose own words best define its character: 'We represent organized terror – this must be said openly – a terror which is absolutely essential in the revolutionary period we are passing through' (Abramovitch 1962: 310).

For those living in places such as Kamenskoye during the four years 1917–1921 mere survival was what counted most, and it was families and households with the best strategies that came out on top at the end of the day. The Brezhnevs undoubtedly belonged to this class; otherwise the oldest son, Leonid, would have been lost to history. If there is no detailed record of the incidents of their everyday life, often enough these would have been extremely harrowing: there was simply no escape for anyone from the horrors of this time. The Brezhnevs were undoubtedly helped by a number of factors: with the foundry employing them able to continue operating when any number of factories had closed (Kenez 1999: 45) Leonid's father, Ilya, retained his position as a skilled foundryman; this was reinforced by both the absence of hostile fellow workmen and neighbours and the relative youth, good health and internal solidarity of his family. If the level of the family's commitment to the new Soviet regime is impossible to judge, objectively, it is more than likely that to working class urban Russians in a place such as Kamenskoye, its local manifestations seemed to be the best game in town – so that life could be planned accordingly.

None of this was incompatible with a man providing a good education for his children. On the contrary Lenin – who had little time for 'proletarian culture' – set a high store by good education, particularly in Russia where it had long been denied to the vast majority of the population. For the time being compromise with established 'bourgeois' standards was an acceptable price. But then, for a family like the Brezhnevs, the new order meant unprecedented opportunity, enjoyed at the cost of the old bourgeois. In demographic terms the times were favourable to families of 'survivors' such as the Brezhnevs, for the Civil War halved the urban industrial working class to which the family belonged, while the rural sector and the peasantry survived better – as related on page 27 their turn for death and devastation would come later. In the Civil War years, 1917–1921, there was also a drastic loss of intellectual and managerial talent (Bullock 1991: 110). In a world that was falling apart the existential problem for an ambitious young man was how best to study and learn. Critically for his own future prospects, the young Leonid was able to remain at a school for 'working men's children' until he was 15 – a comparatively rare privilege. Finding a job in the same foundry as his father when he finished school, the young Brezhnev diligently continued his education part-time: in the circumstances this was a considerable achievement, well beyond the reach of most of his contemporaries. As a boy in his first job, Leonid Brezhnev was unquestionably ahead of the field in what he later described as a 'first class university' where 'the thoughts and hopes of working people and their approach to life – had a decisive influence in forming my world outlook' (Brezhnev 1977: 4]. G.A. Arbatov, a Ukrainian Jew and near contemporary of Leonid Brezhnev's father (although much better educated) described those whose success in life owed everything to the way they adapted to the new regime, as belonging to one of four categories: fanatics, careerists, vicious cynics and moderate believers (Arbatov 1992: 15). The young Leonid fell somewhere between the first and second of these, and stayed the course – and he consistently remained among the front-runners of his generation.

The new economic policy

With the end of the civil war, in 1921, the new Soviet rulers, with Lenin at their head, faced the challenge of organizing the Soviet Russian economy on a sustainable long-term basis, while at the same time applying essential Marxist principles. On March 15, Lenin, at the Tenth Party Congress, introduced his New Economic Policy as the means for achieving this result. This was essentially an exercise in gradualism (Abramovitch 1962: 223), and at this early stage the main focus was on agriculture: this meant, in practice, that the Marxist principles would have to yield to pragmatism. Peasants, after the depredations of the civil war, would once again become independent farmers, subject only to the liability to pay taxes in kind, which was less burdensome than it had been in the days of Imperial Russia. A rural market economy emerged, so that at one and the same time the urban industrial sector – in the impoverished form with which it had survived the civil war – could be fed at affordable prices, while peasants, at least on a modest scale, could acquire consumer goods.

As for the industrial development essential for the survival, to say nothing of increased prosperity, of the Soviet regime, Lenin – as he told the same Tenth Party Congress – trusted, first, in what is now known as 'foreign direct investment', and second, in electrification (Abramovitch 1962: 223). Neither prospect was realistic: the former could hardly succeed when, internationally, the official Soviet policy was notorious from its goal of putting an end to capitalism worldwide; as to the latter, the technical problems involved were far beyond Soviet Russia's drastically depleted resources – both in men and material. If sooner or later education and training would produce men with the required technical and managerial skills, this could not be done in a hurry. If, at the same time, exports of Russia's rich resources in raw materials would eventually pay for the importation of machine tools, experience from Imperial Russia showed that it was wheat produced by the rich black soil of Ukraine that enjoyed the most readily accessible export market. Here, there was a crying need for a drastic increase in agricultural productivity – a result that could only be achieved by mechanization based on machinery, such as tractors, powered by petroleum products. That the supply, at the required level, of both the machinery and the fuel to drive it, would also require unprecedented capital investment, was a matter that Lenin quite ignored at the Tenth Party Congress. Others, such as notably Stalin, who were concerned, had no choice but to bide their time.

Judged pragmatically, if not ideologically, the restoration of the Russian economy to its level in 1916, before its wartime collapse, was more or less complete ten year later, in 1926 (Abramovitch 1962: 226–227). In other words, the essential rationale of the NEP (New Economic Policy), was well-founded. By this time, however, Soviet politics, at the very top level, had been shaken to its foundations. The reason was the decline in the power of Lenin, following two serious strokes in 1922, leading to his death, on 21 January 1924. The inevitable result was a monumental power-struggle between two utterly ruthless protagonists, Trotsky and Stalin.

Shortly after the second stroke, Lenin, in late December 1922 and early January 1923, produced a document, which although now known to history as 'Lenin's Testament', actually consisted of a letter (1922) to his comrades, supplemented by an addendum (1923). As a policy statement it failed critically on two points: the first was the future of the NEP, and second, Lenin's successor (Abramovitch 1962: 284). So long as he was alive Lenin's Testament was in the hands of his wife, Krupskaya, but she sent it to the Politburo immediately after his death. This meant that it went straight to Stalin, the controversial but powerful General Secretary of the Party. Stalin, with the connivance of his supporters in the Politburo, immediately suppressed it – so much so that its existence was unknown to the Soviet people until it was revealed by Khrushchev at the Twentieth Congress of the CPSU in 1956. Stalin could hardly do otherwise, since Lenin's Testament recommended that Stalin be removed as General Secretary. Trotsky was far from Moscow when Lenin died, and he failed to attend the funeral. Whether this was due to mismanagement on his part, or to Stalin's telling him the wrong date, is unknown. His failure, in any case, was fatal. His absence meant that he had little alternative but to support Stalin's declaration that Lenin left no will. The fact that Krupskaya also did so shows something of Stalin's utter ruthlessness.

Following the death of Lenin, an immediate decision was taken to embalm his body and place it in a mausoleum in Moscow's Red Square. This was designed and built, out of wood, in a matter of days: some six years later it was replaced by a more substantial stone structure, long familiar to the world for its roof providing the reviewing stand for top dignitaries on major state occasions – such as the annual commemoration of the October Revolution. In effect Lenin was canonized, to establish what came to be known as Marxism-Leninism as the guiding principle of the Soviet state. Critically for the future of the Soviet Union, Stalin was ruthless in establishing his position as its leading interpreter. Trotsky, together with the group around him, was side-lined. For some three years, 1924–1927, he was able to play a part in the government of the Soviet Union, even after being ousted from the Politburo by Stalin at the end of 1925, and exiled to central Asia in 1927. Although Trotsky, as also his supporter, Zinoviev, were no longer members of the Party's Central Committee, his continued criticisms of the new order were still seen as a threat. He was expelled from the Soviet Union in 1928, a year which also saw the launching of the first *pyatiletka*, or 'five-year plan' (Kenez 1999: 82) – a programme that would transform the Soviet Union in a way that would disrupt, if not end, the lives of an overwhelming majority of its citizens. Stalin, with no serious rivals, had an undisputed hold on power which he would retain until his death 24 years later. Significantly, 1929 was also the year in which Brezhnev became a probationary member of the Communist Party.

According to the principles of Marxist orthodoxy, as enforced by Stalin, the first five-year plan was born out of necessity. Although, with the harvests in the mid-1920s, peasant farmers were well-fed, there was little surplus available either for city dwellers, whose labour was essential for industrialization of the Soviet economy, or for export to provide foreign exchange essential for the import of the capital goods required by industry. The NEP provided little incentive to increase production; on the contrary it provided every incentive for peasants to consume their own produce. Rural over-population meant inefficient labour-intensive agriculture, with minimal investment in machinery, or even horses to pull ploughs or carts for taking the harvest to local markets. Low agricultural production, as Stalin saw it, was mainly the fault of 'kulaks', peasants who had prospered under the tolerant regime of the NEP. In December, 1929, he ordered their liquidation (Snyder 2010: 25), a programme to be carried out by the OGPU, the new secret police that had taken over from Dzerzhinski's Cheka.

For the more fortunate kulaks 'liquidation' meant deportation to special settle-ments in Siberia, Kazakhstan and the northern reaches of European Russia. This was the beginning of the notorious Gulag system, which during the next 25 years would be home to eighteen million Soviet citizens – of whom some ten per cent would never return. The OGPU lost little time in setting up the system: in the first four months of 1930 it was the destination of more than 100,000 Ukrainians, most of whom were sent to work on the Belomor Canal – a favourite project of Stalin – linking the White Sea in the Arctic with the Baltic (Snyder 2010: 27). Some thirty-thousand did not get that far: they were simply executed after being tried locally by *ad hoc* tribunals, known as 'troikas', set up by the OGPU (ibid.: 26). And this was only the first year of a programme that could continue indefi-nitely. Not surprisingly there were peasant revolts across the Soviet Union; more than half were in Ukraine, where many thousands also fled west to Poland. This proved to be critical for the Soviet Union's international reputation; the Polish government, only too ready to support revolt in Ukraine, labelled Stalin a 'hunger Tsar' starving his own people as he exported grain (ibid.: 30).

Stalin, realizing that forcing the pace of collectivization was counterproductive, suspended it in March 1930 (Snyder 2010: 32), leaving the peasants to return to their old ways – or so it seemed. The move was purely tactical. While rural Ukraine, in the summer that followed, produced a bumper wheat crop, Stalin, enclosed in the Politburo, was deciding how to make collectivization effective in

1931. At the heart of the new planned agricultural economy were the new Machine Tractor Stations: although, as their name suggests, their economic purpose was the provision of machinery and equipment for the new collective farms, or 'kolkhoz',[55] this was seldom realized; instead, their main function was as centres of political control, with any number of Party officials and members of the OGPU (ibid.: 28). Confronted with their failure to achieve collectivization in the winter of 1929–1930, Stalin's first move was to purge the lower ranks of the local Communist Parties. This opened the way to use punitive taxation in kind to drive recalcitrant peasants into joining the local kolkhoz. This, in turn was set a harvest quota for 1931 – based on the high yields of 1930 – leaving to its members only what was left over once it had been met. A poor harvest in 1931 spelt disaster, compounded by failure to adapt to the new demands of collectivization when many of the most productive farmers had been deported as kulaks (ibid.: 33). Those allowed to remain on the land were forced to sell their livestock, to be deprived of horses to pull their ploughs while the Machine Tractor Stations, in spite of their name, were quite unable to provide tractors to replace them. At the same time enforcement of the quotas was so drastic that even seed corn was requisitioned. The situation in 1932 was even worse than it had been in 1931. On 20 December 1932 Stalin sent his lieutenant, Lazar Kaganovich, to Kharkov to demand of the Ukrainian politburo that the quotas be met by January 1933. Following an order sent from Moscow a week earlier, many of the local communists had been deported, so those that remained in office knew only too well what was expected of them. Early in the morning of 21 December the Politburo resolved to achieve the impossible and meet Moscow's target (ibid.: 44). The inevitable result was famine on an unprecedented scale, with the number of deaths counted in millions – with ten thousand a day dying in the early months of 1933. In January Stalin sent his own men from Moscow to take over at the top of the Ukrainian Communist Party.[56]

An ambitious and successful young man

Brezhnev, in the years of the first five-year plan, swum with the tide. This was a matter as much of survival as of ambition. In 1926, after finishing at the Management Technical School in Kursk, he found employment as an agricultural surveyor in the Kursk oblast. His first concern was with water-management, advising on both drainage and irrigation – work which on occasion allowed him to visit his paternal grandfather, Yakov Maximovich, who was still a peasant farmer in Brezhnevo. While the old man, a born conservative, had no time for the mechanization of agriculture, his grandson extolled the benefits Stalin's policy would bring to Russian agriculture (Brezhneva 1995: 26). Brezhnev only remained a year in Kursk, for in 1927, when he was still only twenty-years-old, he was sent to work much further afield, first in Belarus, and later in Sverdlovsk – hundreds of kilometres further east and only just in Ukraine. It was in 1927 that Stalin also laid the groundwork for the 'general line', of forced collectivization and accelerated industrialization, which in 1929 would form the basis of the first 'five-year' plan. Also in 1929, Brezhnev, having reached the age limit for membership of the Konsomol, was admitted as a candidate member of the Communist Party, at the same time being elected people's deputy from Bisetsky Rayon of Sverdlovsk Okrug (Brezhneva 1995: 30).

For the next two years, as Brezhnev combined this office with his work in agriculture, he could not escape being a witness to the devastation of the countryside as a result of the five-year plan.[57] Even though Ukraine suffered the most, no part of European Russia was spared: if Brezhnev, like any other ambitious young man in the Communist Party, had much to explain to the rural populations he worked with, he was steadfast in his loyalty to the Party – as is demonstrated by his election to full membership in 1931. This foreshadowed his return to Kamenskoye, to work in the Dzerzhinski Factory, at the same time enrolling as a student at the local metallurgical institute. This marked the end of his career in agriculture, but even so he could not miss the dire consequences of forced collectivization, as even in Kamenskoye starving peasants, vainly seeking to escape from famine, died in the streets – as they did in towns throughout Ukraine. This was not the fate of the Brezhnev family: Leonid, in 1933 – a year described by his niece, Luba, as 'the hungriest . . . in the entire history of Russia' (Brezhneva 1995: 32) — became head of the local workers' evening school.[58] This step identified him as a 'vydvizhentsy', or someone tipped for advancement – a status he shared with Andrei Gromyko and Aleksei Kosygin, who some 30 years later would be part of his administration of the Soviet Union (Figes 2007: 155). There was one setback: his father died as a result of an accident at the foundry where he worked.

For the young *vydvizhentsy*, with a new life focussed on industry, rather than agriculture, prospects could not have been better. Although Bolsheviks accepted the necessity for a mixed economy, the priority of industry was fundamental (Kenez 1999: 89), as could well be see in Kamenskoye, which, in the course of the first five-year plan acquired factories making, among other things, chemicals, cement, electrical equipment and railway wagons (Brezhneva 1995: 37) – all characteristic products of heavy industry. What is more, in carrying out his industrial programme, Stalin insisted there was no need to wait for the collapse of capitalism worldwide. On the contrary, the principle of 'socialism in one country', meant that industrialization could be financed by exploiting the resources of the peasants, a result to be achieved by making them pay more both in taxation and for essential industrial goods (Kenez 1999: 78).

The industrial achievements of the first five-year plan were remarkable. Even before its formal launching in 1929 work had begun, on the lower Dnepr, on what by 1934 would be the world's largest hydroelectric project. At the same time entire new industrial cities, such as the steel centre of Magnitogorsk, were built, while two giant tractor plants, one in Kharkov in Ukraine, emerged to meet – almost always inadequately, the demands of collectivized agriculture. Also in the Ukraine, new metal works built in Krivoi Rug and Zaporozhye, were supplied with coal from the Donbas. This was not all: on almost every day of the five-year plan a new factory opened, to say nothing of more than a hundred kholkoz's

(Matthews 2009: 31). Heavy industry (including armaments), railways, coal and iron invariably had priority, while, with the denial of resources to light industry, few consumer goods were produced for the general population. Improvisation, rather than planning, was the basis of the new order: indeed the earliest show trials in the late 1920s were of local planners who – frustrated by the lack of direction from the centre – had gone their own way. The message was unmistakable: innovation carried a very high risk, while conformity to bureaucratic norms, however perverse, brought promotion. It was not quite that simple: successful innovation might just be rewarded (particularly if a senior man could take the credit), while allegiance to a man higher up could, if he later fell out of favour, also be fatal for subordinates.[59]

In 1935, a year after the completion of the first five-year plan, Brezhnev, having completed his studies at the metallurgical institute, returned to the factory as a shift leader. Towards the end of the year he was called up to become a cadet at an armoured warfare school in Transbaikal Military District. There – as recorded in the official biography – he went on to become a political instructor in a tank company (Brezhnev 1977: 8), suggests official recognition both of his talent for leadership and loyalty to the Communist Party. This is confirmed that the fact that on his release by the military in 1936 he became head of Dneprodzerzhinsk Metallurgical Technical School, to be elected, before the end of year, deputy chairman of the executive council of the Dneprodzerzhinsk City Soviet. Although these were important steps on the way to becoming a typical Soviet apparatchik, with all the associated privileges, they meant also an increased risk of falling from grace at a time when Stalin was purging every level of the state and Party apparatus.

In the autumn of 1937 Brezhnev would discover that the risk was by no means negligible. A neighbour, who was also a member of the NKVD[60] – as the OGPU had become in 1934 – told him that his name was down for investigation; this was an extremely ominous sign. Brezhnev immediately left in an official car for the local airport at Dnepropetrovsk, where with his official status he took a plane to Sverdlovsk, a town which he knew from his days as an agricultural surveyor. There he sought refuge in the same house, which, during his first visit, had been home to a penniless retired Tsarist general. The general had in the meantime been arrested and shot by the NKVD, but his widow was still ready to offer a home to Brezhnev. His stay had only lasted a month or two when a telegram from the same NKVD neighbour informed him that it was safe to return to Dneprodzerzhinsk.

The story of Brezhnev's flight to Sverdlovsk is told by his niece, Luba, who relates neither how the storm arose in the first place, nor why it ended only a short time later. The way the flight was orchestrated also illustrates the power of even a young apparatchik. The incident was plainly forgotten in official circles, for only a year later Brezhnev became a member of the Provincial Soviet of Dnepropetrovsk – listing his nationality, significantly, as Ukrainian. In February 1939 he was elected propaganda secretary of the Regional Committee of the Communist Party of Ukraine (Brezhneva 1995: 65). By this time the fact that his predecessor, Mendel Katayevich, had been executed in one of Stalin's purges, could hardly have surprised him. Luba, his niece, also records (ibid.: 59) how, of the two thousand delegates to the Seventeenth Party Congress in 1934, only 55 attended the Eighteenth Congress in 1939. Brezhnev, however, had the wind behind him; his next assignment, only a year later, was to convert the factories in Dneprodzerzhinsk to armament manufacture: for this task he was promoted to become the Secretary (Defence) of the Regional Committee. With World War II coming to the Soviet Union in June 1941 this was a key appointment: it would test Brezhnev's management skills to the utmost.

The first appearance of Nikita Sergeyevich

Just as Brezhnev's career as an apparatchik was beginning to take off in the manufacturing centres along the lower Dnepr, Stalin appointed a new man as effective ruler of Ukraine. In January 1938 Nikita Sergeyevich Khrushchev arrived in Kiev to take over as General Secretary of the Communist Party of the Ukraine. Given the level of seniority already reached by Brezhnev, his future would depend, to some considerable extent, on how he was regarded by the new General Secretary. Although neither could see it at the time, the tables would turn one day, and Khrushchev's future, some 25 years later, would be determined by Brezhnev. For the time being, however, there is little evidence that Khrushchev was much concerned about how Brezhnev was performing in Dneprodzerzhinsk, although in 1963 he later recalled appointing him as Dnepropetrovsk provincial secretary (Taubman 2003: 614) before the war. There were then more important issues at stake; within four years, both Khrushchev and Brezhnev, together with any number of other top Soviet officials, would leave Ukraine in the face of the invasion, launched by Nazi Germany in June 1941. The events of the years 1938–1941 are still important, however, as a footnote to the lives of both men.

Khrushchev's remit was to continue the purges of disloyal elements in institutions of every kind, and at almost any level: the numbers, in the hundreds of thousands, reflect his willingness to obey Stalin's orders (Taubman 2003: 116). At the top level, only one member of the Ukrainian politburo survived, while the Party leaders in the twelve Ukrainian provinces, together with the corps and divisional commanders of the Red Army, fared no better (ibid.: 117). The NKVD selected the names, but Khrushchev approved the lists (ibid.: 118), which included the name of his predecessor, Stanislav Kossior (ibid.: 119). For Khrushchev it was also a matter of his own survival, for as he recorded it, 'If I don't do this to others, others will do it to me; better I do it than have it done to me' (quoted ibid.: 123).

While Stalin, knowing of Khrushchev's 'love' for mining and industry, and for the Donbas where he had grown up, had warned him not to neglect his 'agricultural responsibilities' (Taubman 2003: 125), Khrushchev, after consultation, did take some steps to mitigate the more draconian demands of collectivization, so that kolkhoz's were able to set their own quotas for certain crops, such as rye. Stalin still warned him, 'If there's not enough rye we'll put someone in prison' (ibid.: 116). Implicit in all this is the assumption that Stalin was satisfied by the achievements of Ukrainian industry – which meant, of course, less pressure on people such as Brezhnev, particularly when they were, as he was, ethnic Russians.

In any case everything changed radically in the late summer of 1939, after Ribbentrop, the German foreign minister, and Molotov, the Russian, had met in Moscow to agree the invasion by both sides of Poland, followed by its partition between them. By the end of September the deed was done. The result, for the Soviet Union, was the gain of a substantial amount of new territory by Belarus and Ukraine. For Khrushchev this meant only an increase in the size of his realm, but the necessity to impose Soviet institutions – such as collectivized agriculture – on populations by no means eager to accept them. To these, in the summer of 1940, was added the Romanian province of Bessarabia, yielded by Bucharest, under pressure from both Berlin and Moscow, at the same time as other parts of Romania were ceded to Hungary and Bulgaria. Of the new Soviet citizens, nearly 10 per cent were deported to the Soviet interior (with some 300,000 dying en route to their final destinations), half a million imprisoned and 50,000 simply executed (Taubman 2003: 136). With such encouragement the national assemblies set up by Khrushchev in the newly acquired territories voted in favour of incorporation into the Soviet Union (ibid.: 137). The General Secretary of the Party in Kiev plainly had his hands full. He still had time to visit Stalin in Moscow, and was there when Paris fell to the Germans in June 1940. Stalin, he recorded, 'nervously swore at the English and French governments for allowing their forces to be routed' (ibid.: 141). Hardly more than a year later this would also be the fate of the forces under his command. A long new chapter was opening, not only in the lives of Khrushchev and Brezhnev, but in those of almost every nationality of eastern Europe, no matter what the status of its members as Soviet citizens.

Notes

1 According to the new Gregorian calendar, introduced in Soviet Russia in 1918, Brezhnev's birthday is 1 Jan 1907 (Brezhneva 1995: 11).
2 This was the main work of village bricklayers; houses were built by carpenters.
3 The familiar *kolbasa* was the most common.
4 This is seen by Bullock (1991: 27) as the classic Marxist proletariat, constituted by workers with 'nothing to lose but their chains'.
5 The term is well recognized but its origins are obscure; note also the Russian *Chernozem*, or 'black land'.
6 According to the Julian calendar; see also note 1.
7 This, a so-called Gimnazia, was foreign-owned (Brezhneva 1995: 13); Bullock (1991: 26) relates how according to the 1897 census only about a millions Russians, approximately 1 per cent the total population, had secondary education.
8 Wikipedia is the source of these figures.
9 This figure takes into account both the Soviet boundaries agreed at Yalta in 1945, and the transfer of the Crimea from Russia to Ukraine in 1954 as related in note 14. It follows that during the time spent by Brezhnev in Ukraine before World War II, its area was considerably smaller.
10 The present area is 603,700 sq km, and population, 49,507,000 (Cambridge Encyclopedia 2000: 1122).
11 Both these ports on Baltic sea were won from Sweden following Russia's victory in the war of 1709.

12 Cf. the United Kingdom's Act of Union of 1706–1707 (Subtelny 1988: 181–182).
13 Such advice, in relation to Lombardy, had earlier been given to his son by King Vittore Amadeo II of Savoy.
14 This ominously foreshadows the Munich agreement of 1938, by which France, Italy and the United Kingdom allowed Nazi Germany to acquire a substantial part of Czechoslovakia, which was not a party to it.
15 This was the first of the modern era in Europe (and the second in the world after that of the United States).
16 Snyder (2010: 185) relates how at the end of 1941 Nazi Germany, following the invasion of Russia in June, occupied the part of world most densely populated by Jews, who then numbered some five million – a number destined to be greatly reduced as a result of the holocaust.
17 This was not done by Jews, who only sold the finished product (Löwe 1993: 29).
18 See also Levine (1991: 258) citing Prince Joseph Czartoryski's *My opinions on the principles of economics*: 'Without the sales of the *propinacja*, we would not be able to assure ourselves of a regular income in currency. In our country the vodka distilleries could be called mints because it is only thanks to them that we can hope to sell off our grain in years when there is no famine'.
19 *Cherta* in Russian.
20 *Sliyanie* in Russian.
21 These were equivalent to the English 'grammar schools', but the years that Brezhnev was a pupil suggest lower average ages for both admission and graduation.
22 Generally 5 per cent but 2 per cent in Moscow and St Petersburg.
23 Census records show a total enrolment of only 104,000 in 1897 (Bullock 1991: 26); already, by the 1880s, the result was that nearly 15 per cent of all university graduates were Jewish, as against slightly more than 10 per cent from gimnaziya's (Löwe 1993: 94).
24 Their bank, Crédit Mobilier, would later finance the Paris metro (Crump 2007b: 251).
25 The main rivals were Greeks and other non-Russians (Klier 1992: 15).
26 By this time, the opening of the Suez Canal, in 1869 – which transformed transport by ship between Europe and Asia in the age of steam – offered new prospects, but even so, in economic terms, Ukrainian policy orientation was still continental, not maritime.
27 The words of Ivan Alexeyevich Vyshnegradsky, Imperial Minister of Finance (1887–1892), 'We may grow hungry, but we will export' (quoted Subtelny 1988: 264) equally define official Soviet policy under the first Five-Year Plan.
28 On one occasion, Tsar Nicholas II, a notorious anti-Semite, being told of increasing Jewish influence in Yekaterinoslav, commented, 'I know, but what is to be done about it?' (Löwe 1993: 111).
29 Count Witte, who reformed Russian state finance at the end of the nineteenth century, was of German descent; indeed, after 1860 there was only one minister of finance with a Russian name (Löwe 1993: 113).
30 In Russian, Krivoi Rog.
31 Apart from such places there was almost no industrial development on the right bank of the Dnepr (Yekelchyk 2007: 55).
32 This is the common abbreviation for the region along the lower Don River containing the main Russian coal reserves.
33 The family of Mikhail Gorbachev, in Stavropol, had a similar pattern of migration, but much earlier in the time of Catherine the Great (Gorbachev 1997: 24).
34 Russian peasants never used a steel plough, such as that invented in America by John Deere, which was used throughout the prairies from the 1840s onwards (Crump 2010: 229).
35 In the ten years, 1896–1905, 1.1 million Ukrainian peasants yielded to government pressure to move to Central Asia, Siberia and the Pacific Coast (Yekelchyk 2007: 54).
36 The Hughes family's New Russia Company in Yuzovka is one instance.
37 A Socialist Revolutionary member of the Duma – the national parliament – since 1912.

38 The Mensheviks arose in 1903 as a separate group among Russian Social Democrats opposed to the Bolsheviks led by Lenin: in the course of time, and particularly after the revolution, they came to represent subversion and disloyalty to the Communist Party (Kenez 1999: 10); this was fatal to their survival.

39 He was succeeded by his brother, the Grand-Duke Michael, whose rule as the last Tsar lasted for one day.

40 Of Marx' two key works, The Communist Manifesto was first published in 1848 and Das Kapital in 1868; the first English translations were published in 1850 and 1887.

41 Lit. 'councils', the key element in the structure of Lenin's socialist state.

42 The full name was Ukrainska Tzentralna Rada; *rada* is equivalent to the Russian *soviet*.

43 The Cossacks and Tartars were both clearly identifiable minority nomadic communities, with the former originating in southern Ukraine and the latter in central Asia: a local designation, such as Don or Crimea refers to groups that split off from the mainstream some time back in history. The Cossacks were Christians, the Tartars, Moslems. Both groups were regarded as deviant and often troublesome, as much in Soviet as in Imperial Russia.

44 See page 6 above.

45 Which included Kamenskoye, Brezhnev's home-town.

46 The Russo-Japanese war of 1905, in which Russia was soundly defeated, justified this concern, at least in Russian eyes.

47 Opportunism, born out of the prospect of taking over German interests in China, was the main reason for Japan joining the allies in World War I (Crump 2007a: 10).

48 The three Baltic states, Estonia, Latvia and Lithuania, also became independent as a result of Versailles. The Soviet Union took them over late in 1939, after it had done the same with eastern Poland, under the terms of the Molotov-Ribbentrop agreement in August.

49 His popularity with Stalin is reflected in the way that the name of Brezhnev's home-town, Kamenskoye, was changed to Dneprodzerzhinsk in 1934.

50 This was named after Lord Curzon, foreign minister of the UK and its chief delegate to Versailles, who had originally proposed it.

51 In the absence of such, a treaty 'war' with Poland continued until 1938 (Lukowski and Zawadzki 2001: 203–204).

52 Kun, later becoming an exile in the USSR, is believed to have died in one of Stalin's purges.

53 This was an operation funded and carried out by American Quakers; Hoover was later (1929–1933) US President.

54 This is the official version of *Soviet Narodnykh Komissarov*.

55 A name derived from *kollektivnoe khoziaistvo* or 'collective enterprise'.

56 The leader of the Ukrainian Party, Stanisław Kosior, was allowed to remain in office, to be replaced by Nikita Khrushchev in January 1938 (Taubman 2003: 114).

57 Brezhneva (1995: 24–25) relates a number of instances when the liquidation of kulaks was reported to her uncle's office in Kursk.

58 The building, having survived World War II, has a plaque commemorating Brezhnev's position at the head of this school.

59 Matthews (2009: 43) relates how in his grandfather, Boris Bibikov, later paid with his life for supporting Sergei Kirov (secretary of the Leningrad Party) at the Seventeenth All Union Party Congress, held in January 1934 to commemorate the successful completion of the First Five-Year Plan ahead of time. Kirov's murder by an unknown assassin in December was the first act in the purge of those associated with him. Kirov's crime was to urge a relaxation of the forced pace of collectivization. In the course of time 1,108 out of the 1,966 delegates to the 1934 Congress would share Bibikov's fate. The implicit warning would not have been lost on young careerists, such as Brezhnev.

60 The initials are for *Narodny Komissariat Vnutrennikh Del*, lit. 'National Committee for Internal Affairs'.

2 Brezhnev and World War II

The Great Patriotic War

Although Stalin, from both intelligence and diplomatic sources, had every reason to expect a German invasion of the Soviet Union in the summer of 1941, when it actually came, in the early morning of 22 June, he was taken by surprise. The results were catastrophic. The forces facing the Germans across the Curzon line in what, until its conquest by Nazi Germany and Soviet Russia in September 1939, had been the independent state of Poland, were little prepared to resist Hitler's armies. By the end of the year, the whole of Belarus and Ukraine were lost to a blitzkrieg carried out on a scale comparable to that which had enabled Germany to conquer and occupy almost the whole of western Europe in the summer of 1940. The initial German advance was so rapid that General Franz Halder, the Chief of Staff, commented at the end of June 1941, that the 'Russians lost this war in the first eight days' (Weinberg 1994: 266). Hundreds of thousands of Soviet troops died in battle or were captured (ibid.: 272), more than a thousand Soviet aircraft were destroyed – mostly on the ground – and other material losses were on the same scale. The Ukrainian capital, Kiev, fell on 16 September (Taubman 2003: 163), but not before the Chief Political Commissar, Nikita Khrushchev, had escaped to Moscow. Although the stubborn Soviet defence of Kiev had held up the German Army Group South, it was not halted: in the next two months it completed the occupation of the whole of Ukraine, and advancing to reach Rostov at the mouth of Don River on 21 November, it had occupied the whole of the north shore of the Sea of Azov (Weinberg 1994: 272), and almost all of the Crimea, except for the key port city of Sebastopol, home to the Soviet Black Sea fleet. In the final days of November a Soviet counterattack drove the Germans out of Rostov: this meant that the oil from the rich Caucasus oilfields was still available for Soviet armies and factories, and so, a fortiori, denied to Germany. On the other hand, the coal of the Donbas and the iron ore from Krivoi Rug were lost to the Soviet Union. Even so, the failure of the Army Group South to hold its foothold on the Don, coupled with that of the Germans' two northern army groups to capture Moscow and Leningrad, meant that their success, on every front, was not complete. Objectives set for 1941 would have to wait until the campaigning season of 1942, and in the meantime the Germans had their own losses to count, which, although not on the scale of those inflicted on the Soviet armies facing them, were still critical. Surviving a Russian winter, for which the Germans were ill-equipped, added to their trials and provided generals with a pretext for their failure to meet the goals set by Hitler. What neither the Reichskanzler, nor his subordinates could admit, was that the losses suffered by their forces meant that their offensive potential was largely exhausted, while, at the same time they had failed to mobilize their society to the level achieved by the Soviet Union (ibid.: 274) – where this new and terrible conflict became known as the Great Patriotic War.[1]

A major goal of the Soviet mobilization of resources, both human and material, was to make good not only the losses resulting from the massive German occupation of Soviet territory achieved before the end of November 1941, but also to create a wartime economy productive of armaments and other essential material at an unprecedentedly high level. The figures show the scale of the problem. The 40 per cent odd of the Soviet population resident in the German occupied territories, as they were in June 1941, produced essential goods out of all proportion to their numbers.[2] They accounted for coke and coal, iron and steel, at levels ranging from 58 to 74 per cent of the total production of the Soviet Union. They produced electricity and railway lines above par, and the same was true of much of agriculture – with a remarkable 87 per cent of all sugar cultivation lost to the Germans (Harrison 1985: 64).[3] If the Soviet Union's massive reserves of oil were beyond German reach, it was still one of Hitler's major objectives to acquire them at almost any cost: this was a defining factor in his strategy for 1942.

Although the Soviet Union was equally intent on keeping its oil, in 1941 more pressing economic matters had to be dealt with: in simple terms this meant evacuating both essential manufacturing capacity and the labour it employed ahead of the advancing German forces. In agriculture it meant getting in harvests in time to meet consumer demand in territories still in Soviet hands. Particularly on the industrial side, the Ukrainian region of Dnepropetrovsk was critical, and here Brezhnev, as a high ranking local official and party member, was bound to play a key role.

Given the concentration of heavy industry in Dnepropetrovsk, Brezhnev, as Secretary (Defence) of the Regional Committee, was involved in both aspects of the rescue operation carried out in the face of the advancing German armies. Although out of sheer necessity he had to make any number of key decisions *ad hoc*, in principle directives from the Council for Evacuation – a new agency in Moscow, set up by the Politburo according to the dictates of Stalin on 24 June – determined the actions to be taken at every stage. This was the first policy resolution 'On the removal and relocation of groups of people and valuable property' (Harrison 1985: 65). The Council worked through three teams: one was responsible for evacuation and relocation of key enterprises and employees from threatened areas (as was the whole region of Dnepropetrovsk), a second for the movement of refugees and a third for transport (ibid.: 66).

Local party secretaries, such as Brezhnev, were responsible for the local supervision of all three operations. In the last six months of 1941 Moscow continually revised the bureaucratic structure in the face of inevitable shortcomings revealed at every stage of the retreat of Soviet forces, but for Brezhnev and those who worked with him in Dnepropetrovsk nothing counted after the end of September 1941 since the whole region was by then overrun, and occupied, by the German Army Group South. None the less there were still about three months during which the plans laid down by Moscow could be implemented. For the right bank of the lower Dnepr, where Dnepropetrovsk was the main industrial city (and that with the largest population) precise daily rates prescribed by the Evacuation Council on 7 August show Moscow's priorities. Every day 3,000 railway wagons would be allocated to the iron and steel industry, 1,000 to agriculture for transporting grain, 400 to transporting refugees (with priority for young children and their mothers), 400 to electricity generation, 100 to the chemical industry and 380 to all other sectors (Harrison 1985: 68). When it came to the evacuation of people, the refugees were essentially a residual case, for the other quotas included provision for evacuating essential workers and their families. Here top officials had the highest priority: Brezhnev, for instance, together with his wife and children, brother and sister and their families, his mother and his grandfather, all escaped in front of the advancing German armies. The fate of those less favoured was much more problematic, but even so, hundreds of thousands of Soviet citizens, from every category, also escaped the Germans, to end up – as often as not separated from their families – at destinations located deep into Russia, where local bureaucratic agencies, equally constrained by directives from Moscow, had to look after them. For men the obvious destination was either military service or employment in an essential war industry (which also defined the life of many women).

None of this directly involved Brezhnev; once he had fulfilled his tasks along the Dnepr, with what degree of success it is difficult to judge, he became separated from his wife and family, and was able to reinvent himself as a political commissar serving with the Soviet 18th Army on the fourth Ukrainian Front (Brezhnev 1977: 15). Having served a year as a cadet at an armoured warfare school, he insisted on joining the troops in the field shortly after the war began, and although his commission is dated 14 July 1941, there must have been some delay before he could leave Dnepropetrovsk – after all he had to look after the safe evacuation of his extensive family,[4] and he also had to ensure that his own considerable local responsibilities were taken over by others. Whenever he finally left, he was then well out of things, in a chaotic and dangerous situation.

By the end of December 1941 two factors enormously strengthened the Soviet Union as a nation at war. First, the Germans had not only failed to reach their objectives – so that both Moscow and Leningrad remained in Soviet hands – but they had also suffered substantial losses in men and materials which they would never make good. Second – and in the long run much more critical – the Japanese, with their attack on Pearl Harbor on 7 December, brought America into the war. In the United Kingdom, the reaction of Winston Churchill as prime minister, was simple. When the news broke, he realized immediately: 'we have won the war' (Churchill 1951: 607). Stalin's reaction was more complicated and much less transparent, since for the Soviet Union the new state of affairs had three different aspects.

First, although throughout 1941 Japan was clearly preparing for a world war, it was not clear where it had set its sights. Where the army favoured war against Soviet Russia, to be launched from the positions already established during five years of war against China, the navy insisted on a war which would bring the whole of south-east Asia, including the island empires of the Netherlands, Britain and the United States, under Japanese occupation. Although some weeks before Pearl Harbor intelligence reports from the Embassy in Tokyo indicated that Japan no longer planned an attack on the Soviet Union, the threat until then was real enough. In the summer of 1939, an invasion by Japanese forces from Manchuria of Soviet territory in Mongolia led to massive retaliation in August, with Soviet forces advancing 30 kilometres into Manchuria, killing 18,000 Japanese and eliminating an entire division (Dear 1995: 636). If this setback was one reason why the Japanese army's war-plan was rejected in 1941, another, and more decisive one, was the Molotov-Ribbentrop agreement of August 1939.[5] This was the state of affairs when the tripartite pact between Germany, Japan and Italy (signed on 26 September 1940) committed the new 'Axis Powers' to the alliance that some fifteen months later was to lead Germany to declare war on the United States ten days after Pearl Harbor. In 1940, however, Japan was told nothing of Germany's planned invasion of Russia, so the news, when it came, surprised Tokyo. Regarding the military threat from Japan Stalin's mind was not set at rest: indeed intensive Soviet diplomacy in Tokyo was directed to ensuring that Japan and the Soviet Union would not engage in another war. Only after Pearl Harbor was Stalin assured that the Soviet Union was no longer threatened by Japan in the Far East: on the contrary Japanese diplomacy then focussed on preserving neutrality between the two great Asian powers.

More immediately, Stalin was free to deploy his very substantial and well-armed forces in the Far East against Germany – an advantage that Hitler was quite unable to match. This was the second aspect of Pearl Harbor, as seen from Moscow. At the same time, new industry in central Russia, far beyond the reach of German forces, steadily increased production of essential war materials, supplying new equipment, such as the T-34 tank, superior to anything the Germans could put into battle. What is more, with Britain, and even more decisively, the United States as allies, the Soviet Union's need for war materials was met, in increasing measure – if at the cost of heavy losses at sea – by these two countries. Somewhat paradoxically, the neutrality of Japan vis-à-vis the Soviet Union, meant that essential supplies could be shipped across the Pacific Ocean to Russian ports, with little danger of loss to German submarines.

The third aspect of Pearl Harbor, as seen from Moscow, was the vast increase in numbers, both of men and materials, of non-Soviet forces available to join battle against Germany, first in the Mediterranean and then in western Europe. From 1942 onwards Stalin – discounting the fact that his two western allies were also engaged in a major war with Japan – waited impatiently for a second front in Europe. The allied invasion of Italy in 1943 relieved some of the pressure on the Soviet forces in eastern Europe, but it was the invasion of western Europe in 1944 which was decisive – although for Stalin it could well have come a year earlier.

In any case, the course of the Great Patriotic War was much more important to Stalin, and derivatively for Brezhnev. This can be summed up quite briefly: during the winter of 1941–1942 the Germans held a line which, in the north and centre was just short of Leningrad and Moscow, and in the south comfortably to the east of Ukraine, although having captured the key city of Rostov at the mouth of the Don river, they could not hold it against a Russian counterattack. None the less they did hold on to several bridgeheads upstream. In the spring of 1942 the Germans planned to continue their advance east beyond the Don (following the recapture of Rostov) towards the oilfields of the Caucasus and the Caspian Sea, and south down the Black Sea coast beyond the Crimea.

Although the new German spring offensive brought substantial gains of territory, the loss of men and material was on a scale at least as high as that of the defending Soviet forces, at the same time being much more difficult to replace. There were no reserves equivalent to the well-trained and well-equipped Soviet soldiers brought from the Far East: on the contrary, such new forces as the Germans mustered – including Romanians, Hungarians, Italians and even a few Spaniards – were of significantly poorer quality than the men they replaced. After all, the Germans, unlike the Russians, were fighting on other fronts – in 1942–1943, in North Africa, 1943–1945 in Italy and 1944–1945 in western Europe. Even so, in the summer of 1942 they reached their line of greatest advance, and although, along the Black Sea coast it went beyond the Kuban (the part of Russia opposite the Kerch peninsula of eastern Crimean) to Novorossiisk, to continue east along the northern foothills of the Caucasus, it was never established along the west bank of the great river Volga, the essential life-line between central Russia and the Caspian Sea.

Both sides knew that the line of the Volga was critical, and for the Germans the obvious place to attack it was the great west-bank city of Stalingrad: to Stalin (after whom the city was named) it was equally obvious that it had to be defended at any cost. On 12 September 1942 Hitler ordered his generals not only to seize Stalingrad, but to go on to the shores of the Caspian Sea (Weinberg 1994: 421). Although the city, west of the river, had already been surrounded for more than a week, it could still be supplied from the east bank of the Volga – notwithstanding heavy German air and artillery bombardment. The Russians held out in Stalingrad, fighting to defend every block in a city steadily being reduced to ruins, and inflicting vast casualties, equal to their own, on the Germans.

In military terms, the German need to concentrate such vast resources on the battle for Stalingrad meant that the city was left at the head of a salient projecting east from the Don river – at its closest only 80 kilometres away. On 12 September 1942, the same day as Hitler commanded his generals to seize the city, Stalin, and his generals, conceived of an operation, code-named 'Uranus', designed to exploit the exposed German position (Weinberg 1994: 424). The plan was for two new Soviet armies to attack the flanks of the salient, one from the north and the other from the south. The attack opened on 19 November, and the capture of the bridge over the Don at Kalach on 22 November, led to the two arms of the pincer movement linking up the next day. The operation succeeded largely because the fronts attacked by the Soviet forces were defended by the remnants of two poorly equipped and demoralized Romanian armies. These were trapped, as were also the greater part of two German armies which were still fighting in Stalingrad. Although an immediate break out, as advised by many senior German commanders, could well have succeeded, Hitler preferred to follow the advice of Göring, his air chief of staff, and von Manstein, recently appointed to command the new Army Group Don, and hold out in Stalingrad. This course of action was disastrous: when the last Germans in Stalingrad surrendered on 2 February 1943, the battle had cost hundreds of thousands of lives on both sides. The loss was critical for the Germans: the defeat at Stalingrad not only meant an end to all Hitler's plans for overrunning the Caucasus, but the beginning of retreat from all the Soviet territory overrun since the first German troops invaded in June 1941. Although in the early summer of 1943 the Germans recaptured some lost territory, in the course of that year it became clear not only that the tide was no longer with them, but that it would never turn. What was still uncertain was just how far the Soviet advance would go, which, as Stalin at least realized, was the only thing that would matter at the end of the day.

The state most concerned to see an end to the fighting between Nazi Germany and the Soviet Union was Japan, and during 1943 Japanese diplomacy, in both Moscow and Berlin, was directed to persuading both sides to an agree an armistice on the basis of the Soviet western frontier as it had been when the Germans invaded in 1941 (Weinberg 1994: 610). If Stalin might just have been interested, Hitler definitely was not: Ukraine, in particular, would not be surrendered at any price. Well before the end of 1943 Stalin's war plans predicated not only the defeat of Germany, but also the advance of Soviet forces into the heart of Europe. This became clear at the Teheran conference at the end of November, when Stalin – leaving Russia for the first time since before World War I – met the two western leaders, Churchill and Roosevelt, to coordinate Soviet strategy with the allied invasion of France planned for the summer of 1944. Although, by this time, the whole of the Caucasus and a very large part of Ukraine (including its capital, Kiev) had been liberated by Soviet forces, nowhere had they overrun territory not part of the Soviet Union as it was at the time of the 1941 invasion.

The three war leaders, Stalin, Roosevelt and Churchill met again, for a week, in February 1945, for a conference at Yalta in the Crimea – where the last German forces had been annihilated in April 1944. By this time the first Ukrainian Army, in a reverse blitzkrieg had reached the Carpathian mountains (Weinberg 1994: 671), and Brezhnev was in the Soviet vanguard.

It is time, therefore, to look at Brezhnev's war once he had left Dnepropetrovsk, in the autumn of 1941, in face of the German advance. At some stage, Brezhnev, no longer involved in the evacuation of men and material from the region where he had been defence secretary, joined the retreating Soviet forces as a political commissar with the rank of colonel.[6] The 18th Army, and the 4th Ukrainian Front, to which Brezhnev was attached, was – for almost the whole first year of his assignment – retreating in face of the German advance along the Black Sea coast to the east of the Crimean peninsula. The Germans captured most of the Crimea before the end of 1941 (Weinberg 1994: 272), but the port of Sevastopol, home to the Soviet Black Sea fleet, held out until the summer of 1942. The naval base then moved to Novorossiisk, some hundred kilometres down the coast, beyond the Straits of Kerch, but although, after a strong defence, the city was lost to the Germans on 6 September, this was almost the limit of their advance; they were never able to use the port. The Soviet Black Sea fleet once again moved its base, to Tuapse, another hundred kilometres further down the coast, but the Germans never got that far – though not for want of trying (Seaton 1072: 285). Novorossiisk – where Brezhnev's services as a political commissar were first formally recognized by the award of the First Order of the Red Banner – would prove to be the turning point: the battle, with heavy losses on both sides, lasted from February to August, 1943 (Brezhnev 1977: 18).[7] The main action took place in a small area of land, known as 'Malaya Zemlya',[8] at the head of the inlet of the sea to Novorossiisk, where the Soviet 18th Army established a bridgehead on 4 February. Brezhnev, with his headquarters on the other side of the inlet, was a frequent visitor, and on one occasion he was thrown into the sea when the fishing boat taking him across the inlet struck a mine.

Once the Soviet forces relieved Novorossiisk, the German forces facing them had lost all power to resist. In the three months from August to November, the Soviet 18th Army, lost little time in advancing up the Black Sea, crossing the Straits of Kerch onto the Crimean north shore, from where they were able to continue their blitzkrieg as far as Kiev, deep into Ukraine. By the end of December the Dnepr was no longer a defensive line for the Germans: before then the Soviet forces had established any number of bridgeheads; one was at Dneprodzerzhinsk, Brezhnev's home town, but there is no evidence that he was involved in this operation. At the end of the day the Russian advance carried Brezhnev right out of the Soviet Union, to the mountains of eastern Slovakia. When his services were recognized by promotion to Major-General on 2 November 1944 (Brezhnev 1977: 26), the army to which he was attached was meeting serious German resistance for the first time since the break out at Novorossiisk more than a year earlier. The retreating Germans, having left behind the vast open plains of Ukraine, Romania and Hungary, established strong defensive positions in the Slanske mountains of Czechoslovakia, where Brezhnev, with his new rank, was finally able to establish himself as a military commander. He also developed a deep affection for the country (Navrátil *et al.* 1998: 23). Following the loss of the key Slovakian town of Kosice on 20 January 1945, there were no German forces left to halt the Soviet advance, which ended only when, in April, it came to face-to-face with Americans forces advancing from the west. By this time, however, Brezhnev, had returned to Russia, to be not only one of thousands taking part in the parade in Moscow[9] – following the final defeat of Germany on 8 May – but also a guest at Stalin's victory banquet. What he had seen in the previous two years must have given him plenty of food for thought. The Soviet lands recovered from the defeated Germans were devastated: buildings were in ruins, agriculture and industry hardly functioned, and millions had died. Then, in the final months Brezhnev saw countries that had never been under Soviet rule, and although the war had hardly left them unscathed, they were in conspicuously better shape than anything Brezhnev could have seen in the Soviet Union.

Yalta and Hiroshima

In the course of the year, 1943, which had started with the decisive Soviet victory at Stalingrad, Stalin's own thoughts turned more and more to how Europe should be reshaped once the Germans were finally defeated. This was a question that also preoccupied the other allied leaders, but in this case there was also the problem as to who counted as such, besides the United States and the United Kingdom. To discuss, if not to resolve, this and other problems a conference chaired by Vyacheslav Molotov, the Soviet Foreign Secretary, was held in Moscow from 19–30 October 1943, with the United Kingdom being represented at the same level by Anthony Eden and the United States by Cordell Hull. The conference was important for considering, for the first time, the establishment of the United Nations (Weinberg 1994: 620). At the same time Molotov and Eden, yielding to Hull, agreed for China to be recognized as a leading allied power, while Hull, yielding to Molotov and Eden, accepted the same status for France. China, France, the Soviet Union, the United Kingdom and the United States, would then be the nations that counted in the post-war world. As to Germany, the three foreign ministers, although agreeing to accept nothing short of unconditional surrender, came to no agreement on such critical matters as its future boundaries and reparations; they were, however, unanimous that Austria should be separated from it.

The process of planning the post-war world was continued at the Dumbarton Oaks conference, held near Washington from 21 August to 9 October 1944, by which time the allied armies were closing in on Germany from both east and west, with almost the whole of both France and the Soviet Union already liberated. If at Dumbarton Oaks the proposed United Nations began to take shape, the conference was essentially preliminary to one planned to take place between the three allied leaders, Stalin, Churchill and Roosevelt early in 1945. This conference, held at Yalta in the Crimea, from 4 to 11 February, is now recognized as the key event in determining the shape of the post-war world. If its historical importance derives from the presence of the three allied leaders, most of the major decisions taken at Yalta were foreshadowed by what had been informally agreed at Teheran and, above all, Dumbarton Oaks.

It is time then to review what Yalta actually decided. Here a distinction must be made between what, in effect, was little more than *realpolitik* in the form of recognizing and accepting what had already been achieved, militarily, in the final stage of a war that would only continue for another three months, and hard planning for both the future of Germany, and that of the world at large.

As for the *realpolitik,* Stalin, at Yalta, was able to present Churchill and Roosevelt with a decisive fait accompli: by February 1945, Soviet forces had driven the Germans out of substantially the whole of eastern Europe and the Balkans. What before the beginning of World War II in September 1939 had been the territory of the independent states of Bulgaria, Czechoslovakia, Hungary,

Poland, Romania and Yugoslavia was occupied by Soviet forces – or soon would be. Stalin's first move was to redraw boundaries to suit the strategic interests of the Soviet Union. This meant that Poland would no longer claim the territory east of the Curzon Line acquired by the Soviet Union following the Molotov-Ribbentrop pact of August 1939, at the same time being compensated for this loss by gaining from Germany the greater part of East Prussia, Pomerania and Silesia – with such important towns as Stettin and Breslau.[10] The Soviet Union would also acquire not only a substantial part of East Prussia, including its capital, Königsburg,[11] but also Ruthenia from eastern Slovakia. One result, strategically important for the Soviet Union, was the gain of a common frontier with both Czechoslovakia and Hungary.[12]

East European frontiers were not only redrawn in favour of the Soviet Union. Romania, in particular, regained provinces which, in 1940, under German pressure, had been ceded to Hungary and Bulgaria – but not, needless to say, Bessarabia, ceded to the Soviet Union at the same time. In a way none of this made much difference, because Stalin was determined to call the shots throughout eastern Europe. None the less, even Stalin had to recognize critical distinctions between the different nations involved. Hungary, Romania and Bulgaria were all German allies, so that their armies had fought in the front line against the Soviet Union. Poland and Czechoslovakia, on the other hand, had never surrendered to Nazi Germany, and, with their governments in exile in London throughout the war, were staunch allies – at least of the western powers. For Stalin, however, the position of Poland vis-à-vis the Soviet Union urgently needed to be rectified: he was not going to be content simply with regaining the territory in Belarus and Ukraine lost to Poland after World War I. Poland, in his book, needed a government that would dance to the Soviet tune, and to this end he orchestrated an alternative government, in the east Polish city of Lublin, which had fallen to the advancing Soviet forces in July 1944 (Weinberg 1994: 708).[13] The result was that by the time of Yalta the 'Lublin Poles' and the 'London Poles' were competitors in taking over the government of Poland. Stalin, needless to say, saw to it that the former won, in spite of agreeing with his allies at Yalta the 'common desire to see established a strong, free, independent and democratic Poland'. None of these adjectives qualified the Poland that actually emerged from the devastation of war. Although history was on the side of Stalin, he was helped by the fact that 'the abject evil of Nazism provided the Soviet system with a beneficent image it would not otherwise have garnered' (Navrátil *et al.* 1998: 1).

Czechoslovakia was a comparable case, although it was only in 1948 that it fell into the Soviet orbit. By this time, its wartime president, Edward Beneš, had sent some 3,000,000 ethnic Germans from the Sudetenland – the region lost to Hitler at Munich but recovered in 1945 – into exile, in a process involving considerable, if no doubt well-deserved, suffering and loss of life. Some 13,000,000 Germans from the regions lost to Poland as a result of the Yalta agreement suffered a similar fate.

Yugoslavia was a special case, since the country had been largely liberated by its own communist leader, Marshal Tito, who, with his strong local roots, was soon able to follow a line independent of Moscow. As for Hungary, Romania and Bulgaria, they were defeated enemies, whose governments had no standing at Yalta. Stalin had little difficulty in finding strong local communists to establish governments utterly subservient to Moscow. Albania, conquered and annexed by Italy in 1938 – with its king fleeing into exile – seemed to go the same way under Enver Hoxha, but he too would eventually leave the Soviet camp.

Everything related above regarding the various countries of eastern Europe, 'liberated' by Soviet forces in the course of 1944–1945 presented itself at Yalta as something that Churchill and Roosevelt were powerless to question: Stalin simply held too many good cards. Things were quite different when it came to setting up the United Nations, or planning the future of Germany, and to a lesser degree that of Japan.

As for the UN, the broad lines had been already agreed at Dumbarton Oaks, while the definitive form would be set at a conference to be held at San Francisco in the summer of 1945. Even so at Yalta the plans both for the actual constitution of the UN and for the future of Germany and Austria (and somewhat marginally Japan) got their imprimatur. Germany (within its new and more constricting frontiers) would be divided into four sectors, to be administered respectively by the Soviet Union, United Kingdom, United States and France. Their demarcation, as agreed at Yalta, left the capital, Berlin, deep inside the Soviet sector: this was simply the result of its geographical location in the east of the country. The city was treated as a special case, with, in principle, a joint administration by the four allied powers, so that in the jeeps of the military police – all too familiar on streets with little other traffic – there was always one Russian, one American, one British and one French soldier. This display of unity was mainly a façade designed to impress the local population. Berlin, like Germany, was divided into four zones, with one allocated to each of the occupying powers, and as time went on their joint administration ceased to be reality. As in the country as a whole the Soviet Union, increasingly represented by a German puppet administration, went one way, and the three western powers, another.

In Austria the position was not much different, at least on paper. With exactly eight provinces two each were assigned to the four occupying powers. Vienna, like Berlin, deep inside the Soviet zone, had its own division into four sectors. The situation of both Austria and Vienna was significantly different: the country was smaller and strategically much less important, there was far less wartime destruction, and there was a solid popular base for repudiating the *Anschluss* of March 1938 that had made it part of Germany. By 1945 most Austrians had conveniently forgotten how many, if not the majority, had then welcomed Hitler.

Yalta also finalized the detailed structure of the United Nations, to be presented to the first plenary session to be held in San Francisco. There was to be a two-tier structure: the General Assembly would be open not only to the big five – China, France, Soviet Union, United Kingdom and United States – but to any allied state that had entered the war against Germany before March 1945; the Security Council would have the big five as permanent members, and six other states chosen for two-year terms by rotation from the other members of the General

Assembly. In both bodies the five permanent members would have a right of veto: Stalin always insisted on this. Among the 'big three' represented at the Moscow conference there was some argument about admitting to the General Assembly, first, the sixteen republics constituting the Soviet Union, and second, the various independent member states of the British Commonwealth. At Yalta Stalin accepted that only two of the Soviet republics be admitted, as against five member states of the Commonwealth.

Japan, at Yalta, was a somewhat problematic issue. Following Pearl Harbor, both Tokyo and Moscow profited from the fact that Japan and the Soviet Union were not at war. For most of World War II there were close diplomatic relations between the two countries. There was hardly a community of interests. Japan's Pacific war, as seen from Moscow, tied up substantial American and British forces which otherwise would be available to fight Germany in Western Europe. The Soviet war against Germany, seen from Tokyo, tied up substantial Germany forces that otherwise would be fighting Britain and the United States. Whatever Moscow might want, Japan was too deeply committed to the Pacific war, to withdraw from it: on the other hand, Japan, enjoying full diplomatic relations with both Berlin and the Moscow, was in principle well-placed to be a peace-broker between them. As already noted on page 39, Hitler was not going to give up at any price acceptable to Stalin, and by 1945 the question was moot anyway. Hitler was losing the war, and Stalin, with Churchill and Roosevelt, was about to win a decisive victory.

It was time for Stalin to take another look at Japan. In spite of continuous setbacks, throughout 1943 and 1944, Japan still seemed set to fight a long war: this, however, would be much shorter if it also confronted battle-hardened soldiers of an army, which had already fought the Japanese in the forgotten war of 1939 (noted on page 37). Soviet forces could now be deployed to attack the Japanese, in China, without the need for the sea-borne invasion in prospect for Britain and the United States. It would certainly be a very valuable ally: the key question was what could it gain in return. This then was another matter on the Yalta agenda, although it was only finally resolved at the Potsdam conference some six months later. The answer for Stalin was that victory, as a combatant, over Japan, would enormously strengthen its hold on China once Japan had been defeated and its army returned home. China was a political vacuum waiting to be filled, and one made even more tempting by the precarious position of Chiang Kai-shek's corrupt and wasteful government in Chungking – which was already confronting communist rebel forces led by Mao Zedong.

This was not all. Stalin could also share in the spoils of victory by taking over, in the seas of Japan, the southern half of Sakhalin and the Kurile islands. Korea, also, conquered and annexed by Japan some 40 years earlier, would be up for grabs. At the same time the Soviet Union might also gain a foothold in the Japanese home islands, by being granted – as it had been in Germany – a zone to govern from Moscow. What then was in it for Britain and the United States? The answer was simple: a shorter war with fewer casualties. With all these factors bearing on the case, it was agreed that the Soviet Union would enter the war against Japan three months after the unconditional surrender of Germany.

This event occurred on 9 May 1945. Roosevelt had died, suddenly, three weeks earlier. The new American President, Harry S. Truman, took the German surrender, and was also committed to attend a conference at Potsdam (just outside Berlin) in July where, together with Churchill[14] and Stalin he would dot the 'i's' and cross the 't's' on what had been agreed at Yalta, and, most important of all, prescribe the exact terms of the Japanese surrender. The conference lasted from 17 July to 2 August. The Japanese surrender terms were enshrined in the Potsdam Declaration of 26 July. By this time Truman, somewhat obliquely, had told Stalin that the United States possessed a weapon of unprecedented destructive power, which was ready to be used against Japan. Stalin took note, but held his cards – whatever they were – close to his chest. He certainly did not tell Truman that he had already learnt a great deal about the atomic bomb from Soviet agents who had penetrated the top secret complex in Los Alamos (New Mexico) where it was being developed. Indeed he had authorized a parallel Soviet programme as early as February 1943 (Ferguson 2006: 576).

On 6 August the news broke that the Japanese city of Hiroshima had been destroyed by a single 'atomic' bomb, with more than 100,000 casualties. 'Little Boy' was the weapon that Truman had mentioned to Stalin at Potsdam (but without telling him that a prototype had successfully been exploded in the New Mexico desert on 16 July). On 8 August Soviet forces, as finally agreed at Potsdam, invaded Manchuria. The next day, 9 August, a second atomic bomb destroyed the city of Nagasaki. On 15 August, the Japanese Emperor, addressing his people by radio, announced that there was no alternative but to surrender according to the terms of the Potsdam Declaration. The formal act of surrender took place on an American battleship, the USS Missouri, anchored in Tokyo Bay, on 2 September. A new world had come into being.

Stalin's new world

As effective ruler of the victorious Soviet Union, Stalin, in 1945, faced unprecedented challenges, which – as he soon realized – could not be met simply by continuing policies shaped, and brutally enforced, in the final years of peace before 1941. The new world confronting Stalin, both at home and abroad, is the subject of the remainder of this chapter. The domestic scene will be first considered, and then the international. The former is also significant for the steady ascent of Brezhnev in the Soviet hierarchy.

The devastation and loss of life in the Soviet Union in the period 1941–1945 can scarcely be exaggerated. The vast areas of land overrun by German armies in the first two years (1941–1942) of World War II and freed by Soviet forces in the last two years (1943–1945) suffered devastation and loss of life on an unprecedented scale.[15] On the home front the first challenge to Stalin was to make good these losses as best he could. If the millions who died could never be brought back to life, there were still many millions more – demobilized soldiers, survivors from the German occupied territory, workers and their families displaced by the relocation of industry in the face of the German advance – with a claim to a normal peace-time way of life. At the same time a ruined infrastructure, both in transport and mains services, together with buildings, both residential and industrial, damaged or destroyed, had to be rebuilt, while the resources available to do so were but a fraction of what they had been in June 1941. In some cases, such as the industry of the lower Dnepr – including the great hydroelectric station at Zaporozhye – policy required not only reconstruction, but unprecedented investment and expansion. The challenge facing men such as Brezhnev in Dnepropetrovsk, or Khrushchev in Kiev, who returned from the war to govern Ukraine was greater than that in any other part of the Soviet Union. One in six, that is some 5.3 million, had lost of their lives while another 2.3 million had been sent to forced labour in Germany; with seven hundred towns and 28,000 villages in ruins, 16,000 industrial enterprises and 28,000 collective farms wholly or partially destroyed, Ukraine had lost 40 per cent of its wealth (Taubman 2003: 179). Life was not going to be easy for local populations, for the war left few resources available for developing a consumer economy – which would never be a priority with Stalin. On the contrary, 1946 brought famine back to the Ukrainian countryside (ibid.: 180).

Zaporozhye, where Brezhnev, on the recommendation of the CPSU Central Committee, had become first secretary of the local party, fared better. The reason for this was its unique importance for Soviet industry, as a key manufacturing city for aluminium and ferro-alloys, and above all, for the Lenin Denpr Hydropower Station. Leninist principle required priority to be given to such a key centre in the Soviet economy, so that the giant Zaporozhye steel plant, left gutted by the Germans, was restored to productivity in a matter of months. It helped, needless to say, that equipment was supplied from factories in Moscow, Leningrad, the Urals and Siberia, with builders and skilled workers recruited from even further afield. Even so, bringing the power station back on stream in the summer of 1947, and other comparable feats, were remarkable achievements. What is more, helped by electricity from Zaporozhye, coal in the Donbas, iron at Krivoi Rug and aluminium at Nikopol, were once more available for Soviet industry. Locally, in the Dnepropetrovsk region, production in the metallurgical industries reached pre-war levels.[16] Brezhnev was clever enough to ensure that he got much of the credit, but then he had the wind behind him. Favoured sectors of the coercive Soviet economy generally obtained the inputs they needed; that was the essential rationale of a Marxist-planned economy. To say that other regions, both inside and outside Ukraine, were not so fortunate as Dnepropetrovsk, would be something of an understatement.

Quite apart from restoring, if not expanding the pre-war industrial economy, Stalin, in the late 1940s, had to create, from next to nothing, a whole chain of enterprises to enable the Soviet Union to join the nuclear arms race. The destruction of Hiroshima and Nagasaki by atomic bombs left him with no alternative. In setting up the Soviet nuclear programme Stalin had two advantages: first, Soviet agents in the United States had communicated to Moscow much of the classified science and technology used in the American Manhattan Project (Newman 1952); second, helped by a number of exceptionally able physicists, nuclear research within the Soviet Union had already covered a great deal of ground. In 1943 Igor Kurchatov, who already in 1939 had alerted Stalin to the possible military use of nuclear fission, was appointed to head a new nuclear research institute just outside Moscow. 'Laboratory No. 2' would then be the Soviet answer to Los Alamos (Rhodes 1988: 502). In the event, when the news of Hiroshima reached Stalin, he was furious with Kurchatov for his failure to be ahead of the Americans: Stalin's dream of 'extending the socialist revolution throughout Europe had collapsed' (Rhodes 1995: 177). After Kurchatov justifiably explained poor performance by pleading the wartime devastation suffered by the Soviet Union, Stalin replied, 'Ask for anything you need. There will be no refusals' (ibid.: 178). To make quite sure, he appointed Lavrentiy Beria, the much-feared head of the NKVD, as overall director of the bomb-project.

Its success would stupefy Washington: in the summer of 1945 leading figures from the Manhattan Project were so disparaging about the prospects of any comparable Soviet project, that the Secretary of State, James Byrnes concluded that 'any other government would need from seven to ten years, at least, to build a bomb' (Rhodes 1995: 650). The Soviet Union needed scarcely four: its first atomic bomb was exploded on 29 August 1949 (Holloway 1994: 216). In the confrontation between the Soviet Union and the United States, already known as 'the Cold War', this event would change everything. Indeed the repercussions would be worldwide, stretching from remote Polynesian islands to the polar ice-caps.

The Soviet Union could not but be involved. The success achieved in September 1949 was no more than a beginning of a process that within barely 40 years would lead to the collapse of the Soviet economy and the end of the Soviet Union. Whatever Brezhnev might have thought when the news broke in 1949, its import would haunt him for the remaining 33 years of his life.

Whatever the Soviet Union might achieve in the atomic arms race, the United States would always be one move ahead. Even after the end of World War II – the direct result of the first and only military use of atomic weapons – Los Alamos, and other associated operations born out of the Manhattan Project, remained in business. At Los Alamos, one scientist, Edward Teller, had no doubts at all about what the next step must be: the development of the 'Super', a bomb based not on the fission of uranium atoms – as had been the case so far – but on the fusion of hydrogen atoms, must start immediately. The rationale was simply that the new weapon would be much more destructive. This proved to be the case: on 2 November 1952, in a remote Pacific atoll the prototype, known as 'Mike', eliminated an entire island, Elugelab, leaving in its place a crater half a mile deep and two miles wide; its explosive power was estimated to be a thousand times that of Little Boy (Rhodes 1988: 777). Stalin's reaction to the news was muted: he was in poor health, and preoccupied by such matters as the Jewish doctors' conspiracy (Rhodes 1995: 517). In any case the Soviet H-bomb was already well on its way: Stalin had authorized the preliminary research, to be carried out at the Physics Institute of the Soviet Academy of Science, in 1947. A 27-year-old physicist was talent-spotted to become research director: although his name, Andrei Sakharov, would in the course of time become well-known – if not notorious – far beyond the bounds of the Soviet nuclear weapons programme, in the early days of the late 1940s it was his 'First Idea' that opened the way to the Soviet H-bomb (Holloway 1994: 298). On 23 November 1955 the first complete test, with a bomb dropped by an airplane, showed the world that in the nuclear arms race the Soviet Union had drawn level with the United States. This was the world that Brezhnev, as he rose in the Soviet hierarchy, to become First Secretary of the CPSU, in 1964, would have to come to terms with.

Internationally, the new post-war world was, in its challenges to the Soviet Union, unlike anything it had to contend with before the 1941 German invasion. One challenge, as already related, was taken up with considerable gain. By 1949, at the latest, in eastern Europe the Soviet Union called all the shots. Even so, in at least one matter Stalin was decisively wrong-footed. In June 1947, with Berlin – under four-power control – deep inside the Soviet Zone of Germany, he decided to block road access (as it had been agreed at Yalta) to the three other occupying powers. His object, which was to force them to abandon the city, was frustrated by an allied airlift of essential supplies to Berlin's Tempelhof airfield, conveniently located in the American sector of the city (Deutscher 1967: 590–591). At the same time, essential services to the Soviet sector were blocked in retaliation. By the end of the year even Stalin had to accept that the blockade was counterproductive; following negotiations between the four occupying powers it was lifted in May 1949, with the airlift continuing to the end of September. In October Stalin's plan for Germany became clear with the emergence of German Democratic Republic (GDR), with its capital located in the Soviet sector of Berlin. The continued presence of a joint American-British-French administration of the rest of the city, made it – as will be related in Chapter 9 – something of an Achilles-heel for the Soviet east-European bloc. This would, in the 1960s, be another problem laid at the door of Brezhnev.

The world outside Europe also changed radically, mostly to the advantage of the Soviet Union – at least as seen from Moscow. The first event to note was the emergence of the State of Israel, proclaimed by its first prime minister, David Ben-Gurion, in 1948. The creation of the new state, carved out of the land of Palestine – a British mandate since the defeat of Turkey in World War I – was bitterly resented by the Arab world, where, in the 1940s, Britain, and to a lesser degree, France, retained considerable political influence. On the other hand the moral case for Israel, after so many millions of Jews had died in the Nazi holocaust, was undeniable – the more so since it would offer a home, not only to the few holocaust survivors, but also, critically, to Jews anywhere worldwide. As things were in the late 1940s, the world's largest Jewish populations were in the United States and that part of the Soviet Union never overrun by the Germans. Both Truman and Stalin supported the recognition of Israel by the UN General Assembly. The United Kingdom, concerned about its substantial economic interests – mainly relating to oil – in the Arab world, abstained from voting. Admitted almost immediately to the UN, Israel was from the very beginning a dynamic state that punched far above its weight: internationally its claim to represent the interests of Jews worldwide was widely recognized, particularly in the United States. This would prove to be a most unwelcome development for the Soviet Union, particularly during the Brezhnev years. That, however, is a story told in Chapter 10.

The world balance of power changed decisively on 1 October 1949 when Mao Zedong proclaimed the founding of Communist China from the Tiananmen Gate in Beijing (Chang and Halliday 2005: 322). Although Stalin had been involved in revolution in China as far back as 1924, when Zhou Enlai, a founder member of the overseas branch of the underground Chinese Communist Party had represented Chinese communists at the Comintern meeting in Moscow, he saw the victory of communism in China, a quarter of a century later, as at best a mixed blessing. Zhou, always a considerable power in his own right, had allied himself with Mao in 1935, and together, from 1937, they would lead the revolution against the nationalist government of Chiang Kai-shek. That Chiang then had to defend China against a brutal Japanese invasion defined the state of affairs in which Mao's rag-tag army, at the other end of the country, opened its own campaign. By doing so, he became not so much an ally of the Soviet Union, but an enemy of the United States, which was unequivocal in its support for Chiang, and its condemnation of Japanese aggression. That is not to say, however, that Mao saw himself, in any sense, as an ally of Tokyo: his plans for the future of China did not contemplate sharing its territory with Japan – or, for that matter, with the Soviet Union. It took Mao twelve years to win the civil war he had started. The Japanese surrender, in 1945, did not save Chiang, in spite of massive material support then given by the United States: the best he could achieve, in 1949, was to establish a government in exile on the island of Taiwan. Although this had become part of imperial China in 1683, it had been annexed by Japan in 1895, so that it was only with the Japanese surrender in 1945 that it reverted to China – where Chiang still ruled. All this meant that Mao never had any support in Taiwan. When, late in 1949, Chiang brought his government there, the United States continued to recognize it as the legitimate government of the whole of China, committed, sooner or later, to defeating Mao on the mainland. It did not matter that this was a quite unrealistic prospect, as was accepted in both London and Paris, and indeed by many in the United States. At this stage, however, in the Cold War it was politically impossible for President Truman to face reality, and recognize Mao's government in Beijing. Critically this meant also that Washington could still count on China in the UN. Stalin – unwisely as events would soon prove – protested by withdrawing the Soviet Union from the Security Council (Crump 2007a: 78).

Victory in 1949 did not, however, leave Mao much peace. The reason was the war that less than a year later broke out in Korea. This remote 'hermit kingdom' consisted of a peninsula off the East Asian mainland, adjoining both Russia and China, but with its far south-eastern end closer to Japan than any part of either of these two giants. Winston Churchill, in the early 1950s, went on record with the words, 'I had never heard of the damned place'. By the end of the nineteenth century some in the outside world had, however, become interested in making something of this unknown, yet strategically located, kingdom – and no state more so that Japan, which in the course of the 1900s incorporated Korea into its empire and proceeded to govern there with a very hard hand. If the Potsdam Declaration would free Korea from the Japanese, it made no further provision for its future – a matter which, while of great interest of the Soviet Union, was of only marginal interest to the United States. At a low level meeting, in 1945, between representatives of these two great powers, a temporary allied occupation was agreed, with two zones, north and south, separated by the 38th parallel north, with the former to be administered under Soviet supervision, based on Pyongyang, and the latter, under American, based on Seoul (Rusk 1991: 102); in principle this was no more than the first stage on the way to a united democratic elected government of the whole of Korea. For their man in Pyongyang the Russians found a young Korean officer, temporarily attached to a Soviet intelligence unit monitoring Japanese forces in Korea and Manchuria: his name was Kim Il-Sung. Following the defeat of Japan, he was part of a small detachment sent to Pyongyang: as the senior Korean officer he was the obvious choice to organize a provisional local administration. The Americans, in turn, sent to Seoul Syngman Rhee, who, since 1905 had been the exiled leader of Korean opposition to Japan in the United States, where his modest supporters' club consisted largely of eminent Presbyterians (Crump 2007a: 75).

Although both Kim and Rhee were dedicated patriots whose only cause was the reunification of Korea, their visions of its future were totally incompatible, and any compromise between them unthinkable. The only principle they shared was that there was no room for both of them in a united Korea. Here, if Kim was more intransigent that Rhee, it was not so much that the ideology he espoused as a dedicated communist was more extreme, but rather that he could claim much closer support from his patrons in Moscow (and indeed in Beijing after 1949) than Rhee could in Washington – which, with regard to Korea, was largely in a state of denial (Crump 2007a: 77).

From the beginning of 1950, Kim, keenly aware of Washington's position, was orchestrating his own policy for reuniting Korea. In January he persuaded Mao to allow some 14,000 Koreans serving in the Chinese People's Liberation Army to return home to join the Korean equivalent; visiting Moscow in April he gained Stalin's reluctant consent to an invasion of South Korea on the clear understanding that Soviet forces would not be actively involved; visiting Beijing in May, he also gained Mao's consent, but only after he misrepresented Stalin' position as one of enthusiastic approval.[17] He also convinced both Stalin and Mao that not only was Syngman Rhee's army too weak to resist the planned invasion (Crump 2007a: 78), but also that the United States would not come to his rescue.

If Kim was right on the first point, he was decisively mistaken on the second. Within hours of his invasion of South Korea, Washington, although caught by surprise, immediately decided to commit American forces to its defence. Although within days the South Korean forces had been driven back to within a small perimeter in the extreme south-east of the peninsula, the first American rein-forcements, commanded by General MacArthur, arrived in early July. This was possible since there was still a considerable American military presence in Japan, with sea and air support on the same scale – and at a level that Kim, even with his air force manned by Russian pilots, could not hope to match. On 7 July, the Security Council, adopting a resolution presented by the United Kingdom, voted to support, militarily, the army of South Korea. The Soviet Union, having withdrawn from the Council, was powerless to use its veto, while Mao's communist China had still not been recognized. The result was that twelve countries joined the United Kingdom and the United States in sending troops to Korea (Crump 2007a: 79).

Inevitably the tide turned against Kim, and within three months his forces had lost all the ground they had overrun, including the South Korean capital, Seoul. Washington told MacArthur that he was to feel 'unhampered strategically and tactically to proceed north of the 38th parallel' and to take on any Chinese forces deployed against him where there was a 'reasonable chance of success'. On 1 October MacArthur issued an ultimatum demanding the surrender of all North Korean forces; unknown to him at the time, on 2 October the Indian ambassador in Beijing learnt of Mao's intention to enter the war in support of North Korea, if UN forces crossed the 38th parallel. This was no empty threat. By the end of November it was clear to the UN commanders that their forces were fighting not Korean, but Chinese soldiers. This changed everything. The UN forces were driven back, and after a winter of bitter fighting between evenly matched armies, new more or less stable battle lines had been drawn across the peninsula, roughly along the line of the 38th parallel (Crump 2007a: 81). Following the decisive defeat of the Chinese, at the battle of Chipyong-ni, on 14 March 1951, President Truman proposed that with South Korea once more cleared of communist forces, the UN should be willing to agree a ceasefire. If this proposal made sense to the Mao who had seen a million Chinese soldiers die in battle, it was not acceptable to Stalin, who had never committed any Soviet forces to the war – though this is not to deny the value of Soviet material and logistic support. Although in the last months of his life he began to realize that an armistice was the only solution, this only came, with a treaty signed at Panmunjom – a small town in the border area between the lines of the two opposed Korean forces – on 27 July 1953 (ibid.: 84).

It is impossible to overestimate the impact of the Korean War. Mao could forget any chance of his people's republic being recognized by the UN: on the contrary the US was now bound to defend the island of Taiwan at any cost, and to keep Chiang's nationalist government in power there. Mao also learnt, as the Soviet leaders did also, that when challenged in its own sphere of interest, the United States was prepared to engage in war. With nuclear weapons deployed on both sides of the Iron Curtain this was not a prospect either side could accept. What is more, in the aftermath of the Korean war the United States enormously strengthened its military presence in the Far East. Here the great beneficiary was a new democratic and demilitarized Japan. It was no coincidence that in the year of Panmunjom, Japan was able to reinvent itself as an independent sovereign state following a peace treaty signed in Washington in September 1951 – but not by any representative of the Soviet Union.

The Soviet Union and the Chinese People's Republic gained little by refusing to sign the Washington treaty, but significantly they were joined by all the independent states of south-east Asia, Philippines, Thailand and Indonesia. In that part of the world – which before World War II had been a happy hunting-ground for colonial powers – in the 1940s the Philippines had been granted independence by the United States, and Indonesia – after a bitterly fought war – by the Netherlands. Thailand, somewhat equivocally, had always been an independent kingdom. Although Malaysia and Singapore were still part of the British empire, and Indochina, of the French, both colonial powers had to contend with communist insurgency, and in Vietnam the French confronted a powerful adversary, Ho Chi Minh, with impeccable credentials and a strong supporters' base in the world of international communism. Together with Zhou Enlai, he was one of the great communist figures to arise out of the world of the pre-war Comintern, and like Zhou, he would be in the vanguard of the communist takeover of east and south-east Asia. Whatever his setbacks, the new world that emerged after World War II offered Stalin, and his successors, many opportunities to fish in troubled waters – and nowhere more so than in south-east Asia.[18]

Where then did all this leave Brezhnev when Stalin died in 1953? In the events involving the Soviet Union outside its boundaries he played no part at all, and his reaction to them is unrecorded. Indeed, none was required in the positions he held, first in Ukraine (as recorded on page 31) and then, from 1950 to 1952 in Moldavia, where as First Secretary of the Moldavian Communist Party, his remit was to impose the Kolkhoz economy on backward, illiterate and no doubt reluctant farmers who had no alternative but to accept it. This was definitely a challenge since Moldavia (which was completely overrun by the Germans in World War II) only became part of the Soviet Union in 1945. At the same time as he was busy with the collectivization of agriculture, Brezhnev embarked on building up local industry, largely linked to the processing of agricultural produce, from scratch, always taking care to establish a sufficient number of show-case enterprises and new towns to impress Moscow.

In Moldavia Brezhnev plainly impressed Stalin, as can be seen from the fact that the Nineteenth Congress of the CPSU elected him a member of the Central Committee (Brezhnev 1977: 50), with additional political responsibilities in both the Soviet Army and Navy following a year later. At the same time he became an alternate member of the Presidium; this was particularly significant, because the 25-member Presidium was a new body created by Stalin to replace the Politburo (Taubman 2003: 222) – a move calculated to check the power of the old guard. Significantly, in the political upheaval following Stalin's death in March 1953, he was removed from the Moscow posts to which Stalin had appointed him, but this is a story for the next chapter.

Notes

1 Великая Отечественная Война.
2 According to an August 1940 report to the German army general staff Ukraine was 'industrially and agriculturally the most valuable part of the Soviet Union (Snyder 2010: 161).

3 The reason here was that Western Ukraine, which had been Polish until 1939, then became the major sugar-producing region of the Soviet Union.

4 Snyder (2010: 182) notes how local Soviet elites escaped to the east in face of the German advance.

5 As related on page 33, note 48.

6 The practice of attaching political commissars to units of the Red Army was initiated by Trotsky during the Civil War of 1918, when shortage of command experience in the field led to a number of former Imperial officers – of questionable loyalty – to be recruited (Brown 2010: 53).

7 In contrast to the numerous studies of the battle for Stalingrad listed in Müller and Ueberschär (1997) little is published about this part of the Russo-German war: Forstmeier (1964) is probably the best source.

8 Малая Земля, lit. 'little land'.

9 As commander of a token regiment of the 4th Ukrainian Front.

10 Renamed Szczecin and Wrocław.

11 Renamed Kaliningrad.

12 This meant, incidentally, that Romania would no longer have a common frontier with either Czechoslovakia or Poland.

13 Majdanek, the easternmost of the German death camps was close by, and liberated more or less intact, allowing the world to see for the first time, the gas chambers, crematoria etc., where more than 300,000 Jews, mainly from Poland and the Soviet Union, had been murdered.

14 Churchill, on the same day as the declaration, learnt that his party had been defeated in the British General Election held following the German surrender. The result was that he returned to London, with the new Prime-Minister, Clement Attlee, replacing him at Potsdam on 28 July.

15 In January 1946, Nikolai Voznesensky, Stalin's economic administrator, told that the Soviet Union had lost 30 per cent of its national wealth (Taubman 2003: 179).

16 The fact that all the facts in this paragraph are from Chapter 3 of the official biography (1977) published, significantly, while Brezhnev was still alive, does not necessarily mean that they are not be trusted. From the beginning both Soviet industry and agriculture could perform spectacularly when Moscow allowed the necessary inputs – as clearly happened in Dnepropetrovsk in the late 1940s.

17 In July 1955, at a plenary meeting of the Supreme Soviet, Khrushchev, at odds with Molotov, blurted out, 'We began the Korean War. Everyone knows we did'. The truth of this allegation – only made public in 1991 – is still problematic (Taubman 2003: 268).

18 See also pp. 53–72 [chapter 3].

3   The death of Stalin and the rise of Khrushchev

Coups d'etat

Suffering conspicuously poor health in the final months of 1952,[1] Stalin, whose behaviour had become increasingly unpredictable, was not expected to long survive into the new year, 1953. The question as to would succeed him as '*vozhd*',[2] or leader, was inevitably much debated at every level, for even those, like Brezhnev, who had no chance of the top job, were inevitably identified with one or other of the few who did. But who, then, were these few?

Following the Nineteenth Party Congress of October 1952, Vyacheslav Molotov, Stalin's foreign minister until 1947 as well as being someone whose voice still counted, identified a 'core group' – a troika whose members were Lavrentiy Beria, Georgy Malenkov and Nikita Khrushchev – as the key to succession once the *vozhd* had died (Taubman 2003: 225). Of these three, Beria, head of the MVD,[3] was both the most feared, and also the one least welcome as Stalin's successor – at any level from the Presidium to the man on the street – as he himself well knew. In the words of Stalin's daughter, Alliluyeva, Beria was 'more treacherous, more practiced in perfidy and cunning, more insolent and single-minded than my father'.

For Stalin this also meant that Beria must be excluded from the succession at any price. He made his wishes clear by seeing to it that Malenkov made the principal report to the Nineteenth Congress, seconded by Khrushchev. This, however, was not enough. Stalin, always paranoid about his health, went on to concoct a plot to kill him among the mainly Jewish doctors attending him in the Kremlin, which Beria would then fail to discover. The doctors 'involved' were arrested in January 1953, with *Pravda* noting the MVD's failure to 'uncover in good time, the wrecking terrorist organization among the doctors' – disregarding the fact that it had never existed in the first place.

The result, so long as Stalin remained alive, was to side-line Beria, even at the cost of a number of innocent doctors fearing for their lives. Then, in the early days of March, as Stalin lay dying, leading members of the Politburo kept watch, at the same time orchestrating the succession. Their decision, which became manifest following Stalin's death, on 5 March 1953, was that Malenkov – nominated by Beria – would be the new *vozhd*, with Beria then continuing as head of the MVD. That Malenkov then chose to be premier rather than First Secretary of the CPSU, suggests that he judged the bloated bureaucracy – a major part of Stalin's legacy – to be a better political power base (Kenez 1999: 188). Significantly, Molotov was then reappointed Foreign Minister. At the same time the Presidium,[4] increased to 25 members at the Nineteenth Congress, was reduced to ten members (ibid.: 187) recruited from the old guard (which, at least for the time being, would leave Brezhnev, and others at the same level, out in the cold). Khrushchev was side-lined, while Beria was jubilant (ibid.: 184). According to Khrushchev, 'there was no power on earth that could hold him back now. Nothing could get in his way' (Taubman 2003: 239). Even before Stalin's death he had already warned Bulganin, a senior member of the Presidium, that Beria only wanted to head the MVD 'for the purpose of destroying us, and he will do it too, if we let him' (ibid.: 238). Although Bulganin agreed, the problem was to find out how many others in key positions felt the same way – and above all, where did Malenkov stand? After all he had been proposed by Beria as Stalin's successor. One thing was clear to everyone: with Beria's MVD informants everywhere the necessary inquiries, and any action that might then follow, were fraught with danger.

The master-mind in the game played against Beria was Khrushchev, whose first move was to persuade Malenkov to keep a tight rein on Beria at meetings of the Presidium, so that other members, in increasing measure, combined to stall his proposals. Beria, greatly frustrated, identified Malenkov as his key opponent, and then disastrously, for his own future, approached Khrushchev for his support. This was just the move that Khrushchev needed to persuade Malenkov that Beria must be destroyed. Acting together, Khrushchev and Malenkov, using every possible means to hide what was up, gained the support of all the members of the Council of Ministers (Taubman 2003: 239) for a coup against Beria.

Khrushchev also orchestrated the actual coup, which took place on 26 July 1953: what, ostensibly, was a routine meeting of the Presidium, was in fact specially convened to set the stage for arresting Beria. With its commandant called away at the last moment, the standard Presidium bodyguard supplied by the MVD failed to react when detachments from the armed forces, specially mobilized for the occasion, entered the meeting, to be ordered by Malenkov, as Chairman of the Council of Ministers, to take Beria into custody, 'pending investigation of charges made against him' (Taubman 2003: 254). (Significantly Brezhnev was part of the small army detachment, led by Marshal Zhukov, involved in the operation (ibid.: 253)). Plans made in advance enabled Beria to be brought to a heavily protected guard-house, before the MVD bodyguards could realize what had happened.

Beria was held in custody until 18 December: then, at the end of a six-day a show trial staged according to standard Stalinist procedure, he was sentenced to death, together with six alleged accomplices. The sentence was carried out immediately in the same bunker as the trial had taken place. The events of that week in December were a foregone conclusion: they had been orchestrated at a meeting of the plenum of the Central Committee of the CPSU in July; this was dominated by Khrushchev, who in an impassioned speech made clear that the struggle for succession was not over. After all, it was Khrushchev who, at very considerable risk, had consistently taken the initiative in the process that led to the downfall of Beria. With this settled just before the end of 1953, the question then was, what would be the Khrushchev's next step.

Malenkov was the man who had most to fear, and in one way or another he was eclipsed by Khrushchev. As early as August 1954 the fact that Khrushchev led an important Soviet delegation to Beijing was a measure of his power, as was also the way that his supporters' club in the Kremlin was then being favoured with key appointments. Brezhnev, notably, was appointed to be second secretary of the Party in Kazakhstan in February 1954, with promotion to first secretary following in August (Taubman 2003: 262). This was particularly significant because in Kazakhstan Brezhnev would be committed to Khrushchev's 'virgin lands' policy, which was anathema to Malenkov and Molotov.[5]

In 1955 the political line-up became clearer: in February Malenkov (who had already, in early 1954, been forced to yield precedence to Khrushchev within the Presidium (Taubman 2003: 164)) was demoted by the Supreme Soviet from his office as prime minister (ibid.: 285 and Hayter 1966: 124),[6] and when, on 7 April Khrushchev informed the Presidium that the Twentieth Party Congress would take place on time, in early 1956, there could have been little doubt about who was calling the shots. If Malenkov still looked for a come-back (ibid.: 124), the endorsement of the prospective party congress by the Central Committee on 12 July made this prospect almost hopeless. He was paying the price of failing to realize, in the critical weeks after Stalin's death, that in the Soviet power structure the government was subordinate to the party, however much Stalin had 'emasculated the party apparatus' (Kenez 1999: 188).

In the summer of 1955, Khrushchev, by ensuring that he represented the Soviet Union at the four-power Geneva summit, presented himself to the world at large as the new *vozhd* (Taubman 2003: 241). What this all added up to for the future of the Soviet Union became much clearer after Khrushchev's 'secret speech' at the Twentieth Congress of the CPSU – the first to be held after Stalin's death. As already decided by Khrushchev in early 1955, the Congress convened on 14 February 1956. In his opening report on domestic and foreign policy, Khrushchev (as First Secretary), by telling the vast audience how the Central Committee 'had resolutely condemned the cult of the individual as alien to the spirit of Marxism-Leninism', could only be referring to Stalin (ibid.: 271).

This was only the beginning. On February 25, listed as the final day of the Congress, the Soviet delegates, headed by Khrushchev, proclaimed an unscheduled secret session. This was taken up by a four-hour speech by Khrushchev denouncing almost every aspect of Stalin's rule, at the same time expressing sympathy and calling for justice for the millions of people who had suffered under it (Taubman 2003: 272). Already, by this time a steady stream of prisoners were returning from the Gulags, to become witnesses to the abuses listed by Khrushchev (ibid.: 275), and the numbers could only increase after the secret speech (Kenez 1999: 193). With the end of the speech many of the Soviet delegates left the Congress Hall in a state of terror, for in one way or another almost all of them were to be counted among Stalin's accomplices (ibid.: 190), and now they had to accept as *vozhd* a man who promised to be guided by his hatred of Stalin. Some, such as Anastas Mikoyan, claimed to have urged Khrushchev, in the months before the Congress, to denounce Stalin; others, such as Molotov and Kaganovich, who had warned him against digging up the past, were left in a very precarious position (Taubman 2003: 278).

Mikhail Gorbachev later marvelled at Khrushchev's 'huge political risk', but after delivering his speech, Khrushchev returned home elated (Taubman 2003: 282). Convinced of its success, he made a point of promoting his supporters, so that Brezhnev not only became once more a candidate member of the Presidium, but also a member of the Secretariat. The speech did not remain a secret for long, if it ever had been so: following the authorized printing of thousands of copies for loyal party members, to say nothing of translations for those from other states in the Soviet orbit, it would certainly reach the free world's press sooner rather than later. In the event the *New York Times* published it on 4 June 1956.

In the new political climate following the wide circulation of the secret speech the Soviet leaders began to lose their hold not so much in their own country, but in the East European satellites (Kenez 1999: 193). Towards the end of the year political unrest, first in Poland, and then in Hungary, reached a level that, as seen from Moscow, could only be contained by Soviet military intervention. After a summer of unrest, set off by the brutal suppression of a strike in Poznań in May, in early October popular demonstrations in Poland got out of hand. Khrushchev showed his anxiety by sending two full members of the Presidium, Molotov and Kaganovich to Warsaw, where Władisław Gomułka, a Polish leader strong enough to stand up to Khrushchev, insisted that he call an end to the Soviet troop movements then threatening Poland. After calling off intervention at the eleventh hour, Khrushchev yielded to Gomułka (and by doing so left Poland with a long-term leader acceptable both to its own people, and as events would prove, to the Soviet Union. Gomułka would remain in office until 1971).

Hungary was much less fortunate. On 23 October Budapest erupted with a massive demonstration called to celebrate Gomułka's triumph in Poland, which Hungarians sought to emulate with their own popular leader, Imre Nagy. It was not to be. Once again Khrushchev hesitated, but persuaded first by the advice of Mao Zedong (conveyed by the head of a Chinese delegation that happened to be in Moscow) and second, by the intervention of British and French troops in Egypt following the Suez crisis (which Khrushchev seriously misjudged),[7] he ordered Soviet troops into Hungary. Nagy, with the public on his side, called upon Hungary to leave the Warsaw Pact.[8] By 5 November the uprising had been put down, but only at the cost of the lives of some 20,000 Hungarians and 1,500 Soviet soldiers (Taubman 2003: 299). At the eleventh hour, János Kádár, a colleague of Nagy, deserted him, and with Soviet support went on to become First Secretary of the Hungarian Communist Party – to remain in office for more than 30 years. Nagy, following a show trial, was executed in 1958.

However self-satisfied Khrushchev was as the result of his achievements at the end of 1956, there was considerable dissatisfaction among the full members of the Presidium, notably Malenkov, Molotov and Kaganovich (Taubman 2003: 315). In the early months of 1957 this 'gang of three', taking a leaf out of Khrushchev's own book, devised a strategy for dethroning him reminiscent of what he himself had done with Beria. The key to its success was a secure majority of eight to three in the Presidium, in which only full members had voting rights. Events then showed that they had misread the script. When the Presidium met on 18 June the alternate members, who supported Khrushchev, defended him in an acrimonious debate that kept it so long in session that there was no decisive vote but an adjournment to the following day. This enabled Khrushchev and his supporters to organize twenty letters from members of the Party's Central Committee (to which the Presidium was answerable) demanding a plenum of all 130 full members to resolve the challenge to Khrushchev. At the same time steps were taken to bring them to Moscow at short notice. On 20 June the session entered its third day, and at 6 p.m. a delegation of 57 members, already in Moscow, presented a signed petition for a plenum. This was a show of strength sufficient to ensure that it be granted.

The plenum began at 2 p.m. on 22 June, and lasted until 28 June. In one speech after another Khrushchev's supporters – most notably Marshal Zhukov – made explicit the complicity of his opponents in all the excesses of the Stalinist era that he had denounced a year earlier in the secret speech. Exact figures were given for the number of executions for which men such as Molotov and Kaganovich were responsible, but as some also made clear, Khrushchev, as Stalin's loyal henchman in the Ukraine, was no less culpable. After all, as Malenkov pointed out, the death warrants were signed by the whole Politburo (Taubman 2003: 321). The number involved, as pronounced by Khrushchev himself, was 681,692, but he went on to say: 'If only Stalin hadn't had two evil geniuses Beria and Malenkov, at his side, a lot could have been prevented' (ibid.: 323). Beria had already been dealt with; Malenkov, inevitably, lost his place both in the Presidium and the Central Committee, but did survive to take up an appointment as manager of a hydroelectric station in Kazakhstan. Another, much younger man, Dmitri Shepilov was banished in the same way, following a speech, made at the plenum, urging that the criticisms of Khrushchev should also be taken seriously (ibid.: 322). This was significant because Shepilov, a contemporary of Brezhnev, had earlier in the year been appointed to succeed Molotov as foreign minister. Andrei Gromyko, whom Khrushchev then appointed as Molotov's successor, remained in office until 1985 (when Gorbachev replaced him with Eduard Shevardnadze). As for Brezhnev, he had prudently kept his head down during the crucial days of late June 1957 and so still counted as a trustworthy Khrushchev supporter. Earlier in the year he had been brought back to Moscow from Kazakhstan (where his achievements in both industry and agriculture had greatly impressed Khrushchev) to be deputy chairman of the Central Committee of the CPSU, with special responsibility for military research and development. In one way or another this involved him, as supervisor, in heavy industry, large-scale construction and space (Zemtsov 1989: 42).

Election as a full member of the Presidium later in the year not only recognized Brezhnev's loyalty (and achievements in Kazakhstan) but also established him firmly in the corridors of power. With key rivals, such as Malenkov, Molotov and Kaganovich out of the way as a result of the failure of the June coup, Khrushchev, at least in principle, was firmly in the saddle,[9] and on the face of things it was in the interest of those close to him, such as Brezhnev, to keep him there – the more so after Brezhnev had been appointed Chairman in 1960 (Zemtsov 1989: 53). Even so, Khrushchev was only to last another four years.

As one day succeeded another, Khrushchev's temperament and behaviour made it clear that he was not master of events, even of those which he had himself orchestrated. Although in the months before his seventieth birthday, on 17 April 1964, he was plainly concerned about who would succeed him, he found shortcomings in all possible candidates. These included two he should not have overlooked: Nikolai Podgorny and Leonid Brezhnev. The former was 'too narrow', and the latter 'not suited either' (Zemtsov 1989: 614). Although, by this time, all Khrushchev's colleagues found him next to impossible (Kenez 1999: 210–211), it was these two who acted decisively against him. Brezhnev, who as chairman of the Presidium (and as such officially head of state), had made the official presentation to Khrushchev on his seventieth birthday, was nominated as deputy Party Leader in July 1964, with Podgorny succeeded him as Presidium Chairman. Also in July, Khrushchev's abusive behaviour and lack of control at a plenum of the Central Committee ensured that no official record was kept of the proceedings, at the same time strengthening the resolve of those present to get rid of him. Mićunović, the Yugoslav Ambassador in Moscow and as good a judge as any of what was going on behind the scenes, was certain that Khrushchev's fall must be attributed to 'internal political reasons' (Mićunović 1980: 441),[10] if only because his successors continued – disastrously as events would prove – his foreign policy. There is no need to be specific about these reasons: it was their cumulative effect that made it essential for Khrushchev to go.

Khrushchev's frequent visits outside Moscow gave every scope for his colleagues in the capital to plot against him. In the event no-one stood by him, and when he left for a Black Sea vacation at Pitsunda, his dacha in Georgia, on 3 October, it was time to act. In his absence, his colleagues in Moscow voted him out of office: he was a sitting duck, and there had been no need for the careful planning of which he himself had proved a master, first with the ouster of Beria in 1953, then with the secret speech of 1956, and finally, in 1957, with his own suppression of the coup against his own person. Historically what is most significant about the events of October 1964 is the way that Brezhnev, although not then the ringleader (Hayter 1970: 29), emerged as the new *vozhd*. His appeal – at least to the party – was simply that once the Soviet Union had recovered from the turbulence of the Khrushchev era he would be committed to maintaining the status quo (which, in the judgment of history, has come to mean the *zastoi*, or 'stagnation', for which he is now remembered). In the Politburo, the 'chief engineer of Khrushchev's fall' was Mikhail Suslov (Zemtsov 1989: 66), a sort of 'High Priest of communism' totally 'devoid of personal magnetism' (Hayter 1970: 29,30; Kenez 1999: 210; Mićunović 1980: 444), whose power behind the scenes contrasted with a low public profile. In Suslov's book, Brezhnev was just the right man to succeed Khrushchev.

In the ten years of the Khrushchev era, a lot of water had flowed under the bridge, coming from many different streams, to create the domain that Brezhnev (together with men such as Kosygin and Podgorny) inherited in October 1964. Because these different streams together define Khrushchev's legacy, they must be looked at in some detail before leaving this colourful yet fatally flawed character.

The space race and nuclear armaments

The final year of World War II witnessed the operational use of two weapons that, once the war ended, would transform the way that any future war on the same scale would be fought – that is, if it ever occurred. These two weapons were first, high explosives carried by rockets, and second, the atomic bombs that in August 1945 destroyed two Japanese cities. The former, developed by Nazi Germany in a project led by Werner von Braun, were used with considerable destructive effect against not only Britain, but also Belgium and France once they had been liberated by Allied Forces in late 1944. The latter were developed in the United States in the joint Anglo-American Manhattan Project. Although during the war the Soviet Union had developed neither rockets as weapons, nor atomic bombs, this was not for want of trying. The way final victory over Japan was achieved in August 1945 resolved Stalin, if any such incentive was necessary, to persevere in developing both rockets and nuclear weapons. Following the North Atlantic Treaty of 4 April 1949 this would also be the top military priority of the NATO powers; indeed the United States had never stood still – so much so that it had moved much of the equipment and personnel of van Braun's German operation, including its leader, to a new American location.[11] At the same time Los Alamos, home to the Manhattan Project, stayed in business, although in 1952 the development of thermonuclear weapons was assigned to the new Lawrence Livermore National Laboratory in California (Rhodes 1995: 496). In all this the Soviet Union was not lagging far behind, even though it was outplayed by the Americans when it came to appropriating the German rocket enterprise. On the atomic side, indeed, it was helped by atomic spies who betrayed many of the results of the Manhattan Project.[12] What was clear to both sides, even before Stalin's death in 1953, was that within only a few years the armed forces of both the Soviet Union and the United States would have long distance rockets with nuclear warheads – at least if both sides decided to embark on this terrifying arms race. In the confrontational climate of the 1950s they were certain to do so.

The race was never between equals. Even before World War II, the Soviet Union lagged far behind the United States on any economic measure,[13] even though they had much the same population.[14] What is more, where the demands made on the US wartime economy led to a substantial increase in the capital value of investment in a country which had suffered neither enemy occupation, nor any material destruction or loss of life within its own frontiers as the result of enemy action, in the Soviet Union – where the territory occupied by German forces, and later regained, was home to about a quarter of the population – some 70,000 villages, 1,700 towns, 32,000 factories and 70,000 km. of railway, were destroyed, leaving some 10,000,000 homeless, to say nothing of 25,000,000 dead as a result of hostilities (with another 2,000,000 dying of famine in the years 1946–1948) (Figes 2007: 457).[15] In short, 'the country was exhausted by war, terror and poverty' (Kenez 1999: 186).

In the Soviet Union, therefore, the simple reconstruction of what had been lost placed a burden on the national economy that the United States never had to carry. If, on top of all this, the Soviet Union was to compete in the nuclear arms race, it would have to mobilize its resources on such a scale that little would be left over to reward its population with a higher standard of living. One likely reason for the fall of Khrushchev in 1964 is that colleagues such as Brezhnev and Suslov could not accept the level of priority he wished for the Soviet consumer economy (Hayter 1970: 30).

For all the obstacles in its way, the Soviet armaments programme after World War II was remarkably successful: in catching up with the US, every stage, such as the first successful test of an atomic bomb, was reached earlier than could have been expected. In the late 1950s and early 1960s the Soviet Union was even ahead of the game: *sputnik*, the first successful earth satellite was launched on 10 October 1957, and on 12 April 1961 Yuri Gagarin became the first man in space. However spectacular these achievements, they hardly added up to the Soviet Union beating the United States at its own game: the hard truth was that both sides were steadily expanding their nuclear arsenals, at the same time increasing not only the range at which rockets, or where appropriate, military aircraft,[16] could deliver warheads, but also their destructive power.

To reach this position the Soviet Union not only had to develop a vast secret military industrial complex, but it also had to find skilled scientists and other professionals to operate it. Here it was remarkably successful. From the end of World War II it was official policy to establish a loyal middle class, rewarded, at the same time, with the sort of material benefits otherwise reserved for top party officials (Figes 2007: 470). This result depended upon a vast expansion of higher education, with 2,700,000 students in the early 1950s, while at the same time there was no repeat of Stalin's terror of the 1930s. Although Khrushchev proscribed that students should also acquire work experience in farms and factories, the policy soon proved to be counterproductive while the laws designed to enforce it were easily circumvented (Kenez 1999: 212). Those most successful in doing so were also the most likely members of a new professional elite, of whom all that was asked was acceptance of the system (Figes 2007: 470). For those recruited to the nuclear arms programme this meant working in remote plants, known only by such cryptic names as Chelyabinsk-40,[17] for an organization that was part of the MVD – and as such until 1953 part of the realm of the dreaded and sinister Lavrenti Beria.[18] If life, by Soviet standards, was privileged and opulent, severe penalties for giving anything away inhibited contact with any outsiders. The whole operation depended upon an elite of top scientists, with internationally recognized names such as those of Kapitza and Sakharov – men who in the end could not be silenced.

The Iron Curtain

On 13 May 1955, Khrushchev set up the Warsaw Pact as a reaction to the admission of West Germany to NATO a week earlier. This was effectively a statement that the signatories to the Pact, East Germany, Poland, Czechoslovakia, Hungary, Bulgaria, Romania and Albania, together with the Soviet Union, formed a single bloc opposed to the NATO powers. In essence, therefore, where NATO constituted the supporters' club of the United States in Europe, the Warsaw Pact did the same for the Soviet Union. A week later the stand-off between the two sides was simplified by the Austrian State Treaty, which, ending the four-power occupation established at the end of World War II, granted independence to a new state of Austria on the basis of neutrality in the Cold War.

If the object of the Warsaw Pact was to create harmony among its signatories, the events in Poland and Hungary related on page 57 soon showed that it was failing to do so. Indeed, one factor leading to Soviet intervention in Hungary in November 1956, was the declared intent of Imre Nagy, the popular Hungarian leader, to withdraw from the Warsaw Pact (Mićunović 1980: 133).

The success of his intervention in Hungary did not long satisfy Khrushchev. What had succeeded in putting an end to popular discontent in Hungary, could not do so in East Germany, the key to the confrontation with the NATO powers. The problem was West Berlin, a NATO foothold in the heart of East Germany, which, at one and the same time, provided a way for its citizens to escape to the West, and a window allowing the West to observe, and then report to the world at large, what life offered, not only in East Germany, but also in the other Warsaw Pact powers.

For Khrushchev the situation was intolerable, and on 27 November 1958, he summoned the western ambassadors in Moscow to the Kremlin, to tell that if the states they represented failed, within six months, to sign a peace treaty on his terms – which critically included turning West Berlin into a demilitarized 'free city' – then control of access to the city would be handed over to East Germany (Taubman 2003: 397). Although in Washington President Eisenhower saw the US position in Berlin as a 'can of worms' (ibid.: 398), he knew he had to stand firm. At the same time, the conflict over Berlin was one between two equally intransigent and solidly established German leaders, Walter Ulbricht in the east and Konrad Adenauer in the west.[19] Eisenhower, in shaping his Berlin policy, was as much beholden to the latter, as Khrushchev to the former. Indeed Ulbricht was an extreme hard-liner among the Warsaw Pact leaders, and – given the strategic importance of Germany – one that Moscow could not ignore.

Although four years later the Berlin question was still not resolved, in the meantime the position taken by Khrushchev did lead to an invitation to visit the United States – an outcome that at the deepest level accorded with his interest in détente. The actual visit took place in September 1959, and ended with two days of talks between Eisenhower and Khrushchev at Camp David (Taubman 2003: 435–439). Although these resulted in little substantial progress, Khrushchev did lift the six-month Berlin ultimatum, and Eisenhower agreed to attend a four-power conference and accepted an invitation to visit the Soviet Union in June 1960. Khrushchev presented all this as evidence of a successful visit – so much so that in February 1960 an official Warsaw Pact statement referred to a new 'phase of negotiations [to settle] major disputed international issues'.

Everything augured well for a Paris summit planned to start on 16 May 1960, but then on 1 May the Soviet air force brought down an American U2 reconnaissance airplane flying at an altitude of some 25,000 metres over the heart of Russia; what is more, the pilot, Gary Powers, parachuted to safety, to be captured on the ground by a *kolkhoz* labourer (Taubman 2003: 466). The U2 flights were part of a CIA (US Central Intelligence Agency) operation that had started in 1956: its main object was to record progress made in the development of advanced weapons within the Soviet military industrial complex. With the prospect of the 1960 summit, Eisenhower, rightly concluding that the flights were known to Soviet intelligence, ordered a seven-month moratorium (ibid.: 444). By April 1960 the CIA was pressing for new flights, with a much improved model of the U2, to detect and photograph possible Soviet intercontinental ballistic missile (ICBM) launching sites near Plesetsk in northern Russia (Taubman 2003: 445).[20] Eisenhower yielded to the CIA, and the resumption of the flights was immediately reported to a very resentful Khrushchev. When, however, the U2 was brought down on 1 May, he was delighted at the prospect of a shamed US President apologizing – and accepting at the same time the trial of a US air force officer – on the eve of the summit. When, on 5 May, Khrushchev finally broke the news at a vast Kremlin meeting of the Supreme Soviet,[21] he added that if Pentagon activists committed 'this vast aggressive act . . . without the President's knowledge', he could go to Paris 'with a pure heart and good intentions' (ibid.: 456). Two days later, on 7 May, with the same audience, he revealed that the U2 pilot was alive and well in Soviet custody. The speech was calculated to make the Americans look ridiculous, at the same time leaving Eisenhower with no alternative to admitting full responsibility as Commander-in-Chief of all US forces: this he did the next day, 8 May (ibid.: 458).

Khrushchev, expressing horror at what had happened, continued in the same vein, even when the heads of state, including Eisenhower, met for the first time in the Elysée Palace on 16 May. He then declared that the Soviet Union – confronted by Eisenhower's failure not only to condemn the US missions, but also to call a halt to them – could not then proceed with the conference, but would be able to do so after a delay of 'six to eight months'. Given the US Presidential Election due in November 1960, this would mean that Eisenhower, even if still in office, would certainly be a 'lame duck' president. Although de Gaulle – host to the conference – did everything possible to put it back on track, Khrushchev's continued intransigence made this impossible, and critically for Brezhnev's foreign policy in the late 1960s ensured that Moscow could count on little support from Paris – whatever the issue (Haslam 2011: 183). Khrushchev devoted a final press conference for 3,000 journalists in the Palais de Chaillot to uninhibited provocation of the western powers, directing his scorn particularly at West Germany (ibid.: 465). It was as if he had always wanted the conference to fail, and that may well have been the truth of the matter. As Ulbricht, the East German leader, confessed to Khrushchev later in 1961 (ibid.: 483), nothing that the conference might have achieved would have helped him maintain his regime, and the same essentially was true for Adenauer in West Germany.

With John F. Kennedy succeeding Eisenhower as US President in January 1961, Khrushchev saw a new opportunity for resolving the Berlin crisis. To his frustration, Kennedy, accepting the status quo as it was after the collapse of Paris summit, seemed to be little interested in further discussion. Then, in April 1961, the ill-fated Bay of Pigs assault – a futile attempt by Cuban irregulars, based in the US, to destabilize Fidel Castro's revolutionary government – was seen by Khrushchev as an opportunity for wrong-footing Kennedy (just as, a year earlier he had wrong-footed Eisenhower following the U2 incident) (Haslam 2011: 493). Khrushchev's plan was to make a proposal for a new summit on Berlin, which, Kennedy, given the circumstances, was certain to reject. When Kennedy, by accepting the proposal showed the world how Khrushchev had miscalculated, the summit went ahead in Vienna in early June 1961. As in Paris, Khrushchev came across as 'ruthless and barbaric', but Kennedy, although generally unconcerned by communist expansion worldwide, held firm on Berlin (ibid.: 498). Then, on returning to Washington, he asked the US Congress to approve funds for a much increased military build-up (including the construction of nuclear shelters to protect the civilian population). The result could only be to increase the American lead, already very substantial, in the nuclear arms race. This, for the Soviet Union, demanded, on one side, much increased military expenditure and on the other an even stronger commitment to 'peaceful coexistence'. To many in the Presidium, including notably Brezhnev (Taubman 2003: 454), this presented the reduction in numbers in the armed forces that Khrushchev had insisted on in 1960 as the result of a dangerous miscalculation. Throughout the summer of 1961 Khrushchev continued to be obsessed by Berlin, the more so given the unprecedentedly large number of those fleeing East Germany as a reaction to his own conduct at Vienna. Ulbricht, who had long seen the construction of a wall separating East and West Berlin as the only way of ending this flight, finally persuaded Khrushchev to agree with him. Starting on 15 August the wall was built in a matter of days. It would only come down, 28 years later, with the collapse of the German Democratic Republic in 1989.

Returning to the summer of 1961, Khrushchev, noting remarkably little reaction from Washington on Berlin, saw another opportunity for getting the better of Kennedy. He would supply Fidel Castro with nuclear weapons for the defence of Cuba. This was another serious miscalculation – indeed the most serious in all the years that Khrushchev was at the helm in the Soviet Union. This is the story in the last section of this chapter. First, however, Soviet involvement in the other side of the world demands our attention.

Mao's China

With the proclamation of the People's Republic of China in October 1949, Stalin gave much of the credit to the support given by the Soviet Union to Mao Zedong's revolution against the Chiang Kai-shek's National Government – the 'Guomindang'. By temperament Stalin, in foreign as much as in domestic affairs, could not act otherwise than as a dictator (Djilas 1969: 103). In his book, therefore, communist regimes outside the Soviet Union could only be supported to the extent that they did not challenge him. This policy worked well enough in the countries of eastern Europe which in 1955 would join together in the Warsaw Pact, for the communist regimes were from the beginning backed by Soviet military force imposed following the defeat of Germany in World War II.

Two cases, however, did not fit this bill. The first was Yugoslavia, where Marshal Tito established a communist state well before the Soviet advance in 1944–1945 had reached its frontiers, and the second, China, where the revolution was by that time well on its way to final victory without any useful Soviet support. While it is doubtful whether Mao Zedong ever saw China as being subordinate to the Soviet Union, this was not the view of Moscow, where the Stalinist interpretation of events was confirmed by the Korean War (1950–1953), which started, even if it did not end, according to a plan dictated by Stalin as much as by Mao. In any case – whoever called the shots in 1950 – it was clear to Mao, after the end of a war in which China suffered up to a million casualties and the Soviet Union next to none,[22] that he must dance to his own tune. Although, even before the end of World War II, Mao's actions had long shown his independence, the Korean War once again made clear that he must trust his own judgment. This, however, was not immediately clear to Khrushchev in the years following both Stalin's death and the Panmunjom armistice in 1953.

Khrushchev's secret speech in February 1957 was interpreted by Mao Zedong, rightly or wrongly, as stating a change in Soviet foreign policy unfavourable to the interests of China. He was confirmed in his views, when, in November 1957, he attended in Moscow the Congress of Communist Parties in Communist Countries. There, in what proved to be Mao's last ever visit to the Soviet Union, he mistrusted Khrushchev not only for his policy of coexistence with the West, but also for his condemnation of the cult of personality. (To Mao, whose public image in China depended on just such a cult, it made no difference that Khrushchev's main target was Stalin). Even so, Mao was still ready to accept Soviet help in developing missiles and atomic weapons.

In 1958, however, Khrushchev pushed his luck too far by proposing that the Soviet Union should combine with China to establish a joint naval force in the Pacific, with an operational area – including essential on-shore installations – that would extend from the Soviet Arctic to the South China Sea. The case presented to Mao was that this 'common fleet' was indispensable for confronting the US Seventh Fleet, which, following the Korean War, maintained a very strong presence in the western Pacific. Khrushchev had not realized that any foreign presence in China was anathema to Mao, who told Khrushchev, in so many words, that 'we do not want anyone to use our land to achieve their own purposes any more' (Taubman 2003: 391). To Mao, the Soviet proposal was no less than a Trojan horse: after all, he could remember, even if Khrushchev did not, how since the early nineteenth century, foreign powers – mainly European – had enjoyed, at the expense of imperial China, extra-territorial rights in the so-called 'treaty ports'.

Mao was not content just to reject Khrushchev's joint defence proposal. In August 1958 he ordered shore batteries in south China to bombard two small islands, Quemoy and Matsu, just off the coast, that were held by Chiang Kai-shek's Guomindang in Taiwan. Although not informed in advance of this action, Khrushchev was bound by the Sino-Soviet Treaty of Alliance of 1950 to declare his support, while Washington threatened war to defend the two islands (Crump 2007a: 31). At the same time Andrei Gromyko, who, as Soviet Foreign Minister, was Mao's guest in Beijing, heard from his host what Chinese strategy would be in the event of nuclear war.

The potentially disastrous consequences for Khrushchev's policy of détente with the west were of little concern to Mao, whose People's Republic enjoyed neither diplomatic recognition by the US and its allies, nor – at this stage – the possession of nuclear weapons. And if there was to be nuclear war, the Soviet Union was bound to be involved. Confronted with this horrifying prospect Khrushchev, intent on mending fences, went to Beijing at the end of September 1959, to attend the celebration of the tenth anniversary of the founding of the People's Republic: the visit was a disaster, and ended with an acrimonious confrontation with Mao (Taubman 2003: 394). The Soviet delegation, led by Khrushchev, stayed for only three days rather than seven as planned.

In his approach to China Khrushchev did no better in 1960 than he had in 1959. With a surprise attendance at the Third Congress of the Romanian Communist Party in June, his intention was to ensure the presence of the leaders of other communist parties (Taubman 2003: 470). The calculated absence of Mao Zedong (which left Peng Zhen as head of the Chinese delegation) did not deter Khrushchev from making a vituperative attack on Mao at the final closed session, describing him as a 'Buddha who gets his theory out of his nose' (ibid.: 471), and so provoking a bitter reply from Peng. Khrushchev reacted by withdrawing all Soviet experts and advisers from China, repudiating any number of contracts and scrapping almost as many joint projects in science and technology. His ambassador in Beijing was 'amazed' by this drastic step, while, significantly, for Brezhnev, Khrushchev's outburst marked the decisive break with China (although five years later his attempt to repair it was equally ham-fisted).[23] Then, in October 1961, Zhou Enlai, leading the Chinese delegation to the 22nd Congress of the CPSU, made a point of leaving early, but not before paying tribute in Red Square not only to Lenin, but also to Stalin (ibid.: 540) (whose body, on Khrushchev's instructions, was removed from the mausoleum on Red Square on the last night of the Congress (ibid.: 515)).

The rift between China and the Soviet Union would never be mended so long as Mao lived.[24] His rejection of Khrushchev's strategy of a joint Sino-Soviet naval presence in the western Pacific seriously restricted the Soviet Union's capacity to establish a significant presence in east and south-east Asia – which, of course, suited Mao's book very well. If, in his dealings with the Soviet Union Mao presented himself as an unreconstructed Stalinist, his differences with Khrushchev and the Soviet leaders that came after him were not purely ideological. So long as the integrity of his People's Republic was not threatened, Mao saw no reason to involve China operationally in worldwide revolution: events should be left to take their own course, and if this proved favourable to China, then so much the better. This approach to foreign policy, however, was never that of the Soviet Union: the next section shows what this would lead to in a number of different parts of the world.

Fishing in troubled waters

A commitment to establishing communism worldwide was always essential to the ideology of the Soviet Union (Hayter 1970: vii); seen in this light the success of the October revolution of 1917 could only be a first step towards achieving this end. According to strict Marxist principle, communist regimes would emerge outside Russia, as local parties succeeded in overturning established capitalist and imperialist governments. Soviet support, essential for achieving this purpose, defined the role of a special organization, the Comintern, which, with its head-quarters in Moscow, became home to representatives of communist parties in countries outside Russia awaiting the day when they would finally be in power. If, as a result of the pre-World War II international political line-up, the countries that counted in the Comintern were mainly European, Zhou Enlai still came to Moscow from China and Ho Chi Minh from Vietnam. Even so, there was little prospect for communism in Chiang Kai-shek's China, and even less in Vietnam – which was still part of the French colonial empire. In the aftermath of World War I prospects were far better in Italy, France, Germany and Spain, so that top European communists like Palmiro Togliatti from Italy or Walter Ulbricht from Germany regularly attended Comintern meetings in Moscow. In the event, none of them ever came near to power in these critical times; on the contrary, with Mussolini in Italy (1922), Hitler in Germany (1933) and finally Franco in Spain (1939), coming to power as right-wing totalitarian dictators, communist parties went underground with many of their leaders, such as Ulbricht and Togliatti becoming exiles in Moscow. This was not necessarily a safe haven, for Stalin's purges of top party members were not confined to Soviet citizens. By this time, anyway, it was all too clear how little the Comintern had actually achieved. Stalin, who had never thought much of it, wound it up shortly after the German invasion in 1941.

With the end of World War II the political line-up of Europe – largely the result of what had been agreed at Yalta (as related in Chapter 2) – meant that Stalin, some years before his death in 1953, had established a solid Soviet bloc in eastern Europe (which after May 1955 comprised the Warsaw Pact powers). This was destined to be the high tide of Soviet power in Europe, as had long been apparent when Khrushchev was ousted in 1964.

Although after Stalin's day there was nothing more to be gained by the Soviet Union in Europe, the world outside Europe was being transformed in a process that began with defeat of Japan in August 1945. Although the decline, if not the collapse of European colonial empires largely defined this transformation, it extended to parts of the world – such as notably Latin America – which, in principle, comprised a large number of independent sovereign states. In this process the colonies least likely to revert to their subordinate pre-war state were those that had been conquered by the Japanese. Seen from the Kremlin every such case presented an unprecedented opportunity for the emergence of new communist powers, beholden to Moscow rather than Washington.

Four south-east Asian colonial empires fall to be considered in this light. The simplest case is that of the Philippines, a vast archipelago which, in 1898, became an American overseas territory as a part of the spoils of victory in the Spanish–American war. The whole territory was lost to the Japanese in the first five months of the Pacific War, but with the end of the war in 1945, it was granted independence with its first president, Manuel Roxas, elected on 23 April 1946. Less than a year later Roxas, well able to recognize a powerful ally, granted the US 99-year leases on 22 military bases, of which Subic Bay, for the US Navy, and Clark Base, for the air force, were of major strategic importance (Crump 2007a: 207). At the same time Filipino nationals were granted privileged immigration status in the US (where they had already settled in considerable numbers), while exports to the US – mainly of plantation crops – enjoyed preferential tariffs. The price paid for all this was a succession of inefficient, corrupt and self-seeking governments, who did little for a poor and rapidly growing population. Locally communist insurrection, led by Hukbalahap guerrillas who – unlike many government supporters – had actually fought against the Japanese, enjoyed considerable popular support, but it was never going to be a successful revolution. Its activities simply meant more American money for the Filipino armed forces, the government's essential power base. Moscow (and Beijing for that matter) could give nothing beyond moral support. Washington was plainly not going to allow the Philippines to go at any price.

Although the British, whose south-east Asian empire comprised Malaya, Singapore and a part of Borneo, were able to restore their rule after World War II, they did so in face of the Malayan Communist Party fighting a war of independence, with terrorist attacks on mines, plantations and lines of communication claiming numerous Malayan and British lives. Its members, mainly recruited from the minority Chinese population, were inspired by Mao Zedong's success in China (Crump 2007a: 189). The British, however, succeeded in suppressing the revolt, first by winning the hearts and minds of the majority Malay and Indian population – stressing the Chinese contempt for Islam – and then by setting a time-table for independence, starting in 1957 with self-rule for Malaya (ibid.: 192). It helped also that British military-aid was essential for resisting Indonesian claims made on Malaysian territory in Borneo. With local communists beholden to Beijing, Moscow never had anything to gain in Malaysia (which throughout the Brezhnev years was a rock-solid capitalist bastion).

Where the British in Malaya in the end lost little in the new post-colonial world of south-east Asia, the Netherlands, with its vast East Indies empire on the other side of the Malacca strait, lost everything. For four years, 1945–1949, the Dutch fought hard to recover their empire, but in the end they had to concede defeat to the Indonesian nationalist leader, Ahmed Sukarno. Indonesia became an independent sovereign state (with a population of more than 100,000,000) – which from an orthodox Marxist perspective – was born out of a successful struggle against capitalist imperialism. This was an opportunity for Moscow, and Sukarno was ready, to a degree, to play along. Internationally, however, the cause closest to his heart was non-alignment, which meant that the nations committed to it – mainly former European colonies, but including Yugoslavia – refused to be beholden to either the Soviet Union or China on one side, or to the United States, and other western powers, on the other.

In April 1955, Sukarno, by orchestrating a major conference, attended by leading politicians from 29 states, in the Indonesian city of Bandung, was able to profile himself as the leader of the non-aligned movement. China, represented by its prime minster, Zhou Enlai, inevitably played a dominant role, while the Soviet Union did not even qualify for an invitation. On the contrary, the general consensus, condemning 'colonialism in all its forms', extended to the Soviet Union's hold on eastern Europe.

Sukarno, with his own policy of 'guided democracy', did his best, internationally, to play off east against west, while at the same time guiding Indonesia, domestically, towards economic chaos. For ten years after Bandung Sukarno held on to power, but in the end corruption and chaos provoked a reaction: in the late summer of 1965, a military coup led by General Achmad Suharto, deposed Sukarno and took over the government (Crump 2007a: 209).

Suharto's regime lasted for more than 30 years. One reason for his success was that from the start he encouraged western investment, while at the same time, his brutal suppression of communism in Indonesia – leaving tens of thousands dead – showed whose side Indonesia was on in the stand-off between East and West.

When, in October 1964, Brezhnev took over from Khrushchev in Moscow, he had less than a year to deal with Sukarno, and by this time it was already clear that the Soviet Union had little to gain in Indonesia. Under Suharto, Brezhnev – and for that matter Mao Zedong – had to accept that Indonesia offered next to nothing. In a region of critical international importance – broadly defined by he western Pacific and the South China Sea – the balance of power had tipped decisively against them.

Even so, in this region there was still one battle to be fought, not in one of the vast island states, but in the former French colony of Indochina, which was part of continental south-east Asia: here Moscow would be involved, but always in competition with Beijing, and then in a confrontation in which it had the weaker hand.

While French involvement in Indochina goes back to the early nineteenth century, the definitive establishment of the Union of Indochina, comprising Vietnam, Cambodia and Laos, dates from 1887. While the three component states all had a long recorded history in south-east Asia, the most important of them, both politically and economically, was Vietnam: this was essentially a quite narrow strip of land stretched out between latitudes 8°N and 24°N, with a coastal strip of well over 1,000 km along the South China Sea and an interior defined by ranges of hills covered in tropical vegetation. In two vast areas, one in the north around the colonial capital of Hanoi in the flood plain of the Red River, and the other in the south, around Saigon, in that of the Mekong River, millions of peasants cultivated rice, as also did many more in the hill country; this was also the basic agricultural economy of the ancient kingdoms of Laos (an entirely inland state) and Cambodia.

Like the British in Malaysia or the Dutch in Indonesia the French exploited Indochina by maintaining a typical dependent colonial economy, based on the export of primary commodities – mainly plantation crops. Although French concern for the welfare of local populations went no further than what was necessary to ensure their optimal exploitation as a source of labour, there was still a 'mission civilisatrice' ensuring that some at least of the children went to school, to be educated in French ways. One of these, a Vietnamese boy called Nguyen That Than, born in 1892, did so well that in 1912, he was able to leave home and travel the world (Crump 2007a: 125). After visiting London and New York, he settled for Paris in 1918 and immediately became active in radical politics – so much so that in 1922 he was one of the founder members of the French Communist Party to become, in 1924, a member of the Comintern in Moscow, along with Zhou Enlai and another notable characters. With this background he returned home in 1930 with a new name, Ho Chi Minh, to found the Indochinese Communist Party. He went on to take an active part in local popular uprisings against the French, who lost little time in declaring the Communist Party illegal, followed by the arrest, and, where appropriate in their judgment, the execution of its members. Ho always escaped, where necessary by taking refuge outside Vietnam. None the less what he had seen in Vietnam convinced him that there would be strong grass-roots support for a Communist takeover. In the late 1930s all Ho needed to do was bide his time.

The position changed radically in his favour following the defeat of France in 1940, and the establishment of a new government in Vichy on terms dictated by Germany. In Vietnam this meant accepting a Japanese military presence, in what would remain a French colony. With the Japanese mainly concerned with their war in China, and the French deprived of all support from Paris, the time was ripe for Ho Chi Minh to establish a more solid base in Vietnam. This he did by organizing a new resistance movement, Viet Minh, to fight the Japanese, and later, the French. In March 1945, the final year of the Pacific War, the Japanese occupying forces turned on the local French administration, both military and civil, in retaliation for the declaration of war by General de Gaulle, who had established a new government in Paris following the liberation of France in 1944. This, to the Japanese, turned the status of the French in Vietnam from friend to foe. The Japanese reaction was brutal: the French, first turned out of their offices, were then imprisoned, and in some cases executed.

With the defeat of Japan in August 1945, the formal surrender on 2 September provided the occasion for Ho Chi Minh to return to Hanoi and proclaim the independence of the Democratic Republic of Vietnam – in much the same way as Sukarno, two weeks earlier in Jakarta, had proclaimed that of Indonesia. At this stage the local French administrators, locked up by the Japanese in March, were still in prison. When, on 9 October, regular French forces finally reached Hanoi, their commander, General Sainteny, had to negotiate with the local Viet Minh commander, the formidable General Giap, Ho Chi Minh's right-hand man.

This was the beginning of a process that was to last for more than seven years, during which the French, facing mounting resistance from the well-organized Viet Minh forces, tried to restore their authority in Vietnam. Finally, in the spring of 1954, General Giap decisively defeated the French Army in the battle of Dien Bien Phu, deep in the interior of North Vietnam. It was then plain to all that North Vietnam was lost to the French, who threatened to lose the south also unless they received considerable material and political support from the US. Washington, however, made it clear that this required a firm French commitment to granting independence to a new state of South Vietnam. In the event, a treaty signed in Geneva in June 1954 provided for Vietnam to be divided in two, with North Vietnam conceded to Ho Chi Minh and the Viet Minh, while South Vietnam would also become an independent state (Crump 2007a: 133). The two would be separated by a demilitarized zone along the 17th parallel, a line some 70 km long, from the South China Sea in the east to Laos in the west. All this was too much for the French: after evacuating their army from North Vietnam during the winter of 1954–1955, they were no longer interested in maintaining any sort of presence in South Vietnam.

While it was clear that France's old colonial empire in south-east Asia had gone for good, it was equally clear that a new state of South Vietnam would never be viable without substantial outside support, which could only come from the US. Although President Eisenhower was persuaded that the South's army 'was prepared to do a first class fighting job' he accepted the need for American support, not only material but also human in the form of military advisers. The hard truth was that Ho Chi Minh was intent on uniting the whole country under his rule, a not unrealistic goal given his extensive grass-roots support from local 'Viet Cong'. What is more, this army of peasant farmers could be supplied from the north with arms sent through the mountains of Laos, just across the frontier with Vietnam, along the 'Ho Chi Minh trail'. One way or another, the war against North Vietnam was one that South Vietnam was never going to win, but in the late 1950s Eisenhower preferred to believe that 'the Communists will eventually stew in their own juices' (Kissinger 2003: 159).

Whatever Eisenhower may have thought, by the time he was succeeded by President Kennedy circumstances of the ground left no choice other than to increase the American military presence, so that during his short time in office the number of US troops in Vietnam increased from 1,000 to more than 16,000, without there being any notable gains by South Vietnam's own army in the field. This was the position when Lyndon Johnson, following the murder of Kennedy on 22 November 1963, became US President. Within nine months the stakes were enormously increased, as a result of the so-called Gulf of Tonkin incident. This, as reported to the press by US Defence Secretary McNamara, was a 'deliberate, unprovoked attack' on a US warship 'on routine patrol in international waters' (Ellsberg 2002: 12). The attack was in the Gulf of Tonkin, off the coast of North Vietnam, and the attackers, North Vietnamese patrol-boats. Johnson immediately ordered US carrier-based bombers to attack North Vietnamese targets on land, while Secretary of State Rusk told Congress that 'the attacks were no isolated event . . . [but] part and parcel of a continuing Communist drive to conquer South Vietnam . . . and eventually dominate other free nations of South East Asia' (McNamara 1995: 135–136). This was followed almost immediately by a US Senate Resolution effectively authorizing 'the President to take all necessary measures to repel any armed attack against the forces of the United States and to prevent further aggression'. All this happened in the space of three days. It did not matter that the statements made by McNamara and Rusk could well have been untrue: the die was cast, and the way was open to the unrestricted escalation of the war in Vietnam.

Within two months Brezhnev had become First Secretary of the CPSU. What then was he to make of the new turn in the war in Vietnam? Although the answer to this question is left to Chapter 11, one point is worth noting: in all that Ho Chi Minh achieved in Vietnam he received remarkably little support from Beijing. One reason is that when Mao declared final victory on 1 October 1949, the Viet Minh had already been established in Vietnam for more than four years. Ho's success could have owed little to Mao, for during almost the whole of this period the part of China with a common frontier with Vietnam had been ruled by the Guomindang. Although, after 1949, Mao did provide some material help to Ho, his attitude to an independent communist Vietnam was much the same as Stalin's to Yugoslavia after 1948. Both had to deal with a communist state which was beyond their control: Mao no more called the shots in Hanoi than Stalin did in Belgrade, and the position hardly changed in his favour after October 1949. What is more, Vietnam had for centuries been a traditional enemy of imperial China. All in all, Brezhnev could look upon the history unfolding in Vietnam as providing the opportunity for the foothold in south-east Asia that circumstance had denied to the Soviet Union in the Philippines, Indonesia and Malaysia.

Cuba

Fidel Castro (1927–) found his vocation as a revolutionary at a young age. His immediate target was the corrupt dictatorship of Fulgencio Batista which had ruled Cuba since 1952. Although his first attempt to lead an uprising, in 1953, ended with betrayal and imprisonment, he returned to Cuba in 1956, with a small band of insurgents, and although once more betrayed, succeeded in escaping into the Sierra Madre mountains of eastern Cuba, from where, with the help of his younger brother, Raul, he carried out a relentless guerrilla revolt against Batista's government.

To begin with there were few successes, but then the government forces were finally defeated in the final months of 1958, to the point that Batista fled to exile in the US on 1 January 1959, while, on the same day, Castro proclaimed a 'new revolution' under which North Americans would no longer be masters – as they had been, in effect, since the American liberation of Cuba from Spain in 1898. A week after Castro's proclamation his forces finally entered the Cuban capital, Havana, and his new government was formally recognized by Washington.

This opened the way for Castro to visit Washington three months later: there, granted a long meeting with Vice-President Nixon, the plans he revealed for Cuba's future led Nixon 'to become a leading advocate for the overthrow of Castro' (Bay of Pigs 1998: 267), who clearly intended to establish 'a dictatorship of the far left', at the same time supporting 'other revolutionary movements in Latin America'. By January 1960 President Eisenhower had already decided that Castro must be overthrown, so that two months later the CIA began training a small force of Cuban exiles, to provide the nucleus of a force that, in a covert operation, would land in Cuba as the first step on the way to bringing down Castro (ibid.: 270).

Castro's January, 1959, victory in Cuba aroused little immediate interest in Moscow, where, following Stalin, Latin America affairs were seen as a side-show (Taubman 2003: 532). In September, while Khrushchev was in Washington, the Presidium, following the advice of Gromyko, decided against providing military aid to Cuba. Once back in Moscow, Khrushchev, rejected his foreign secretary's advice, ordering Warsaw Pact weapons to be sent to Cuba without regard to possible adverse reactions in Washington. This then was the background to Eisenhower's decision to overthrow Castro.

From this point on Khrushchev hardly missed any opportunity to welcome Castro into the communist fold, describing Cuba as 'a beacon, a hopeful lighthouse for all the unfortunate, exploited peoples of Latin America'. Castro, for his part, helpfully declared that even as a student he was already a Marxist (ibid.: 533). The US–Soviet stand-off over Cuba was beginning to take shape.

Kennedy, inaugurated as US President in January 1961, took over Eisenhower's policy of overthrowing Castro, and more specifically adopted the CIA plans for landing an exile force in Cuba as the first step. The result was the Bay of Pigs fiasco in April, only three months later. With strong US support, a guerrilla force of Cuban exiles, trained by the CIA, landed on a remote stretch of coast in southern Cuba on the night of 16–17 April; they were brought there by landing craft with Cuban crews to make the point that this was a Cuban, not an American operation. It was, in any case, a complete failure: Castro soon mobilized forces more than sufficient to defeat the invaders, who finally surrendered at 2 p.m. on 19 April (Kornbluh 1998: 319).

The US reaction to the humiliating failure of the Bay of Pigs invasion was to find other means of making life difficult for Castro. In January 1962 Washington orchestrated trade sanctions against Cuba and its expulsion from the Organization of American States (OAS) (Dobrynin 1995: 71).[25] At the same time Khrushchev decided that nuclear-tipped weapons should be sited in Cuba, and sent a special representative, Aleksandr Alexeyev, to Havana to sound out Castro. At this stage Alexeyev, returning home, had to inform Moscow that Castro was unwilling to risk Cuba being isolated from the rest of Latin America. Sent back to Havana as Ambassador, Alexeyev, presenting Khrushchev's decision as no more than a proposal, sold it to Castro on the basis that the only reason for it was to defend Cuba against possible American aggression (ibid.: 73). After definitive agreement in May 1962, little time was lost in carrying out the plan. Its scale was breath-taking: 42 intermediate range nuclear missiles were to be stationed in Cuba together with some 40,000 Soviet troops and technicians; 85 ships were earmarked for transport form the Soviet Union.

At this stage, although photographs taken from the U2s showed that launching sites were ready, there was no sign that missiles had actually reached Cuba. On the other hand, naval intelligence revealed that leading vessels of the vast Soviet transport fleet had already reached the western Atlantic. With little time to lose, Kennedy, after long deliberations with members of his cabinet and others close to him, decided on a 'naval quarantine': this meant that the US Navy would ensure, if necessary by force, that none of the Soviet ships would reach Cuba. The decision was made public with a radio and TV address by Kennedy on the evening of 22 October; for Dobrynin, who had been shown the text an hour before, this was the first he knew of the whole operation.

If, until then, secrecy was the name of the game on both sides, Kennedy's address ensured unparalleled media interest for future developments in the so-called 'Cuban missile crisis'. Moscow's first reaction to the quarantine, on 24 October, was to reject it – even to the point of sending submarines to protect their cargo ships. On the next day, however, their ships started to turn back (Rusk 1991: 209). By this time, also, US troopships were bringing vast reinforcements to US Army bases in Florida, and on 26 October a personal message from Khrushchev suggested to Washington that he was ready to withdraw the missiles in exchange for a US pledge not to invade Cuba (ibid.: 211). Two days later, on 28 October, Khrushchev – having learnt from Dobrynin of a last-minute conversation with Robert Kennedy suggesting this as the basis of a settlement – announced that he would withdraw the missiles under UN supervision (Dobrynin 1995: 89). In a personal letter, already delivered to the US Embassy in Moscow, he informed Kennedy that he had 'given a new order to dismantle the arms which you described as offensive, and to crate and return them to the USSR' (Taubman 2003: 575). In his reply Kennedy welcomed Khrushchev's 'important contribution to peace'.

The crisis was over. The settlement was favourable to both sides. Kennedy had restored the status quo ante in Cuba while Khrushchev was assured that there would never be a US invasion of Cuba. (Now, some 50 years later, with Castro as the sole survivor of the crisis, his regime in Cuba is still in power. Whether, after the crisis, the balance of advantage had tipped in favour of Cuba, is somewhat problematic. It has yet to be readmitted to the OAS, and with the Soviet Union, after 1991, no longer paying high prices for Cuban sugar, the Cuban people have seen little economic progress. Castro remains unrepentant.)

The Cuban adventure was fatal to Khrushchev's position at the head of the Soviet Union. In the following months his Kremlin colleagues began to see the justice of a Chinese charge that his Cuban policy added up to 'adventurism' leading to 'capitulationism'(Taubman 2003: 578). The succession of blunders, in the two years following the Cuban crisis, related on page 64, confirmed Khrushchev's failings as a leader. As part of his political legacy, the obligation to support Castro's regime tied Khrushchev's successors to a commitment that cost the Soviet Union dearly, without Cuba contributing anything useful to the Soviet international agenda. If, from the perspective of revisionist history, Khrushchev's Cuban missile adventure put paid to any US venture that might have toppled

Castro, then, even if this had happened – as was intended with the Bay of Pigs invasion – the loss to the Soviet Union would not have been critical. On the contrary, the fact that it never could happen after the missile crisis, involved the Soviet in endless and unrewarded trouble and expense.

If, to the question as to why the Soviet Union so readily committed itself to Castro's Cuba there are a number of answers, one given – shortly after the crisis has passed – to US Secretary of State, Dean Rusk, by Anastas Mikoyan, a long-time member of the Politburo, is particularly telling: 'You Americans must understand what Cuba means to us old Bolsheviks. We have been waiting all our lives for a country to go communist without the Red Army, and it happened in Cuba. It makes us feel like boys again' (Rusk 1991: 217). If, however, to Bolsheviks of Mikoyan's generation, Cuba confirmed Lenin's classic view that once started, the communist revolution would spread out over the whole world, they had still had to wait a generation or more for Castro's successful revolution. Although the failed Cuban adventure soon led to Khrushchev's downfall, this did not mean that those, such as notably Brezhnev, who then took over, learnt the right lesson: quite simply, to see the odd successful communist revolution in the developing world – such as later occurred in Ethiopia and Angola – as confirming the Leninist view was a mistaken interpretation of history. What is more, economic and political support for the regimes that then followed, was a wasteful use of Soviet resources that in the end could lead only to bankruptcy. As the following chapters will show, this is an important part of the Brezhnev story: it was a tragedy for the Soviet Union that he never got the right script.

Notes

1 As early as 1948, those who dealt with Stalin noted how much his health had deteriorated since the end of World War II (Djilas 1969: 118).
2 Vozhd, being a title that Stalin claimed for himself, was for this reason discredited so long as Khrushchev was First Secretary of the CPSU. It was revived by Brezhnev in 1978, the same year as he was appointed Marshal of the Soviet Union (Zemtsov 1989: 121).
3 In 1946 the NKVD (see chapter 1, note 60) was replaced by the MVD, Ministerstvo Vnutrennikh Del (Ministry of Internal Affairs).
4 Essentially this was no more than the Politburo under another name.
5 Although the success of this policy is questionable, the virgin lands ultimately accounted for more than a third of Soviet grain production, an achievement for which Khrushchev was ready to give those, such as Brezhnev, who carried it out, much of the credit. The price was paid by traditional agricultural areas, such as Ukraine, which were deprived of machinery essential for increased production (Kenez 1999: 197–198).
6 He was succeeded by Nikola Bulganin.
7 See pp. 164–170.
8 This Pact, agreed between the East European satellites in 1955, was the Soviet Union's answer to NATO (North Atlantic Treaty Organization) as agreed by the Western powers in 1949.
9 As can be seen from the fact that he also became premier in March 1958 (Kenez 1999: 194).
10 As early as late 1953, only months after Stalin's death, the British ambassador noted how Soviet internal policy was much more interesting than its foreign policy (Hayter 1966: 122).

11 This was first Fort Bliss, Texas, and then, from 1955, Huntville, Alabama (where it still is). With this final move more than a hundred Germans, including von Braun himself, became American citizens (Crump 2001: 97). It was only after von Braun retired in 1973 that the Germans no longer dominated Huntsville.

12 Newman (1952) is the standard text.

13 Even in the last twenty years of the Soviet Union, the gross domestic product (GDP) per head of the population never exceeded 36 per cent of that of the US. In the immediate postwar years the figure would have been much lower.

14 Between 1945 (the end of World War II) and 1991 (the collapse of the Soviet Union), its population nearly doubled, from 171,000,000 to 293,000,000. The rate of growth was much the same in the USA, where the population was consistently between 80 and 90 per cent of that of the Soviet Union.

15 See also the figures cited on page 46 [chapter 2].

16 This meant approval of the Tu-16 medium bomber, which was deployed in large numbers, but not of the intercontinental Tu-95, whose slow cruising speed made it much too vulnerable (Holloway 1994: 322).

17 In this case the name indicated a location somewhere close to the industrial city of Chelyabinsk, which was actually 80 km away (Holloway 1994: 184). The number, 40, was simply a code, that later distinguished this plant from Chelyabinsk 70, a rival plant set up much later some 40 km away (ibid.: 322).

18 See Sakharov (1990: 145–146) for a description of his first private meeting with Beria.

19 Ulbricht (1893–1973) was Secretary General of the Communist Party in East Germany (retiring in 1971), while Adenauer (1876–1967) was the West German chancellor (retiring in 1963).

20 At this time Plesetsk was the site of the Soviet Union's only four complete and operational ICBM launching sites.

21 This was a body with more than a thousand deputies convened, quite infrequently, on special occasions, to provide a forum for events such as that staged by Khrushchev on 5 May 1960. It had no power to initiate, or even criticise, official policy.

22 This was the official Soviet figure, while the Chinese, officially, only admitted to 152,000; Deng Xiaoping, however, later admitted to 400,000 (Chang and Halliday 2005: 378, note).

23 See page 90.

24 When Mao died in 1976 Brezhnev still had another six years in office before his own death in 1982.

25 The OAS was set up in 1948 under the UN Charter to co-ordinate the work of various inter-American agencies. With its head office is in Washington the OAS is often presented as essentially an instrument of US foreign policy. The benefits of membership have long ensured, however, that almost all qualifying states in the Americas belong to the OAS.

Part II

Brezhnev's domestic politics

4 Brezhnev's life at the top

In Soviet Russia there were two ways to rise to the top. One was the Communist Party, and the other, the government bureaucracy (Zemtsov 1989: 79). Both involved climbing up a pyramid of power, an ascent that required the favour of the right men higher up, which if denied, could not only block further progress, but also lead to downfall. The fall could go a very long way, which in Stalin's day could end at the executioner's block. At local level, a career in Party or government started at the level of the '*raion*' – where the gate-keeper could be either the secretary of the '*raionkom*' (the lowest level organ of the CPSU) or the director (who could also be a 'People's Commissar') of the local office of one of the proliferating national ministries (whose personnel, constitution and functions were subject to continuous change).[1] Once Brezhnev – following the ouster of Khrushchev in 1964 – had completed his planned government reorganization, there were altogether fifty-six ministries, allowing any number of different career paths for ambitious young men.

Where the executive branch of government was organized according to the designated functions of a particular ministry, or more often a local base where it had a specific task to perform, the Communist Party was organized geographically, so that at the level above the *raion* – the *oblast* or *krai*,[2] it still had a relatively modest presence with the 'first secretary' and 'second secretary' at the head of the local party bureaucracy. With each step up to the higher levels of republic and nation the party had substantial additional powers and responsibilities, with – needless to say – a much larger number of personnel and party members. Because the power base was always at the top, a party secretary at any level was constantly involved with the same office at higher levels – so much so that the first secretary of a republic would also be assigned both an office and a home in Moscow.[3]

All this together added up to what was known as the 'apparat' (Gorbachev 1997: 140), with its officials, known as 'apparatchiki', recognized as responsible both for carrying out and shaping policy. Although the realm of *apparatchiki* extended as low as the *raion*, some in the highest levels of government were outside it. This was particular true of Soviet diplomats in countries outside the Soviet bloc, so that neither Andrei Gromyko, a former ambassador who was Foreign Minister from 1957 until 1985, nor Anatoly Dobrynin, Ambassador in Washington from 1962 until 1986, were *apparatchiki* (Hayter 1970: 31).[4] The key to this paradox was that the power to control – the essential *raison d'être* of the CPSU – hardly extended beyond the Soviet bloc, so that, for instance, the Ambassador in Warsaw was much more an *apparatchik* than, say, the Ambassador in London.[5] In practice the Soviet Foreign Minister, as seen from London or Washington, was more like a permanent official (ibid.: 32). However great his influence and knowledge of the world outside the Soviet Union, he decided little.

That the domain of the *apparat* was essentially domestic meant that those who reached the top had no need for any experience of the outside world. How then did someone like Brezhnev reach the highest levels? Once again, nothing counted for more than support from the top. Although this is true also of the non-Soviet world, in the Soviet Union the way the principle operated was much more drastic. Until his death in 1953 the top was Stalin, so that until the end of the Khrushchev era the *apparatchiki* who governed the Soviet Union were all 'Stalin's creatures' (Hayter 1970: 27). This was certainly true of Khrushchev, who was never out of favour with Stalin. Brezhnev, on the other hand, owed everything to Khrushchev. It could hardly have been otherwise: with Khrushchev as First Secretary of the Ukrainian Communist Party, Brezhnev's steady climb to the top of the party pyramid, from the mid-1930s onward, would have been impossible without strong support from Khrushchev.[6] In the jargon of Soviet bureaucracy, Khrushchev was recognized as Brezhnev's *krysha*, or 'roof'.[7] Indirectly Brezhnev was also Stalin's man, even though the name meant little to Stalin.[8] As recorded by Sir William Hayter, British Ambassador in Moscow in Brezhnev's day:

> The apparatus at that time was the way to power, but the way to death too. No body of men in the U.S.S.R. was more ruthlessly and repeated purged than the *apparatchiki*. Those who survived, like the present leaders in Moscow, did so because of their willingness to join in betraying their colleagues and persecuting the rest of the population. Passivity under Stalin was not enough; active participation in terror was required, and the survivors must have terrible burdens on their conscience. This hideous background must never be forgotten in estimating the present Soviet leaders.'
>
> (Hayter 1970: 28)

Of the leaders at the time Hayter's book was published, Brezhnev, as General Secretary, was unquestionably dominant. Even so, loyalty to Stalin and Stalin's men would not have been sufficient to reach that height. As he climbed up the pyramid Brezhnev would have to have done more than just accept party policy as it affected his domain – whether Ukraine, Moldavia or Kazakhstan – but also to make it work, or at least satisfy Moscow that he had done so (which was not necessarily the same thing). In Kazakhstan, therefore, Brezhnev had to be able to report success, measured in terms of annual harvests, in implementing the controversial virgin lands policy. This meant that recent settlers on land that had not previously been ploughed had to meet production targets set by Moscow, which, for any number of reasons, could be completely unrealistic. Brezhnev, therefore, needed first the agricultural bureaucracy on his side, and particularly the directors of the collective farms where the wheat would actually be harvested. Crucially, at grass-roots, the labour force had to respond by actually growing wheat in the quantities laid down in the overall plan. Where this was next to impossible, various expedients were at hand, both for the First Secretary and, derivatively, for his subordinates right down to the level of *kolkhoz* labourers who concealed agricultural inventories and forged the transfers of land to the collectivization programme (Zemtsov 1989: 23). Inevitably, then, information reaching successively higher levels of the *apparat*, was subjected to 'whitewashing' (*ochkovtiratel'stvo*) so as to confirm what they wanted to hear rather than what they needed to know (ibid.: 30);[9] nor was there any more reality in what came down to the lower levels from above (ibid.:xv).

In a difficult year, the obvious answer was to persuade Moscow simply to accept that circumstances, such as weather, beyond the control of the local *apparat*, made reaching the planned target impossible.[10] This could well be inevitable when too many local *kolkhoz* managers failed to deliver. A single manager could, however, well hesitate before making such an approach, simply out of fear of being condemned, higher up, for finding a pretext for his own poor performance. The alternative was to orchestrate a cover-up, say by false accounting; if, then, the problem was the need to involve others, it could be solved on the understanding that favours would be returned. In this way whole networks, based on such mutual support, operated behind the scenes, incidentally giving vast scope for corruption and betrayal. All this was by no means marginal: for those involved it was taken for granted. The inflexible bureaucratic system allowed no alternative. Under Brezhnev corruption flourished as never before, particularly in the Caucasus and Central Asia, with top party men becoming millionaires, able to salt away their fortunes in dollar accounts (Kenez 1999: 218).[11]

Success for a man like Brezhnev, as he climbed the pyramid, required not only meeting the targets set by those higher up – or at least appearing to do so in a convincing way – but also the choice of subordinates who would work the informal networks without compromising their superior. Here Brezhnev (who must have been skilled in covering his tracks) combined the advantage of being popular and approachable (Zemtsov 1989: 72) with exceptional managerial skills (Arbatov 1992:xi), so that people worked with him rather than against him. At the same time he was always genuinely orthodox in applying Marxist-Leninist principles – in other words a good advertisement for the system. His gifts were clear at an early stage: A. A. Arzumanyan, who had worked with Brezhnev during the war years to become in the 1950s a leading academician, said of him, 'You don't need to teach this man anything as far as the struggle for positioning and power is concerned' (ibid.: 119)

Brezhnev's record of success, while First Secretary in Kazakhstan (1952–1956), in implementing the virgin lands policy was critical for his promotion to candidate member of the Politburo early in 1956. This meant that he became a member at the top level of the Moscow 'nomenklatura', and this in turn provides a key to understanding the Soviet power system. The *nomenklatura* was a distinctive new class characteristic of society in the Soviet Union. As described by

Djilas (1957: 39) '... it is made up of those who have special privileges and economic preference because of the administrative monopoly they hold'. Stalin, with his commitment to industrialization from the early 1920s onwards, thought that his plans 'would come to nothing if the new class were not made materially interested in the process, by acquisition of some property for itself' (ibid.: 49). This, in practice, was no more than a statement of policy, which was carried out in parallel to the implementation of the first Five-Year Plan (1929–1934). As the number of members of the Party increased from less than a million to nearly two million, they provided the base from which the new class emerged, to enjoy privileges which ;were expanding more rapidly than industrialization itself'.

Such were the origins of the *nomenklatura*, which at the end of the day was to have nearly half a million members (Kenez 1999: 217). Like the Party and every other organ of government, it was a pyramid, with a number of clearly recognized levels, each one entitled to its own privileges. Even at the lowest levels these were sufficient to ensure for members a lifestyle unattainable for non-members. In the early 1930s, while Ukrainian peasants were starving, the local *nomenklatura* wanted for nothing (Matthews 2009: 40; Kenez 1999: 217). This was then the world of Brezhnev, but by the time he arrived in Moscow some twenty years later, membership of the top level of the *nomenklatura* – which was then his by right – meant a much more opulent and privileged lifestyle. Brezhnev's niece, Luba, devotes a whole chapter of her book (Brezhneva 1995: 225–247) to the *nomenklatura*, which, in her own words, 'refers to a list of those key positions, in every sphere of Soviet life from economics to culture, that were deemed so important that aspirants could be appointed to them only with special party approval' (ibid.: 225). A spacious apartment, a private car and chauffeur, special aircraft for long distance travel,[12] a well-appointed dacha, special schools for children, shops with high quality goods, privileged access to higher education, high-grade medical care, sanatoria in prime holiday locations, even reserved cemeteries, defined a world so enclosed that the *nomenklatura* seldom encountered the common people. Even at the lowest levels members enjoyed something of these benefits, if on a more modest scale, but at the top level – mainly to be found in Moscow – they defined an entirely separate world, in which neighbours, whether of the city apartment or the country dacha, were certain to belong to the same party elite. This, in Luba Brezhneva's words (ibid.: 226), was surrounded by 'an ever-expanding octopus' – to quote from Gilbert and Sullivan's *HMS Pinafore* – of 'his sisters, and his cousins and his aunts . . . whom he reckons up by dozens', to say nothing of old friends from back home.[13] Indeed the key to success in the Soviet hierarchy for a man with any ambition was to build up a supporters' club by securing as many senior posts, honours and decorations for subordinates from every stage in one's career; no-one did this more successfully than Brezhnev (Zemtsov 1989: 68), who was also quite unashamed about the scandalous jet-set lifestyle enjoyed by membership of the top levels of the *nomenklatura*.[14] One reason for Brezhnev's survival in office was that, unlike Khrushchev, nothing he did ever threatened the vested interests of the *nomenklatura* (Kenez 1999: 217). At the same time he always covered up for loyal subordinates.

The amenities provided for the highest level of the *nomenklatura* ensured easy contact between its members: if one wanted an informal meeting with another, the chance was good that both lived almost next door to each other in Moscow, or had dachas on the same stretch of the Moscow River, or took the cure at the same elite Black Sea spa (Sakharov 1990: 215). A Kremlin discussion between members of the Politburo could easily be adjourned to a dacha outside Moscow, a practice much favoured by Stalin who could then keep his guests eating and drinking until the small hours of the morning (Djilas 1969: 85ff). In all this families could also be involved, both under Stalin and his successors (Alliluyeva 1967: 31, Taubman 2003: 556). The price paid, as noted by Brezhnev's niece, Luba (Brezhneva 1995: 226), was almost complete alienation from the grass-roots: no member of the Politburo ever had to confront constituents who might vote him out of office.

The result for policy was that much was decided outside any formal setting, such as the 10 Downing Street cabinet room or the White House Oval Office, and without any notes being taken: it was as if Chequers or Camp David, or some vacation retreat, was the place for important decisions, but with the additional factor that almost any politician who counted enjoyed comparable facilities. Although distinctively Russian, this was a country-house lifestyle reminiscent of Edwardian England or Theodore Roosevelt's America.[15] In the Soviet Union the county-house was typically a Crimean sanatorium reserved for the top *nomenklatura*, where policy could be discussed and made at private meetings lasting far into the night.[16] The critical difference was that almost all those involved were self-made men, beholden to no historical legacy beyond Marxist-Leninism, as it evolved in Stalin's day. For Brezhnev – and he was not alone – this was holy writ.

Significantly, during the eighteen years that he was *vozhd*,[17] Brezhnev never had to mobilize support in the Supreme Soviet or the Central Committee of the CPSU, in the manner described in Chapter 3, first, for the fall of Beria, second, for Khrushchev to survive the failed coup of 1957 and third for ensuring his downfall in 1964. If, as appears from the judgment of Brezhnev's fellow members of the Politburo, he was always a safe pair of hands (Haslam 2011: 215), his years in office fall into three distinct phases.

In the first phase (1964–1968), Brezhnev was constrained to share power with others (Haslam 2011: 214), notably Aleksei Kosygin (prime minister), Anastas Mikoyan (head of state until 1965), Nikolai Podgorny (Mikoyan's successor), Yuri Andropov (head of the KGB)[18] and Mikhail Suslov (Second Secretary of the CPSU from 1965). One extremely sensitive problem for Brezhnev was his ranking in Soviet diplomatic protocol below the head of state and the prime minister. When, in 1965, Podgorny became head of state, he was in a position, if he combined with Kosygin, to block Brezhnev. For reasons of *realpolitik* Podgorny consistently preferred not to oppose Brezhnev, but support him,[19] while Brezhnev in turn sowed discord between Podgorny and Kosygin (Zemtsov 1989: 103). This meant that Brezhnev saw Kosygin as his principal rival, and the latter, indeed, as Chairman of the Council of Ministers had considerable power as head of the Soviet Bureaucracy: this was, however, limited by the fact the political commissars, with a specific function at every level of the bureaucracy, were subordinate to

Brezhnev, as General Secretary. Khrushchev avoided this problem by holding both offices, as Stalin had. When Brezhnev succeeded Khrushchev as *vozhd*, the new oligarchy took care to ensure that he would not have this advantage (ibid.: 79). On the other hand, in 1966, the 23rd Party Congress upgraded Brezhnev from 'First' to 'General Secretary' of the Party, at the same providing for the Presidium to revert to Politburo (ibid.: 87).

Although Kosygin remained Chairman of the Council of Ministers until his death in December 1980, Brezhnev was able to ensure that his power declined throughout the 1970s. The process was already under way at the 24th Party Congress in 1971, where Brezhnev was clearly recognized as leader of the Politburo (Zemtsov 1989: 119); his position – particularly vis-à-vis Kosygin -was then greatly strengthened in 1977 when he orchestrated his own succession to Podgorny as Chairman of the Presidium of the Supreme Soviet, while at the same time remaining General Secretary of the CPSU.

In relation to Soviet politics, the question to ask, is to what extent all this added up to something more than palace intrigue, in which Brezhnev – always hungry for power – came out on top? Did Kosygin attempt to mobilize support for policies that antagonized Brezhnev? The answer is to be found in the seven years leading up to the 24th Party Conference in 1971, when Kosygin's own power base still counted in Soviet politics. In this period economic reforms, initiated under Khrushchev, and focussed on restricting Moscow's intervention in the day-to-day management of local enterprises while at the same encouraging the growth of the consumer economy, had considerable success, for which Kosygin willingly took the credit. On the other side Brezhnev's policy was to give priority to trade with the west, using export revenue from Soviet oil and gas to pay for hi-tech imports, notably computers (Suri 2006: 139]. Pursuit of this policy led to such trade (particularly with West Germany) doubling in Brezhnev's critical first seven years (ibid.: 140), even before Willy Brandt's Ostpolitik (as outlined in Chapter 7) had found its feet. Once it was clear that this was at the cost of retarding the development of local industry and new house construction (ibid.: 141) central to Kosygin's reforms, these could be presented by Brezhnev as having failed. Brezhnev and Kosygin, were at cross-purposes, and Brezhnev was coming out on top. It mattered little to him that the Soviet consumer economy paid the price.

The more Kosygin lost out to Brezhnev, the more Brezhnev also turned against Podgorny, a process ending with his removal from office on 16 June 1977. As for Andropov, Brezhnev's consistent support for the KGB was sufficient to ensure loyalty; in the event Andropov's steady success in the Soviet hierarchy as head of the KGB – largely attributable to unquestioning identification with Brezhnev (Suri 2006: 100; Haslam 2011: 217) – was such as to ensure that he succeeded to the office of First Secretary when Brezhnev died in 1982. As for Suslov, he was always content to be number two; even so, he was always very powerful behind the scenes, having, like Brezhnev, a seat both in the Secretariat and the Politburo. Whereas in 1970 Suslov (who had played a major part in the deposition of Khrushchev) combined with other members of the Politburo to frustrate attempts by Brezhnev to remove Kosygin from office, he reversed his position well before 1977. By this time, although Brezhnev's health was steadily deteriorating, neither Suslov, nor any of his fellow members of the Politburo, were minded to act as they had with Khrushchev. For them Brezhnev's was still the best game in town, and remained so until his death in 1982. What then mattered is which informal coalitions, within the Politburo, called the shots at any one stage of the game – such as notably the Afghan crisis of 1979, as related in Chapter 11.

The interaction between almost all the personalities named above, together with many others subordinate to them, was such that after the end of the 1960s, Brezhnev's dominance was hardly questioned. One reason for this was his ability, first to identify the shifting membership of informal factions in the Politburo (where decisions depended on a simple majority vote by full members), and then to replace those who, in this kaleidoscope of power, were least reliable, with his own nominees. In this way Andropov, Gromyko and Grechko became full members of the Politburo in 1973 (Zemtsov 1989: 104).[20] For the purposes of Brezhnev, as General Secretary, the Politburo was becoming increasingly subservient over the course of time (ibid.: 81), but the game, none the less, had to be played with extreme circumspection.[21] In the late 1960s another development also helped Brezhnev: this was the mass recruitment of new members of the CPSU who would recognize him as its undisputed leader (ibid.: 92).

This process was already under way when, in January, 1969, Richard Nixon was inaugurated as Lyndon Johnson's successor as US President. For more than six years (1969–1975) (which define the second and most important phase of Brezhnev's time as *vozhd*) this meant that in pursuing the causes dearest to his heart, international détente and nuclear disarmament, Brezhnev was dealing with a fellow soul while at the same time enjoying solid political support back home. It also meant that he could deepen his understanding of the world outside the Soviet Union, which, for so long as Khrushchev was in power, he only knew from short visits to Afghanistan, Iran, Finland, China and Syria (Zemtsov 1989: 63) and one to western Europe.

The first steps on the road to détente were taken at the Glassboro conference in June 1967,[22] where the limitation of anti-ballistic missiles was just one topic discussed by US President Lyndon Johnson and Soviet Prime Minister Kosygin: although no agreement was reached, the amicable 'spirit of Glassboro' promised well for future negotiations.

Although at Glassboro Kosygin had sufficient power to insist on representing the Soviet Union, it is a measure of Brezhnev's ascendancy that this was the last time this happened. Once Nixon had become president in January 1969, it was Brezhnev who represented the Soviet Union at international summits. If, like Khrushchev, he had little previous international experience, he was just as able to learn his way about. The Nixon years, 1969–1975, were then the period that both Brezhnev's standing in the outside world and his power in the Soviet Union were at their height. He himself took the credit for a consistent foreign policy which had redeemed the crises – Cuba and Berlin – of Khrushchev's final years, and won trust internationally (Haslam 2011: 175).

At the same time, however, Brezhnev was paying the price of his demanding lifestyle, and became increasingly dependent on tranquillizers. The third and final phase (1975–1982) was therefore one of decline, in which he largely lost control of events (as witness the Soviet invasion of Afghanistan in 1979, which belied his strong long-term commitment to the avoidance of hostilities). None the less, even at the 26th Party Congress in 1981, the last before Brezhnev's death a year later, every speaker praised him with words such as 'the true continuer of the immortal work of Lenin' (Haslam 2011: 120). He was awarded the Lenin Peace Prize, the Order of Victory and the title of Marshal of the Soviet Union (ibid.: 121). Judged in the light of history, this meant little more than that Brezhnev was presented as the public face of power in the Soviet Union, with the achievements attributed to him being essentially the work of men operating behind the scenes; the more interesting question is how much this was also true of his failures – in Czechoslovakia, the Middle East, Africa, China, and so on – as related in the following chapters. Domestically, *zastoi*, or 'stagnation', still remains a fair description of what was achieved – or, indeed, failed to be achieved – during Brezhnev's years in office. Here, however, it is worth noting that Soviet populations expected no better, so that today, many older people, when looking back on the Brezhnev years remember good times, rather than bad. Although they did not see it, they were, under Brezhnev – and largely as a result of policies pursued in his name – living on borrowed time.

Notes

1 In Harrison (1985: 268–276) the list of ministries operating in the period 1938–1945 takes up nine pages. These ministries ranged from the general (e.g. Foreign Affairs) to the highly specific (e.g. cellulose and paper industry). The former were the so-called 'All Union' or 'Union' ministries, the latter, 'industrial' ministries.
2 An *oblast* (best translated as *region*) could well have a population counted in millions. In certain parts of the Soviet Union, mainly in remote or frontier areas, the *oblast* was replaced by a *krai*, but administratively they were at the same level.
3 Taubman (2003: 143) describes the luxurious flat in Moscow, close to the Kremlin, assigned to Khrushchev as first secretary in Ukraine.
4 Significantly Dobrynin only joined the Politburo in 1971, and Gromyko in 1973.
5 That the Politburo paid a high price for appointing *apparatchiki* to East bloc embassies can be seen from the reports sent to Moscow by the ambassador to Czechoslovakia, Stepan Chernovenko, at the time of the Prague spring in 1968; these consistently asserted that Soviet military intervention would be welcome – the opposite of the truth, but still what Moscow what wanted to hear. True reporting of the actual situation could well have led to this disastrous and costly policy not being carried out (Coleman 1997 91). Much the same happened with the Hungarian uprising in 1956, when Yuri Andropov was ambassador in Budapest: note, however, how he went on to become, first, head of the KGB, and then, in 1982, Brezhnev's successor as General Secretary.
6 Given the character of Khrushchev, the fact that, on occasion, he enjoyed making fun of Brezhnev (Taubman 2003: 598,614) cannot be interpreted as a sign of disapproval.
7 Having Brezhnev as his *krysha* was the key to the success of Chernenko, who later, at one step remove, succeeded him as First Secretary of the CPSU (1984–1985).
8 According to Prof. Stanislav Kulchitsky, author of a standard text on communism in the Ukraine (Kulchitsky 1996), Brezhnev was entirely Khrushchev's man and not Stalin's.

9 There was a special word 'pripiski' for doctored production output reports.

10 When, in 1961, Podgorny, First Secretary of the Party in Ukraine, attributed a poor wheat harvest to bad weather, he fell from grace when Khrushchev reacted by attributing the losses to 'pilfering', but was restored to favour after a good harvest in 1962 ('The leading contenders to succeed a tired Khrushchev', *Time*, 29 June 1962)

11 After the fall of the Soviet Empire in 1991 such accounts were an important source of capital for the new business oligarchs (Prof. Aleksandr Dvukhzhylov, personal communication).

12 Sakharov (1990: 212) relates how, when Mikhail Pervukhin (deputy chairman of the Council of Ministers) visited the secret installation producing nuclear weapons, he arranged for a second airplane carrying several refrigerators and a private stock of delicacies.

13 Among those promoted by Brezhnev were Andrei Kirilenko, Nikolai Tikhonov and Nikolai Shchelokov, all of whom came from the Dnepropetrovsk *oblast* where Brezhnev had once been First Secretary of the Party. In at least one case Brezhnev failed: the promotion of Volodymyr Shcherbitsky to First Secretary in Kiev to succeed Nikolai Podgorny was blocked by Podgorny himself to make room for his own man, Petr Shelest (Zemtsov 1989: 69).

14 Brezhnev's own daughter, Galina, was notorious in Moscow for her relationship with a circus artist, who secreted vast sums of money abroad, while Galina's husband, General Yury Churbanov, was second in command of the Soviet police (Kenez 1999: 217; Zemtsov 1989: 174).

15 Even to the point of providing suitable female company, as Chernenko, in the early 1960s, did for Brehznev (Zemtsov 1989: 53). To suggest that Brezhnev was a sort of Soviet Berlusconi *avant la lettre* would, however, overstate the case.

16 E.g. an evening in 1965 with Washington Ambassador Dobrynin at prime minister Kosygin's Black Sea *dacha* (Dobrynin 1995: 135).

17 See Chapter 3, note 2.

18 The KGB (Komitet Gosudarstvennoi Bezopastnosti), or 'Committee of State Security', was the successor to the NKVD: see Chapter 1, note 60.

19 The power of the head of state counted for little, given that the Supreme Soviet, of which he was President, although formally an elected legislature, was hardly more than a forum for making public legislation decided upon by the Council of Ministers, as required – in the final analysis – by the Presidium. In other words, the formal order of precedence was the reverse of that in the actual Soviet power structure. The need for Podogrny to support Brezhnev came from the fact that never having been part of the decisive 1964 conspiracy against Khrushchev it was critical for his future to assure Brezhnev of his loyalty (Zemtsov 1989: 74); indeed as soon as the coup against Khrushchev succeeded, those behind it made clear to both Podgorny and Mikoyan that they must either support it, or go the same way as Khrushchev (ibid.: 75).

20 Brezhnev had appointed Andrei Grechko as Minister of Defence in 1967.

21 One factor here was the thousands of letters from ordinary Soviet citizens received by the Central Committee; these, more often than not cries of desperation born out of the crimes of local Party organizations and their members, were kept on file, ready for use when counteraction was judged to be in the interests of overall policy. During the Brezhnev era the power so to act was Chernenko's (Zemtsov 1989: 94).

22 The site of the conference, Glassboro State College in New Jersey, was chosen for being half way between Washington (convenient for Johnson) and New York (where Kosygin had come to address the UN).

5 Confronting the military industrial complex

Conventional weapons

By the time Brezhnev succeeded Khrushchev as First Secretary of the CPSU in 1964 the direction of the Soviet economy had long been determined by the paramount need to meet the demands of a military industrial complex, whose purpose was to ensure that the Soviet Union could hold its own, if not be ahead, in the arms race with the United States and its NATO allies. Although a single event, the decisive operational use by the United States of two atomic bombs in August 1945 to bring about an unexpectedly rapid end to the Pacific War, added an entirely new dimension to warfare, Stalin presented his post-war armaments policy as essentially an extension of the manufacture of conventional weapons, such as had played a decisive part in the final defeat of Germany in 1945.

The priority given to investment in heavy industry – for Stalin a key Marxist-Leninist principle – dates back to the earliest days of the Soviet Union. Foreseeing the end of the New Economic Policy, Stalin emphasized the need for accelerated industrialization at the 15th Party Congress in 1927. Then, in December 1929, increased investment in heavy industry became an essential part of the first five-year plan, with priority for aircraft, armour and artillery for the Soviet armed forces (Holloway 1983: 6). Two years later, in 1931, Stalin showed how urgent the need was:

> 'We are fifty or a hundred years behind the advanced countries. We must make good the distance in ten years. Either we do it or they crush us.'
>
> (Stalin 1947: 213)

If this goal was not achieved, then 'socialism in one country', as Stalin conceived of his regime in the Soviet Union, was doomed (Holloway 1983: 7). The programme continued, but at a very high price, with Stalin's purges of 1936–1938 costing the lives of more officers than the Soviet Union lost in combat in World War II (ibid.: 10), to say nothing of key civilians working in the military industrial complex. The success of the German invasion during its first months (when the territory lost to the Soviet Union contained 40 per cent of its population, while producing 40 per cent of its grain and accounting for 60 per cent of its metallurgical industry) made only too clear how Stalin's policies, both military and industrial, had failed (ibid.: 11) – as Khrushchev later revealed in his 1956 secret speech (as related on page 56).

Notwithstanding these appalling losses, it was still possible to evacuate some ten million Soviet citizens (with priority for those working in essential war industries), together with some 1,300 industrial plants, in face of the German advance – an operation in which Brezhnev, as First Secretary in the Dnepropetrovsk *oblast*, played a part. This achievement meant that Soviet heavy industry relocated in new sites hundreds of kilometres east of the furthest extent of the German advance. This new war industry then produced the new modern armaments, such as the T34 tank, which the Soviet forces needed to defeat the Germans. Its location, deep inside Russia, far to the north and east of Moscow, meant that few questions were asked about what its operation involved in human terms. There is little doubt, however, that the labour force included any number of Gulag prisoners (Hill and Gaddy 2003: 86–88) – and so it continued, after World War II, when the military industrial complex turned to nuclear weapons. Its programme then included not only the production of warheads, but also of the means of delivery: here the Soviet defence industry concentrated mainly on rockets, which brought the additional advantage of potential use for space travel. At the same time the production of conventional arms continued at a high level. This was necessary to equip not only the forces deployed along Soviet frontiers, including that defined by the European Iron Curtain – to say nothing of the even longer frontier with China – but also the forces of a remarkable number of foreign states beholden, one way or another, to the Soviet Union. Brezhnev, from his first days as *vozhd*, consistently gave priority to the production of advanced tanks, aircraft and artillery (Parrott 1983: 183),[1] down-playing – in contrast to Khrushchev and Kosygin – the demands of the consumer economy (Cousins 1972: 35). On one critical question, the need to acquire western technology, Brezhnev took the orthodox Stalinist line that the Soviet Union, being technologically more dynamic, could look after its own interests (ibid.: 188). The debate was not confined to the military industrial complex. A major factor was the demand for western technology, civilian as much as military, by Warsaw Pact countries, and Brezhnev was duly concerned by the possibility of unacceptable diplomatic bargains being made with the West (ibid.: 191). To a degree the extreme Soviet position was relaxed by making a distinction between technology transfer from western Europe and that from the US. At the end of the day the crucial need for western technology could not be denied. The figures speak for themselves: in the five years from 1966 to 1970 Soviet industry bought five times as many foreign licences than it had in the 20 years from 1946 to 1965; there was a corresponding increase in the number of Soviet scientists and technologists visiting both the west and the other countries in the Soviet block (ibid.: 208). If Brezhnev could not turn back the tide, he had considerable misgivings about its advance. In the 1960s these related to the struggle for power with, among others, Kosygin and Podgorny. The fact that by the 1970s, Brezhnev's position had become much stronger, goes a long way to explain the stagnation (*zastoi*) with which his name is now associated.

Exports of armaments, as much as the technology transfers that made them possible,[2] were always crucial to the Soviet economy. At different stages of Soviet post-war history these fell into a number of separate categories. First of all, following immediately upon the defeat of Germany in 1945, came all the East European states that in May 1955 were to sign the Warsaw Pact. The next case, that of the People's Republic of China, was much more problematic. In the years before October 1949, when Mao Zedong finally proclaimed victory in Beijing, the material support of the Soviet Union was equivocal. In principle, the Soviet occupation of Manchuria following its declaration of war on Japan on August 1945, should have been a considerable boost to Mao, but Stalin's main concern was to plunder whole factories as 'war booty', while often demolishing the industrial installations that had to be left behind. Even so, vast Japanese arms depots were left behind for Mao, who was also free to recruit into his army hundreds of thousands of men left unemployed as a result of the plunder by Soviet forces (Chang and Halliday 2005: 284). As related in Chapter 11, the Korean war (1950–1953) decisively changed the relationship between the Soviet Union and the People's Republic. When, following Stalin's death, the new Politburo told Mao of the decision to end the war, he dragged his feet, even after the Soviet leaders promised to reward his acquiescence with some ninety-one arms enterprises promised by Stalin. What Mao wanted from the Soviet Union was the atomic bomb. Given that US President Eisenhower, in his first inaugural address on 2 February 1953 had suggested that the atomic bomb might be used against China, Mao had a strong case. While it was soon clear that he would not get an actual bomb, the Soviet leaders did agree to send top level scientists and engineers to China, together with key blue-prints. These were the men that Khrushchev repatriated after the final break with China in 1960 (page 66). China was then on its own, and its first successful nuclear weapons test at Lop Nor came only on 16 October 1964, two days after Brezhnev had become the new *vozhd*.[3] If, then, there was any chance of mending fences, it was forfeited by an ill-advised insult to Mao, made three weeks later to Zhou Enlai by the Soviet Defence Minister, Rodion Malinovsky, at a Moscow reception to celebrate the 47th anniversary of the October Revolution (ibid.: 490). Thereafter, the stand-off between the Soviet Union and the People's Republic was not only irreparable, but also had a nuclear dimension. However, this new factor may have influenced Soviet or Chinese policy, both sides were compelled to maintain substantial forces along their 7,000 km long common frontier (Coleman 1997: 147), and equip them with state-of-the-art conventional weapons.

Soviet involvement with China also extended, critically, to two of China's neighbours, North Korea and Vietnam. Following the Panmunjom armistice, finally agreed on 27 July 1953, the Soviet Union remained committed to Kim Il-Sung to supply essential arms for his North Korean forces. Although, in principle, the arms were sold on commercial terms, these counted for little with North Korea near bankruptcy. In the result, supplying arms represented a considerable economic burden for the Soviet Union until its final collapse in 1991: Brezhnev, during his 18 years as *vozhd* could do little to improve the situation.

Vietnam was a different case. As related on page 72, the Gulf of Tonkin resolution, adopted by the US Congress only two months before Brezhnev became *vozhd*, effectively committed the US to war in Vietnam: the enemy was first the Viet Minh, who, under Ho Chi Minh,[4] governed North Vietnam (as agreed at Geneva in 1954 (Crump 2007a: 133)) as a communist state, and second, the Viet Cong, insurgents in South Vietnam, who, with considerable popular support in the countryside, were intent on defeating the US-backed government, so as to extend the rule of Ho Chi Minh to cover the whole country, North and South. Essential supplies (including arms) for the Viet Cong were sent south through Laos and Cambodia, the two states west of Vietnam, sharing a long north–south frontier, inland from coast of the South China Sea and running through hills covered in dense forest. The operation of a supply route along the 'Ho Chi Minh Trail' was, needless to say, orchestrated by the Viet Minh. The arms themselves came from a number of sources, but with the escalation of the war after the Gulf of Tonkin resolution, the Soviet Union became a leading supplier once it was clear that the People's Republic, with a long history of hostility to Vietnam, would not assume this role (Hosmer and Wolfe 1982: 19, Coleman 1997: 204). The cost to the Soviet Union was considerable, not only because, given the circumstances, Ho Chi Minh hardly had the means to pay for arms – whatever their source – but also because of the high costs of shipment from Soviet Baltic ports along a sea-route leading round South Africa and across the Indian Ocean to the final destination, the North Vietnam port of Haiphong.[5] This operation was a challenge to the US air force, which had to take care not to damage Soviet merchants ships, nor injure crew-members, whether in harbour at Haiphong or on the open sea. The point had become critical after some Soviet sailors were injured (Dobrynin 1995: 247), but in practice US precision bombing was sufficiently accurate to avoid this happening (Kissinger 1982: 24). The Soviet Union continued supplying North Vietnam until the South, under US pressure, conceded defeat in 1975,[6] so allowing the whole country to be united, with the southern capital, Saigon, being renamed 'Ho Chi Minh City'. Even after 1975 the Soviet Union accepted the new Socialist Republic of Vietnam as a major trading partner, but compared to North Korea, there was relatively little economic cost involved. It should be noted, however, that in the late 1970s, wars against both China and Cambodia, required considerable expenditure on new armaments, which could only come from the Soviet Union. In June 1978 Vietnam joined the Council for Mutual Economic Assistance (COMECON), an international trading block originally set up by the Soviet Union in 1949 for the benefit of communist states, which at that time were mainly in Eastern Europe. By 1978 it had already expanded to include Mongolia and Cuba in the developing world; Vietnam, by joining, led China to withdraw all economic aid,[7] and indeed the countries were at war within a year (Crump 2007a: 153). For the Soviet Union, this foothold in south-east Asia was too valuable, politically, to be abandoned: enhanced economic aid, and not only for the purchase of armaments, was the price that had to be paid.

In terms of armament supply the most controversial case, inevitably, arose with Khrushchev's attempt (related in Chapter 3) to supply nuclear weapons to Fidel

Castro's Cuba. The fact that Khrushchev, under overwhelming international pressure, drew back, did not end the Soviet commitment to supply Cuba with conventional weapons. Economically this made little sense, for Cuba could only offer in exchange agricultural produce, such as cane-sugar and rice, for which the Soviet Union had little need.[8] The position became even more difficult after 1975, when – as related in Chapter 10 – Castro chose to send a large military force to Angola to support the new communist regime established after the Portuguese had ended their colonial administration. Once again, as with North Korea and North Vietnam, the Soviet arms industry had been committed to loss-making exports. As always, a high price had to be paid for whatever political advantage was gained.

Quite apart from states such as Cuba and Vietnam where the Soviet military industrial complex was bound by an inescapable long-term political commitment to supplying conventional weapons, there were any number of others where dependence on Soviet arms had, in the circumstances of the day, a clear political advantage for both sides. This often related to a local war of independence fought against European colonialism, at least in the perception of Moscow. In this context Soviet arms were supplied to Algeria in the critical first two years (1962–1964) of independence from France, and to Angola and Mozambique, in the first four years (1975–1979) of independence from Portugal.[9] As to the Arab states of the Middle East, Soviet policy was largely a question of fishing in troubled waters, although as seen from Moscow these states were judged according to their potential to contribute to the victory of communism; neither Khrushchev nor Brezhnev were ready to be satisfied with the status quo in international affairs (Pleshakov 2000: 233– 235). A country was an appropriate recipient of Soviet arms to the extent that its policies vis-à-vis the historic imperialist powers, the UK, France – and by extension the US – were hostile, at least as seen from Moscow. This explains the Soviet arms supplied to Guinea, Ghana and Mali in 1959–1961, Egypt and South Yemen in 1962–1963,[10] Syria in 1982, Laos from 1960–1970, Libya from 1970 onwards, Ethiopia in 1977–1979, Lebanon in 1982 and Iraq from 1980. In many cases, also, Israel was a key factor, as a result first of its defeating Egypt, Jordan and Syria in the six-day war of 1967, and second of its defeating Egypt and Syria in the Yom Kippur war of 1973. Israel, then, lies behind the massive sale of Soviet armaments to Egypt, Syria and Yemen in the period, 1969–1976.[11] In many of these instances the arms sales could well have benefitted the Soviet economy, simply because the purchasers could afford to pay a fair market price (Hosmer and Wolfe 1982: 44); this was certainly the case with Libya, which, under Colonel Qaddafi, made a fortune from selling oil (Anderson 2011: 51).[12] There were, moreover, economies of scale following from increased production for the export market, while, at the same time, the use by many of the purchasing states of the arms in actual combat situations helped the Soviet military industrial complex evaluate their performance, and where necessary improve upon it. After the Yom Kippur War of 1973 the Soviet Union, as a major producer of oil, also benefitted from the substantial increase in the world oil price enforced by the Organization of Petroleum Exporting Countries (OPEC).[13] The price paid was the enduring hostility of Israel,[14] which could always count on US support. The far-reaching repercussions not only for the Soviet Jewish population, but derivatively in negotiations with the US for détente in the nuclear arms race, are the subject matter of Chapter 8.

Nuclear weapons, missiles and the space race

However much the Soviet Union invested in conventional weapons, the top priority of the military industrial complex was consistently defined in terms of nuclear weapons and the means to deliver them (Haslam 2011: 196).[15] In contrast to conventional weapons, their role was always seen, at least by Brezhnev, as essentially strategic; they were cards in his hand in dealing with the US and the name of the game was 'parity' (Zaloga 2002: 102). The game, as Brezhnev played it – against a background of infighting within the Kremlin – involved the Soviet Union in costs substantially higher than in Khrushchev's time. This, indeed, was one reason why Brezhnev (as related in Chapter 8) was so committed to strategic arms limitation (ibid.: 140–144).

The Soviet nuclear programme's first landmark was the successful test of a plutonium 'fission' bomb on 29 August 1949 – hardly four years later than the first US test in July 1945.[16] A year later, on 18 December 1950, US President Truman approved the development of a thermonuclear, 'hydrogen' bomb,[17] and the fact that the first successful thermonuclear test-explosion followed in October 1952 indicates how advanced and efficient US nuclear weapons technology had become since the days of the wartime Manhattan Project. The same is true of Soviet achievements in the thermonuclear field, as is shown by there being only ten months between the first US test and the first Soviet test in August 1953.[18] This was just the beginning: 22 November 1955 was the day of the first successful test of a Soviet superbomb (Holloway 1983: 25). This then established the standard for both sides in a nuclear arms race, in the course of which the competing states – not just the US and the Soviet Union – would between them produce well over two thousand of these horrendously destructive weapons.[19] The great majority were produced, in more or less equal numbers by the US and the Soviet Union, during the 18 years that Brezhnev was *vozhd*. With nuclear weapons escalation triggered by such critical events during Khrushchev's watch as the Cuban weapons crisis of 1962, Brezhnev, from his earliest days in power accepted the compelling need for nuclear arms limitation, in one form or another.

This, however, was only half the story. Nuclear weapons still needed some means to bring them to their destined targets. While the atom bombs that devastated Hiroshima and Nagasaki in August 1945 were dropped from airplanes, German rocket-engineers had already, before the end of World War II, developed the V2 rocket, which from bases in occupied France and Belgium, were successfully launched on London. Although, following the end of the war, Werner von Braun with most of his team of rocket-engineers and scientists, moved to the US to form the hard core of rocket technology and development (Crump 2001: 99), the Soviet Union – with the help of a much smaller number of Germans – was intent on surpassing the Americans. The first long-range (300 km) rocket, the

R-1 – based on the German V2 – was tested in October 1947 and the R-2 (600 km) followed in 1950 (Holloway 1983: 23). In 1957 the Soviet Union, by conducting the first ever test of an Intercontinental Ballistic Missile (ICBM), effectively established the dimensions of any future nuclear war (ibid.: 39) – which were horrendous. The US soon caught up, and by 1965 Soviet Union was significantly behind (ibid.: 43).[20] As early as the 20th Party Conference in 1956 Khrushchev had stated that there could never be a nuclear war, and after 1964 this position was also that of Brezhnev, whose foreign policy – above all vis-à-vis the US – was consistently centred on nuclear disarmament. As shown in Chapter 8, this led to a series of negotiations with the US, focussed on achieving this end, which continued almost to the end of the Brezhnev era.

Although Soviet nuclear strategy consistently favoured long distance rockets above aircraft for delivering nuclear weapons,[21] it is not easy to know how this affected the balance of capital investment between rockets and nuclear weapons. What counts is that the combined sums involved were simply enormous, as they were in the US. Participation by both sides in the space race made costs even higher. If, then the Soviet Union was ahead in launching sputnik, the first successful earth satellite, on 10 October 1957, and having Yuri Gagarin as the first man in space on 12 April 1961, these triumphs were gained at a price that was much harder to bear than it would have been for the much more prosperous US industrial economy. This was bound to tell in the not so long run: judged in the light of future developments, these first two moves in the space race were relatively low-cost. By the end of the 1960s the US was ahead when the Apollo Space Programme, launched by US President Kennedy on 20 May 1961, brought the first three men to the moon on 20 July 1969. This defined another field of battle in which the Soviet Union, under Brezhnev, was forced into unequal competition with the US.

Apart from the attempt to establish nuclear missile bases in Cuba in 1962 (related in Chapter 10), under Khrushchev such bases were restricted to the territory of the Soviet Union. In 1965, however, an agreement made with Czechoslovakia allowed the Soviet Union three bases in the west of the country for the permanent storage of nuclear weapons (Kramer 2010: 33). With the bases still under construction at the time of the Soviet invasion of 1968 (related in Chapter 7), they were also a relevant factor in the decision to launch it.[22]

Brezhnev – once again in contrast to Khrushchev – also adopted a programme submitted by Admiral Sergei Gorshkov to construct nuclear-powered submarines equipped to launch missiles, and by 1972 the Soviet Navy had 34 'Navaga' submarines (Zaloga 2002: 153). Although advanced by Soviet standards, the Navaga had critical shortcomings. The short-range of its R-27 missiles meant that it would have to be deployed close to the shores of any land-mass containing their designated targets – which, needless to say, were likely to be located far inland (as they were in the US). Because the Navaga was so noisy any such deployment was bound to be detected by acoustic sensors – so much so that US Naval Intelligence knew almost immediately of any sailing from the Soviet home-base.

During the 1970s the shortcomings of the Navaga led to the development of new submarine designs that would overcome them. The advanced Murena submarine first went to sea in 1972, with 18 constructed by 1977; in the same year they were armed with the new extended range R-29 missiles. Then, in 1981, an enterprising Soviet captain took one under the Arctic ice, to reach an open stretch of water to conduct a simulated missile launch – a feat not then achieved by the US Navy (Zaloga 2002: 157). Despite this success the Soviet Navy had to come to terms with the US MIRV solid-fuel Poseidon missile with a range of 5,000 km.[23] The Soviet answer, the R-31, was no match; it was no better than the US Polaris missiles first deployed in the 1960s. The Murena then evolved into the Kalmar, the first Soviet submarine to carry missiles with true MIRV warheads; of these 14 were deployed in 1981, the last full year in the life of Brezhnev. The problem was that the Kalmar cost more than four times as much to build as the Navaga (ibid.: 159). If the Kalmar had brought the Soviet nuclear submarine capability closer to parity with that of the US, it went no further than that at a time when the US was actively using new technology to develop its own force.

Clearly, by the end of the Brezhnev era, the burden on the Soviet economy was becoming insupportable. Nuclear submarines were only part of the story. In spite of the time and trouble devoted by both the Soviet Union and the US to nuclear disarmament during the 1970s, both sides continued to add new and ever more expensive weapons to their arsenal. At the end of the day the world contained more than two thousand nuclear warheads, mostly in the possession of either the Soviet Union or the US, with not only every single nuclear power, but also the world at large, living under their shadow. Almost to the very end, the military industrial complex, both in the Soviet Union and the US, had sufficient political influence to ensure that these weapons continued to be developed – regardless of cost. This was a major factor in the final disintegration of the Soviet Union in 1991, which, incidentally, was also one year after its last nuclear test, and one year before the last carried out by the US at the Nevada test-site.[24]

The Soviet Union in space

The production of rockets for delivering nuclear warheads was closely linked to the Soviet space programme. That much of the essential technology was shared meant that the development of spacecraft, from the first earth-satellites onward, also belonged to the military industrial complex – as it did also in the US. Inevitably, then, the cosmonauts were serving officers in the Soviet Air Force, while, at the same time, their activities were subject to the same security, enforced by the KGB, as the nuclear weapons programme. One result was that only the successes of the space programme were made public. This, at least until the mid-1960s, was sufficient to assure citizens that the Soviet Union was ahead in the space race. They soon learnt, therefore, of Luna 2 being the first spacecraft to impact on the moon, or Luna 3, the first to transmit images of the hidden far side and of Luna 9, the first to make a soft landing. What remained untold (at least until Gorbachev's *glasnost* in the late 1980s) were disasters, such as the death of a leading scientist, Vladimir Komarov, in the Soyuz 1 crash, and more seriously, the explosion, on four successive launches, of the N1 rocket, specially developed for manned lunar landings. In the event, the American Apollo 11 became, on 20 July 1969, the first spacecraft to land men on the moon – an event impossible to conceal from the Soviet public. Worse still, the Soviet space programme never landed men on the moon, and in the early 1970s all attempts to do so were abandoned. On the other hand the Soviet programme did include the very successful 'Soyuz' series of spacecraft, with the first unmanned space mission accomplished on 28 November 1966. After the collapse of the Soviet Union in 1991 the Soyuz spacecraft came into their own as shuttles between earth stations and the International Space Station (ISS).[25] This new role was commercial, which it never was in Brezhnev's time; the ISS dates only from 1998, seven years after the collapse of the Soviet Union in 1991. Under Brezhnev, whatever the merits of 'Soyuz', the programme was still an exceptionally heavy burden on an essentially stagnant national economy. Although as spacecraft go, the Soyuz was remarkably low-cost and with, as of today, more than 1,700 completed missions, highly reliable, the capital investment required by such a large-scale enterprise is still enormous. What is more, the remoteness of the two locations – one, the Baikonur Cosmodrome in the middle of the barren Kazakh steppe,[26] and the other, the Plesetsk Cosmodrome, in the *taiga* south of the Arctic city of Archangelsk – from which all Soviet (and after 1991, Russian) spacecraft have been launched, added enormously to the cost of maintaining the space programme.[27] However well-chosen for the secure testing of long-range missiles, the purpose for which both Baikonur and Plesetsk were originally established in the mid-1950s,[28] the cost of the transport infrastructure necessary to service such remote and inhospitable locations was also very substantial. That one day the Soyuz rockets might just earn their keep as international space-shuttles could never have been foreseen by Brezhnev. In economic terms, the Soviet space programme, as much as that devoted to long-range missiles and nuclear warheads, was a dead loss. Significantly also, from the end of the 1960s the space programme, like the nuclear submarine programme, always lagged behind what the US was achieving – and never looked like closing the gap.

Nuclear power

After the end of World War II in 1945, the Soviet Union – committed almost from its earliest days to the slogan 'Communism equals Soviet power plus electrification of the entire country'[29] – was a world-leader in realizing the usefulness of nuclear reactors for generating electricity. When, in 1954, the Obninsk nuclear power station, some two hours south of Moscow, went on stream, it was two years ahead of the UK (with its first nuclear power at Calder Hall opening in 1956), with the US (1957) and France (1962) lagging even further behind. Even so, US President Eisenhower, in a speech made in New York on 8 December 1953, had already announced an 'atoms for peace' programme, worldwide in scope. In the Soviet Union Khrushchev readily adopted the same slogan (Josephson 2000: 4), and in many ways the Soviet Civil programme was wider in scope that that of the US. Although this meant that it was extremely expensive, it also had priority in access to essential resources equivalent to that enjoyed by the military industrial complex, to which it was closed linked. From a Soviet perspective this was a new field offering unprecedented opportunities of demonstrating the superiority of communist government. The problem was that in a country with abundant resources of fossil fuel, unit capital costs for nuclear power stations were never brought down to the level of conventional thermal power. The advocates of nuclear power, noting the remoteness of the major sources of fossil fuel, mainly in Siberia, argued that the extremely light weight of nuclear fuel meant a vast saving in transport costs to generating stations located close to the main industrial centres in European Russia. At the same time economies of scale could be realized by adopting only two basic models for the construction of huge generating stations, grouped together in 'reactor parks' near to major industrial users of electricity.

From its earliest days the Soviet nuclear power programme had its own momentum, which, so long as Brezhnev was alive, it never lost. What this meant in practice is well-illustrated by the Ukrainian nuclear programme, whose time-span was almost exactly that of Brezhnev's watch. Although the original initiative, in January 1965, came from the Ukrainian Council of Ministers, Shchelest, the Party Secretary in Kiev, lost little time in gaining the necessary approval from Moscow for what, in September, 1966, would become the 'Plan for Construction and Operation of Atomic Energy Stations, 1966–1975' – to be located in the Kiev region (Josephson 2000: 253). In November a government commission was established to select a site for the first reactor, and by February 1967, the decision was made to build two units at a site on the Pripyat River, some 80 km north of Kiev. The official recommendation, dated 2 February, referred to the 'Chernobyl Atomic Regional Electrical Power Station'. The RBMK model was adopted for the reactors, because it was substantially cheaper than the alternative VVER model. The ground-breaking ceremony took place in January 1970, and in September 1977, Unit 1 was supplying electricity to the Ukrainian grid. By this time the plan had been extended to four units, which took much less time to complete – so much so that when the Kiev Party secretary, Vlad Tsybalko visited in 1979 he was able to rename, the whole completed project 'Lenin Chernobyl Atomic Energy Station', to commemorate Lenin's hundred and tenth birthday. This was not the end: Tsybalko successfully promoted two new units, 5 and 6, to add to the reactor park, which were still under construction when,[30] on 25 April 1986, a poorly carried out experimental shutdown of Unit 4 led to an explosion that reverberated across the world, and sealed for good the fate of the Lenin Chernobyl Atomic Energy Station.

Although by this time, Brezhnev had been dead for four years, it is still relevant to ask what position he took with regard to the whole Soviet nuclear electric power programme. The answer is simple: he was consistently impatient to accelerate and extend it, a matter which at a plenary meeting of the Central Committee in November 1980, he called 'quite feasible' (Josephson 2000: 46). Here he was encouraged by physicists of the Kurchatov Institute, whose livelihood depended largely on developing new nuclear technology, such as that related to fast breeder reactors (ibid.: 58, 66) – which were hardly to prove viable in any part of the world.[31]

Atomic powered surface vessels

From very early days, both in the US and the Soviet Union, atomic scientists were exploring possible uses of nuclear reactors to provide the power for transport. It was always clear that the weight of even the smallest reactor meant that such use would be confined to transport by water, particularly over open seas. Then in 1953, if not earlier, Soviet scientists and engineers, claimed that nuclear reactors, if installed in ice-breakers in the Arctic, would make possible much larger ships, capable of breaking through thicker layers of ice, at greater speeds than any conventional ice-breaker. At the same time the exceedingly low weight to power ratio of nuclear fuel would allow such vessels to continue operating at sea for exceptionally long periods of time, a decisive advantage along coasts where the ports were few, liable to be ice-bound, and difficult to link to any transport infrastructure overland. In this realm, where geography favoured the Soviet Union over any possible rival, the way was open to achieving spectacular successes in the peaceful use of atomic energy. If the technical problems, which were considerable, could be solved, the construction of nuclear-powered vessels – not only ice-breakers – was a commercial project ideally suited to demonstrate the superiority of the Marxist planned economy, and by doing so providing Moscow with invaluable political capital, both at home and abroad. The first ship planned was the *Lenin*. From the first designs on the drawing board in 1953 to laying down the keel in the Admiralty Factory on 24 August 1956, three years were needed for the project; although a matter of considerable national pride the launch which then followed on 5 December 1957 was rather less successful than that of the sputnik a month earlier, for inspections required before sea-trials could be approved revealed any number of defects to be dealt with (Josephson 2000: 121). This meant that the first sea-trials only took place in December 1959: even so, 'the creation of the first in the world nuclear ice-breaker *Lenin*' earned all those involved effusive congratulations from Moscow, and wide coverage in the Soviet Press. In May 1960 the *Lenin*, closely shadowed by NATO surveillance aircraft, finally reached Murmansk in the Baring Sea, destined to be its home port until it was finally decommissioned in 1990.

The achievements of the *Lenin* were remarkable, and although no-one was more impressed by their performance than Brezhnev, it was only in the 1970s that a programme for eight new, and much improved ice-breakers, was adopted (Josephson 2000: 125).[32] Until then Soviet ship-building resources were mainly deployed for building nuclear submarines – eighty-nine in the period 1961–1971 – while the nuclear reactor industry was kept fully stretched by the demands of new electricity generating stations (as at Chernobyl). Although by the end of the 1970s Soviet ice-breakers were making it possible for shipping to cross from Murmansk to Vladivostok at any time of year, their full economic potential was far from being realized. If the sea-lanes were being kept open, too few nuclear-powered giant freighters were built to exploit them. What is more, both ice-breakers and freighters had to share inadequate and poorly maintained shore facilities with the Soviet Northern Fleet. The key Atomflot base in Murmansk was quite unable to meet the demands made upon it, so that even after Brezhnev's time, new giant freighters such as the *Sevmorput*, were barely 50 per cent operational. At the same time, the nuclear-powered fleet, whether civil or military, was an environmental disaster, with both shore facilities inadequately protected against nuclear contamination and spent fuel dumped in the Arctic sea representing long-term hazards.

Just as with electric power generation, the bottom line of the nuclear shipbuilding programme – which Brezhnev consistently promoted with the same level of enthusiasm – reveals a substantial loss rather than any gain to the Soviet Union. This is just another case of policy, favoured by Brezhnev, contributing to the Soviet economy as a whole little that would save it from stagnation: it was still *zastoi* all the way. If, to be fair to Brezhnev, it must be conceded that the success of such programmes, even in the western world, was always problematic, the price paid in the west was just about affordable; it is part of the tragedy of Brezhnev that it never was so in the Soviet Union.

Notes

1 Here he was supported by Suslov and Shelepin, but not by Kosygin.
2 Coleman (1997: 153) gives examples of such transfers in the military field.
3 At one stage Brezhnev's Politburo even considered a pre-emptive strike against Lop Nor (Coleman 1997: 76).
4 Ho Chi Minh died in 1969, but his successor, Le Duc Tho, was equally formidable in pursuing his policies.
5 Until 1967 Soviet arms had been sent to North Vietnam by rail through China: that the Chinese then closed this route confirms their hostility to both the Viet Minh and the Soviet Union (Coleman 1997: 69). The sea-route, if slower, did not necessarily cost more.
6 Brezhnev, while US President Nixon's guest at San Clemente in June 1973, claimed that the Soviet Union had stopped supplying arms to Hanoi following the Paris agreement of January 1973, whose purpose – in the event never realised – was to end hostilities between North and South Vietnam. (Kissinger 1982: 295). During the same visit Brezhnev had already made clear his hatred of the Chinese and his mistrust of Mao Zedong.
7 Up until 1961 China, as an observer, had attended COMECON sessions.
8 Note also that Cuba joined COMECON in 1972.
9 Mozambique, in its war of independence against Portugal, had also received Soviet arms in the years 1967–1969.
10 Under a $250,000,000 agreement initiated by President Nasser Egypt first received Soviet armaments in the mid-1950s, although for political reasons Czechoslovakia was initially named as the actually supplier (Hosmer and Wolfe 1982: 11).
11 Significantly, on 18 July 1972, President Anwar Sadat ordered the withdrawal of all Soviet military personnel from Egypt; his object was two-fold: first, the Soviet Union would no longer be an impediment to an attack on Israel (such as took place in September 1973), and second, Egypt would be strengthened, diplomatically, vis-à-vis the US (Kissinger 1982: 205).
12 Haslam (2011: 313) estimates that in the period 1978–1982 three quarters of all arms sales were to the Middle East and paid for in hard currency.
13 OPEC started with six members in 1960 (of which only Venezuela was not in the middle East), but by 1973 had been joined by six more (of which four belonged to the Arab world).

14 Somewhat ironically Stalin, in 1948, strongly supported the admission of the new state of Israel to the UN, recognising a chance to follow a line that would discredit British imperialism.

15 In 1946 the first post-war five-year plan provided specifically for priority for nuclear weapons, rockets, radar and jet-propulsion (Holloway 1983: 21).

16 The first successful test of an uranium bomb was in 1951.

17 Truman at the same time converted an existing US Air Force base into the Nevada Test Site, where almost all subsequent nuclear tests would be carried out – the last being in 1991.

18 In a sense this brought the Soviet Union ahead of the US, because the Soviet test was of an actual bomb, which could have been used operationally. The first US test (code-named 'Castle Bravo') of a practical hydrogen bomb was on 1 March 1954 at the Bikini atoll in the Marshall Islands.

19 By the mid-1960s all five members of the UN Security Council had tested nuclear weapons, with the UK from this time on sharing the Nevada Test Site with the US. They were later joined by Israel, India and Pakistan, while at one time or another, Argentina, Iran, Iraq, Libya and South Africa all had nuclear weapons programmes.

20 This was certainly the message conveyed to the west in 1961 by the Soviet defector, Colonel Oleg Penkovsky, who had unusual access to military secrets (Haslam 2011: 196). However, it was only in January 1977 that a speech by Brezhnev made clear that parity, not superiority, in nuclear weapons was acceptable to the Soviet Union – a position restated at 26th Party Congress in 1981 (Holloway 1983: 48).

21 Three quarters of all US strategic warheads were planned to be delivered by bombers, not rockets (Holloway 1983: 50).

22 At the time the bases, always under strict Soviet military control, were a very well kept secret, which only came to light after the fall of the Soviet Union in 1991.

23 MIRV – Multiple Independently targeted Re-entry Vehicle.

24 China and France carried out tests in 1996, India and Pakistan in 1998, and North Korea, possibly, in 2009.

25 After the final flight of the US space shuttle, *Endeavor*, on 20 May 2011, only the Russian Soyuz spacecraft still operated as the earth-link to the ISS.

26 The site, measuring east–west some 90 km, and north–south, 85 km, is also home to the Tyuratam Missile Test Range, discovered, incidentally, by US air reconnaissance on 5 August 1957.

27 The fact that it is now used exclusively for the civilian Soyuz programme does not mean that a new more accessible location might be chosen for it. Kazakhstan has agreed with Russia a lease of the Baikonur test-site until 2050.

28 Although Baikonur was the earlier test-site, the operational advantage of Plesetsk was that US targets would be within the range of new R-7 missiles launched from this site. The Soviet government commissioned the first launch-pad in December, 1959, at the same creating the Strategic Missile Forces within the Soviet Army. All this explains why, as related on page 63, the American U2 reconnaissance airplane brought down by the Soviet Air Force on 1 May 1960 was then on its way to photograph Plesetsk – having already photographed Baikonur.

29 Josephson (2000: 6).

30 By the time of the Chernobyl explosion another four units were being planned for the site (Josephson 2000: 243).

31 Phenix and Superphenix in France, Monju in Japan, Dounreay in the UK, Clinch River in the US, and Kalkar in Germany all proved to be failed projects.

32 The first new ship, the *Arktika*, having entered operations in 1974, became the first ice-breaker to reach the North Pole in August 1977.

6 Dissidence and human rights

Khrushchev's legacy

If in the Soviet Union, as seen from the outside world during the Brezhnev years (1964–1982), the activities of so-called 'dissidents' played a key historical part, this was not a judgment shared by Brezhnev and his colleagues at the top of the Soviet hierarchy. For them dissidents were essentially marginal, and had to be taken into account not so much because of the trouble they caused within the Soviet Union, but rather because of the way their activities influenced the foreign policy of the United States and its allies. Mikhail Gorbachev, in a very long book of memoirs (Gorbachev 1997), hardly mentions them. In September 1978, Anatoly Dobrynin, present, as Soviet Ambassador in Washington, at a meeting in the White House, heard Andrei Gromyko, the Soviet Foreign Secretary, ask President Carter, 'who is Shcharansky?' (Dobrynin 1995: 399). That a Russian mathematician, serving a long prison sentence as a result of his dissident activities, was known to the American president – who was much concerned about his fate – but unknown to a key figure in the Soviet government, reflects the vast difference in political climate between the US and the Soviet Union.[1]

The year, 1978, came at a very late stage in Brezhnev's time as *vozhd*. Already General Secretary of the CPSU for nearly 14 years, his health was so poor that he governed largely by default: decisions, if made in his name, were initiated by others. Even more serious was Brezhnev's failure to keep up with events after Nixon's departure from the White House in 1975. In particular, he realized the impact neither of the Helsinki Accords of 1975 – to which he was a party – on the human rights movement in the Soviet Union, nor that of the emigration (which he tolerated if not encouraged) of a substantial part of the Soviet Jewish population.

Shcharansky, more than anyone else, was the link between these two themes: the imprisonment that followed his protests against official refusal to allow him to move to Israel – the destination of the majority of the Jewish emigrants – identified him as the most prominent victim of the systematic denial of human rights within the Soviet Union. This link, however, is the subject matter of Chapter 9; the focus of the present chapter is on the dissidents, not necessarily Jewish, active on Brezhnev's watch, particularly in the early years when he had to come to terms with Khrushchev's legacy in the field of human rights and freedom of expression.

In today's popular English usage *dissident* is a word that almost immediately evokes a Soviet citizen, generally prominent in literature or the arts, who was officially presented as 'no longer recognising the authority of the state to which he had previously submitted'.[2] Essentially the dissident was a heretic in world governed by principles – in the case of the Soviet Union, those of Marxist-Leninism – rigorously enforced by the political hierarchy, which, until his death in 1953, simply meant Stalin.

Identification as a dissident had serious consequences both for the individual, and for his public. Here it should be noted particularly that dissidents had names; this, indeed, is what made them so dangerous, for a name is something that people can identify with. The composer, Shostakovich, the nuclear physicist, Sakharov, and the writer, Solzhenytsin, are well-known instances, but there are many more. The result, however, of the individuality of dissidents, was that much time passed before they constituted a single recognizable movement, with some sort of co-ordination. Notwithstanding allegations made officially, dissidents were seldom conspirators. They disagreed among themselves on everything except for the right to be heard freely (Rubenstein 1980: xi, foreword by Harrison E. Salisbury). This meant that the Soviet authorities, in dealing with dissidents, were constrained to act in any number of separate cases, with the risk that any one of them might attract just the sort of attention that they were most anxious to avoid. Two writers, Yuli Daniel and Andrei Sinyavsky, who were arrested in 1965 – Brezhnev's first year as *vozhd* – and tried and convicted in February 1966, are now known to history mainly for this reason. What is more, the fact that the prosecution evidence consisted mainly of excerpts from their published work, inevitably meant that this became much better known. This was not a welcome precedent for the KGB, which had initiated the whole process. Significantly the Judge later described the offence for which the authors were convicted as 'blasphemy' (ibid.: 38); the word occurs nowhere in the Soviet Criminal Code, but in Russian it clearly indicates an offence against God.[3] This supports equating *dissidence* with *heresy*.

For the Soviet hierarchy the problem of dissidence was inherent in the official policy of promoting literature and the arts, at least so long as the works produced affirmed the principles of 'socialist realism' and spurned every trace of 'bourgeois decadence'. Inevitably the constraints inherent in this policy – as in that of any other strict government control of the arts – discouraged the creativity which is the hallmark of any great artist, and encouraged the production of works which were banal and uncreative (of which any number were produced in the 80-odd years of the Soviet Union). In the result, although many members of, say, the Union of Soviet Composers, had gained their place as a reward for orthodoxy – reflected, for instance, in music composed for patriotic films – it was impossible to deny membership to such towering figures as Sergei Prokofiev and Dmitri Shostakovich.

This is not to say that they had an easy ride, as is shown by the history of Shostakovich's opera, *Lady Macbeth of Mtsensk*, consigned to limbo in 1936 simply because Stalin did not like the music and only fully restored to favour under a new name, *Katerina Ismailova*, in 1962. Although by this time Khrushchev had long been in power, Shostakovich's music could still arouse official disapproval, as he was to discover with the first performance of his 13th symphony, 'Babi Yar', on 18 December 1962. This was a choral work, in which the words sung in the first movement came from 'Babi Yar', a recent work of a young poet, Yevgeny Yevtushenko. Although the title to his poem came from the horrific murder of the Jewish population of Kiev after the city fell to the Germans in September 1941, it was also, quite unmistakably, a critique of contemporary Soviet anti-Semitism. For Khrushchev it was not the music, but the poetry that went too far; indeed he can take credit for restoring Shostakovich, along with Prokofiev, to good grace (Volkov 1979: 115). Even so, the symphony's first performance in Moscow provided the occasion for demonstrating against the government (ibid.: 24, note 31). Before the symphony could be performed again Yevtushenko had to add new lines to his poem, so as to record not only Soviet solidarity during World War II, but also the fact that not all who died at Babi Yar were Jewish.

Significantly, the first performance of the 13th symphony was also the last occasion on which any work of Shostakovich encountered official disapproval. After adapting his score to a revised version of 'Babi Yar', Shostakovich was no longer officially treated as a dissident, despite, during the 1960s, a close association both with the English composer, Benjamin Britten (who also visited the Soviet Union) and the Russian cellist, Mstislav Rostropovich, who, having refused to condemn Pasternak in 1958 (Rubenstein 1980: 13) and in 1964 declared his support for Sinyavski, finally emigrated, under KGB pressure, in 1974. By this time, however, Shostakovich, after years of poor health, was within a year of his death: in his case, at least, the authorities appreciated that in the world of music, both inside and outside the Soviet Union, a high price would be paid if Russia's leading composer were to be harassed at so late a stage in a life that started in the same year as that of Brezhnev. Given how easily the language of music can cross frontiers, it is significant that the two works – *Lady Macbeth of Mtsensk* and 'Babi Yar' – that caused Shostakovich the most trouble were both choral. When it comes to dissidents, therefore, it is now time to look at the written word.

A good place to start is Appendix A of Mandelstam (1976), where, over some 33 pages, the author, Nadezhda Mandelstam, lists the persons mentioned in the text of a book which has as much to tell as any other published during the 70-odd years of the Soviet Union's history about the fate of individuals judged to be dissidents. Of the names listed, not all are those of writers, and of those that were, a few belong to men who, like Shostakovich, successfully rode out the storm of Stalin's terror. As witness the Moscow show trials of the late 1930s, this was never an easy ride, and even those who escaped the death sentence could still be sentenced to years of imprisonment in one of the notorious Gulags, where, like Nadezhda's husband, Osip Mandelstam, and many others, they might never be heard of again.

The Gulag system was formally established in 1929 with the object of providing the labour force needed for the exploitation of remote and inhospitable regions of the Soviet Union, which were still, none the less, rich in natural resources

(Hill and Gaddy 2003: 83). In the mid-1930s, Nikolai Yezhov, head of the NKVD, ensured that a steadily increasing number of prisoners, were sent to the Gulags – so much so that by 1938 the number of those imprisoned exceeded two million (ibid.: 86). (Yezhov, far from being rewarded for this achievement, was himself a victim of the Great Purge of 1938; he was succeeded by Beria.) Although the number of Gulag prisoners declined during World War II, it rose again, to some two-and-a-half million before Stalin died in 1953.

Needless to say, within such a large population, prominent dissidents, such as Mandelstam, were very few in number. Except for their close associates their absence from Soviet society went unnoticed. By the end of the war, the total number of Gulag prisoners was hardly more than a tenth of the 20 million odd lives lost in it, one way or another. The existence of the Gulags, let alone the actual names of prisoners prominent in the literature and the arts, was hardly reported in the rigidly controlled official media. When, after the war such men once more ended up in a Gulag, this would have been of little concern to those millions who had survived – often with the loss of young members of the family – even if they had known (Deutscher 1967: 580). Given the total absence of independent media, such knowledge was not widespread.

With the death of Stalin, the climate in which writers and artists worked, changed immediately for the better. A new period of unprecedented freedom opened; this came to be known as the 'thaw' after the title of a book by Ilya Ehrenburg, one of the best-known Soviet writers. *Thaw* was first published in the leading Soviet literary journal, *Novy Mir* (New World), in 1954, together with articles criticizing Communist Party attitudes towards culture. Within a few months this led to the dismissal of its editor, Alexander Tvardovsky. Although this was seen as a sign that the thaw was over, Tvardovsky, rehabilitated, was reappointed editor in 1958. As Editor-in-Chief during the whole of the 1960s, he was inevitably involved in the way that Soviet leaders, particularly Brezhnev, dealt with dissidents. This is significant, because where Khrushchev's name is associated with the thaw, Brezhnev is remembered for his largely ineffectual attempts to retard it. Almost inevitably the problems that Brezhnev faced in the 1960s were a legacy from the Khrushchev years. The question, therefore, is what then were the events that counted?

In the literary field the way was opened by Vladimir Dudintsev's *Not by Bread Alone*, a novel published in 1956, during the second 'Khrushchev thaw', as the period of only a few months between the secret speech and the Soviet invasion of Hungary came to be known. What counted was the remarkable popularity, both in the Soviet Union and – in translation – abroad, of a satirical work describing a corrupt bureaucracy, in which the subservient earn promotion, while this is denied to those of any real merit. Even if the thought never occurred to him, Brezhnev belonged unmistakably to the former category.

In Khrushchev's final years as *vozhd* Dudintsev was largely eclipsed following the publication of two books which achieved worldwide fame: the first was Boris Pasternak's *Doctor Zhivago*, the second, Alexandr Solzhenitsyn's *One Day in the Life of Ivan Denisovich*.

Pasternak had in Stalin's day been censured by the Union of Soviet Writers, he still remained a member. Stalin's death, and the first Khrushchev thaw, meant freedom to write as never before. Pasternak was already working on Doctor Zhivago, and although *Novy Mir* published ten poems from the book in 1954, a year later the full text was judged unsuitable for publication. Pasternak had, however, also sent a copy to a leading Italian publisher, Feltrinelli, who was also a member of the powerful Italian Communist Party. Feltrinelli not only published the book in Italian in November 1957, but arranged for translations in other European languages. All this was little noted in the Soviet press, but then, on 23 October 1958, the news broke that Pasternak had been awarded the Nobel Prize for Literature – accepted by him two days later. Within the Soviet Union all hell was let loose. Official Soviet bodies lambasted him, speakers at mass meetings (of which one was attended by Khrushchev (Rubenstein 1980: 12)) denounced him, and the Union of Soviet Writers expelled him. The pressure was too much for Pasternak. Within a month he wrote to Khrushchev apologizing for his book and notified the Swedish Academy that he was renouncing the Nobel Prize.

The official reaction to *Doctor Zhivago* proved to be overkill on a massive scale. Outside the Soviet Union leading authors – several of them, like Feltrinelli, Communists – publicly supported Pasternak, and although such support was inconceivable within the Soviet Union, many in the Union of Soviet Writers still protested, off the record, against his expulsion (Rubenstein 1980: 13).

Inevitably copies of the foreign translations of Doctor Zhivago began to circulate,[4] surreptitiously, within the Soviet Union, but even more important, in the long run, was the fact that it was the first full-length book to be distributed as 'samizdat'. This so-called 'self-publication', based on the distribution of typewritten copies of literary works, had started in the late 1950s with the unofficial literary magazine, *Syntax*, edited by Alexander Ginzburg. The *samizdat* publication of *Doctor Zhivago* was a critical breakthrough into what, in the course of the 1960s, would become something of a mass market.

Ginsburg, belonged to the Lianozovo group of artists and intellectuals, named after one of the few places close to Moscow where former Gulag prisoners, denied permission to reside in the city itself, were allowed to live (Zubok 2009: 188). This was extremely significant in the years immediately following Stalin's death, because of the steady release, under Khrushchev, of the majority of those imprisoned in the Gulags (accompanied by the gradual unwinding of the whole system). At the same time millions more who had been deported to new territories, such as the virgin lands of Kazakhstan so favoured by Brezhnev, whose exploitation was central to Stalin's economic policy (Taubman 2003: 275), were also released. The result of so many millions returning to their former homes was that even the smallest village could learn, at first hand, about the horrors of the Gulag system and mass deportation. Among those released were writers who had stories to tell, which only confirmed what Khrushchev had revealed in the secret speech (ibid.: 271).

If, to begin with, publication by 'deviant' writers, including those released from the Gulags, was by *samizdat*, Alexander Solzhenitsyn's *One Day in the Life of Ivan Denisovich* was a decisive breakthrough into the world of officially sanctioned publishing. At the 22nd Congress of the CPSU in February 1962 Khrushchev publicly denounced Stalin in terms even more extreme than those of the secret speech six years earlier. For Solzhenitsyn this suggested that the time had come to find a publisher for *Ivan Denisovich*, so he submitted the manuscript to Tvardovsky, as editor of *Novy Mir*. Although Tvardovsky much liked the book, from previous experience he knew that the way to publication was hazardous. Fortunately Vladimir Lebedev, one of Khrushchev's aides, could be persuaded to present it to the *vozhd*. This he did by reading passages aloud to Khrushchev while he was on holiday at his Black Sea *dacha* in September 1962. The book won spontaneous approval – so much so that Khrushchev wanted to invite its author for an immediate visit. Prudently thinking better of this idea, he decided to consult the Presidium of the Supreme Soviet. This he did in early October, when, with Suslov as the only open opponent, he carried the day and went on to receive Solzhenitsyn and Tvardovsky officially on 20 October (ibid.: 527). Not only was Solzhenitsyn cleared for publication, but so incidentally was the much younger Yevgeny Yevtushenko, whose poem 'The Heirs of Stalin' was published in *Pravda* the next day (ibid.: 528).[5] In Brezhnev's final years 'Stalinist orthodoxies were discarded, and there was a recovery of intellectual vitality unknown in Soviet life since the 1920s' (Kemp-Welch 2010: 220).

Brezhnev's estate

Even when the established Stalinist orthodoxy was falling apart under Khrushchev, his successor, Brezhnev, consistently remained loyal to the principles of Marxist-Leninism that he had embraced as a young man in Ukraine. When, therefore, he succeeded as *vozhd* late in 1964 he had to come to terms with a world in which science, literature and the arts, had succeeded, quite conspicuously, in deviating from these principles. The question, then, from a very early stage, was what would Brezhnev do to reverse this process? Would he go so far as to rehabilitate Stalin?

Even before the end of his first year in power Brezhnev was confronted by what would prove to be a cause célèbre. As already related on page 102, on 8 September 1965 the KGB arrested, two authors, Andrei Sinyavsky and Yuli Daniel; during four days in February 1966 they were tried and convicted for 'anti-Soviet agitation and propaganda'.[6] The evidence against them was derived mainly from the contents of stories in which the action took place before Stalin died. Both authors, however, had published abroad, and under pseudonyms. What is more Sinyavsky, barely three months before his arrest, had published a lengthy introduction to a volume of poetry by Pasternak – a man he much admired. Both he and Daniel had been pall-bearers at Pasternak's funeral in May 1960. Both had put their trust in the new freedom following Khrushchev's secret speech, and their arrest led many to fear that Brezhnev was intent on rehabilitating Stalin. While the suggestion made by two Marshals of the Soviet Union, shortly after the trial of Sinyavsky and Daniel, that it was 'time to re-evaluate Stalin's wartime role' may have justified this fear – as did also Brezhnev's condemnation of 'hack artists who specialize in smearing our regime' at the 23rd Party Congress – demonstrations in Moscow against the conviction of the two writers, combined with loud foreign protests, were a warning that such proceedings against authors could be counterproductive. As with Pasternak much of the work of Sinyavsky and Daniel had already been published officially, while much of what remained circulated either as foreign translations or as *samizdat*.

If the trial of Sinyavsky and Daniel was a signal to the world that Brezhnev was intent on turning the clock back, this was not true of every action he took with regard to dissidents in his first year. Joseph Brodsky was a poet who, following the denunciation of his work as 'pornographic and anti-Soviet' by a Leningrad newspaper in 1963, was twice committed to a psychiatric hospital. Then, in 1964, he was put on trial for 'social parasitism' and sentenced to five years hard labour. Khrushchev, whatever he might have done for Solzhenitsyn and Yevtushenko, did nothing to help Brodsky. In 1965, after a secret transcript of the trial had been leaked to the outside world, Brodsky's sentence was commuted. His case had become a cause célèbre, with Yevtushenko, Shostakovich, Akhmatova and Jean-Paul Sartre all demanding his release from the Gulag.[7] Brezhnev, in so far as he was involved, found it prudent to consent – perhaps as a result of the problems he had faced with Sinyavsky and Daniel. Even so the authorities did not make life easy for Brodsky after he returned to Leningrad, but his poems were still widely published abroad and as *samizdat*, with only four judged as suitable for official Soviet anthologies. After consistently refusing Brodsky's requests to be allowed to emigrate to Israel, the Soviet authorities, in 1972, put him on a plane to Vienna. This followed advice given by Andrei Snezhnevsky, a psychiatrist and expert on 'paranoid reformist delusion', in whose opinion Brodsky was 'not a valuable person at all and may be let go' (Brintlinger and Vinistky 2007: 92). From Vienna Brodsky proceeded not to Israel, but to the United States. There he remained for the rest of his life, producing his best work; this led to a Nobel Prize for Literature and appointment as national Poet Laureate, to say nothing of countless other honours – not bad going for a 'paranoid deluded reformist', but what a loss to the Soviet Union. Brezhnev no doubt wondered what all the fuss was about.

During the Brezhnev years one man above all, Andrei Sakharov, established his name as a Soviet dissident. It was a process that took some time to get started. Involved in the Soviet nuclear weapons programme from its earliest days, Sakharov, by showing his masters how to achieve a thermonuclear explosion, earned the title 'Father of the Hydrogen Bomb'. This work was achieved at what Sakharov always referred to as the 'Installation', a secret location some distance from Moscow, where, in 1949, Sakharov was ordered to work by NKVD Chief, Lavrentiy Beria. He had earlier been sounded out by a Beria subordinate, General Malyshev, who had urged him to join the Communist Party. Sakharov refused, on the grounds that he could not accept some of the party's recorded actions, mentioning specifically 'the arrest of innocent people and the excesses of the collectivization campaign' (Sakharov 1990: 104). If this identified him as a dissident *avant la lettre*, the point was overlooked by Beria. Sakharov's potential contribution to the nuclear weapons programme was simply too valuable – as indeed was reflected by his high ranking in the *nomenklatura* after he had moved to the Installation. His standing was recognized in October 1953 when the Soviet Academy of Sciences, quite exceptionally, voted unanimously to elect him a full member (ibid.: 179). (Beria was by then imprisoned and awaiting trial).

In 1955 Sakharov was involved in Soviet nuclear politics at the highest level. Khrushchev, still concerned about his ascendancy over Malenkov, proposed a second Installation for the development of nuclear weapons. Officially, the argument was that competition between the two would produce better results. One of Malenkov's alleged shortcomings was that he had dragged his feet, so that nothing was done; this was all the more frustrating given that Malyshev, who had been Beria's man, was still involved in the security of the first Installation (although he would soon lose his job). At the same time there were thought to be two many Jews at the top level, even though some, such as Yuli Khariton, the scientific director, were internationally acclaimed nuclear physicists. Among the bureaucrats of the Ministry of Medium Machine Building responsible for the administration of the Installation its dining-room was informally known as 'the synagogue'. The fact that the second Installation was known as 'Egypt' (Sakharov 1990: 184) tells all.

In the event, the two institutions operated independently of each other, so that critically, they each carried out their own weapons tests. In the late 1950s, when the pace of the nuclear arms race was continually increasing, atmospheric tests were carried out by both the Soviet Union and the US. Here, however, President Eisenhower had suggested a treaty banning all tests other than those conducted underground (Sakharov 1990: 230). What is more, Sakharov, went on record by making a similar proposal in the Soviet Union.

In the Soviet Union the question became critical, with tests carried out in the autumn of 1962. The first of these, being carried out by the first Installation, inevitably involved Sakharov, who, while accepting that it was essential to the Soviet nuclear weapons programme, noted also the possibility of 'long term casualties running into six figures' (Sakharov 1990: 226). Seeing no justification for a new test, to be carried out by the second Installation, Sakharov did everything in his power to prevent it. After Khariton declined to help – on the grounds that any intervention would only alienate Efim Slavsky, the Minister of Medium Machine Building – Sakharov got through to Khrushchev, who was unwell, in Turkmenistan, after attending an official event. After Khrushchev promised to consult Frol Kozlov, a key member of the Presidium, Sakharov got through first, but once again he got nowhere, for Kozlov, like Khariton, did not wish to get across Slavsky (ibid.: 229). This is significant because Kozlov's power base was the Presidium, and Slavsky's, the Council of Ministers. At the same time the first Installation was the protégé of the Presidium, and the second, that of the Council. Although the former counted more as a power base, as appreciated by both Khrushchev in the 1950s and Brezhnev in the 1960s (in their opposition, respectively, to Malenkov and Kosygin), in principle they were still bound to work together. In the case of the 'second test' what probably counted, in the end, was a common perception that Khrushchev preferred, in any conflict of interests, to support the second Installation – which was created on his watch – above the first. The fact that this might lead to 'hundreds of thousands' of lives being put in jeopardy quite unnecessarily, exasperated Sakharov, but, as events showed, he could nothing about it. The second test was carried out successfully on 26 September 1962.

As to the rivalry between Slavsky and Sakharov, the story had a happy ending. Early in 1963, Slavsky called Sakharov, to tell him of interest, at the very highest level, for his proposed test ban treaty. This was confirmed by Khrushchev in a speech in Berlin on 2 July 1963, which led to *The Treaty Banning Nuclear Weapons in the Atmosphere, Outer Space and Under Water* being signed in Moscow on 5 August. This, as seen by Sakharov, significantly reduced the risk of a thermonuclear war.

In the summer of 1964 Sakharov, on his own initiative, was involved in an event that was to have important political consequences. This occurred at the regular meeting of the Academy of Sciences for electing new members. Before this happens each separate department fulfils its quota of members by secret ballot, and at the general meeting each one is proposed by a senior member in appropriately laudatory terms.

In the years leading up to 1964 orthodoxy in Soviet biology was defined by the theories of Trofim Lysenko – a protégé of Stalin who had dominated the field for 30 years. Lysenko maintained that changing environmental conditions could alter the basic nature of plants and animals, contradicting the established genetic theory of inheritance, as it was accepted worldwide. With Lysenko's theory leading to such practical proposals as mobilizing chickens to exterminate sugar beet weevils in Ukraine, it found favour with Stalin (Taubman 2003: 131). Worse still, Lysenko's main scientific opponent, the world-renowned Nikolai Vavilov, was arrested and sent to a Gulag, never to come out alive. When, in 1964, the biologists in the Academy of Sciences nominated Nikolai Nuzhdin, a followed of Lysenko, as a full member this was too much for Sakharov. Contrary to normal practice he opposed full membership for Nuzhdin. The final paragraph of Sakharov's speech left no room for doubt:

> Together with Academician Lysenko, [Nuzhdin] is responsible for the shameful backwardness of Soviet biology and of genetics in particular, for the dissemination of pseudoscientific views, for adventurism, for the degradation of learning, and for the defamation, firing, arrest, even death, of many genuine scientists.
>
> (ibid.: 234)

Unprecedented applause and uproar greeted this speech. Three more academicians followed Sakharov, all vehemently opposing Nuzhdin's election. Lysenko, in turn, supported it, as was only to be expected; Mstislav Keldysh, President of the Academy, adhering to protocol, also did so, but directly addressing Lysenko, affirmed Sakharov's right to state his views. The academicians left the meeting to cast their votes in the ballot boxes in the lobby outside the hall; Nuzhdin was not elected.

Believing that Lysenko enjoyed Khrushchev's favour, Sakharov wrote a letter containing a popular outline of genetics, and describing the Soviet biologists' involvement in politics. Khrushchev, much displeased, ordered his guest at his Black Sea *dacha*, KGB chairman Vladimir Semichastny, to gather compromising material about Sakharov, an operation justified by the fact that 'first Sakharov tried to stop the hydrogen bomb, and now he's poking his nose again where it doesn't belong' (Sakharov 1990: 237). With Khrushchev's fall from power two weeks later, one of the things held against him was his concealment of Sakharov's letter from the Presidium. Semichastny, although refusing to help Khrushchev, was still removed from office by Brezhnev, with Yuri Andropov appointed to succeed him. All this meant the end of Lysenko. In 1966 Nikolai Dubinin, an internationally respected geneticist, disgraced under Lysenko, succeeded him as director of the Institute of Genetics.

From the history of occasional dealings between Sakharov and Brezhnev during the Khrushchev years, it is fair to conclude that when need be Brezhnev was able to help Sakharov, while in such matters as Sakharov chose to be involved – such as a nuclear test ban treaty or the discrediting of Lysenkoism – he had Brezhnev on his side. It must, indeed, have been clear to Brezhnev that Sakharov was a man of considerable standing, and that not only within the Soviet scientific community. In part this derived from official honours, such as being three times awarded the medal of a 'Hero of Socialist Labour'. On the last occasion, in March 1962, Sakharov was effusively greeted by Brezhnev, who at the dinner following the ceremony also sat next to him, with Khrushchev on the other side (Sakharov 1990: 224). Sakharov was undoubtedly well-connected, and he knew how to take advantage of this. Indisputably the Soviet Union had every reason to be grateful to the 'Father of the Hydrogen Bomb'.

Under Brezhnev this distinction was prima facie less valuable, if only because the fundamental problems involved in producing hydrogen bombs had already been solved – mainly by Sakharov. By the mid-1960s the production of hydrogen bombs, essential for achieving parity with the US in the nuclear arms race, was well under way. With escalating production, both in the US and the Soviet Union, both sides began to focus on the potential of anti-ballistic missiles (ABM). In the Soviet Union this inevitably involved Sakharov, who, together with a majority of his professional colleagues, soon concluded, first, that any ABM system could be neutralized, and second, that its deployment, by increasing the minimum number of nuclear weapons needed for mutual assured destruction (MAD), would only make this horrific event more likely to occur. Sakharov, horrified by this prospect, realized that the military, technical and economic problems were secondary, while the fundamental issues were political and ethical.

With all this in mind, Sakharov, in 1968, decided to make a 'wide-ranging public statement on war and peace and other global issues' (Sakharov 1990: 268). This was the year of the 'Prague Spring', where, led by men such as Vaclav Havel, the people of Czechoslovakia were on the way to establishing 'democracy, including freedom of expression and abolition of censorship, reform of the economic and social system and curbs on the power of the security forces' (ibid.: 281). This, at least was the perception of Sakharov, providing at the same time an incentive to go ahead with his own public statement. And Czechoslovakia, needless to say, was still counted upon in the Soviet Union as a committed Warsaw Pact state.

Sakharov's statement took the form of a long essay entitled *Reflections on Progress, Peaceful Coexistence and Intellectual Freedom*, with a preface quoting from Goethe's *Faust*:

> He alone is worthy of life and freedom
> Who each day does battle for them anew.

By mid-April the essay was almost complete, and in May the typescript was ready for Sakharov to show to trusted friends, such as Zhores Medvedev, but also for circulation in *samizdat* (Sakharov 1990: 284) – with Medvedev himself promising to produce at least a dozen copies. On 18 May Sakharov, visiting Khariton at his dacha, told of his essay and of his intention to give it to *samizdat*; before the end of the month the KGB office at the Installation knew of its existence (ibid.: 284). Early in June, Sakharov, travelling to the Installation, was invited to join Khariton in his private railway carriage. There he learnt that Andropov, head of the KGB, having acquired a copy of the essay, showed it to Khariton without allowing him to read it. Khariton insisted that Sakharov withdraw the essay, to be told that it was far too late to do so. Instead Sakharov sent a slightly revised copy to Brezhnev.

Samizdat worked only too well. Andrei Amalrik (who later became a well-known dissident)[8] gave a copy of Sakharov's essay to Karel van het Reve, the Moscow correspondent of a Dutch newspaper, *Het Parool*, which published it in translation on 6 July – the news reaching Sakharov four days later via the BBC Overseas Service (which also reported Sakharov's work on the hydrogen bomb). On 22 July the *New York Times* published the essay, and before the start of 1969 18 million copies had been published worldwide (Sakharov 1990: 288), a number exceeded only by the works of Lenin and Mao Zedong. Then, in August 1968, Soviet troops invaded Czechoslovakia, and within the days the Prague Spring was over.

In spite of this setback, Sakharov did not give up in what he had come to identify as a struggle for human rights. In particular, he intervened in any number of individual cases, abroad as well as at home. Following the publication of *Reflections on Progress* Sakharov had any number of contacts with the outside world; the foreign media representatives in Moscow were constantly ready to support him when need be. The more active Sakharov became, the more the Soviet authorities took steps – refusing permission to travel, depriving him of office or reducing his salary – to make his life more difficult. Then, on 15 August 1973, he was summoned to the State Procurator's Office, to be warned that he might be liable to prosecution for 'anti-Soviet statements' (Sakharov 1990: 385). A report of what happened, made by Sakharov immediately after the interview, then appeared in the *New York Times* on 29 August. But by then, on 21 August, Sakharov had already held a press conference in his Moscow apartment, where he was asked about dissidents and human rights, détente and the risk of war.

Sooner or later there was bound to be an official public reaction. This first took shape in a letter published in the newspapers of 28 August, in which 40 members of the Academy of Science denounced Sakharov. This was the beginning of an orchestrated press campaign with letters not only from institutions such as the Academy of Soviet Writers, but others from individuals – even including miners and milkmaids. What was significant, while all this was happened, were the names of those who had not signed the letters, such as notably, Aleksandr Solzhenitsyn (already a Nobel prize-winner for literature) and Pyotr Kapitsa (a future Nobel laureate, internationally recognized for his work in low-temperature physics).

The main charge against Sakharov was that he was an enemy of détente, the cause upon which Brezhnev, in the early 1970s, was building up his international reputation – as related in Chapter 8. Brezhnev had cause for concern, for Sakharov had any number of contacts with the United States. Even so Sakharov's human rights campaign may still have been marginal to what Brezhnev was trying to achieve with US President Nixon (which is certainly how Brezhnev regarded it), but then, as was suggested by the *New York Times*, with Watergate simmering in Washington (but still hardly mentioned in the Soviet press), there could well have been 'a de facto Nixon–Brezhnev alliance against dissent in each other's country'(Kissinger 1982: 988). It is an interesting thought. None the less, at the same time a letter to Moscow written by the President of the US National Academy of Science certainly made clear the potential adverse affect of Soviet policy on dissidents on future scientific collaboration with the US. Mstislav Keldysh, president of the Soviet Academy, in a reply published in *Literaturnaya Gazeta* – a journal known for its adherence to the strict party line – while affirming the academicians' letter, added his assurance that 'Sakharov had not been, and is not now, subject to any kind of harassment' (ibid: 390).

In 1975, after two more difficult years engaged in the struggle for human rights, Sakharov devoted the first six months to a new book, *My Country and the World*, which was essentially a programme for a radical reform of the Soviet Union on the basis of 12 wide-ranging human rights principles (Kissinger 1982: 425). Then, on 9 October, the announcement was made that Sakharov has been awarded the Nobel Peace Prize. In an immediate media reaction he linked the honour bestowed upon him with 'the whole human rights movement', hoping at the same time 'for an improvement in the lot of political prisoners in the USSR and for a worldwide political amnesty' (ibid.: 429). As he expected, Sakharov was denied the exit visa necessary for him to attend the official presentation in December, but his wife, Elena Bonner, who was in Italy for medical treatment was able to go to Oslo and read his acceptance speech,[9] entitled – provocatively by Soviet standards – *Peace, Progress and Human Rights*. Unlike Pasternak, in the late 1950s, Sakharov did not recant.

During the 18 Brezhnev years Soviet authorities found various expedients for controlling, if not suppressing, dissidence. Two factors explain why over time, trial and imprisonment – the fate of Sinyavsky and Daniel – increasingly became measures of last resort. First, reactions both at home and abroad, showed how easily this could prove to be counterproductive. The fact that as late as 1978

Gromyko (as related on page 101) had never heard of him does not mean that the imprisoning Shcharansky was a price worth paying for the suppression of dissidence. By this time any number of other cases proved the contrary, as some at least of those close to Brezhnev – such as notably KGB Chief Andropov – had long appreciated. The second factor was that there were other ways of dealing with dissidents.

The simplest alternative was simply to allow dissidents to emigrate, as hundreds of thousands of Soviet citizens did, quite officially, during the 1970s. The narrow doctrinal objection, which would have been decisive in Stalin's day, was that was any such policy could be read as evidence that Soviet citizens could find a better life outside the Soviet Union – which of course was no less than the truth. For Andropov, and others like him, turning a blind eye could well be a price worth paying for seeing the last of potential trouble-makers – particularly since the right to emigrate had itself become a major dissident cause.

Claiming the right to emigrate was a hard-fought cause among two minorities, both of which had a specific destination in states only too willing to welcome them: these were Volga Germans and Jews. If, in both cases, the prospective new home, whether Germany or Israel, was one which almost none of these Soviet citizens had ever been able to visit, it still represented a promised land to be reached at any cost. In the 1970s Soviet Jews, by and large, found it easy to obtain exit visas (Zubok 2009: 311). This was a policy favoured by KGB-head, Andropov, for purely pragmatic reasons (ibid.: 313). Soviet Jews, although no more than 1 per cent of the population, were disproportionately over-represented in art, science and professional life, so that, for example, a fifth of all writers and journalists were Jewish (ibid.: 311). Inevitably a disproportionate number of dissidents were also Jewish, so that emigration meant a substantial loss to the dissident cause – precisely the result envisaged by Andropov. On the other side, however, the loss of talent, particularly to Soviet science – with 7 per cent of recognized practitioners being Jewish – threatened to be critical. The result was that top men, if they were Jews asking for exit visas, could well be refused. This identified a new class of 'refuseniks', of which the best-known, Anatoly Shcharansky was going to be a considerable thorn in the flesh for the Kremlin – as will be related in Chapter 9. In such cases it was not only a question of the loss of a first-class scientist, trained at state expense, but also one of the inherent risk of secret military technology being communicated to foreign governments – like that of Israel. In such cases trial and imprisonment – the eventual fate of Shcharansky – offered the only solution.

In the event, an alternative was found to imprisonment: this was compulsory in-patient treatment in a mental hospital – a practice widely condemned in the world outside the Soviet Union almost as soon as it was adopted. The case of Joseph Brodsky was by no means an isolated one. Zhores Medvedev – an internationally recognized biologist and a friend of Sakharov – after suffering the same fate, produced with his brother, Roy, a memoir, *A Question of Madness* (Medvedev and Medvedev 1971) in which chapter 4, 'Medicine Standing on its Head', reveals what this gross abuse of medical practice added up to. Although the official line was that Medvedev had been consigned to the Kaluga Psychiatric Hospital for medical reasons, he soon had every reason to believe that this had been instigated by the KGB (ibid.: 92). The object, according to Medvedev's well-founded hypothesis, was to discredit his published work (particularly that part of it published abroad) as the 'pathological delusions of someone suffering from mania, etc.' What Medvedev went through in the hospital was pure 'theatre of the absurd', as he, his friends and family, realized from the very beginning of his stay.

Medvedev's experience as a 'psychiatric' patient was also extremely disagreeable. Worse still was the fact that thousands of other ordinary Soviet citizens, without a supporters' club such as that enjoyed by Medvedev, were as 'dissidents' subjected to the same processes. The principle applied by the Soviet authorities was that dissidence, as it manifested itself in art or science, was 'the consequence and the proof of a mental illness' (de Meeus, undated: 7). Although, following the 20th Party Conference in 1956, a special commission reported that under Stalin 'hundreds of healthy people were interned in psychiatric hospitals' (ibid.: 9) – a practice that enabled Khrushchev to claim that 'there [are] no political prisoners in Russia, only persons of unsound mind' – the use of 'repressive' psychiatry for treating dissidents only became widely known in 1963; the 'patient' was the writer Valery Tarsis who, in a story published abroad, had said that Khrushchev 'was a man in whom a superficial knowledge of the cultivation of potatoes took the place of culture' (ibid.: 11).[10] However, 1963 was Khrushchev's last full year as *vozhd*, and it was only on Brezhnev's watch that the use of psychiatry for treating dissidents came into its own.

It is not easy to know how many Soviet citizens were subjected to repressive psychiatry, for whether they were in-patients in ordinary mental hospitals, or in institutions for the criminally insane – a less common case – their identity was lost in ways that would have been impossible if they had been subjected to a criminal process (de Meeus, undated : 63). In the Soviet Union, just as elsewhere, medical records have a different character to court records; the former are essentially confidential, the latter, public. At the same time committal to hospital, by its nature, is not 'news' in the same way as committal to prison; it is moreover part of the life of ordinary law-abiding citizens, in a way that imprisonment is not. For those concerned to suppress dissidence hospitalization also has other advantages: there is no fixed term, supervision and restrictions on a patient's life after discharge are routine, and – much more sinister – medication can be prescribed to alter a patient's state of mind (ibid.: 46).

In the early 1970s, as evidence accumulated abroad from a select few of those who had been released from mental hospitals, human rights organizations outside the Soviet Union estimated that some seven to eight thousand were subject to repressive psychiatry at any one time. Most of them, far from being prominent, were ordinary citizens recorded as deviant in a way unacceptable to Soviet orthodoxy. In particular this meant religious believers, such as Baptists and Jehovah's Witnesses, professing a faith that found little sympathy among main-line Christians, who, if anything, were inclined to regard them as heretics.

It was some time before the use, or rather misuse, of psychiatry to control dissidents, was noticed, let alone criticized, outside the Soviet Union. With such well-documented cases as those of Joseph Brodsky and Zhores Medvedev, this was bound to happen sooner or later. The first whistle-blower came, somewhat improbably, from British Columbia. In January 1971, Dr Norman Hirt, Chairman, for the province, of the Canadian Psychiatric Association, presented a resolution to its Board 'condemning the political misuse of psychiatry and inviting medical associations everywhere to protest to the USSR and to any other country guilty of such malpractice' (de Meeus, undated : 51). Dr Hirt was nothing if not provocative, for his resolution also noted how, but for the failure of the medical profession to condemn medical malpractice as an instrument of state policy in Nazi Germany, '. . . it is more than probable that the entire idea and technique of the death factories for genocide would not have come into being'.

Dr Hirt had set the ball rolling. Later in 1971, 44 British psychiatrists, helped by new documentation, presented an address to the Congress of the World Psychiatric Association in Mexico City condemning the Soviet misuse of psychiatry; in 1972 the cause was taken up by psychiatrists in Belgium, Switzerland and France, and in September, 1973, Dr Alfred Freedman, President of the American Psychiatric Association, in a letter to Andrei Snezhnevsky, President of the Association of Soviet Psychiatrists, asked him to receive a delegation of US psychiatrists, to discuss – in conditions assuring medical confidentiality – charges made of 'involuntary psychiatric confinement . . . used unjustly and without regard to human rights' (de Meeus, undated : 72).

Snezhnevsky, in the first round, proved to be a masterly apologist for Soviet psychiatry, and, in particular, for the Serbsky Institute of Forensic Psychiatry in Moscow, which was inevitably involved in the treatment of the criminally insane. A high-level US delegation came to the Soviet Union, where Snezhnevsky saw to it that they met all the right people, and saw all the right places. He was so successful that the US delegation accepted that 'concerning forcible treatment . . . the Russian standard is the same as the American' (de Meeus, undated: 55). Little did the American psychiatrists realize that both Snezhnevsky and the Serbsky Institute were deeply involved in the practices that the delegation were meant to investigate, but signally failed to expose to the light of day.

Although Snezhnevsky was a master in obtaining foreign endorsements, in the 1970s climate of international concern over human rights – largely the result of leading Soviet activists such as Sakharov and Medvedev – his statements steadily lost all credibility. For one thing, too many awkward questions were asked of Soviet psychiatrists attending international conferences,[11] and there were too many people – even including former Soviet psychiatrists[12] – who had seen too much. Sakharov arranged for a letter from Viktor Fainberg, a dissident confined in appalling conditions in a Leningrad psychiatric hospital, to be delivered to UN Secretary-General Kurt Waldheim. By the mid-1970s Soviet authorities could no longer conceal the true state of affairs – and this was just the time when, as a result of the Helsinki Final Accord, the Soviet Union could no longer maintain a state of denial in the face of human rights charges. This, once again, is a story told in Chapter 9.

On the question of the confinement and treatment of dissidents in mental institutions – as on so many others concerning the misuse of scientific and medical institutions for purposes contrary to their principles – one is left wondering about the involvement of the Supreme Soviet, and its General Secretary. With the example of the Khrushchev's fall before him, Brezhnev, at least until the end of the 1960s, was obsessed by the need to avoid mistakes that would cost him his job (Spechler 1982: 228). Among Khrushchev's mistakes, as perceived by Brezhnev – largely on the basis of what others told him –was that Khrushchev too readily allowed the publication of works portraying the down-side of life in the Soviet Union, even in the days of Stalin. It is not for nothing that Khrushchev fell only a week or two after his remarkably positive endorsement of Solzhenitsyn, as related on page 106. When, in his Victory in Europe day speech of May 1965, Brezhnev praised Stalin's conduct of the Great Patriotic War (Brezhnev 1965: 2) this was intended as a condemnation of political and ideological deviance, and as such was a signal to those in authority that action taken to suppress dissidence was likely to win official approval. Brezhnev was never going to make his own *secret speech*. It is significant also that publication of Solzhenitsyn's later works became steadily more hazardous, to the point that Tvardovsky – who had always remained true to him – in 1970 finally had to resign from being editor of *Novy Mir* (Spechler 1982: 227).

Given Brezhnev's character, whatever his awareness of what was happening, he was never much concerned to intervene one way or the other in the suppression of dissidence. It was sufficient that he, where necessary, made his own views clear, as in the VE day speech. As for the mental hospital programme, its relatively small-scale suggests that there was no reason for Brezhnev to be directly involved: where millions had passed through Gulags, the dissidents confined in mental institutions only numbered thousands. If the level of international condemnation (to say nothing of that within the Soviet Union) may have seemed disproportionate, this was because the abuse took place in institutions at the heart of any civilized society – that is those dedicated to the care of the sick.[13] Even according to their own lights, those responsible for the abuse could have achieved little: as every year went by the dissidents' message resonated more clearly, both in the Soviet Union and in the world outside. Brezhnev, in all probability, neither noticed nor cared. The damage to the Soviet Union's international reputation passed Brezhnev by, even when it made achieving the goals he had made his own much more difficult.

The one man who must have known what was involved was Andropov, head of the KGB, and, on Brezhnev's death, his successor as General Secretary of the CPSU. Andropov, essentially a pragmatist (as was his protégé, Mikhail Gorbachev), must have supported – even if he not initiated – the confinement of dissidents in mental hospitals as an expedient worth trying in solving a wide-ranging problem. Andropov, however, is better remembered for another expedient – allowing Jewish emigration on an unprecedented scale. Here the consequences reached much further, for once in Israel – the chosen destination of most of the emigrants – they soon established their own political identity, which they used particularly effectively to influence not only Israel's Soviet policy, but also that of many other countries – most notably the USA. Just what this involved is a main subject of Chapter 9.

Notes

1 Gromyko, referring to this incident in his own memoirs (1989: 376), notes how 'it later transpired that the person in question was a dropout, someone who had moreover been convicted and sent to gaol for breaking the law'.
2 These words come from the French of *Le Petit Larousse Illustré* (1997).
3 God is *Bog*, and blasphemy, *bogokhul'stvo*.
4 Publication abroad then became known as 'tamizdat', lit. 'publish-it-over-there' as opposed to *samizdat* (Zubok 2009: 190).
5 Even so – as related on page 103 – there were still to be problems with Khrushchev, as witness the first performance, in December 1962 of Shostakovich's 13th Symphony 'Babi Yar'.
6 For the full definition of this offence see *Ugolovnyi Kodeks RFSFR*, Moscow, 1962, pp.47–48. It includes 'the production . . . of literature . . . denigrating the Soviet state . . . with the purpose of subverting or weakening the Soviet regime'.
7 Anna Akhmatova (1889–1966) was one of the greatest Russian 20th century poets; also one of the most courageous, she was a good friend to any number of dissidents and to many, including her first husband, who died in the Stalinist terror – the subject of *Requiem*, her greatest work.
8 Later author of *Will the Soviet Union Survive until 1984?* (London: Penguin).
9 This in itself required a long struggle, with massive foreign support, for permission to go abroad for a critical eye-operation not available in the Soviet Union. Elena Bonner was a herself a notable dedicated and courageous human rights activist.
10 Tarsis was in any case the first to publish his story abroad (Tarsis 1965): he eventually succeeded in emigrating to Switzerland.
11 In one case, that of the Oslo conference in 1973, this meant that the Soviet delegation never turned up (de Meeus, undated: 56).
12 One of these, Dr F. Yaroshevsky, who was allowed to emigrate to Canada, launched an appeal for an International Tribunal 'with a view to judging those responsible for political internments in the USSR'.
13 This can be compared to today's (2013) widespread disgust at the sexual abuse of children in educational institutions of the Roman Catholic Church.

Part III

International politics

Peacemaker under pressure

7 The Soviet Bloc, the Brezhnev doctrine and Ostpolitik

When Brezhnev assumed power in 1964 the Soviet Union was tied to Albania, Bulgaria, Czechoslovakia, Hungary, Poland, and Romania by a Treaty of Friendship, Cooperation, and Mutual Assistance agreed in Warsaw in 1955 as a Soviet-led reaction to West Germany joining NATO.[1] Although the treaty continued to operate, with no change in its membership, throughout the eighteen years (1964–1982) that Brezhnev was in power,[2] it was, in advancing his global strategy during this period neither a hindrance nor much of a help – particularly in arresting the decline of the Soviet Union that set in during the late 1970s. For the main theme of this book, therefore, it is essentially background.

What counts is that for Moscow, from the 1950s onwards, the re-armament of West Germany and its incorporation into NATO represented a critical threat to a key element of Soviet foreign policy – preventing the resurgence of a powerful German nation, the more so if this new Germany was to be allied to the US and the other Western powers. Although the Warsaw Pact was part of the strategy for preventing this happening, in the critical events of the late 1950s and the 1960s in the East-West confrontation, in Poland, Hungary, Czechoslovakia, East Germany, and above all, Berlin, the Pact counted for little beyond providing a forum for Soviet leaders, including Brezhnev, to justify actions already taken. As shown later in this chapter, this was essentially the role it played after the Soviet-led invasion of Czechoslovakia in 1968 – now remembered, mistakenly, by many as a Warsaw Pact operation.

From its earliest days the Warsaw Pact was of little help in preventing major unrest, first in Poland and then in Hungary. In both cases there were calls for Soviet military intervention. As to Poland, a popular leader, Władisław Gomułka – appointed First Secretary of the Polish Communist Party at the eleventh hour – persuaded Khrushchev to call off military intervention, having satisfied him that the proposed reforms were purely internal, with Poland having no intention of repudiating treaties – which included the Warsaw Pact – with the Soviet Union. The price paid was a decade of stagnation (Kemp-Welch 2010: 219).

Hungary, inspired by Poland, followed the same path, but went even further, with its own popular leader, Imre Nagy, announcing withdrawal from the Warsaw Pact on 1 November – a move denounced by Gomułka. This time Khrushchev did send Soviet forces, which crushed the revolution and arrested Nagy, who in 1958 was hanged for treason.

Although Hungary was not a Warsaw Pact operation it did lead Khrushchev to reassess the role of the Pact in relation to the security of the Soviet state. Instead of withdrawing from Hungary the two Soviet divisions sent there in 1956, he sent in two more. The loyalty of the Hungarian army could not yet be counted on. With the same being true of Poland, Czechoslovakia was perceived as the most dependable Warsaw Pact ally of the Soviet Union. (In the late 1950s East Germany had yet to establish its military usefulness in Moscow). While all this was happening Khrushchev's main preoccupation was, as related in Chapter 12, with China. Within the Warsaw Pact, Albania, in 1962, chose to ally itself with China, and withdrew, and the Soviet Union, with no common frontier, was powerless to intervene. The best Khrushchev could do was to use Warsaw Pact meetings to mobilize support against China and Albania, but geography ensured that this would little help the Soviet Union. The more immediate problem was to find a way of using the Warsaw Pact to inhibit further defections. At the same time the Pact would become a cover for what were essentially Soviet operations,[3] even if this meant – contrary to what the Pact laid down – intervention in the domestic affairs of the non-Soviet Warsaw Pact (NSWP) states. According to the formula then to be applied, events requiring such intervention, being the result of Western imperialist provocation, constituted external aggression. Needless to say, in any such case, Soviet diplomatic pressure would ensure that any action taken was accepted as falling within the terms of the Pact. In the event this never happened.

Although Brezhnev, after he took over from Khrushchev in 1964, was well aware of events and developments in Poland, Hungary, Romania and East Germany from the 1950s onwards, he had little premonition about what the future had in store. The test came first – not in any of these states – but in Czechoslovakia.

In Brezhnev's early years he confronted in Czechoslovakia – regarded as 'one of most reliable and trustworthy' of the NSWP states (Gromyko 1989: 297; Navrátil *et al.* 1998: 23) – an irritating degree of independence on the part of the government of President Antonin Novotný, relating both to its foreign and domestic policies. Bonn (which had never recognized the Czechoslovak Union of Socialist Republics) had been approached for financial credits, while people on the streets enjoyed a degree of freedom so far beyond that of any other NSWP state that Brezhnev was beginning to fear 'counter-revolution' (Haslam 2011: 246). Seen from Moscow, Novotný – never regarded as a strong leader (Alexandrov-Agentov 1994: 145) – was losing control.[4] In December 1967 a street demonstration in Prague led Brezhnev to make a special visit to the city, where Novotný asked him for help; exasperated at the end of an 18-hour meeting with leading officials of the Czech presidium he could only reply 'act as you wish' (ibid.: 147) – thereby sealing not only Novotný's fate but determining also a course of events that would keep Czechoslovakia in the headlines throughout 1968. The Communist Party elected, on 5 January 1968, a new reformist First Secretary, Alexander Dubček, whose radical proposals 'to make a new start to socialism' (Kemp-Welch 2010: 222) not only increased anxiety in Moscow, but led Novotný to resign as President on March 22;[5] the following day, at a meeting in Dresden, convened by Brezhnev, and attended by Dubček – together with Bulgarian, East

German, Hungarian and Polish leaders – Brezhnev made his displeasure clear, pointedly asking Dubček, 'Have you not had democracy until now?' (Navrátil *et al.* 1998: 65). Insisting that 'we cannot leave here without results', Brezhnev demanded decisions 'which unequivocally state that the counter-revolution will not succeed in Czechoslovakia . . .' (ibid.: 67).

Dubček was unmoved: five days later the Central Committee of the Czechoslovak Communist Party adopted an Action Programme (Navrátil *et al.* 1998: 83) to give effect to his proposals – to establish 'socialism with a human face', a prospect that resonated also among young people in Moscow (Kemp-Welch 2010: 36), while greatly displeasing Brezhnev and alienating leaders of the other Warsaw Pact states (Navrátil *et al.* 1998: 426, 141). To realize this 'third way' (Judt 2010: 441) a new government, installed with massive popular acclaim on 25 April, relaxed almost all formal controls restricting freedom of speech, including press and media censorship – a most unwelcome development for Moscow (Navrátil *et al.* 1998: 115). If at this stage Brezhnev was guardedly in favour of the reform programme (Suri 2006: 148), he changed his mind after the publication, on 27 June, of the 'Two Thousand Words' manifesto,[6] which urged that the Communist Party abandon its monopoly of power (ibid.: 149). Although for Dubček this was also a step too far (ibid.: 150), he had still allowed, if not encouraged, a situation to develop which both Moscow and the Czechoslovak politburo (Navrátil *et al.* 1998: 194) viewed with foreboding, even though it was accepted that the situation in Czechoslovakia was substantially different from that in Hungary in 1956 (Kramer 2010: 23). Dubček believed that there would be no Soviet intervention so long as Czechoslovakia avoided Hungary's fatal mistake of leaving the Warsaw Pact. Dubček miscalculated:[7] by early summer, with protests from top Communist leaders in Ukraine, Poland and East Germany reaching Moscow (Haslam 2011: 246), Yuri Andropov, head of the KGB, was already talking of 'concrete military measures' while the Minister of Defence, Andrei Grechko, was drawing up plans for what would become known as 'Operation Danube' (Navrátil *et al.* 1998: 187; Kramer 2010: 26). On 14 July five Warsaw Pact party leaders, meeting in Warsaw, sent a letter to the Czechoslovak Party, warning it of the threat of counter-revolution and indicating the measures to be taken to prevent it (ibid.: 39) – which, in the event, were almost immediately set in train (ibid.: 40). Starting on 29 July Brezhnev met Dubček for three days in a small town on the Slovak–Soviet frontier, before proceeding, on 3 August, to a Warsaw Pact meeting at the Slovak capital, Bratislava – where Romania, significantly, was unrepresented[8] – as it had also been at earlier meetings in Warsaw (Kemp-Welch 2010: 223) and Karlovy Vary (Kramer 2010: 10). With little regard for Dubček, Brezhnev, in Bratislava, stated the doctrine now known by his name: 'Each Communist Party is free to apply the principles of Marxism-Leninism and socialism in its own country, but it is not free to deviate from these principles if it is to remain a Communist party . . . The weakening of any of the links in the world system of socialism directly affects all socialist countries, and they cannot look indifferently upon this'.[9] Although the implicit warning to Dubček was unmistakable, the decision to invade Czechoslovakia was adopted by the Soviet

Politburo quite late in the day.[10] Outside pressure for intervention by Gomułka in Poland and Ulbricht in East Germany (Kramer 2010: 17) – both of whom feared contagion from Czechoslovakia[11] – could well have been decisive. It also counted in Moscow that Sakharov and other dissidents had welcomed the Prague Spring (Sakharov 1990: 282). At all events Dubček failed to take steps that would satisfy Brezhnev and the Politburo,[12] and on 21 August, 500,000 soldiers – mainly from the Soviet Union, but with some 80,000 from Bulgaria, Hungary, and Poland – marched into Czechoslovakia. Except for a token liaison unit, it was agreed that – to avoid highly adverse historical connotations – none should come from East Germany (Kramer 2010: 48).

The soldiers had been led to expect that they would be welcomed as 'liberators' – which indeed was the advice given to Moscow by Soviet representatives in Eastern Europe (Arbatov 1992: 139), including the ambassador in Prague.[13] Although the soldiers were disillusioned as soon as they crossed the frontier, their entry into Czechoslovakia was unopposed (Kramer 2010: 49). The 'sacred duty' of acting on behalf of 'socialist solidarity' counted for more than Czech sovereignty (Kemp-Welch 2010: 226). Although this was not strictly a Warsaw Pact operation, the Brezhnev doctrine seemed to be a carte blanche for Soviet interventionism involving the NSWP states (ibid.: 227; Kramer 2010: 62).[14] In 1968 Moscow also claimed – without any supporting evidence – that events in Prague had been orchestrated by 'American and West German imperialists'[15] (Alexandrov 1968: 4). The position was made even more critical by the fact that the Soviet Union, following a secret agreement made in 1965, was in 1968 busy constructing nuclear weapons sites in western Czechoslovakia (Kramer 2010: 33); what was going on in Prague could jeopardize a process essential to the rationale of the Warsaw Pact.

The Prague Spring had turned to winter.[16] None the less Brezhnev had to come to terms with the almost complete and unexpected failure of his intervention to win public support in Czechoslovakia, to the extent even of setting up an alternative government to that headed by Dubček (Kramer 2010: 51). The only outcome for Brezhnev was to allow Dubček to remain in office for a few more months, in face of mounting protest by Ulbricht and Gomułka, to say nothing of fellow members of the Soviet Politburo. On the other hand the bilateral *Treaty of Temporary Presence of Soviet Troops in Czechoslovakia*, signed in October 1968 allowed five Soviet divisions from the invading force to remain in Czechoslovakia: this was important for Moscow, for ensuring first that Soviet troops were present along the entire Soviet bloc frontier with West Europe, and second that the nuclear sites were secure (ibid.: 54). The price paid was the loss of any meaningful Czechoslovak contribution to the Warsaw Pact forces (ibid.: 55), while at the same time the performance of the Polish, Hungarian, Bulgarian and East German troops in the invasion was judged to be less than satisfactory – and that in a situation where was no fighting at all. These troops were demoralized from the start. Romania, which had opposed the invasion, was further alienated from the Warsaw Pact, to the point that it could no longer be expected to play a meaningful role (ibid.: 58).

The political failure of the Soviet invasion was also a factor in leading Zhou Enlai, a year later, to label the Soviet Union as China's 'main enemy'. At the same time the allegiance of the Communist parties of Western Europe was forfeited – a critical loss seeing that the fall of the right-wing dictatorships in Spain and Portugal in the mid-1970s might otherwise have opened the way to a key role in government. On the other hand, vis-à-vis the US and West Europe, the Soviet intervention in Czechoslovakia did have the advantage for Moscow of making clear that Ostpolitik, such as that promoted by Will Brandt in West Germany, would get nowhere except on the basis of the frontiers of the East European states established at the end of World War II (ibid.: 60).

Finally, in April 1969, pro-democracy demonstrations following the defeat of the Soviet team at an ice-hockey match provided the pretext for replacing Dubček with the more compliant Slovak leader, Gustáv Husák (Judt 2010: 445), who proceeded, relentlessly, to bring the autonomous student and worker unions, which had been restive all through the winter, back under party control (Kemp-Welch 2010: 229).

However enfeebled Brezhnev later became, in 1968 he was definitely in the ascendant and he cannot escape responsibility for what then happened in Czechoslovakia – however much he was constrained by other members of the Politburo.[17] Although the Soviet-led invasion was not strictly a Warsaw Pact operation, the provisions of the Pact were rewritten in such a way as to strengthen the Soviet hand if any comparable situation should recur. Although the new version of the Warsaw Pact remained in force until the end of the 1980s, it was of little help to Brezhnev either in controlling events in the NSWP states, or – equally if not more important – in dealing with the West. In the short term, however, the 1968 invasion of Czechoslovakia – as seen from Moscow – had the advantage of making clear to the West that recognizing the status quo in Europe was a non-negotiable precondition for any progress in East–West relations (Haslam 2011: 250).

Three months after the Soviet intervention in Czechoslovakia, Richard Nixon was elected to be Lyndon Johnson's successor in the White House from January 1969. In foreign affairs Nixon followed two key policies vis-à-vis the world's communist states: of these one focussed on Europe and the other on Eastern Asia. The key to the former was the principle of détente, to be realized in a series of bilateral treaties between the United States and the Soviet Union providing for nuclear disarmament (as described in Chapter 8); the key to the latter was the rapprochement between the United States and China under Mao Zedong and negotiated between Henry Kissinger and Zhou Enlai (as described in Chapter 12). As to détente in Europe, Brezhnev had every reason for not antagonizing Washington, so that military operations under the Warsaw Pact were on a very modest scale. As for China, the Soviet Union, in the course of the 1970s, was completely side-lined, together with all its Warsaw Pact allies.

In 1969, at much the same time as Nixon's Republican administration took over in Washington, Willy Brandt, leader of the Social Democratic Party in West Germany became Chancellor following the defeat of the Christian Democrats in the Federal elections: with the Free Democratic Party joining the Social Democrats in a coalition Brandt was able to form a majority government in the Reichstag (Haslam 2011: 250). Where Konrad Adenauer – Chancellor from 1949 to 1963 – had always insisted that the Federal Republic of Germany (whose territory consisted of the three western zones under American, British and French military administration following the end of the war in 1945) was the only legitimate German state, Brandt was ready to change course (Judt 2010: 497). For Adenauer, recognition of the German Democratic Republic (whose territory comprised the former Soviet zone) was unthinkable. Indeed, he went further, by claiming that the cession of considerable German territory to Poland after the war was not definitive, so that the land could still revert to Germany: with this claim having no chance of ever being acceptable to either Moscow or Warsaw, Adenauer ensured that German reunification would never take place on his watch.[18] His policy was based on the Hallstein doctrine, according to which West Germany would never have diplomatic relations with any state that recognized East Germany. The one exception was the Soviet Union, with diplomatic relations established in 1955 following a visit to Moscow by Adenauer: the Hallstein doctrine was then a clear policy statement that West Germany would not deal with any state that recognized East Germany.[19]

After Adenauer resigned as Chancellor in 1963, it became increasingly clear that strict adherence to the Hallstein doctrine was counterproductive, so much so that support from the other NATO powers – including the US – became problematic. At the same time, Willy Brandt, the Social Democratic mayor of West Berlin, argued that Hallstein did little either to undermine the communist regime among East Germans or to improve their standard of living; change for the better was more likely to come by increasing trade and other contacts with East Germany. This encouraged Khrushchev to engage with West Germany – disregarding the misgivings both of Ulbricht in East Germany and of fellow members of the Politburo in Moscow – and his acceptance, on 2 September 1964, of an invitation to visit Bonn was one of the factors leading to his downfall a month later (Haslam 2011: 213); Brezhnev, needless to say, let the matter drop.

In 1966 the West German right-wing coalition collapsed, to be succeeded by one which included Brandt's Social Democrats, with Brandt himself as Deputy Chancellor and Foreign Minister. In 1967 the death of Adenauer, out of office since 1963, deprived Hallstein of its most uncompromising defender. At the same time, Brandt was promoting his own policy of Ostpolitik, and in 1969, with Social Democrats winning the federal elections, the way was open to enforce it.

In 1970, Ostpolitik led to the Treaty of Moscow, which recognized Bonn as the legitimate government of West Germany (Mastny 2005;42), and the Treaty of Warsaw, which formally recognized the People's Republic of Poland. In 1973, following a general election in 1972, in which Brandt won a somewhat uncertain victory, the Reichstag approved the Basic Treaty, according to which East and West Germany recognized each other's sovereignty and agreed to establish diplomatic relations.[20]

For Moscow all this meant a much more favourable climate in dealing with Western Europe, so that Brezhnev would lose little by not enforcing, strictly, the doctrine bearing his name, just as – at least in the perception of Willy Brandt – West Germany, lost little by abandoning Hallstein. Given that the Warsaw Pact was originally set up in 1955 – in the same year as Hallstein formulated his doctrine – its usefulness to Soviet policy in Eastern Europe was, throughout the 1970s, extremely problematic.[21] For some thirteen years, from 1969 to 1982, Moscow had the advantage of Social Democratic governments in West Germany, first under Brandt, and then, after 1974, under Helmut Schmidt. When Helmut Kohl became Chancellor on 1 October 1982, Brezhnev had only six weeks to live. As for Soviet relations with West Germany, the 1979 invasion of Afghanistan was condemned by Schmidt as much as by any other Western leader.[22] The operation of the Warsaw Pact was, however, little affected.

Before this time, Soviet relations with Europe, both East and West, had taken a new direction as a result of the Helsinki Conference, and above all the final accord of 1975. The conference, which effectively extended the principles of Brandt's Ostpolitik to the whole of Europe, is the subject matter of Chapter 9. Even though the Helsinki Final Act was signed in 1975, the process of implementation, in which the Soviet Union was constantly involved, continued with a series of meetings first in Belgrade and then, during Brezhnev's last years, in Madrid.

Although these meetings overshadowed anything that might happen within the Warsaw Pact – which, after all, fell within the same geographical remit as that of Helsinki – the NSWP states were involved in two other matters not directly the concern of Helsinki: the Third World and the Catholic Church. As to the Third World, from the 1960s onwards the Soviet Union became increasingly involved in a number of states, mainly in Africa, which, as related in Chapter 10 – often as a result of revolution or a military coup – had revealed themselves as committed to Marxist-Leninist government, and by doing so, as opponents of the US-led Western world. In some cases, such as that of Angola, the revolutionary process was not complete, and even where it was so, as in Ethiopia, after the mid-1970s, there still remained the threat of counter-revolution.

Moscow made it clear to the NSWP states that they too should recognize these new states as allies, so enhancing, worldwide, the role of socialism. In effect the NSWP states became proxies for the Soviet Union in carrying out certain of its Third World policies. On Brezhnev's watch this meant commitment – at one time or another according to circumstances largely beyond the control of Moscow – to Angola, Ethiopia, Libya, Mozambique, South Yemen and Syria. From the perspective of Moscow the most valuable form of cooperation was to supply arms, but this was acceptable only to Bulgaria, Czechoslovakia, and East Germany,[23] all of which supplied Soviet-manufactured equipment and spare parts to various Third World armies,[24] at the same time training their personnel. Hungary's and Poland's Third World commerce did not include armaments. Although by the late 1970s the world economic crisis had led all the NSWP states to reduce their aid, their involvement in the Third World at the behest of Moscow allowed them to establish, independently of the Soviet Union, relations with other countries. None the less, in the context of the Warsaw Pact, involvement in the Third World was never more than a side-show, and there was no question of any Third World 'People's Democracy' joining the Pact.[25] When in the early 1980s the troubled situation in Poland made clear to Moscow how essential the other NSWP states were for maintaining the Soviet hold on Eastern Europe, involvement in the Third World inevitably became less important.

One key factor affecting the operation of the Warsaw Pact was the entrenched position of the Roman Catholic Church in three, if not four, of the NSWP states. Particularly after the loss of their Jewish populations in the holocaust, a great majority of the citizens of Czechoslovakia, Hungary and Poland were Catholics, and as such belonged to a church that had dominated public life for centuries. The Habsburg empire, to which all had belonged – at least in part – at the beginning of the twentieth century was uncompromisingly Catholic, and the Church retained the allegiance of Czechs, Slovaks, Poles and Hungarians even after they became citizens of independent states following the Treaty of Versailles of 1919. After 1939, when Eastern Europe was overrun first by Germany, and then – with changes in the tide of war – by the Soviet Union, the Catholic Church remained not only a powerful institution, in its own right, but one which was indispensable in fields such as the care of orphans, the old and the disabled – whom religious orders, more often than not composed of women, had looked after for centuries.

Although post-war Soviet policy confronted the Catholic Church mainly at the level of the senior hierarchy, a number of whose members, such as the Hungarian Cardinal Mindszenty, were tried and imprisoned for treason, the rank and file of Catholics, supported by parish priests and members of religious orders, remained loyal to the Church. The price paid was not so much persecution, but deprivation of any chance of advancement in society; in this way, NSWP states forfeited the services of countless professionals and academics, to say nothing of writers and artists opposed to communism. Institutions of higher learning, such as the 600-year-old internationally renowned Jagiellonian University of Kraków were closely tied to the Catholic Church,[26] and Poland has not forgotten how the university was closed by Nazi Germany during World War II (with nearly 200 professors deported to the Sachsenhausen concentration camp) nor how after it had reopened in 1945, its faculty, in 1954, was suppressed by the hard-line communist government of President Bolesław Bierut – an unreformed Stalinist noted for signing the death sentences of Church leaders.[27]

That Catholics in the NSWP states not only regarded themselves as subjects of a secular state, allied to the Soviet Union, but also accepted the authority of the Pope in Rome, head of his own government in the Vatican, posed a problem to Moscow for which Marxism-Leninism provided no adequate solution. The Pope, from the perspective of Moscow, was far from accepting – as he ought to have done – that his Kingdom was 'not of this world';[28] seen from Rome the secular world cried out for intervention, particularly that part of it behind the Iron Curtain with substantial, if not majority Catholic populations. Although the Soviet government under Brezhnev, did not regard the Catholic Church as a key actor in international politics,[29] the Church itself, as a social force, was – following the policy of *aggiornamento* introduced by Pope John XXIII – changing quite radically. (This pope's years in the Vatican were almost the same as Khrushchev's in the Kremlin.)[30] What is more, two leading Catholic clerics, Archbishop König of Vienna, and Archbishop Casaroli from within the Vatican, were active in establishing closer ties with the Catholic Church behind the Iron Curtain (Melloni 2006: 10); both cases, needless to say, were closely monitored by Moscow, with local KGB *rezidents*, at the same time, reporting potentially subversive church activities back to Moscow (Corley 1994: 39). Also on Brezhnev's watch a number of low-level agreements between the Vatican and NSWP states led to more freedom of action for both laity and clergy (ibid.: 22), so that the 'Church of silence' of Stalin's day began to have a voice that was heard by the world at large. Then, just as Brandt was launching Ostpolitik in West Germany, the Vatican, inspired by Cardinal König, was moving in the same direction (Barberini 2006: 49).

That the success of Vatican *Ostpolitik* was far from uniform was the result of the history of the Church and of its standing in each separate NSWP state. A key factor was the extent to which each such national church was tainted by its past. The close historical ties of the Hungarian hierarchy to the Habsburg emperors could, even after World War II, be used to discredit its popular appeal (Hanson 1987: 221, 233), particularly after 1956, when its intransigent primate, Cardinal József Mindszenty, was granted political asylum in the US Embassy in Budapest after being freed from prison (where he was serving a life sentence imposed by a communist show trial in 1949) during the 1956 popular uprising (ibid.: 217). In Czechoslovakia the Church had to come to terms with the fact that during the war years Slovakia, set up by Nazi Germany as a separate state in 1939, had, as its president, a Catholic priest, Monsignor Jozef Tiso, who, collaborating with Hitler, facilitated in Czechoslovakia the 'final solution' to the Jewish problem (Barberini 2006: 61).

In Poland the Catholic Church suffered from no such handicaps. On the contrary, during the long period (1795–1919) of subjugation to either Russia or Germany, the Catholic Church, to which most Poles belonged, became closely identified with the cause of Polish independence (Hanson 1987: 202). When this finally came with the Treaty of Versailles in 1919 the Church had no equal as a social or political force. Far from collaborating during World War II, its clergy were active in the resistance, with many dying in German extermination camps (ibid.: 203).[31]

In 1950 the Polish primate, Cardinal Wyszyński, on his own initiative, negotiated an accord with the Communist government which recognized the legitimacy of the Church as a major operator in public life. That the Vatican, which only learnt of the accord from press reports, was not pleased, was essential to its success, which depended upon a tacit understanding by both parties that Rome would not intervene in Polish politics; there was no papal nuncio in Warsaw (Hanson 1987: 71).[32] The result, in the days of the Warsaw Pact, was that Wyszyński, helped by direct contact with the Party leaders, was able to stand up to the Communist government. If, in 1950, the accord was seen as achieving no more than a modus vivendi, it had proved to be the charter for 'the political power of the Polish church under Communism' (ibid.: 76) long before Brezhnev took over in the Kremlin.[33] As is shown by statistics cited by Chadwick (1992: 104) the Church in Poland was at this stage numerically far stronger than in any other Communist state. In Brezhnev's day the Polish church first suffered a setback in 1966 when a proposed visit by Pope Paul VI to the shrine of the Black Madonna of Częstokowa was turned down by Warsaw, but then, a year later, Archbishop Casaroli, representing the Pope, was allowed not only three visits to Poland, but also direct contacts with clergy.

If, in the course of time, the Communist regime, accepting that cooperation with the Church was indispensable, allowed the hierarchy a free hand to an extent unthinkable in either Catholic Czechoslovakia or Hungary, in 1978 it had to come to terms with an event which it had not foreseen: on 15 October, Karol Wojtiła, Cardinal Archbishop of Kraków, was elected Pope.

For Warsaw, and Moscow even more, it was not a good time for such an event.[34] Wojtiła, was seen as subversive and reactionary, at a time when US President Carter had declared himself a protagonist for human rights everywhere, including the Soviet Union – a stance ensuring that of all five American presidents on Brezhnev's watch, Carter would be the one he particularly disliked. Brezhnev's distrust extended so far as to convince him that Wojtiła's election was the result of Archbishop John Krol of Philadelphia enrolling the support of the other American cardinals in the Rome conclave of October 1978; this, on the second day, was sufficient to ensure Wojtiła's election. It was no coincidence that not only Krol, but also Carter's national security adviser, Zbigniew Brzezinski, was of Polish descent (Corley 1994: 41). At the same time, Brezhnev, was constrained, for diplomatic reasons, to join the rest of the world in congratulating Poland on the election of the first non-Italian pope in more than 400 years.[35]

Worse was to come in 1979, when the new Pope John Paul II proposed to visit Poland for the celebration of the nine-hundredth anniversary of the death of St Stanisław, recognized as the founder of the Polish church. Brezhnev himself is on record for asking for the visit to be banned, although, given his poor health, it is doubtful how much this counted for.[36] At all events the visit did take place, and its resounding success led the KGB to be concerned that the new pope intended to use the Church in Poland, Hungary and Czechoslovakia as a springboard for religious revival in the NSWP states (ibid.:p.42).[37] This concern extended even to the Soviet republics, Lithuania, Belarus and Ukraine (Hanson 1987: 212–213),[38] with substantial Catholic populations. Various tactics devised by the KGB were used to subvert the Catholic Church's plans, even to the extent of looking for support from Orthodox Christians and members of the World Council of Churches (which Rome had never joined) (ibid.: 45). Local KGB *rezidents* in NSWP states were also asked to report in greater detail activities of local churches (ibid.: 46) – particularly in such sensitive areas as labour relations (ibid.: 51).

The Pope's 1979 visit to Poland came at a time when the country was ripe for social upheaval. Ever since 1970, when Edward Gierek succeeded Gomułka as First Secretary of the Communist Party of Poland, a faltering consumer economy had caused unrest, which the government could assuage only by means of short-term measures, such as borrowing heavily abroad (Judt 2010: 587). By the end of the 1970s, when such expedients were palpably failing, workers in industry began to organize 'free trade unions', which, in December 1979, adopted a 'Charter of Workers' Rights' from the underground Workers' Defence Committee (KOR) set up in June 1976 as a reaction to government suppression of a popular protest against rising prices. Although the price rises were cancelled, the Committee did not disband, but continued its work to play a key role in ending communism in Poland. In the summer of 1979 it provided crucial support for industrial workers engaged in organizing free trade unions: one of these, an electrician in a Gdańsk shipyard, was Lech Wałęsa. The government reacted to the adoption of the Charter in December 1979 by imprisoning the intellectuals at the head of the Defence Committee, and dismissing the workers involved from their jobs. These included Wałęsa, who remained in Gdańsk, spending the early months of 1980 mobilizing the workers in the shipyards. In a widely reported interview with the West German *Spiegel* (4 August 1980) KOR leader Jacek Kuron added fuel to the flames by stating that the activities of Solidarność were intended to have a political impact. This became clear when, during a strike on 14 August, held as a protest against increased food prices, Wałęsa broke into the Lenin shipyard and led the strikers to occupy it. With this dramatic move not only inspiring further strikes, first in Gdańsk, and then nationwide, but also attracting worldwide support, Wałęsa organized a Strike Coordinating Committee to confront the government. On 31 August – with the strikers offering assurances that they 'intended neither to threaten the foundations of the socialist regime . . . nor its position [internationally] . . .' (Ouimet 2003: 137) – this led to the Gdańsk agreement, which both recognized the shipyard workers' right to strike and permitted them to organize their own union. The coordinating committee became the *National Coordinating Committee of the Solidarność Free Trade Union*, with Wałęsa as its chairman adding a whole new dimension to politics, not only in Poland (Kemp-Welch 2010: 229), but throughout the Soviet bloc where what was happening in Poland could be seen as challenging 'the very foundations of communist rule' (Ouimet 2003: 136). *Solidarność* grew so rapidly that it soon had some ten million members, with Wałęsa's leadership rewarded, in 1983, by the award of a Nobel Peace Prize.

In the context of Poland, around the year 1980, one question immediately arises: where did the Catholic Church come in? Wałęsa, who always wore a badge from the shrine of the Black Madonna of Częstochowa, never concealed his allegiance to the Church (Hanson 1987: 199), and the same was undoubtedly true of many other members of *Solidarność*. Wałęsa also had any number of contacts with the clergy including with the Pope himself.[39] At the same time *Solidarność* was emboldened by the way the Pope's 1979 visit had led millions of Poles to demonstrate their allegiance to the Church. That these millions and the millions belonging to *Solidarność* were much the same people was reason enough for many in the communist hierarchy – in the Soviet Union as much as in Poland – to ascribe the success of *Solidarność* to some sort of conspiracy originating in the Vatican.[40] For all this, whatever the Church may have done behind the scenes, it was never a front-line actor in the struggle for Poland – as Brezhnev himself accepted.

Both to the Soviet Union and the NSWP states on one side, and to the US and NATO on the other, the dramatic chain of events leading to the emergence of *Solidarność* as a major actor in Polish politics – with significant international repercussions – was a call to action, but how then did they respond to it? If, as is now recorded by history, the short answer is by doing nothing – so that the Polish government was left to work out its own salvation – one is still left to ask, first, why there was no intervention, beyond words, from outside Poland, and second, how the crisis was dealt with inside Poland.

In the first instance, outside intervention involving the use of force would come either from the Soviet Union acting alone, as in Hungary in 1956, or as the result of joint action sanctioned by the Warsaw Pact. In either case the voice of Moscow would be decisive. The East German and Czechoslovak leaders, Honecker and Husák, consistently urged intervention, but this was opposed by the other NSWP states (Mastny 2005: 50). In April 1980, the Politburo decided to shelve intervention in Poland (ibid.: 52). There were no doubt hawks in the Kremlin, but Brezhnev (who had just become honorary Commander-in-Chief of Warsaw Pact forces) preferred to follow Suslov's principle of no troops in Poland 'under any circumstances' (ibid.: 53), and together with Andropov and other Politburo members they had a majority. One key factor was the absence of any satisfactory exit strategy once Soviet, or Warsaw Pact troops had moved into Poland. There was no Polish Husák waiting to take over from Gierek, for as Brezhnev later observed, 'We see no real personality who can assume command ... there is no other way than strengthening the present leadership and bringing pressure to bear on the healthy forces' (Byrne 1998: 125). Seen from Washington, the August 1980 success of *Solidarność* combined with steady deterioration of the Polish economy, created a situation so 'intolerable to the Soviet Union' that intervention was inevitable some time around the turn of the year – so much so that in early December Carter sent a hot-line message to Brezhnev, warning of 'the very grave consequences to US–Soviet relations' (Gates 1996: 167). Intelligence reports of unprecedented Soviet military exercises just short of the Polish frontier added to US concern.

Although 1981 passed without any Soviet military intervention, on 11 December a successful coup d'état by General Wojciech Jaruzelski brought to power a man closer to Brezhnev's heart than any of his predecessors. Under Soviet pressure Jaruzelski declared martial law three days later and ordered the imprisonment of hundreds of members of *Solidarność*, including Wałęsa. Where this brought a sense of relief to the NSWP states, for Moscow the need to rely on Jaruzelski was humiliating – there was simply no better game in town (Saltoun-Ebin 2012: 54). Economically Jaruzelski's coup brought no good to Poland: Washington, having imposed a variety of sanctions on the one NSWP state which had consistently maintained close economic ties with the US, also blocked the rescheduling of Poland's foreign debt and its access to the International Monetary Fund (Neier 2012: 251). This, then, was the state of affairs when Brezhnev died less than a year later.

Notwithstanding Carter's hot-line message to Brezhnev in December 1980, the White House consistently played a waiting game, confident that time was on its side (Neier 2012: 79). President Reagan's policy reflected the advice given by Cardinal Casaroli on a visit to the White House just a week after Jaruzelski's coup (ibid.: 89).[41] Under Jaruzelski the Pope expected neither executions, nor Soviet intervention (ibid.: 86),[42] but rather modest liberalization – even in a climate of increasing apathy about religion among the youth in Eastern Europe. Washington, then, as much as for Moscow, left Poland under Jaruzelski to solve its own problems. Neither side had much choice, but the winner, even before the end of the 1980s, was clearly Washington.

Quite apart from Poland, the balance of advantage to Moscow which the Warsaw Pact was designed to achieve was extremely problematic. The whole modus operandi of the Warsaw Pact opened the way for NSWP states to form coalitions to frustrate Soviet policies, so that in case of need an individual member state could call on support in any confrontation with Moscow. For Brezhnev, on the other hand, the Warsaw Pact had become a forum where Moscow had to justify any claim for support, whether it related to détente, the Third World or NATO, to say nothing of Poland. What is more, economic aid and subsidized trade with the NSWP countries was a severe drain on resources for which, in economic terms, there was much better use. Selling arms to Arab countries, such as notably Syria, was much more profitable than using them to modernize the armed forces of NSWP states – a policy which was recognized as unnecessary and prohibitively expensive long before Brezhnev died. That inevitably the NSWP armed forces lagged far behind the Soviet Union in modern equipment and weapons systems could only mean that their deployment in offensive operations against NATO was no longer part of Soviet strategy – as was well appreciated in Washington. At the same time détente was long past revival, and when Brezhnev died in 1982, arms parity – whatever it might have been in the 1970s – had been irretrievably lost (Mastny 2005: 56).

Notes

1 Moscow's choice of Warsaw was part of a general policy to use Polish cities as 'launching pads for various Soviet sponsored activities' (Wandycz 1994: 293).

2 The Pact's duration was set at twenty years with an automatic ten-year extension, provided that none of the member states renounced it before its expiration. In the event this ensured that it would be in force when Brezhnev died in 1982. (The treaty also provided for disbanding, simultaneously with other military alliances, such as NATO, once East–West agreement about a general treaty on collective security in Europe was reached – in 1955 something of a pipe-dream.)

3 As seen by the Czechoslovak general, Václav Prchlík, in the summer of 1968, '. . . the joint command of the Warsaw Pact . . . consists solely of marshals, generals and other [Soviet] senior officers . . . while the armies of the other member states have to make do with mere "representatives" . . .' (Navrátil *et al.* 1998: 241). This prompted a letter to Dubček (first secretary of the Czechoslovak Party) from the Soviet Marshal Yakubovsky, accusing Prchlík of distorting the true position (ibid.: 259).

4 Speaking, in 1968, from his own experience in suppressing the Hungarian uprising in 1956, the Hungarian leader, János Kádár, saw the Prague spring as the culmination of

a long process: 'You have to do many things badly for many years for the situation to become so deplorable' (Navrátil *et al.* 1998: 137).

5 A week earlier Andropov, head of the KGB, had already noted at a meeting of the Soviet Politburo, that events in Czechoslovakia were 'very reminiscent of what happened in Hungary [in 1956]'; Brezhnev, who was involved in the Hungarian crisis at a high level, agreed, and warned Dubček accordingly by telephone (Kramer 2010: 15).

6 Navrátil *et al.* (1998: 177–181) is an English translation.

7 Research in archives only open after the collapse of the Soviet Union in 1991 proves that the Soviet decision to invade Hungary predated Hungary's declared intent to leave the Warsaw Pact (Kramer 1998).

8 This meeting, where Mikhail Gorbachev was a Soviet delegate, provided him with the only occasion for mentioning in his memoirs the operation of the Warsaw Pact in Brezhnev's time (Gorbachev 1997: 128).

9 The substance of the doctrine is to be found in a statement by Gromyko reported in *Pravda* on 28 June 1968 (Kramer 2010: 60), which clearly derives from what Brezhnev had said in Dresden in March (Navrátil *et al.* 1998: 65).

10 In deciding whether or not to approve such action, Brezhnev, knowing that Lyndon Johnson would shortly leave the White House, took into account the need to establish, internationally, a strong moral basis for a new Soviet policy vis-à-vis Vietnam (Gaiduk 1996: 175) – a matter of little concern to the NSWP states.

11 Students demonstrating on the streets of Warsaw carried signs reading 'Polska czeka na swego Dubczeka', or *Poland awaits its own Dubček* (Kramer 2010: 18). In East Germany Ulbricht introduced specific measures to reduce contacts with Czechoslovakia, fearing particularly that the Czechs would follow Romania and establish diplomatic relations with West Germany (ibid.: 19) – a possibility that also alarmed Moscow (Navrátil *et al.* 1998: 116, 170).

12 Concerned that the loss of Czechoslovakia could threaten his own position as CPSU General Secretary (Alexandrov-Agentov, A.M. 1994: 149) Brezhnev had to take into account the influence, within the Politburo, of potential rivals, such as particularly Kosygin (ibid.: 88). It is significant how at this stage on Brezhnev's watch both Kosygin and Podgorny were involved in top level discussions (ibid.: 132). According to a newspaper interview in 1990, a US Intelligence Assessment of the summer of 1968 suggesting that divisions among the top Soviet leaders could work in Dubček's favour (ibid.: 169) was one about which he himself would have been extremely sceptical: 'The advent of Brezhnev's regime [after the fall on Khrushchev in 1964] heralded the advance of neo-Stalinism, and the measures taken against Czechoslovakia in 1968 were the final consolidation of the neo-Stalinist forces in the Soviet Union, Poland, Hungary, and other countries' (ibid.: 306, and see also p.425). As for Brezhnev, however he stood in the 1968 Politburo, his position would become much stronger in the 1970s.

13 See Chapter 4, note 5.

14 Note Crump (2011: note 95) citing from the Minutes of the Romanian Communist Party Politburo Session of 16 March 1969 words spoken by politburo member Gheorghe Stoica relating to an impending Warsaw Pact meeting: 'It was not said that [the invasion of Czechoslovakia] was an action of the Warsaw Treaty [per se], but it was seen as the action of five states allied within the treaty and this fact was always in the foreground [of the debates].' The Romanian leader, Ceausescu, had already taken the line that since there was no longer a single 'model' of socialist development, the Warsaw Pact had no right of intervention to end 'deviations'. When Czechoslovakia was invaded, Ceausescu later condemned the action. (Kemp-Welch 2010: 223).

15 Critical for Moscow was the fact that Czechoslovakia was the only NSWP state to actually border on West Germany, which Grechko feared it would no longer be able to defend if no action was taken by the Soviet Union (Navrátil *et al.* 1998: 102, Kramer 2010: 30). As Kosygin said at a meeting in Czechoslovakia on 29 July 1968, 'This is a border we will never surrender to anyone' (Navrátil *et al.* 1998: 296).

16 A month later Brezhnev (1968) was published in Moscow to justify the Warsaw Pact intervention.

17 The crisis, none the less, did take a serious toll on Brezhnev's health (Kramer 2010: 45; Haslam 2011: 299).

18 Although at the Potsdam Conference in the summer of 1945 France, the Soviet Union, the UK and the US agreed that two rivers, the Oder and the Neisse, should define the eastern frontier of Germany, with the land beyond this new frontier to be ceded to Poland, it was accepted that this would only become definitive with a final peace treaty with a recognized German government with full national sovereignty. This stage was only reached in 1990, when the Treaty on the Final Settlement with Respect to Germany was signed in Moscow by the Federal Republic of Germany and the German Democratic Republic on one side, and the four great powers present at Potsdam in 1945 on the other. This 'Two Plus Four Agreement', which opened the way to the reunification of Germany, contained the condition that the eastern frontier agreed at Potsdam was recognised as definitive.

19 Walter Hallstein, a top civil servant and close confidant of Adenauer, was part of the German delegation to Moscow in 1955. On the flight home the delegation deliberated over how Germany should proceed in relation to East Germany and the other East European communist states. The Hallstein doctrine was the result. Hallstein later became the first President (1958–1967) of the European Economic Community.

20 The East German leader Walter Ulbricht, a Stalinist strongly opposed to improved relations with West Germany, used Warsaw Pact councils to attack the Soviet détente policy openly. This led to his removal from power, in 1971, to be succeeded by the more flexible Eric Honecker, who became the first East German head of state to visit West Germany. This was only after Brezhnev had warned him that 'the GDR cannot exist . . . without the Soviet Union, its power and its strength' (Haslam 2011: 254).

21 Although, after 1972, joint Warsaw Pact exercises, organized on the principle of a 'deep strike' – an attack behind the front lines of battle, far into NATO's rear areas – took place every year. The underlying rationale was that Soviet nuclear force developments increased the likelihood that a European war would remain on the conventional level. All this did little to enhance the political significance of the Pact, which remained low so long as Brezhnev was alive; the final years under Gorbachev are a quite different story, but one beyond the scope of this book.

22 Schmidt was already angered by the recently deployed Soviet Medium Range Missiles whose only possible targets were in Western Europe (Haslam 2011: 308).

23 In August 1955 the sale of a large quantity of arms by Czechoslovakia to Egypt was one reason why the US refused to help finance the Aswan Dam. As a member of the Warsaw Pact Czechoslovakia never sold arms to any Third World country.

24 In the early 1970s the Soviet Union also used these countries to transship weapons to North Vietnam.

25 The Soviet Union did, however, build an informal alliance system in the Third World during the 1970s, making use of their experience in setting up the Warsaw Pact, and calling its new allies 'people's democracies' and their armed forces 'national liberation armies.'

26 In 1364, the permission of Pope Urban V was essential for the royal charter granted by King Casimir III. In 1400 the University's future was assured after it inherited all the personal jewellery of Saint Jadwiga, Queen of Poland – making possible the enrolment of 203 students.

27 These were seldom if ever carried out.

28 New Testament, John xviii: 36.

29 Works that play down the role of the church are listed in Melloni (2006: 4, note 3).

30 This is the main theme of Cousins (1972).

31 One priest, Maksymilian Kolbe, who by dying in Auschwitz in 1941 saved the life of another Polish prisoner, was canoniszed by Pope John-Paul II on 10 October 1982.

32 In 1974 Poland and the Vatican agreed to permanent diplomatic exchange at a lower level (Barberini 2006: 74). Significantly the Vatican never broke off diplomatic relations with Cuba.

33 It was not all plain-sailing for the church; in the mid-1950s clergy were imprisoned, including even Wyszyński, who was only released from house arrest in October 1956.

34 The dramatic return of Ayatollah Khomeini to Iran four months earlier was an additional reason for concern in Moscow (Hanson 1987: 210).

35 In 1979, the Soviet Embassy in Rome, did not, as had become customary, invite a Vatican representative to the yearly celebration of the October Revolution on 7 November. It is worth noting, also, that Pope John Paul II could speak Russian.

36 In contrast to his immediate successor, Yuri Andropov, Brezhnev was indifferent to religious affairs – at least according to an interview with Vladimir Kuroyedov (head of the Soviet Committee for Religious Affairs), reported in *Lyudina I svit* (Kiev), no.1,1992 (Corley 1994: 61). Significantly the Committee for Religious Affairs fell under the jurisdiction of the KGB, where Andropov was the head.

37 Referring to the election of a Polish pope in his Russian memoirs Gromyko wrote: 'Perhaps the Holy See itself does not fully realise just what strength it possesses' (Corley 1994: 56).

38 A letter written by the new Pope to the Ukrainian Cardinal Slipyi (who had suffered years of persecution under Stalin) caused Moscow particular disquiet. The ban on the Ukrainian [Greek] Catholic church was finally lifted by Gorbachev.

39 In January 1981 the Pope celebrated a private Mass in the Vatican for a *Solidarność* delegation led by Wałęsa. A month later, in a letter to Brezhnev, the Pope threatened that if Soviet troops invaded Poland, he would stand between the Soviet tanks and the Polish people.

40 On 21 December 1981, US Secretary of State, Alexander Haig, said at a White House meeting, '[Wałęsa] is a protégé of Cardinal Wyszynski. They don't dare kill him at this time' (Saltoun-Ebin 2012: 101).

41 At the first consistory, in 1979, of the new Polish Pope, John Paul II, Archbishop Casaroli was promoted to Cardinal, being appointed as Vatican Secretary of State at the same time. This clearly recognized his long diplomatic experience in Eastern Europe, culminating in his chairmanship of the Helsinki Conference in 1975.

42 KGB chief Yuri Andropov: 'We do not intend to introduce troops into Poland . . . I don't know how things will turn out in Poland, but even if Poland falls under the control of Solidarity, that is the way it will be', Minutes of CPSU CC Politburo, 10 Dec 1981, Document No. 21, p.166.

8 US Presidents and the nuclear arms race

From 1969 onwards Brezhnev, a strong believer in personal diplomacy, negotiated directly with three – Richard Nixon, Gerald Ford and Jimmy Carter – of the five men occupying the White House during his 18 years in power. The process of high-level face-to-face contacts started earlier, in 1967, at a meeting at Glassboro, New Jersey, between US President Lyndon Johnson and Soviet Prime Minister Aleksei Kosygin. Their talks, with nuclear disarmament as the main subject of discussion, could achieve little after Kosygin dismissed as 'ridiculous' a suggestion made by Johnson, that one key category, that of anti-ballistic missiles (ABMs), be renounced by both sides (Kissinger 1982: 261). Despite this setback, there still remained a favourable climate for further negotiations. Brezhnev, having been convinced that little could be achieved with Johnson, saw new cause for hope once Nixon became President in January 1969. This was justified: Nixon was also convinced that progress could be made, and a year later – after Nixon's freedom to negotiate was established by a one-vote majority in the US Congress – ABMs were the only subject that Moscow wanted to negotiate. This was a critical step towards achieving the first Strategic Arms Limitation Treaty (SALT 1). For Brezhnev this meant détente, the constant *leitmotiv* of his foreign policy: what then did it all add up to?

Although the history of the nuclear stand-off between the Soviet Union and the US goes back to Stalin's time, the situation, worldwide, as it was when Brezhnev came to power in 1964, was the result of events on Khrushchev's watch during the preceding ten years; the most important of them for world peace, the signing of the Limited Test Ban Treaty in Moscow on 5 August 1963, took place in his last year in power. A year later, Brezhnev made clear that continuing this process of negotiating – and implementing – treaties designed to reduce the possibility of nuclear warfare was to be the main goal of Soviet foreign policy. This then was 'détente', a policy designed to transcend Khrushchev's legacy of 'peaceful coexistence'.

A number of issues defined the nuclear weapons world of 1964. First, both the Soviet Union and the US each had by this time more than 2,000 thermonuclear warheads ready for deployment. On both sides this had required vast investment in the military industrial complex, of which research and development (RD) counted for at least as much as production and deployment. Testing new types of warhead – at every stage essential to the RD process – had by the 1960s led to massive international concern about its harmful consequences for the environment. This had culminated in the 1963 Treaty, which restricted testing to underground explosions: by this time both the Soviet Union and the US had developed vast remote testing sites for this purpose, implicitly accepting that nothing was to be gained from atmospheric, surface or undersea tests, such as were carried out, particularly by the US, during the 1950s.

On Brezhnev's watch the 1967 *Outer Space Treaty* became the first international agreement restricting the use of nuclear weapons. [1] Specifically, it prohibits stationing them, or any other weapons of mass destruction, in orbit round the Earth, or on the moon or any other celestial body; the prohibition extends to tests of any kind, and – outside the nuclear realm – to conducting military manoeuvres and establishing military bases, installations and fortifications. The treaty, however, does not extend to conventional weapons. Although the Treaty also declares the realm that it governs to be the 'Common Heritage of Mankind' – so that no single state can claim sovereignty to any part of it – it does provide that a state that launches a space object is liable for any damage it may cause, at the same time being responsible for ensuring that it does not contaminate space or celestial bodies.

In 1967, the *Outer Space Treaty* was remarkable for providing for the regulation of a realm in which none of the signatories could operate at all ten years earlier; it was simply beyond their reach. Even so, by 1967 both Soviet and US space operations, involving artificial satellites, were well underway, while, in December 1968, the US Apollo 8 mission brought a manned spacecraft successfully into orbit round the moon (so that the far side was seen for the first time); a year later the Apollo 11 mission achieved an actual landing on 20 July 1969.

Throughout the 1960s the state-of-the-art technology of rocket propulsion was being established at a level that allowed nuclear warheads, of almost any size, to be delivered over any distance on Earth, so as to destroy any designated unprotected target. This made real the possibility, in any nuclear war, of Mutually Assured Destruction (MAD). If, intuitively, the appropriate counteraction was to install missile defence systems capable of intercepting ballistic missiles with nuclear warheads, this was easier said than done.[2] Such ABM would have to be 'guided' throughout their trajectories, which meant in turn much more advanced, and inevitably expensive control systems linked by radio to ground stations – which themselves would be obvious 'first strike' targets. In the mid-1960s the Soviet Union was already designing two ABM networks, one around Moscow and the other around Tallinn in Estonia (Dobrynin 1995: 148). In Washington, President Johnson's Secretary of Defence, Robert McNamara, opposed an American ABM programme on the grounds that any such defence system could be overwhelmed by increasing the number of offensive weapons it had to deal with – a view shared by Brezhnev (ibid.: 150). Then, in June 1966, Johnson proposed, somewhat informally, a high-level meeting; although this never took place, the possibility of an agreement on ABMs was raised (as noted on page 85) by Johnson at the Glassboro summit of 1967. There was no useful reaction, if only because Prime Minister Kosygin, representing the Soviet Union, did not have a sufficient mandate from the Politburo (ibid.: 167). Significantly, when nuclear arms limitation was once more on a summit agenda, Brezhnev himself would represent the Soviet Union.

So long as Lyndon Johnson (1963–1969) was in office McNamara's assessment of ABMs prevailed, in part because two Democratic Senators, Robert Kennedy and Hubert Humphrey, agreed with it to the point of being ready to block any ABM programme in the US Senate. Even so, Washington did disclose plans for a 'thin'[3] ABM system for neutralizing the Chinese threat; this was in part a response to criticism from congressional Republicans accusing Johnson of 'inactivity' (Dobrynin 1995: 166).

After Richard Nixon became President in 1969, his National Security Adviser, Henry Kissinger, was strongly in favour of ABMs, partly as a means for strengthening US nuclear diplomacy (Hanhimäki 2004: 50) at a time when Nixon was content with 'sufficiency' not 'superiority' in nuclear weapons (Schulzinger 2010: 379). It also counted that newly developed MIRVs (Multiple Independently-targetable Re-entry Vehicles) would allow many warheads to be carried by a single missile, so that however effective the Soviet anti-missile defence might prove to be there would still be a very considerable chance of one MIRV warhead reaching its target (ibid.: 51; Dobrynin 1995: 153). This, for Kissinger, was a new means of increasing US diplomatic leverage. This may well have been the case: following a Washington meeting between Nixon and Soviet Ambassador Dobrynin on 17 February 1969, a secret back channel was set up between Kissinger and Dobrynin, to discuss possible nuclear disarmament (Hanhimäki 2004: 34). A month earlier, Dobrynin, Brezhnev, Podgorny and Kosygin, meeting in a sanatorium near Moscow, had worked out the strategy that Dobrynin would try to sell to the new US President (ibid.: 37). If successful, then for Brezhnev this would open the way to détente, even though his Minister of Defence, Marshal Grechko, and Suslov – behind the scenes the most powerful member of the Politburo – were not in favour. Since, however, progress would depend on negotiating with Washington, the support of both of Dobrynin and Foreign Minister Andrei Gromyko counted for much more. At this stage Nixon raised the problem of linkage (Schulzinger 2010: 377), stating it in terms that warned Moscow that 'crisis or confrontation in one place and real cooperation in another cannot long be sustained simultaneously' (Hanhimäki 2004: 35). Few then suggested that the US could also be prone to linkage. In 1969 the critical case was the war in Vietnam where the US and the Soviet Union supported opposite sides with massive military aid (Haslam 2011: 222,261); here, however, neither Washington nor Moscow saw fit to relate events in Vietnam to nuclear disarmament. Until well into the 1970s this principle, somewhat shakily, would continue to hold in relation to events in Israel and its Arab neighbours,[4] to say nothing of other troubled corners of the world.[5] When linkage became critically disruptive, as it did in the mid-1970s, it was because of political events in the US (related later in this chapter). In 1969, however, with Kissinger and Dobrynin calling the shots, substantial progress was made towards agreeing the terms of nuclear disarmament.

Although Kissinger accepted that the United States had lost the dominant world position of the earliest days of the Cold War (Schulzinger 2010: 374), it was still important for him to negotiate from a position of strength (Hanhimäki 2004: 39). Convinced that the decline in American power was absolute rather than relative, Kissinger believed that this position had been achieved by the US. (This was partly the result of his own high-handed treatment of both Congress and other cabinet colleagues.) Once the dialogue relating to a possible treaty was underway, negotiations lasting the whole of 1970 and 1971 were conducted at a lower level in a series of meetings between US and Soviet diplomats in Helsinki and Vienna, with a definitive treaty, SALT I, ready to be signed by Brezhnev and Nixon in Moscow in May 1972; the ABM treaty was signed on the same occasion. The circumstances were propitious: Soviet leaders, mindful of what American diplomacy was achieving in China (as related in Chapter 12) were very strongly inclined to reach agreement with the United States (Schulzinger 2010: 378; Haslam 2011: 214, 263) – so much so that they also agreed to convene a Conference on Security and Cooperation in Europe, finally to recognize the international borders established in Europe after World War II (Schulzinger 2010: 381). This, a real can of worms, is the subject matter of Chapter 9.

Essentially SALT I provided for a stop to any increase in the number both of launchers for 'intercontinental ballistic missiles' (ICBM) located in the Soviet Union and the US or of launchers contained in submarines for 'submarine-launched ballistic missiles' (SLBM). In this latter case, actual numbers both of launchers (950 for the Soviet Union and 710 for the US) and of submarines (62 for the Soviet Union and 44 for the US) were specified in a protocol. The treaty also contained an undertaking, by both parties, to continue 'active negotiations for limitations on strategic weapons'; this was critical since the treaty also provided that it would only remain in force for five years. The agreement was supplemented by a number of agreed statements relating to the modernization and replacement of launchers. There were also unilateral statements from both sides: Moscow wished to provide for possible SLBMs held by US allies in NATO, while Washington was concerned, first, about the result of failing to reach within five years a permanent agreement providing 'for more strategic offensive arms limitations', insisting that such failure would then 'constitute a basis for the withdrawal from the ABM treaty'; second, about the development of 'mobile land-based ICBM launchers'; third, about obstacles to the verification of concealed nuclear submarine bases and fourth, about failure by Moscow to agree a definition of 'heavy' ICBMs, which if deployed, would go beyond what the treaty allowed for.[6]

The ABM treaty, after defining an 'ABM system' in broad terms, provides for both the Soviet Union and the US to deploy no more than two such systems, one in defence of the national capital, and the other located according to strategic defence principles as conceived of in the respective states. At the same time the development, testing or deployment of 'ABM systems which are sea-based, air-based, space-based or mobile land-based' is prohibited. Although the treaty is quite short, it still contains a number of provisions designed to close possible loopholes; compliance is then one of the tasks entrusted to a Standard Consultative

Commission. Critically, the treaty – in contrast to SALT I – is of 'unlimited dura-tion'[7] (although provision is made for extraordinary events justifying withdrawal from the treaty).[8]

With the benefit of hindsight, it is now clear that SALT I was a high-water mark in the history of treaties relating to nuclear disarmament agreed between the Soviet Union and the US. When, however, it was signed in 1972, both sides intended it as no more than a first step on the way to a comprehensive and perma-nent treaty, SALT II. This explains the period of five years explicitly provided for in SALT I before the treaty should expire. This then defined, at least in principle, a deadline for SALT II in 1977. In the event SALT II was not ready to be signed in 1977, and when, finally, it was signed in 1979, it never came into effect as a result of the US Senate failing to ratify it. At the end of the day, therefore, a disappointed Brezhnev had to be content with the ABM treaty as the sole endur-ing achievement of the Moscow summit of 1972. Détente had proved to be a failure. What then went wrong? And to what extent did the blame lie with Brezhnev and the power base that supported him?

Nixon was riding high as he approached the 1972 presidential election. If something of an overstatement, the American political world, at least as defined by the Congress, was at his feet. Although the Democratic Party had yet to find a convincing challenger, Nixon, by temperament, was not a man to take victory for granted; his unease was shared by his staff in the White House. As history would later confirm, he was a party to the June 1972 break-in at Democratic headquarters located in a vast Washington building known as 'Watergate' – an operation orchestrated by the Committee for the Re-election of the President (Haldeman 1994: 471). Occurring only a month after the SALT summit in Moscow this was the first in a chain of events which two years later would lead to Nixon's downfall, with Gerald Ford succeeding him as President in August 1974. As for the Watergate story, it is sufficient to note how at every stage Nixon's power and influence, both at home and abroad, inexorably diminished – a process diligently reported back to Moscow by Ambassador Dobrynin. During this period, other events, notably the start on 28 January 1973 of a ceasefire in Vietnam (agreed in Paris between Kissinger and Viet Minh leader Le Duc Tho) and the Yom Kippur war (as related in Chapter 10) at the end of the same year, occupied both the White House and the Kremlin. Once the year 1973 had ended Nixon's hands were tied by the need to survive Watergate, a prospect that became every day more uncertain. The point of no return was reached in April 1974, when it became clear that the Judiciary Committee of the US House of Representatives was set on impeachment. None the less, détente was still more or less on track: the US–Soviet *Treaty on the Limitation of Underground Nuclear Weapons Tests* (the Threshold Test Ban Treaty) was signed on 3 July, just five weeks before Nixon resigned as President. By this time Gromyko – for whom '. . . the United States *was* world politics' (Haslam 2011: 220) – had inquired of Kissinger what procedures would then follow relating to the succession (Kissinger 1982: 1026).

In the event Nixon's successor, Gerald Ford, intent on reviving the moribund negotiations relating to SALT II, agreed to meet Brezhnev in Vladivostok on 23

November 1974, after only three months in the White House: the meeting could then follow a long-planned visit to Tokyo. By this time, however, SALT – at least as Kissinger saw it – was 'no longer part of a broader, coherent security policy or an overall strategy . . . it was doomed above all by the inability of the President [Nixon] to supply leadership during his Watergate travail' (Kissinger 1982: 1029). At the same time a substantial Democratic majority in both houses of Congress following the 1974 mid-term elections was certain to restrict Ford's prospects of bringing the SALT II negotiations to a successful conclusion, the more so given the fact that he could not lose sight of the presidential election due in November 1976. Here two factors were critical: the first was the potential opposition to the nomination of Ford as the Republican candidate; the second was the candidate to be chosen by the Democratic Party in an election which it had a good chance of winning. On the Republican side, Governor Ronald Reagan of California threatened to be a formidable challenger to Ford, while on the Democratic side, the man with the highest profile in the mid-1970s was Senator Henry ('Scoop') Jackson of Washington.

While Reagan was certain to make capital out of any questionable concessions to the Soviet Union in the SALT negotiations, Jackson established the principle of 'linkage' based on restrictions in the Soviet Union on the emigration of its Jewish citizens. Significantly, both Reagan and Jackson came from west-coast states with a massive stake in the US armaments industry – names such as Lockheed (California) and Boeing (Washington) represented a very powerful lobby. Economically at least, arms reduction was not a vote-winner. Jackson, indeed, was the Senate's strongest supporter for the arms industry (Bourne 1997: 388). On the other hand, on 28 May 1976, Ford and Brezhnev did sign the *Underground Nuclear Explosions for Peaceful Purposes Treaty*,[9] a follow-up to the Threshold Test Ban Treaty that had come into force on 31 March.

None of this was of much help, politically, to Ford – a matter of some regret to Brezhnev, who had got on well with him. In 1976 the winner at the end of the day was Jimmy Carter – governor of the east-coast state of Georgia – who won the 1976 presidential election for the Democratic Party; this did little to make good the damage done to détente by Reagan and Jackson. Above all, it was the impact of Jackson that had the most drastic consequences in the mid-1970s: this was because of his focus on an issue, the civil rights of Soviet Jews, that resonated not only within the US but worldwide. With the full history related in Chapter 9, it is sufficient to note here that Carter, as president, would find it difficult to equal Nixon's successes in foreign policy vis-à-vis the Soviet Union, let alone China. On the other side of the line this meant that seen from Moscow, Brezhnev's prospects with Carter were no more promising (Haslam 2011: 305). Accepting that the Soviet invasion of Afghanistan in December 1979 (as related in Chapter 11) would ensure that nothing would be achieved during the last year (1980) of the Carter presidency, SALT II was still on the agenda during Carter's first three years in office. In principle it should have become operative in 1977 after the five-year term provided for SALT I had expired, but this goal eluded Carter. Why then did he fail, and indeed had he ever any prospect of reaching it?

With Carter stating in his inaugural address that '... we will move this year a step towards our ultimate goal – the elimination of all nuclear weapons from this earth' (Walker 1996: 45) it must have seemed to Moscow that his heart was in the right place, so that negotiations relating to SALT II could proceed along the promising path laid down by Ford and Brezhnev in Vladivostok in November 1974. At that time, however, Ford's presidency still had more than two years to run, and in this period Soviet foreign policy, with somewhat marginal involvement by the US, was mainly focussed on the negotiations that led to the Helsinki final accord (as described in Chapter 9), while Ford, in increasing measure, was concerned with his bid for a second term as President. When, therefore, Carter won in November 1976, time had been lost in relation to SALT II, and there was no certainty that Carter would follow the same path as Ford.

In the event Carter's concern for human rights, and in particular for the welfare of the Nobel Prize-winning physicist, Andrei Sakharov – the leading protagonist in the Soviet Union – infuriated Brezhnev (Bourne 1997: 387; Gates 1996: 177),[10] who saw the US President as intent on derailing détente. Indeed with Zbigniew Brzezinski, Carter's National Security Adviser, urging a tougher US stance in arms negotiations, Brezhnev must have regretted that, with the defeat of Ford, Kissinger was out of office. Worse still, when Cyrus Vance, Kissinger's successor as Secretary of State was in Moscow to continue the SALT II negotiations in March 1977, his proposals – particularly those relating to the advanced Soviet SS-18 MIRVs – were so objectionable that Brezhnev, after only one meeting, cancelled all those planned to follow it (Bourne 1997: 389).

This was not all. Carter increased the US military presence in western Europe, and by equipping US forces with new state-of-the-art tactical nuclear weapons made clear to the world the steadily increasing US lead in the nuclear arms race (Bourne 1997: 390).[11] A US-backed Israeli attack on Syrian airbases in the Bekaa Valley, in which 70 of the most advanced Soviet airplanes – MiGs and Sukhois – were destroyed without any loss to the attackers brought the same message to Moscow. Carter proceeded to the formal diplomatic recognition of China on 1 January 1979, a step that Kissinger could never take, and then, when war broke out between China and Soviet ally Vietnam, unequivocally supported the former. In all this Brzezinski, at least, made clear the implicit warning against further Soviet expansion (ibid.: 440). In a new world of realpolitik, Brezhnev – who had come to despise Carter (Walker 1996: 268) – was left in little doubt about how Beijing and Moscow stood in relation to Washington. None the less, negotiations relating to SALT II continued, even after Brezhnev had to contend with a strong attack on Soviet policy made by Deng Xiaoping on a visit to Washington in early 1979. In June both Carter and Brezhnev spent five days together in Vienna to finalize the treaty – actually signed on 18 June – on terms limiting both sides to 2,250 nuclear weapons.

Following the Soviet invasion of Afghanistan in December 1979, Carter's hard line continued with his support for mujahidin resistance in Afghanistan to say nothing of the American boycott of the Olympic Games in Moscow in 1980. By this time, however, it was clear to Carter that the two-thirds majority in the US Senate required for the ratification of SALT II was beyond his reach, particularly in a year when he would be standing for re-election. He had no alternative but to ask for the resolution to be tabled (Bourne 1997: 457), so that, at the end of the day, Brezhnev never achieved the treaty for which he was worked so hard and so long. None the less, both the Soviet Union and the USA adhered to the limits agreed at Vienna.

With the benefit of hindsight, it can said, quite simply, that in the negotiations between the Soviet Union and the US relating to nuclear weapons, both sides were overtaken by events in the late 1970s. For some, such as the Iran hostage crisis of 1979, and to a lesser extent, the international oil crisis orchestrated by OPEC (Organization of Petrol Exporting Countries), neither Brezhnev nor Carter were responsible; that both the Soviet Union and the US were victims shows that the leaders of these two great powers still could still have feet of clay – at least as seen from the non-aligned world.

For Carter it was largely a question of priorities. The Camp David Accords of 1979, which brought peace to both Israel and Egypt after 30 years of conflict (and Nobel Peace Prizes for the two countries' leaders, Menachem Begin and Anwar Sadat), were the culmination of a lengthy diplomatic process in which Carter invested considerable political capital. The same had been true of the 1977 treaty between Panama and the US which provided for Panama to assume full control of the Panama Canal – exercised by the US since 1903 – on 31 December 1999. Although Camp David did indirectly involve the Soviet Union, this could hardly be said of the Panama Canal treaty; on the other hand opposition in the US Congress meant that Carter once again had to pay a high price for getting his way. It is no wonder, then, that he held back, at the end of the day, from confronting the US Senate over SALT II.

At the end of his term of office Carter's stance vis-à-vis the Soviet Union was confrontational rather than accommodating.[12] Although the Soviet invasion of Afghanistan was the main reason other factors also counted: in particular the fall of the Shah in Iran early in 1979, and the success of the Islamic Revolution led by Ayatollah Khomeini, greatly weakened the US presence in the Middle East, at the same time offering new openings to the Soviet Union. Carter's response is to be found in his final State of the Union speech on 23 January 1980:

> Any attempt by any outside source to gain control of the Persian Gulf region will be regarded as an assault on the vital interests of the United States of America.
>
> (Bourne 1997: 457–458)

These words could only be intended for Moscow. By this time, however, Brezhnev – in very poor shape, both physically and mentally – was described by one doctor as having 'only minimal comprehension of his surroundings' (Gates 1996: 117). This then was the man, who from January 1981, would be dealing with the new US President Ronald Reagan.

Dealings between Brezhnev and Reagan were entirely by letter,[13] which, while addressed to and signed by the two world-leaders, were plainly statements of policy, together with proposals based on them, which were the largely the work of senior advisers – generally members of the Politburo on one side, and of the US Cabinet on the other. So much was this the case with the ailing Soviet leader that Reagan sometimes doubted whether Brezhnev had even read the letters he signed.[14]

The most significant of the letters was handwritten by Reagan, on 24 April 1981, while recovering in hospital from an assassination attempt that had nearly cost him his life. Its first sentence refers to the only occasion that Reagan and Brezhnev ever met face-to-face. This was in June 1973, when Reagan, then governor of California, was invited to Nixon's 'summer White House' at San Clemente when Brezhnev was the president's guest. Reagan, in his letter to Brezhnev nearly eight years later, ended the first paragraph with the words, 'Never had peace and good will among men seemed closer at hand', to recall, in the third paragraph, how Brezhnev was 'dedicated . . . to fulfilling [the] hopes and dreams . . . millions of people throughout the world' (Saltoun-Ebin 2012: 15). Brezhnev, in his reply (which was not handwritten) referred to the time of the San Clemente meeting as belonging to a golden age in US–Soviet relations (ibid.: 24); he then attributed their subsequent deterioration to the policies of the Carter administration, noting that so far, under Reagan there had been little improvement.[15]

The correspondence between Reagan and Brezhnev, continued until the summer of 1982, by which time there was little doubt about Brezhnev's terminal decline. As late as 7 May 1982, Reagan wrote to Brezhnev proposing a new round of talks relating to nuclear weapons (Saltoun-Ebin 2012: 154); this was read in Moscow as implying that the Soviet Union still led the arms race. The letter sent in reply, repeated the standard Soviet denial of any such advantage,[16] of any such advantage, and proposed that both sides consider freezing the actual state of their respective nuclear arsenals; Reagan, after reading the letter, wrote, next to Brezhnev's signature, 'I have, and it's an apple for an orchard . . . He's a barrel of laughs'[17] (ibid.: 155).

In fact the character of the nuclear stand-off was changing. While SALT II was still on hold, Richard Allen, Reagan's National Security Adviser, proposed a new initiative to be known as START, an acronym for Strategic Arms Reduction Treaty. Its purpose was to take into account the deployment of Theater Nuclear Forces (TNF) armed with intermediate range weapons. This was a process by which the ground forces of both NATO and Warsaw Pact states were to be equipped with tactical nuclear weapons, such as American Pershings for the former and the Soviet SS-range for the latter. Here grass-roots opposition to TNF encountered by Reagan in Western Europe provided the background to a letter sent to Brezhnev on 17 November 1981, stating that the US was ready to accept parity in both conventional arms, and intermediate and strategic nuclear weapons (Saltoun-Ebin 2012: 74). The letter foreshadowed a high-level meeting held in Geneva on 30 November, when the US delegates offered to pull back the Pershing IIs, if the Soviet Union did the same for the SS-4s, SS-5s and SS-20s.[18]

Brezhnev, writing to Reagan the following day affirmed both the need to eliminate the threat of nuclear war and the principle that reciprocity should be central to any agreement reached at Geneva, while refusing to withdraw the SS-weapons.[19] At the same time verification, seen as critical to the success of the SALT treaties, had yet to satisfy Soviet requirements. Although correspondence between Reagan and Brezhnev continued intermittently during the winter, 1981–1982, it related mainly to non-nuclear issues – such as Soviet intervention in Cuba and Ethiopia, and critically, Poland (as related in Chapter 9). This was not what Brezhnev wanted; as he said in his letter of 25 December 1981, 'the US and the Soviet Union should confine discussion to important matters like the arms race' (ibid.: 122). Reagan finally responded, in a letter of 7 May 1982, proposing a new line of disarmament talks based on START for Geneva in June, when there would be a special session of the UN. Brezhnev instead proposed a meeting in October in either Finland or Switzerland. By this time Brezhnev's poor health plainly ruled out any personal diplomacy, so that San Clemente in 1973 would remain the only occasion he ever met Reagan face-to-face. It could well be that, in the eighteen months of written exchanges between the two leaders, Brezhnev was little more than a figure-head – which was certainly not true of Reagan.[20] In the short period he was corresponding with Brezhnev, he was just finding his feet in dealing with the Soviet Union. In a closed Washington meeting on security on 24 May 1982, Reagan noted how the Soviet Union was 'economically on the ropes' (ibid.: 164); after returning from the Geneva summit, he told how the Soviet Union is 'more vulnerable today than we have ever known it to be' (ibid.: 165); on 9 August, at a meeting devoted to START he suggested telling the Soviets 'If we find even one [violation on agreed verification], we're back in the arms race and we'll out-build you' (ibid.: 168).[21]

By this time. it must have been clear to Moscow that if détente was ever to be back on track, Washington would call the shots. At the beginning of the 1970s, when Brezhnev was at the height of his powers, a Soviet claim to be ahead of the game was just about credible; indeed it was widely accepted in the world outside the Soviet bloc. By the end of the 1970s the stance taken by President Carter had shown that in Washington such a claim was no longer taken seriously; it certainly did not inhibit Carter's Soviet policy in any way. For Brezhnev the position under Reagan showed no sign of improvement, whatever he may have hoped from the new administration. When Brezhnev died late in 1982 the détente that he had set his sights on in the 1960s was further away than ever. If, with the benefit of hindsight, it is clear that Washington always had a better hand, Moscow still held some good cards, such as its claim to the moral high ground when the US was still fighting to save Vietnam. Brezhnev, with the invasion of Afghanistan in 1979, irretrievably forfeited any such claim. Even more disastrous was the way that the new relationship between China and the US, initiated by Nixon and sealed by Carter, bypassed the Soviet Union.

In the whole nuclear disarmament process there were only two protagonists, the US and the Soviet Union. It made little difference that China, France, the United Kingdom, and even Israel, all had small nuclear arsenals. The states belonging to

NATO or adhering to the Warsaw Pact had little choice but to accept – reluctantly in such cases as that of the TNF – what was agreed between Moscow and Washington. The same was true of the non-aligned world. In a sense all these states were spectators in a contest between two giants; by the time Brezhnev died on 10 November 1982, there was little doubt which of the two had won. In the fall of the Soviet Union Brezhnev has much to answer for, not least – as this chapter shows – for his failure to achieve détente, the goal closest to his heart.

Notes

1 The full name is Treaty on Principles Governing the Activities of States in the Exploration and the Use of Outer Space.
2 According to the Merriam-Webster's Dictionary *ballistic* defines 'a missile guided in the ascent of a high-arch trajectory and freely falling in the descent'.
3 The word comes from the US State Department's own report on SALT I: see [URL] http://www.state.gov/t/isn/5191.htm[/URL].
4 Nixon did mention both the Middle East and Vietnam at the initial meeting with Dobrynin, but when asked whether he meant 'linkage' to prospective arms talks, he said no more than 'that progress in one area is bound to have an influence on progress in all other areas' (Hanhimäki 2004: 38).
5 The Moscow summit of May 1972 (which was largely concerned with peace in the Middle East) took place only two weeks after the US had resumed the bombing of North Vietnam and the mining of its harbours, but even so there was never any question of withdrawing the invitation to Nixon.
6 The official US Department statement relating to SALT I, as of 20 January 2001, is to be found at [URL]http://www.state.gov/www/global/arms/treaties/salt1.html[/URL].
7 The text of all treaties between the Soviet Union and the US relating to disarmament can be found via [URL]http://www.fas.org/nuke/control[/URL].
8 This actually happened when on 13 December 2001 US President George W. Bush officially announced that this step would be taken.
9 Although nuclear detonations, for such purposes as building canals, were contemplated on both sides of the iron curtain, neither side ever went beyond this point.
10 After Truman Carter was the first US president to 'challenge directly the legitimacy of the Soviet government in the eyes of its own people' (Gates 1996: 95).
11 In the early 1970s Moscow was reassured by the Soviet Union's superiority in conventional weapons in Europe, and the long distance separating the NATO forces there from their essential logistical bases on the other side of the Atlantic (Haslam 2011: 197). This view reflects the invariably Americocentric focus of Moscow's policy vis-à-vis the West (ibid.: 198).
12 In February 1980, a worldwide briefing submitted to the US Congress by Admiral Turner, head of the CIA, stated how 'Under Brezhnev, and especially since the mid-1970s, an assertive, global Soviet foreign policy has come of age' (quoted Bourne 1997: 171).
13 During his eight years in the White House Gorbachev was the only Soviet leader (out of four) that Reagan actually met face-to-face (Reagan 1990: 634).
14 After reading one letter from Brezhnev dealing with arms control, Reagan asked, 'Do you suppose he really believes all the crud – or did he even write it?' (Saltoun-Ebin, J. 2012: 65)
15 Gromyko (1989: 191) noted in his autobiography how 'In practical terms only Nixon and Ford gave any attention to the issue of disarmament'.
16 See Brezhnev's letter of 1 December 1981 (Saltoun-Ebin 2012: 77).
17 This phrase was borrowed from President Kennedy.

18 The SS-20s, designed to replace the S-4s and S-5s, were the most advanced of these weapons; after their first top-secret deployment – unknown even to the politburo – in the late 1970s they were much feared by NATO and particularly by Bonn, and as such were a strong Soviet bargaining counter in disarmament negotiations (Haslam 2011: 303–4).

19 Here it seems that the Politburo had overruled Brezhnev while Carter was still US President (Haslam 2011: 312). See also note 21.

20 Haslam (2011: 300) relates how at this stage '. . . the substance of power [had] tacitly passed to a troika: Andropov, Gromyko and Ustinov . . .'

21 In a National Security Study Directive (NSSD 1–82) Thomas C. Reed, an NSC staffer advised 'The bottom line is we are helping encourage the dissolution of the Soviet Empire' (Saltoun-Ebin 2012: 137). By the time he wrote his memoirs, Reagan (1990: 594), it seems, only became convinced of the American 'position of strength', after Chernenko had come to power in the Soviet Union in February 1984.

9 The mixed blessings brought by Brezhnev's new German friendship

The Helsinki conference and its aftermath

At much the same time as Brezhnev came into power, in October 1964, the first tentative steps were being taken towards a conference which would definitively settle the internal frontiers of Eastern Europe as they had been agreed at the Yalta and Potsdam conferences in 1945, where – apart from the Soviet Union – none of the countries involved were represented. Yalta and Potsdam confirmed the western frontier of the Soviet Union so as to include the part of eastern Poland which (as related in Chapter 2) had belonged to Russia before 1919,[1] extended the western frontier of Poland to the Oder–Neisse line so as to include a substantial part of eastern Germany, and provided for what then remained of Germany to be divided into four zones, to be occupied by the four great powers, with on one side – as the course of history would soon determine – the Soviet Union, and on the other, the United States, the United Kingdom and France. The Iron Curtain would then be the frontier between the two sides – East and West – which in 1949 were reconstituted as, respectively, the German Democratic Republic (GDR) and the Federal Republic of Germany (FRG).[2]

Although Berlin, left deep inside the Soviet zone of Germany, was in principle subject to a joint four-power administration, in practice the city was divided in the same way as Germany, with each power with its own zone to administer. Although the Soviet occupation forces had never left the city, East Berlin had also been adopted by East Germany as its capital. Where, however, the frontier between East and West Germany had been effectively closed by the end of the 1940s, in Berlin the same result was achieved only in August 1961, when Walter Ulbricht, the East German head of state, acting on a request from Moscow (Haslam 2011: 189), constructed, almost overnight, a wall separating East from West Berlin. This was then closely guarded, with East German frontier guards, posted in watch-towers all along the wall, instructed to shoot any attempting to cross over to the West. Effectively, this completed the incorporation of East Berlin by East Germany. Although there was no counteraction by West Germany, with the capital remaining in Bonn (where it had been established in 1949), the construction of the Berlin Wall was condemned throughout the western world. With nothing that could be done about it, the West had little choice but to accept the revision of the European status quo that it entailed. This, in the event, would prove to be a blessing in disguise: where, before 1961, Berlin had been the focus of any number of crises involving both East and West in Europe, none of any significance occurred after that year.[3] By the time Brezhnev took over from Khrushchev (who had instigated many of the crises occurring before 1961) the political division of Europe between East and West promised to be stable indefinitely.

For Moscow, the question was whether a position that had been established de facto could acquire international recognition *de jure*. A partial answer to this question has already been given in Chapter 7: in 1970, the Treaty of Moscow formally recognized the FRG, and the Treaty of Warsaw, the de facto frontiers of Poland as they had been since 1945; in 1973 East and West Germany agreed to recognized each other's sovereignty on the same principle, agreeing, also, to establish diplomatic relations.

What then was lacking – at least from the perspective of Moscow? The answer must be that whatever had been achieved in the early 1970s did not add up to a comprehensive settlement of Europe's international boundaries, nor establish détente as the fundamental principle governing relations between European states. The underlying principle can be traced back to a suggestion made by the Polish Foreign Minister, Adam Rapacki, in November 1956, to create 'a definite region in Europe of greatly reduced forces and armaments' including Denmark, Belgium, France, the Netherlands, Luxembourg, Germany, Poland and Czechoslovakia (Wandycz 1994: 289). This was the essence of the 'first' Rapacki plan presented to the UN on 2 October 1957. Predictably it was categorically rejected in Bonn by Adenauer and in Washington by US Secretary of State, John Foster Dulles, who saw it as 'highly dangerous' and containing 'totally unacceptable risks' (ibid.: 299–300). None the less Rapacki persevered, presenting a second plan in 1959 and a third in 1962 (ibid.: 310), and even after failing to have them adopted he continued along the same lines until he retired in 1968. With all his plans totally incompatible with the Hallstein doctrine, he was bound to fail so long as Adenauer was Chancellor in Bonn. If, in his last few years, with a new regime in West Germany, prospects were brighter, he died in 1970 without reaching the promised land. By this time, however, the initiative was no longer confined to Poland; the principle behind Rapacki's plans was beginning to appeal to Moscow, where Soviet leaders – none more than Brezhnev – were beginning to welcome the prospect of making 'détente irreversible, giving it concrete form and substance and [opening] . . . a window on to the future of Europe' (Israelyan 2003: 277).

In the event, an initiative by the Finnish government in 1969 started a chain of events directed to achieving just this end. The NSWP states approved it in 1970, and NATO followed in 1971. At the same time Brezhnev set his sights on what, from 1973 to 1975, would be the Conference on Security and Cooperation in Europe (CSCE). This led to informal talks in Helsinki in November 1972: the result was the production of 'The Blue Book' containing a programme for a three-stage conference. The conference was broadly conceived, so that not only almost all European countries would be represented, but also the United States, Canada and – critically – the Vatican.

The first stage, opening in Helsinki on 3 July 1973, lasted only five days, and did little more than adopt the Blue Book as the basis for negotiations. The serious business of the conference took up the whole of the long second stage, held in Geneva from 18 September 1973 until 21 July 1975. The result was the draft of what is now known as the Helsinki Final Act; this was adopted by all the 35 participating states during the short final third stage, held in Helsinki from 30 July to 1 August 1975.

The conference's choice of Archbishop Agostino Casaroli, representing the Vatican, as its chairman for the third stage, was extremely significant. As related in Chapter 7, Casaroli was the key exponent of the Vatican's own version of Ostpolitik, which had, essentially, the same focus as that of Willy Brandt. Somewhat to the distress of Brezhnev, in May 1974 Brandt had to resign as the result of an espionage scandal involving East Germany; the new Chancellor, Helmut Schmidt, if less enthusiastic for Ostpolitik, did not abandon the policy. The combination of Casaroli and the West German Chancellor remained extremely favourable to Brezhnev's claim to a key role in the whole Helsinki process, played out at much the same time as he was negotiating the SALT treaties with Washington – as related in Chapter 8. It is little wonder then, that at this stage many Americans saw the Helsinki process as a European sell-out to the Soviet Union (Gates 1996: 96, Davy 2009: 4), while Brezhnev was in a state of euphoria (Walker 1996: 239). From his perspective, his meeting with the new US President Gerald Ford in Vladivostok in November 1974 had confirmed that the good relations with Washington promoted by Nixon were still intact; it is significant here that not only Brezhnev, but Ford also, came to Helsinki in the summer of 1975 to sign the Final Act. The event was, however, much more important for Brezhnev, whose high-profile welcome of the Final Act confirmed his good relations with western Europe – most particularly in Bonn. A photograph of Brezhnev signing the Helsinki accords appeared on the front page of *Pravda*, which also printed the entire text – an unintended gift to human rights activists in both the Soviet Union and the NSWP states. If, from 1973 onwards, the status wished upon the latter by Moscow during the Helsinki process was that of spectators rather that participants, so that Brezhnev's acceptance of the Final Act could simply be presented to them as a fait accompli (Alexander 1998: 16), events would soon show that they had a mind of their own (Davy 2009: 13,15). In 1971 in East Germany support from Moscow had helped replace the intransigent Walter Ulbricht with the much more accommodating Erich Honecker as First Secretary of the Communist Party, while in Poland the same could be said of Edward Gierek, who had succeeded Władisław Gomułka as First Secretary in 1971. János Kádár in Hungary and Gustáv Husák in Czechoslovakia consistently followed the dictates of Moscow (which was always their power base). In all these states relatively liberal economic policies brought unprecedented prosperity in the early 1970s, that is, in the years leading up to the Helsinki Final Act. But then, when the day came, what counted most at Helsinki was the signing of the Final Act by both Honecker (for East Germany) and Schmidt (for West Germany) (Kenez 1999: 236).

At this time Brezhnev was also strong domestically: his was the voice that counted in the Politburo, much more than that of former rivals such as Kosygin or Podgorny. There was little evidence of the pronounced deterioration in his health that was to become all too apparent before the end of the 1970s.[4] The short third stage at Helsinki presented to Brezhnev a supreme opportunity for grand-standing, and he made the most of it. If, thereafter, it was downhill almost all the way until his death in November 1982, what went wrong?

It is time then to look at what was actually agreed at Helsinki in August 1975. The substance of the Helsinki Final Act is to be found in 'four baskets':[5]

- Basket I: Questions relating to Security in Europe
- Basket II: Cooperation in the Field of Economics, of Science and Technology and of the Environment
- Basket III: Cooperation in Humanitarian and Other Fields
- Basket IV: Follow-up to the Conference.

For Brezhnev the most important part of the Act was Clause (a)(III) of Basket I headed 'Inviolability of Frontiers' which in his view confirmed the de facto frontiers agreed at Yalta and Potsdam in 1945. This, the essential precondition for the success of West Germany's Ostpolitik, opened the way for the NSWP states to enjoy normal political and economic relations with any other signatory state – and in particular West Germany. All this was spelt out at length in Basket II. For Brezhnev Clause (a)(VI) of Basket I, 'Non-intervention in internal affairs', would also prove to be important, if not in relation to 'terrorist . . . or . . . subversive activities directed towards the violent overthrow of the regime of another participating state' which prima facie was its main focus. Principle (a)(VII), 'Respect for human rights and fundamental freedoms, including the freedom of thought, conscience, religion or belief', would also have been critical for Brezhnev, even accepting that its main provisions were extended – and spelt out in much greater detail – in Basket III. It is worth noting, however, that the final paragraph of this clause commits the participating states to 'act in conformity . . . with the Universal Declaration of Human Rights', referring in the next sentence to the 'declarations and agreements in this field . . . by which they may be bound'. But what then does *may* signify, when the Soviet Union, together with Ukraine, Belarus, Poland and Czechoslovakia, were among the eight states that abstained from signing the Declaration when it was laid before the UN in 1948.[6] In practice, however, Moscow hardly questioned this provision in Basket I: after Helsinki human rights issues in the Soviet Union almost always turned on the application of Basket III, in which the first section 'Human Contacts' and the second 'Information' proved to be critical (Davy 2009: 13–15).

As to Human Contacts, paragraph (b), 'The Reunification of Families', and to a lesser extent, paragraph (h) 'Expansion of Contacts', contained the provisions that would prove to be the Achilles' heel of Soviet human rights policy. In particular, paragraph (b) was critical for one articulate, well-educated and well-organized class of citizens – the Jewish population of the Soviet Union. Jews shared three key attributes: first, more than any other Soviet citizens, they had family members resident outside the Soviet Union, with whom they sought to be reunited; second, Jews were disproportionately over-represented in the arts and higher education, science and technology; third, internationally, Jewish interests were defended – indeed actively promoted – by the state of Israel and the powerful Jewish lobby in the United States. There was one dominant reason for this policy: in both Israel and the US there were countless Jews not only ready to welcome members of their families resident in the Soviet Union, but also to use any means to win outside support.

The right to emigration, to the extent that it was even recognized by Soviet law, was subject to any number of hazards; even applying for the necessary visa was a step noted by the KGB, so that, for instance, future career prospects – always uncertain for Soviet Jews – could be impaired. None the less, Brezhnev approved a relatively accommodating stance to be adopted by the Soviet authorities, for as he had remarked to Kissinger at his Zavidovo dacha in May 1973, 'All those who want to can go . . . It's peripheral' (Hanhimäki 2004: 342). So Jews discovered that emigration was possible, if not for those, such as nuclear physicists like Sakharov – not himself a Jew – whose work made them a living repositories of state secrets (Gessen 2005: 356). Nixon's quiet diplomacy probably secured the greatest number of Jewish emigrants (Saltoun-Ebin 2012: 89) – so much so that in 1973 Sadat complained to Moscow about the threat to Egypt resulting from the corresponding increase in the population of Israel (Golan 1977: 45), with the Palestine National Council demanding, a year later, that Moscow end emigration to the occupied territories (Bourne 1997: 235).[7] Even with Carter (whom Brezhnev abhorred) in the White House 118,551 Soviet Jews were allowed to emigrate (ibid.: 390). By the end of Brezhnev's watch Jewish emigrants from the Soviet Union numbered some 300,000 (Kenez 1999: 231) – a far greater number than that of those allowed to emigrate before he came to power in 1964.

Notwithstanding the figures cited above, the world was not impressed by Brezhnev's human rights record in the years after 1975. This was largely the result of the consistent Soviet suppression of any spontaneous movement to enforce the human rights provisions in Basket III. Following the signing of the Helsinki Final Act it soon became clear that there would be no essential change in government human rights policy in any Warsaw Pact state, in spite of the obligation imposed by Basket IV '. . . to pay due regard to and implement the provisions of the Final Act', which would soon prove to be 'profoundly embarrassing' to Moscow (Davy 2009: 13). Spontaneous high-profile protest came almost immediately in Poland and Czechoslovakia, with significant intervention by the Catholic Church (Thomas 2001: 105), while in August 1975, in the Soviet Union, a group of dissidents asked the members of a visiting US Congressional delegation to help hold 'the Kremlin accountable for its commitments under the Final Act' (ibid.: 100). This led a group of prominent activists, headed by Yuri Orlov, a leading physicist, to establish an independent organization in Moscow to monitor compliance; on 12 May 1976 the formation of 'the Group to Assist the Implementation of the Helsinki Agreements in the USSR' – soon to become known as 'the Moscow Helsinki Group' – was announced (ibid.: 107). By this time Moscow was beginning to be concerned, so that, for instance, in December 1975 Brezhnev, referring to the Final Act in a speech made at an official Polish workers' congress, warned that 'it is important to see and understand the significance of this document as a whole, in all its parts, without succumbing to the temptation of pulling out separate pieces which some believe to be more convenient to themselves in tactical terms' (Maximov 1976). Brezhnev's intended meaning became all too clear when a leading physicist, Mikhail Kazachkov, was imprisoned for using the Final Act to justify an application for an emigration visa (Thomas 2001: 103). It was clear, as Ambassador Dobrynin had noted in Washington, that the Final Act was being adopted as 'the manifesto of the liberal and dissident movement' (Dobrynin 1995: 346). If the lines were being drawn for a battle which Brezhnev was destined to lose, how then did it proceed once the Moscow Helsinki Group became influential in a way totally beyond the imagination of the Soviet leadership?

Critically, with the US leading the way, support for the enforcement of both Basket I and Basket III became a formidable political and popular issues in the West – to the point that the hand of those fighting this cause in the Soviet bloc was greatly strengthened. As a result, the Soviet leadership was forced to engage in a contest subject to rules substantially different from those which governed the SALT negotiations. Where for Brezhnev Helsinki was the end-point of a political process (as evidenced by the official publicity), for many western leaders, such as notably US President Carter (who was elected in the year following Helsinki) it proved to be the beginning of a new approach to the Soviet bloc (as was to a degree inherent in the provisions of Basket IV). As this happened, *détente* – the key to Brezhnev's policy in dealing with the West – yielded to *human rights*, a field where his weakness was already apparent before the end of 1975. The fate of SALT II in 1979 can be seen as the 'last gasp of détente'. Carter reacted to Afghanistan in 1979 by 'dismantling the whole weakened edifice of the detente of the 1970s . . . a major turning in the Cold War itself' (Garthoff 2001: 336).

The story must now be told in greater detail. There are essentially two sides to it, one American and the other Russian. The American story begins with the local contacts made by, Millicent Fenwick, a junior member of the 1975 congressional delegation to the Soviet Union who was impressed by the trouble taken by refuseniks (introduced on page 113) to contact the American congressmen. After an unofficial meeting with Orlov she was persuaded that appropriate political action in America based on the Helsinki Final Act would help the human rights cause in the Soviet Union. Before Ms Fenwick left Moscow her raising of a number of particular cases with Brezhnev at a final press conference led him to describe her as 'obsessive'.

In this case Brezhnev got things right: on returning to Washington, Ms Fenwick, although only a first term Representative, initiated a process leading to the establishment of a Congressional Commission on Security and Cooperation in Europe, whose remit was to monitor compliance with the Final Act in the Soviet Union (Thomas 2001: 125). At first President Ford's administration, which had faced considerable criticism for its participation in the Helsinki process, was hostile to Ms Fenwick's initiative, but 1976 was a crucial election year, and as the months went by it was becoming clear that key categories of voters, such as members of Polish, Czech and Hungarian émigré organizations, were strongly in favour of the proposed commission. Critically they were joined by key Jewish organizations (ibid.: 128), while at the same the media took up the cause. In the Congress, where the Republican Party (to which Ms Fenwick belonged) was in a minority, Dante Fascell, the Democratic Chairman of the Foreign Affairs Committee, changing his original adverse stance produced a Bill that would establish the commission. President Ford, facing a strong challenge by Reagan for the Republican nomination for president, accepted the Bill, if only for reasons of political expediency: it became law on 3 June. By this time its proponents were helped by the fact that this prospect had already caused considerable distress to Brezhnev, whose report to the 25th Congress of the CPSU in February had noted how 'Certain quarters are inclined to emasculate and distort the very substance of the Final Act adopted at Helsinki, and to use this document as a screen for interfering in the internal affairs of the Socialist countries, for anti-Communist and anti-Soviet demagogy in cold war style' (Brezhnev 1979: 106). Substitute 'the US and its allies' for 'certain quarters', and 'justification' for 'a screen', and Brezhnev's observation was no more than the truth – accepting the tendentious use of the words 'emasculate and distort'. As for American politicians, and their European counterparts, it was just a matter of 'if the cap fits, wear it'. Three months after Brezhnev's *cri de coeur*, NATO reported a council meeting as follows: 'Ministers . . . emphasized the importance they attach to full implementation of all parts of the Helsinki Final Act by all signatories, so that its benefits may be felt not only in relations between states but also in the lives of individuals'.[8]

When it came to the run-up to the 1976 US Presidential election, while both candidates, Ford and Carter, were initially unenthusiastic about the Human Rights Commission, the position changed when, in a televised debate Ford apparently suggested that Eastern Europe was not subject to Soviet domination. This was immediately taken up by Carter, who, by criticizing Ford – for the first time – for failing to press for Soviet compliance with the human rights provisions of the Final Act, initiated a public controversy in which he came out on top. Carter's quick reaction could well have been decisive in traditional Republican areas, where voters preferred his commitment to human rights, above Ford's perceived commitment to détente.

In January 1977, Carter's inaugural address repeated his commitment to human rights. If this was just one of many policy commitments that a new president made in his inaugural, Carter, in this case, was soon overtaken by events. Before the end of the month the Czech government had cracked down on the signatories to Charter 77, a new human rights initiative just discovered by western media. Public criticism by the US State Department of this violation of the Final Act was seen as a landmark in the development of Carter's human rights policy (Thomas 2001: 136). A week later the State Department reacted in the same way to the arrest of the Soviet activist, Alexander Ginzburg, a member of the Moscow Helsinki Group.

On 21 January 1977, the day following the inauguration of the new US President, Jimmy Carter, in Washington, an American lawyer, Martin Garbus, called unexpectedly on Andrei Sakharov in Moscow. Noting the President's three references to human rights in a relatively short inaugural address, Garbus suggested to Sakharov that he write a letter to Carter, naming ten Soviet dissidents imprisoned for their stand on human rights. In a hurriedly written letter Sakharov, after actually naming sixteen, went on to insist – as he had already done publicly in Moscow – that Soviet authorities had no justification for blaming dissidents for a recent explosion that had claimed several lives on the Moscow metro on 8 January (Sakharov 1990: 464). What Sakharov had intended as a private message was then published in the *New York Times* on 29 January. Although Carter's own reaction to the letter was at first somewhat non-committal, he did send to Sakharov – via the US Moscow Embassy – a written reply affirming American commitment to human rights, and in particular 'the release of prisoners of conscience' (ibid.: 687).

Sakharov (as related in his *Memoirs*) continued to maintain a high profile in the cause of human rights, with his intervention in any number of specific cases attracting considerable publicity – particularly outside the Soviet Union. At the beginning of 1980 this had become too much for a Politburo already tied up by the Soviet failure to achieve a quick and decisive victory in Afghanistan; on 22 January Sakharov, on his way by car to a scientific seminar, was waylaid by KGB agents and brought to the office of the State Procurator. There he was confronted with an official decree depriving him of his title as Hero of Socialist Labour and all his state awards (Sakharov 1990: 511), at the same time banishing him to the city of Gorky – specially selected for being closed to foreigners. The original decree has been signed by Brezhnev, but for the General Secretary it was much too late in the day to undo the damage done by Sakharov – who had been active in the cause of human rights throughout almost all the sixteen years of Brezhnev's time as *vozhd*.[9]

With others such as Ginzburg and Orlov active in the field Sakharov was far from being the only high profile protagonist for human rights. One, above all, was to cause endless frustration at the highest levels of government: this was Anatoly Shcharansky, who, if not as eminent a scientist as Sakharov, was not only much younger but also Jewish. Notwithstanding the large number of Jews allowed to emigrate on Brezhnev's watch, Shcharansky was never going to be one of them: the level he had already reached in Soviet science meant that he had far too much to tell if ever he left the Soviet Union – to say nothing of the usefulness of his talents to the scientific establishment. In the spring of 1973 he applied for an exit visa, with the intention of emigrating to Israel (Sharansky 1988: xv). Although it was refused, in the summer of 1974 Shcharansky's fiancée, Natasha Stieglitz was granted a visa to allow her to join her brother, Misha, in Israel.[10] With the visa due to expire on 5 July, there was no time for a civil marriage, but on 4 July, a rabbi performed the appropriate religious ceremony in Shcharansky's Moscow apartment (ibid.: 85). Shcharansky, although a refusenik, hoped to follow within a few months; this was quite unrealistic, and it was only in February 1987 – after ten years in prison and more than four years after the death of Brezhnev – that he joined his wife in Israel, expelled from the Soviet Union, stripped of his citizenship and condemned as an American spy (ibid.: 403).

Shcharansky's imprisonment, which started in 1977, was almost inevitable given not only his active participation in the human rights movement, but also his many contacts in Moscow with western journalists.[11] After the Helsinki Final Act in 1975 Shcharansky, together with other refuseniks, became a founding member of the Moscow Helsinki Group joining such well-known dissidents as Orlov. Highly articulate and fluent in English, Shcharansky's every move was followed by the KGB; what is more his Israeli friends did everything to ensure that his message was not lost to the outside world. Like Sakharov he enjoyed the personal support of President Carter, who (as reported on page 101) in September 1977 took up his cause face-to-face with Soviet Foreign Minister Gromyko (Dobrynin 1995: 399). In his negotiations relating to SALT II, Cyrus Vance (Carter's Secretary of State), was already making clear to Moscow that the climate of détente was changing (Bourne 1997: 300).[12]

The success of the international human rights movement in the years following the Helsinki Final Act in 1975 must be judged in the light of the Soviet claim to the moral high ground, particularly in the non-aligned world. As revealed by the full story (as told in Chapter 10) this claim was based on the Soviet contribution to the independence achieved, often as a result of long and bitterly fought wars, by such countries as Vietnam, Ethiopia, Angola and Cuba, while at the same time the US could be represented as having worked hard – and successfully in countries such as Guatemala (1954), Indonesia (1965) and Chile (1973) – to block this process, and in doing so bring to power ruthless military dictators such as Jacobo Arbenz, Achmad Suharto and Augusto Pinochet. In advancing the interests of the state it served, the CIA could be portrayed as being just as extreme as the KGB in its disregard for human rights and national sovereignty.

Helsinki added a new dimension to this process. For Brezhnev, signing the Final Act in 1975, was the culmination to negotiations in which the Soviet Union had actively participated. Even though the Final Act was not 'a treaty or any other form of legal instrument' (Davy 2009: 4), as a critical stage on the way to securing a permanent international settlement of frontiers which had been recognized, de facto, for 30 years, it had considerable advantages both for the Soviet Union and the NSWP states – or so it seemed at the time (Schulzinger 2010: 381). The ghost of Adenauer was laid; the Hallstein doctrine would never be revived. Brezhnev had not foreseen how the Final Act would open the Soviet bloc to international pressure relating to law and order issues previously accepted as purely domestic. This was the card that Shcharansky played when claiming his right and that of other Jews in the Soviet Union to emigrate. More generally, the international movement to enforce Baskets I and III of the Final Act – by the encouragement it gave to Charter 77 in Czechoslovakia,[13] in Czechoslovakia, *Solidarność* in Poland, and Human Rights Watch committees in East Germany and the Soviet Union – reversed the moral defeat of the West, and discredited Soviet attempts to proclaim it. Given the climate in Washington in the late 1970s, the denial of human rights by Brezhnev – highlighted by the way men such as Shcharansky were treated in the Soviet Union – also proved to be a key factor in blocking progress towards continuing nuclear disarmament. It is no wonder then that Brezhnev could not stand Carter, a US President on record for stating that 'Human rights is the soul of our foreign policy' (Neier 2012: 152). By accepting the Final Act 'Brezhnev and his colleagues had inadvertently opened a breach in their own defences. Against all expectation it was to prove mortal' (Judt 2010: 503), for even without the force of law '. . . it was treated subsequently no less seriously than legally substantive agreements' (Haslam 2011: 268). If, in the early 1970s, the Soviet leaders had listened to Henry Kissinger (who saw little advantage for the US in the prospective CSCE conference), they would have realized that they had already got most of what they really needed from Willy Brandt in 1970 (Davy 2009: 3; Kemp-Welch 2010: 231).

Notes

1 This was recovered by the Soviet Union under the Molotov–Ribbentrop pact of August 1939, which provided for the division of Poland after the invasion by both Nazi Germany and the Soviet Union planned for September.
2 In German, Deutsche Demokratische Republik (DDR) and Bundesrepublik Deutschland (BRD).
3 Taking the crises in Czechoslovakia and Poland related in Chapter 8 to be internal events within the Soviet bloc, however great the concern of the West.
4 Lord Owen (personal communication). For Brezhnev's poor health record, going back as far an angina attack in 1956, see Haslam (2011: 299).
5 This is the common term, but the word does not occur in the actual text of the Act, for which the most convenient reference is [URL]http://www.hri.org/docs/Helsinki75.html[/URL].
6 The other three non-signatory states were Saudi Arabia, South Africa and Yugoslavia. Note also that at this stage Bulgaria, Hungary and Romania were not members of the UN.
7 The claim made by Libyan media in February 1974 that Moscow had allowed 2,486,000 Jews to emigrate to Israel was wildly exaggerated (Bourne 1997: 200).
8 North Atlantic Council, *Text of Final Communiques*, Volume 2, 45.
9 Sakharov himself was never committed explicitly to the refusenik cause (Dobrynin 1995: 158).
10 This was the name by which she was known in Russia: once in Israel she adopted a new name, Avital, which Shcharansky also used consistently. Once is Israel, some thirteen years later, Anatoly Shcharansky became Natan Sharansky.
11 Note how in the Final Act (Basket III (2. Information) (c) Improvement of Working Conditions for Journalists) requires the participating states to '. . . increase the opportunities for journalists . . . to communicate personally with their sources . . . enable journalists . . . to transmit completely, normally and rapidly . . . the results of their professional activity . . . for the purpose of publication . . .'
12 Gromyko (1989: 366) had already noted how President Ford preferred 'peace through strength' to 'détente' (which was Nixon's word).
13 Charter 77 was a 'virtual' organization, without rules for membership, subscriptions or administration, open to all those 'united by the will to strive, individually and collectively, for the respect of civic and human rights in our own country and throughout the world' (Schulzinger 2010: 233).

10 Brezhnev's blind spot: Africa and the Middle East

The Soviet Union discovers Africa

At the end of World War II, the world outside the Soviet Union, Europe and North America, as seen from Moscow, had changed little from before the war. This was a world of capitalist imperialism; vast continents were divided up into separate colonies by a small number of West European states: Belgium, Britain, France, Holland, Italy and Portugal. Government in each one of them was directed from the European capital cities, each with its own ministry for the colonies – which the British chose to call the 'Colonial Office', with the 'Colonial Secretary' at its head. This directed, in the field, as many separate administrations as there were colonies, with each one headed by a governor appointed by the Colonial Secretary, and supported by a local hierarchy of British expatriate colonial civil servants. France and the other lesser colonial powers maintained comparable structures, each reflecting suitably adapted metropolitan principles of government, which in some cases, such as France but never Britain, went so far as to provide for colonial constituencies to be represented in the national legislature. In 'Soviet-speak' the system depended on as many local expatriate *nomenklaturas* as there were colonies.

In the imperial exercise Britain was, by any measure, whether demographic, economic or political, much the most successful of the imperial powers, if only because – more often than not – it was first in the field. In the late nineteenth century Belgium, France, Germany and Italy established their colonies in sub-Saharan Africa in territories not claimed by Britain. Portugal was exceptional both for having started its African colonial adventure in the fifteenth century, and for retaining Angola and Mozambique, its two most important colonies, until the 1970s. Germany, defeated in World War I, was forced to abandon its colonial empire, which in Africa comprised the Cameroons, South West Africa, Tanganyika and Togoland. This was provided for in the Treaty of Versailles, but in the imperial climate of 1919 there was no question of these former colonies becoming independent self-governing states; instead they were effectively added, as 'protectorates' or 'mandated territories' to the colonial empires of the victorious allied powers.

Although the metropolitan powers each had their own guiding principal, whether it was *Pax Britannica* or *Mission Civilisatrice*, the underlying rationale of colonial expansion was always economic.

The industrial revolution, which by the end of the nineteenth century was largely complete in Europe, brought with it not only an unprecedented demand for raw materials, but also the means – steamships, railways and the electric telegraph – for exploiting natural resources in almost any location worldwide. This was not all: the new infrastructure developed for this purpose also made possible strong and effective colonial government directed, in the British case, from Whitehall, and carrying out policies made in Westminster. In extreme, but rare cases – such as the Ashanti and Zulu wars of the late nineteenth century – this could mean the deployment of the colonial military to deal with a local uprising. Because the combat was always unequal,[1] such insurrection was always put down, and *Pax Britannica* restored.

For Africa, above all, this could mean a European presence wherever there were valuable mineral resources or land and climate suitable for plantation agriculture. The question then is, what did this mean for local indigenous populations? The orthodox Marxist answer, which is what counted in Moscow throughout the whole 70-year history of the Soviet Union, was expropriation of their land and employment as unskilled labour, at starvation wages – in other words, the destruction of the local community.

This was at best no more than a half-truth. As often as not ground expropriated for mines and plantations had little intrinsic value for the local population, who at the same time welcomed the chance of earning wages and so becoming part of a cash economy – so much so that Africans often walked to destinations far from home for just this purpose.[2] Much more than land, the critical factor was the living conditions of indigenous labour, which could vary considerably between different colonies.[3] By the beginning of World War II, however, working conditions on mines and plantations reflected the fact that they operated, to some degree, in a free labour market. Inevitably, as local African economies developed, cities and their literate populations grew larger, radical political movements – with their base in Europe – began to make their impact, the more so, as a number of Africans acquired professional and academic qualifications in the metropolis. This meant, almost inevitably, coming into contact with radical political leaders. Once back in their own country, returning Africans could easily resent the privileged status of the colonial *nomenklatura*, coupled with their own lack of opportunity.

Before World War II, the impact of such discontent was limited, but even so a number of Africans who would be a force to be reckoned with after the war, were already contemplating independence. From British Africa, the names that would count most were Kwame Nkrumah (1909–1972) from Ghana and Jomo Kenyatta (c1890–1978) from Kenya, from French Africa, Léopold Senghor (1906–2001) from Sénégal, Sékou Touré from Guinea and Félix Houphouët-Boigny (1905–1997) from the Ivory Coast, and last but not least, Agostinho Neto (1922–1979) from Portuguese Angola. At one time or another all these spent time – either before or directly after World War II – mainly devoted to study or acquiring professional qualifications, in the capital city of the colonial empire of which they were unwilling subjects. Living in Europe meant an opportunity to meet radical politicians sympathetic to the then unpromising cause of colonial freedom.

Although these new acquaintances certainly included local communists, who declared themselves willing allies in the fight against imperialism, this does not mean that these young expatriate Africans became uncritical apologists for the Soviet Union. For one thing, Soviet diplomacy left them on one side: direct contacts with the Soviet Embassy in Paris and London were almost certain to be counterproductive. For Moscow, with no diplomatic presence in colonial Africa, and little in the way of economic involvement, prospects of sowing the seeds of proletarian revolution, anywhere in Africa, were negligible.[4] For Moscow, almost the whole continent, at least south of the Sahara, was terra incognita.

If, when it came to involvement in Africa, Moscow had no alternative but to bide its time, the same was true the other way round for putative African leaders, who might, when the time was ripe, find Soviet support useful in achieving their aims – a possibility that led to some unrest in European capitals in the post-war years. In London, at least up to the end of the 1940s, the principle of independence for British colonies was anathema to the Foreign Secretary, Ernest Bevin, even though the government he served did grant independence to India and Pakistan in 1948.

This intransigent position, which was also that of France, to say nothing of Portugal, could not withstand the tide of history. For one thing, European colonial empires were not popular in Washington,[5] and at a time when European recovery from the devastation of World War II depended on economic aid under the American Marshall Plan, this was a factor that could not be disregarded – so much so that it left the Netherlands with little choice but to grant independence, after more than 300 years, to its vast and profitable empire in the East Indies.[6]

While the need to meet the demands of the allied war economy meant that World War II had a palpable impact on parts of Africa remote from any battlefield, two parts of the continent were in the front line, North Africa and the Horn of Africa. Both would be critically important for post-war Soviet foreign policy in its attempt to subvert the colonial powers and extend the Soviet bloc. Even before the German invasion of the Soviet Union in 1941 made it an ally of Britain and the US, two key events in the summer of 1940 radically changed the politics of colonial Africa. The first was Italy's declaration of war on France and Germany on 10 June 1940; the second was the surrender of France, two weeks later, on 24 June, followed by the establishment of a new government, which, from its capital at Vichy, was entrusted by Germany with the government of a substantial part of Central and Southern France, including its whole Mediterranean coastline.

The consequences for Africa were far-reaching. Egypt, which since the nineteenth century had been subject to British military occupation, was central to British war strategy. Italy's declaration of war meant that Libya, adjacent to Egypt, would become a battlefield. The same was true of the Italian colonies of Eritrea and Somalia, together with Ethiopia, an ancient independent state conquered by Italy in 1936. The status of the French colonies was equivocal: while any sort of government from the metropolis was out of the question, the local French administrations were certainly not going to renounce their allegiance to Vichy. They had no alternative but to play a waiting game. While the same was true of the colonies comprising French West Africa, in August 1940 the colonies of French Equatorial Africa, led by the governor of Chad, Félix Eboué, declared their allegiance to the Free French government of Charles de Gaulle – a remarkable course of events given that Eboué was a native African (and the first ever to be appointed a colonial governor).

Although the Italian army, with strong German reinforcements from 1941 onwards, fought hard to defend the African colonies, the entry of the US into the war at the end of the year proved to be decisive in favour of the Western Allies. By May 1943, following the final surrender of the German army in Tunisia, the whole of Africa was under their control. By this time it was clear that Italy was a spent force, with defeat in Africa a critical first step in turning the tide of war against Germany.

All this had an unmistakable message for local African populations: quite simply, whoever claimed the right to govern Africa from some European capital had feet of clay. This was true even of the British, for the war in Africa, as seen from Cairo – always the centre of operations – was a close-run thing. Even if on a lesser scale, the same perspective held in Nairobi (Kenya), Khartoum (Sudan), Freetown (Sierra Leone), all colonial capitals, which – though far from any battleground – were essential to allied war strategy. For one thing, locally recruited African soldiers, fighting in the front line, witnessed how Europeans could be defeated in battle.

While the final defeat of Germany in May 1945, as seen from London and Paris, opened the door to the restoration of the pre-war colonial administrations in Africa, the war itself had worked a sea-change so fundamental that sooner or later this would prove to be impossible. For one thing, communications had been transformed: long distance air transport would soon transform towns such as Dakar (Sénégal), Kano (Nigeria), Léopoldville (Congo), Entebbe (Uganda) and Johannesburg (South Africa) into hubs in a worldwide network, helping, at the same time, a new cosmopolitan Africa to emerge.

In spite of the lack of vision of such men as Ernest Bevin, even before the end of the 1940s, it was becoming clear that colonial Africa could not be taken for granted. The British Colonial Development Corporation was established in 1948 to invest in projects designed to bring local economies – not only in the African empire – into worldwide markets. At the same time the means were found to allow much larger numbers of young Africans to obtain university degrees or professional qualifications in Britain. France, although following a parallel course, faced the need, in Algeria, Tunisia and Morocco, to accommodate very considerable entrenched European populations, who did not welcome the prospect of coming to terms with new indigenous academic or professional élites. (This was also true of South Africa, but with one critical distinction: South Africa had always been an independent state, even if a member of the British Commonwealth).

Until the early 1950s, the *leitmotiv* of African colonial policy, in both London and Paris, had been gradualism, if not restraint. The same was true in Brussels and Lisbon. In one place, however, this was impossible: the final defeat of Italian forces in the Horn of Africa in 1941, and in North Africa, in 1943, left an empty space on the colonial map of Africa that could not be filled by expedients similar to those adopted for the former German colonies in 1919. Ethiopia was straight-forward – or so it seemed: the defeat of Italy in 1941 opened the way for the Emperor Haile Selassie to return from exile and take over the government in Addis Abeba. By the end of the war he had come to be regarded as an important strategic ally of Britain and the US: from this advantageous position he laid claim to both Eritrea and Somalia. With strong US support – and at a time of mounting Soviet interest in Africa – Ethiopia was granted Eritrea, with little regard for the former colony's own desire for independence. By this time there was also a Soviet Embassy in Addis Abeba – the first ever, outside South Africa, in sub-Saharan Africa. This was critical for future involvement in Africa, because according to Soviet practice, an embassy, as the base for political relations was also the centre of intelligence operations, with the KGB having its own presence behind the mask of accredited diplomats. In a place like Addis Abeba, discovering their identity was a constant preoccupation both of western embassies and the national govern-ment. For the Soviet Union, intelligence and diplomatic operations in Ethiopia provided a useful trial run for potential operations in the rest of Africa, for which, from the perspective of the 1960s, there was every prospect – as would be con-firmed before the end of the decade. The long-term result – unforeseen by Brezhnev in 1964 – was that on his watch, the Cold War would be 'cold in Europe and hot in the periphery' (Mitchell 2010: 75).

The heat was first felt in Somalia, which, for historical reasons, was bound to be a problem. In 1897 the Emperor Menelik, with strong British support, incorporated the Ogaden, a vast ethnic Somali province, into Ethiopia. After World War II this ruled out all possibility of Somalia joining Eritrea, on any terms, as part of an extended Ethiopian empire. In 1945 it was not, however, ripe for independence, at least in the judgment of the UN. Instead, in 1949, the UN Trusteeship Council decided to appoint Italy as trustee for a period not exceeding ten years. In the event Somalia became independent on 31 July 1960, to join the former British colony of Somaliland, granted independence five days earlier, to form a new Somali Republic, which, following a popular referendum, adopted a new constitution on 20 July 1961. This was the position when Brezhnev, in October 1964 succeeded Khrushchev as *vozhd*. Little could he have known of what the future had in store for him in this remote corner of a continent in which he had seldom shown much interest.

By this time, however, much had been happening in the rest of colonial Africa, in a process, referred to by the British Prime Minister, Harold Macmillan, in 1960, as a 'wind of change'.[7] These words were rightly interpreted as a proclamation that under Macmillan the process of granting colonies independence would con-tinue. Although, before the 1960s, Ghana was the only British African colony that had reached this stage, in 1958 it was joined by a number of French colonies; of these all but Guinea chose to join a new French community of nations, with the advantage of substantial future investment. Guinea, under a maverick leader, Sékou Touré, chose for complete independence; having aligned itself with the Soviet Union it proved to be an unreliable ally – more trouble than it was worth, as would be the case with any number of former European overseas colonies. By this time Khrushchev had also come to see the decolonizing world as essentially transitional, with time on the side of the Soviet Union (Latham 2010: 264) – and Mao, in Beijing, thought the same way with respect to China (ibid.: 267). What is more, Soviet engagement with the Third World continued under Brezhnev along the lines laid down by Khrushchev (ibid.: 273).

For the future of Africa, one event, far outside the continent, would prove to be critical. This was Fidel Castro's successful revolution in Cuba in 1959, followed by an alliance with the Soviet Union not at all welcome to Washington. US policy, deliberately hostile to Castro's Cuba, led to the unsuccessful Bay of Pigs operation in 1961 and the Cuban Missile Crisis in 1962. Although the history, up to the resolution of the crisis, is related in Chapter 3, the decisive factor, for the future of Cuba, was that Castro would remain in power into the indefinite future – indeed his regime long outlived the Soviet Union. Castro made his allegiance clear in 1965 by founding the Cuban Communist Party, of which he would be the first secretary. Plainly his regime could only survive and prosper with substantial Soviet economic help. This meant that the Soviet Union would import Cuban sugar, and other commodities, at advantageous prices, which in turn would enable Castro to maintain a modern army equipped with state-of-the-art Soviet armaments. What is more, Castro – a convinced internationalist – was ready to deploy his forces outside Cuba in support of Soviet expansionist policy.

In the event, Castro's willingness to support the Soviet Union was to involve Cuba in armed conflict in Africa. There were two critical cases: Somalia in 1969 and Angola in 1975. Since both occurred on Brezhnev's watch, he must have approved the Soviet policy decision in favour of military intervention, even if he had not initiated it. In both cases, however, the policy was reactive rather than proactive; in other words it was formulated to take advantage of political developments, in Europe as well as Africa, favourable to the Soviet Union – at least as seen from Moscow.[8] In the event, Moscow, in both cases, was to get more than it bargained for.

On 15 October 1969 President Abdirashid Ali Shermarke of Somalia was shot dead by one of his own bodyguards. He had become, in 1961, Somalia's first Prime Minister, to succeed to the Presidency in 1967. A week after the assassination, Major-General Mohamed Siad Barre, commander-in-chief of the army, took over the government of Somalia in a bloodless *coup d'état*. As head of the new Supreme Revolutionary Council, he dissolved parliament, abolished the supreme court, suspended the constitution and renamed his country the Somali Democratic Republic. The name, correctly reflecting Siad Barre's commitment to orthodox 'socialist' principles, was an invitation to the Soviet Union to become involved in Somali politics. Somalis, however, had two goals not directly relevant to Soviet interests. The first was a strong commitment to Islam, the Arabic World and Africa – so that in 1974 Somalia joined the Arab League, while Siad Barre became chairman of the Organization of African Unity. Although such ties could be useful to Moscow, exploiting them would be a considerable challenge to Soviet diplomacy.

Siad Barre's second commitment was one that could only spell trouble to any ally of Somalia: it was to recover Ogaden, the province lost to Ethiopia in 1897. When, after seizing power in 1969, Siad Barre willingly accepted Soviet military aid, he always had in mind that Soviet armaments, if necessary, could one day be used in war against Ethiopia. In principle this could be a welcome prospect for Moscow, for Ethiopia, under the aged Emperor Haile Selassie, was a firm African ally of the US. In practice, it did not matter to Moscow either way who owned the vast sparsely populated desert of Ogaden, which was never going to be an area of any strategic importance.

So long as Haile Selassie was in power Siad Barre knew that US support would ensure that Ethiopian forces would defeat any invasion by Somalia. For the Soviet Union, on the other hand, unreformed imperial Ethiopia was a country ripe for revolution. In the early 1970s massive corruption, mounting inflation and widespread famine, led to massive discontent, not least among the rising middle classes in Addis Abeba. In 1974, a committee – known as the 'Derg' – of middle-ranking officers seized power in the name of 'socialism', deposed the Emperor and executed 59 members of his government, including two former prime ministers. By the end of 1975 the old emperor was dead, and Lieutenant Colonel Mengistu Haile Mariam, after eliminating two of his predecessors as chairman of the Derg, declared himself head of a new Marxist state. In December 1976 a military assistance agreement with the Soviet Union was signed in Moscow, and in April 1977 the agreement with the US was repudiated and the US military mission expelled. While all this was happening the vast estates of landlords and the Coptic Church were nationalized, and through 1977 and 1978 a purge known as the 'red terror' accounted for the torture, imprisonment and death of tens of thousands of suspected enemies of the Derg. Stalin could hardly have done better.

Mengistu was not destined to have an easy ride. Long before he seized power Ethiopia was threatened by the loss of Eritrea, where from 1972 onwards the well-armed and well-led Eritrean People's Liberation Front (EPLF), which consistently defeated government forces in battle, was effectively in control of much of the country. The fall of the imperial government did not lead to any change of heart in Eritrea. Mengistu, confronted by the Eritreans, determined to defeat them, and to achieve this end he relied not only on massive arms supply from the Soviet Union but also on a force of 20,000 men sent by Castro from Cuba. Although with such support he did succeed in recovering a substantial part of the territory lost to the EPLF, the campaign inevitably weakened his hold on the rest of Ethiopia. In the spring of 1977 Soviet President Podgorny, visiting the Horn of Africa accompanied by Fidel Castro, proposed federation between Ethiopia and Somalia (Hosmer and Wolfe 1982: 61). Siad Barre rejected this futile proposal, and instead, in July, ordered his forces to invade Ethiopia with the intent of recovering Ogaden. They were at first extremely successful; by September they had occupied some 90 per cent of the province. When, however, Mengistu, turning from Eritrea, deployed his 20,000 Cubans, supported by countless Soviet 'advisers', to fight Siad Barre, he recovered all the lost ground. Siad Barre, who had started by declaring his allegiance to the Soviet Union, now repudiated it (Haslam 2011: 314), at the same time ordering the departure of all 2,500 Soviet advisers in Somalia (Hosmer and Wolfe 1982: 61). This was the price that the Soviet Union had to pay for choosing to support Mengistu rather than his sworn enemy, Siad Barre.[9] The choice was pure *realpolitik*: Ethiopia was simply a much bigger prize than Somalia.[10] When Brezhnev died in 1982, Ethiopia still held Ogaden and Eritrea, but the latter would still be lost by the end of the 1980s. Taking the view most favourable to the Soviet Union, its involvement in the Horn of Africa from 1969 (when Siad Barre seized power in Somalia) until 1982 (when Brezhnev died) had achieved nothing beyond establishing a disastrous and bloodthirsty regime in Ethiopia, with little strategic advantage in relation to the rest of Africa.[11] The role of the Soviet Embassy in Addis Abeba went beyond just subverting Haile Selassie's empire. It was from the end of World War II a foothold exploited by the Soviet Union to establish a presence in Africa extending far beyond the frontiers of Ethiopia. The intelligence staff of the western embassies in Addis Abeba knew quite well what the Soviet Embassy was working to achieve, and consistently warned the Emperor – who always had close ties to Britain and the US – accordingly. By the 1970s this was not enough: there were simply too many others like Mengistu, ready to join him in overthrowing the regime they served, and when the time came the Soviet Embassy was able to provide essential support.

If, however, bringing down the imperial government must be reckoned a diplomatic and intelligence success for the Soviet Union, in the end much too high a price was paid for all that it had led to by the end of the 1970s. Just for two years of war between Ethiopia and Somalia, arming 75,000 Ethiopian soldiers and maintaining 20,000 Cubans and 1,500 Soviet advisers in the field on the other side of the world, to say nothing of the cost of 23 aircraft, 139 tanks, 108 armoured personnel carriers and 1,399 other vehicles lost in battle,[12] was never going to be a good investment, whatever the political gain. The cost of Soviet military involvement in Eritrea was on a comparable scale. At the same time, both Somalia and Eritrea could count on support from the Islamic world; the former had an ethnically uniform Muslim population and the latter a substantial Muslim component, particularly along the Red Sea coast. Above all, the events in the Horn of Africa in 1978–1979, revealed how the Soviet Union was not an ally to be trusted: supporting Ethiopia meant becoming Somalia's greatest enemy, when earlier it had been its greatest benefactor (Heikal 1978: 281). It must be recognized, however, that the Soviet Union's large-scale military operation in difficult African terrain was a logistical triumph, which even the US might have found difficult to equal (ibid.: 282); however that may be, it was still a pyrrhic victory.

The Horn of Africa was not the only scene of costly Soviet military involvement in Africa. In the mid-1970s, far from Ethiopia and south of the equator on the other side of the continent, the ancient Portuguese colonies of Angola and Mozambique became a much more extended battleground. While history, in relation to Soviet involvement, ran much the same course in both, the case of Angola is more instructive.

Unlike Ethiopia, Angola's contacts, mainly economic, with the outside world, were substantial, which explains why Portugal, having discovered it in 1482, never let it go.[13] Portugal, neutral in World War II, was only marginally involved in the process by which one European colony after another was granted independence in the 1960s. On the contrary, Portugal was intent not only on exploiting the considerable natural resources of the colony in its own interests, but also in settling large numbers of its own citizens there – a policy strongly supported by Angola's southern neighbour, South Africa, where the successive National Party governments represented only the interests of a minority white population numbered in millions. In the early 1970s, the Portuguese Prime Minister, Marcelo Caetano, and the South African Prime Minister, John Vorster, had much the same political outlook, particularly when it came to the suppression of communism at any price.

For Caetano, fear of communism, both in Portugal itself and its African colonies, was well-founded. The man he had most to fear was a charismatic African leader, Agostinho Neto (1922–1979), who, significantly, was born in rural Angola but died in Moscow. Allowed, because of his exceptional gifts, to study medicine in Portugal, once there he was soon involved in revolutionary activities. Arrest by the security police led to a seven-year prison sentence in 1951, but after being released in 1958 he was able first to complete his studies and then, a year later, to return to Angola. There he combined medical practice with being president of the Popular Movement for the Liberation of Angola (MPLA), which incorporated the Angolan Communist Party. He was plainly a man to be watched, both by the security police and by Moscow, where he was rightly regarded as a useful future ally. In spite of periods of exile and imprisonment imposed by the Portuguese government, Neto was still able to establish a high international profile, meeting Fidel Castro several times in Cuba, but failing, in Washington, to win the support of the Kennedy administration. At the same time he continued – even *in absentia* – to lead the MPLA in a guerrilla war against the Portuguese army in Angola. Time was plainly on his side.

From the end of the 1960s Caetano's government was paying an increasingly high price for retaining its hold on Angola. The war against the MPLA meant higher taxes, retarded economic development, a break on immigration and considerable resistance not only from conscript soldiers, but from their officers. Caetano, like General Franco in Spain, was not keeping up with the times. Throughout Portugal there was a strong sense that Caetano's days were numbered, while illegal political activity went unchecked. On 25 April 1974, a bloodless *coup d'état* staged by young officers, belonging to the self-styled 'Armed Forces Movement', led to the downfall of a regime that had been in power for more than 50 years, and opened the way to a new democratic government. At the same time an end was declared to the wars in Angola and Mozambique, which, together with a number of smaller colonies, were granted independence in 1975.

Politically everything was up for grabs, both in Portugal and its former African colonies. In Portugal, during the two years directly following the fall of Caetano, there was a prospect of a government formed by communists, but in the event, the first elections held under a new constitution in 1976 brought a centre-left socialist government under Mario Soares to office.[14] The Communist Party, although not suppressed, was never invited to join a coalition government. Portugal had become, and remains to this day, a western liberal democracy. For Brezhnev this must have counted as a missed opportunity, but then Angola would offer the Soviet Union a much better prospect.

With the MPLA declaring independence for Angola on 11 November 1975 – the same day as the Portuguese abandoned the capital, Luanda – Neto, in principle, became the first president of the new independent African republic. In practice the position was much more involved, with little prospect of resolution. The MPLA, although the most powerful and best organized of the forces fighting for independence, was not alone; it had to contest the right to govern with two other groups, the National Front for the Liberation of Angola (FNLA) and the National Union for the Total Independence of Angola (UNITA). Although Angola bordered on three other African states, South Africa, Zaire and Zambia, Neto and the MPLA could only count on the support of Zambia, the least powerful of them. While Zaire strongly supported FNLA, South Africa supported UNITA, whose leader, Jonas Savimbi (1934–2002) would do anything to bring about the downfall of the MPLA. This distribution of support also reflected the division of Angola into land under the military occupation, respectively, of FNLA, UNITA and MPLA. Critically for Neto, and the future of Angola as a communist state, the MPLA held the capital, Luanda, and a substantial part of the territory inland from the long Atlantic coastline and the border with South West Africa. (This also meant that a much greater part of the population was subject to Neto, who also commanded a much larger share of the economy.)

Critically for Neto, UNITA, led by Savimbi, occupied a vast inland area, also accessible to South Africa. This represented an extremely serious threat: that South Africa under Prime Minister John Vorster was implacably opposed to communism meant it would spare neither trouble nor expense in making life difficult for any communist state, such as Angola under Neto. For Vorster the communist threat was doubly dangerous, because of the presence of a strong African revolutionary movement, SWAPO, in South West Africa, the only South African province bordering Angola. After the loss of Angola to Portugal, this meant that Vorster had plans made to deploy units of the well-trained and well-armed South African army to help Savimbi in his fight against Neto. When the time came, in 1979 – following an incursion by MPLA forces into South West Africa – such support was more than welcome, even from a country whose all white government maintained strict apartheid.

Neto knew well that his regime equally could not survive without outside help on the same scale. There was only one possible source: the Soviet Union and its allies. Brezhnev, if his commitment to colonial liberation was to be credible in Africa, if not elsewhere, also had to support his side in the contest – which meant Neto and MPLA – regardless of cost. Escalation in what was essentially a proxy war between the US and the Soviet Union in Angola was a comparatively slow process, that was far from complete when Brezhnev died in 1982. Apart from Angolans on both sides, the forces confronting each other came on one side from Cuba (supporting MPLA) and on the other, South Africa (supporting UNITA).

Throughout the 1970s the US was inhibited from providing military aid to UNITA as the result of the 'Clark' amendment,[15] adopted by the US Congress in 1976, that prohibited US government support for private military operations abroad. Significantly, at the same time, Israel had long been supplying arms to FNLA through Zaire, and also training its soldiers.

As for the Soviet Union, Neto had refused to allow military bases to be set up in Angola, a policy that led to Soviet support for an unsuccessful *coup d'état*, led by Neto's Interior Minister, Nito Alves, after he had returned home from attending the 25th Congress of the CPSU in Moscow in February, 1977. Neto, like President Carter in Washington, was a dove, not a hawk. Even so, Neto had welcomed 25,000 Cuban troops sent to support MPLA in 1975, as part of a commitment entered into by Castro long before the 1970s. At the same time, Vorster, in South Africa, approved not only the secret provision of some $14 million worth of arms to FNLA and UNITA, but also raids on SWAPO bases in Angola by the South African Defence Force.

With the death of Neto in September 1979, the civil war escalated as a result of more aggressive policy on the part of his successor, José dos Santos. MPLA forces raided across the border with South West Africa on 31 October, and on 12 May 1980 South African forces invaded the southern Angolan province of Cunene. A month later South African intelligence tried to orchestrate a *coup d'état* to overthrow dos Santos. The coup failed, and back-fired on South Africa when three days later it was condemned by the UN Security Council, an outcome claimed by Moscow as a triumph of Soviet leadership in the cause of Third World liberation (Latham 2010: 277). As all this was going on new troops came from Cuba: inevitably the cost of providing their arms was borne by the Soviet Union, to reach $2,000,000,000 by 1984.

The cost to South Africa was at the same level, but 'it was the price that had to be paid to stop the expansion of Soviet influence in southern Africa' (de Klerk 1998: 59). This was important not only in South West Africa, but also for the future of white South Africa, where the illegal Communist Party was perceived to have a strong influence on the African National Congress (ibid.: 170). The Cuban presence in Angola justified holding up the grant of independence for South West Africa, the only cause that counted for SWAPO – which was always supported by MPLA. Significantly, when the last Cuban soldiers left Angola in 1989, South West Africa became the independent state of Namibia only a year later. Even so, with negotiations between South Africa and the UN Security Council going back to 1978, this was a long time to wait.

It is something of a paradox that both the Soviet Union and South Africa were able to make political capital out of the long drawn-out war in Angola – which lasted sporadically into the twenty-first century. The Soviet Union could claim that it was fighting for colonial freedom and against capitalist imperialism, South Africa, that it was fighting against international atheistic communism. Significantly both regimes collapsed in the 1990s, a process in which the vast costs of years of fighting in Angola certainly played a part. The costs to the people of Angola, whether they supported MPLA, FNLA or UNITA, were immeasurably higher. By the end of the war half a million civilians had lost their lives, more than four million – a third of the population – suffered internal displacement, 80 per cent lacked basic health care, 60 per cent had no access to fresh water, 30 per cent of all children died before the age of five, and general life expectancy was less than 40 years.

What part did Brezhnev play in all this? Two points must be made: first, the history related above only got under way when Brezhnev's poor health prevented him from being an effective leader; second, the worst in Angola only came after he died. But Angola was simmering even when Brezhnev took over from Khrushchev in 1964. After all it was the unacceptably high cost of controlling local insurgency in Portugal's African colonies that led the young officers in Lisbon to bring down Caetano's government in 1974. Seen from Moscow this was always a process that the Soviet Union could profit from, and so enhance its standing in the non-aligned world.

Israel and the Arab world

Until the end of World War II the Soviet Union had been only marginally involved in the Arab world. The reasons were both geographic and historical. As for geography, the Arab world – defined in terms of the language spoken by the majority of the indigenous population – divides into two parts: North Africa and the Middle East, with Egypt having a foot in both camps.

From the Atlantic to the Red Sea, Arab North Africa, extends some 5,000 km along the whole length of the southern shores of the Mediterranean, from the Straits of Gibraltar to the Suez Canal. In 1945 it comprised, first, three French colonies, Morocco, Algeria and Tunisia, administered from Paris mainly in the interest of substantial French populations descended from nineteenth century European settlers; second, Libya, which until World War II had been an Italian colony since 1912, and third, Egypt, under British military occupation since 1882 and with a long Red Sea coast. Whereas, for all these North African countries, the northern frontier was the Mediterranean coast, the southern frontier was a line, far inland, across the Sahara desert. Although there were ancient and well-trodden caravan routes across the Sahara, twentieth century North Africa was tied politically and economically to Europe and not to the lands south of the Sahara.

At the end of World War II, the Arab Middle East, extending, from the eastern Mediterranean to the Indian Ocean, comprised three small, but critically important states with Mediterranean coastlines, Syria, Lebanon and Palestine, and a much larger number with either a coastline on the Red Sea or one on the Persian Gulf; the Arabian peninsula, with its long Indian Ocean coastline, separated the two. The relation to the sea was much more complicated than in North Africa. Although a traveller overland along the coast from the Red Sea in Egypt to the Persian Gulf in Kuwait would have passed through every Arab state except Syria, Lebanon and Palestine, this roundabout journey was one seldom, if ever, undertaken in practice: in many places, local politics to say nothing of the topography, would have made it impossible. At almost every stage, desert comes down to the sea – even more than in North Africa. On the other side, however, of the Arab world of the Middle East, communications over land, to outside states, were critically important to it. There were only two such states directly adjacent to the Arab world: Turkey and Iran. The former, with a long coastline on both the Black Sea and the Mediterranean, was the gateway to Europe, while the latter, with a much shorter coastline on the Indian Ocean was the gateway to India; both were a gateway to Russia, with which they shared a common frontier.

Turning now to history, North Africa and the Middle East are once again separate cases, with Egypt, however, playing a key part in the history of both parts of the Arab world. At the beginning of World War II, in 1939, the position in North Africa – at least on the surface – had been more or less stable since the end of World War I in 1918. Although Egypt, under King Farouk, was nominally independent, the British military presence effectively ensured that its considerable strategic importance for the United Kingdom was not jeopardized. This was based on the Suez Canal, the 'life-line to India'. As noted at the beginning of this chapter the position changed radically in the early summer of 1941 with the fall of France and the entry of Italy into the war on the side of Germany. It was then clear to London that Egypt must be held on to, so that large numbers of troops, many from India, were sent to secure it at any cost in the war against Germany and Italy. On the other side it was clear to both Berlin and Rome that Egypt was a prize worth capturing at an equally high price. This objective was never realized, although in 1941 it was a close-run thing. With the entry of the US into the war as a British ally, the combined German and Italian forces in North Africa were finally defeated in April 1943. With France liberated in 1944, Paris once again took over in Morocco, Algeria and Tunisia, and remained – if somewhat precariously – in control until the early 1960s.

Given Italy's history in the war, there was no question of its regaining Libya. Instead, with a modest British military presence to help maintain law and order, it became an independent state, with at its head a king, Idris I, chosen from a leading desert tribe – for the British a typical African colonial solution for a local political problem.[16]

Egypt in the post World War II world was a much bigger problem. For the British a corrupt, inefficient and unpopular government, with King Farouk as head of state, was the best game in town. Britain's main priority was to ensure that its economic interests were not impaired: of these the Suez Canal, owned jointly with the French, was much the most valuable, for strategic as much as for commercial reasons. Significantly, the Soviet Union had opened a Legation in Cairo in 1943, its first ever in Africa. Although a Soviet finger in the African pie was hardly welcome to the British, the implicit threat was one that could be contained so long as the immediate post-war status quo continued.

In the 37 years (1918–1945) leading up to the final defeat of Germany after two world wars, two developments were to change, radically, the politics of the Middle East, and that in a way that would have considerable repercussions for the Soviet Union (as much as for the rest of the world) throughout Brezhnev's 18 years (1964–1982) as *vozhd*. The first of these was the discovery and exploitation, in the course of the years leading up to World War II, of what would prove to be the world's richest oilfields. The way opened in 1906 with the discovery of oil in Iran. Here, Whitehall almost at the eleventh hour, decided to support the British company set up to exploit the country's oil resources. If, the decision – born out of concern that otherwise Russia might step in – was political rather than economic, the economic benefits that followed in the course of time were vast: Iran proved to be a leading world-producer of oil, as it is to this day.

Iran was only the beginning of big oil in the Middle East. Equally important oilfields were found in Iraq in 1927, Bahrain in 1932, Kuwait and Saudi Arabia in 1938. The main actors were British, French and American; Soviet Russia, with considerable oil resources of its own, was neither able nor particularly concerned to be involved. For the time being it was sufficient for its embassies in Turkey and Iran to hold a watching brief; until 1944, when Soviet legations opened in Beirut, Damascus and Baghdad, there was no other Soviet diplomatic presence in the Middle East. There the diplomats were well-placed to observe the final stages of a process whereby Britain and France, in the years after World War I (and the defeat of the Turkish empire, which had been allied to Germany), had orchestrated the emergence, in Turkey's former Arab provinces, of independent states that could be relied upon to safeguard the oilfields in the interests of foreign investors. As in Libya after 1945, this process involved setting up kingdoms, sultanates and emirates, with hereditary heads of state chosen from dominant local tribes. If, in 1945, this meant the Turkey was the only secular republican state in the Middle East, the way in which this example was followed in a number of critical cases, Syria, Iraq and Iran, is an important part of the history of the region. It is not one, however, in which the Soviet Union had much influence.

The second radical development in the Middle East in the interwar years, 1918–1939, was the arrival of tens of thousands of European Jews in Palestine with the intent of finding a permanent new home there. This immigration, which went back to the nineteenth century, was inspired by the cause of Zionism, whose objective was to re-establish a Jewish state, with its capital at Jerusalem, such as had existed in biblical times. By this time the historical evidence contained in the bible – both supported and contradicted by archaeological research – was hardly sufficient to determine the actual frontiers of King David's Kingdom. Up until the beginning of World War I in 1914, this hardly mattered: Palestine was a remote province of the Turkish empire, with little sense of national identity (Wheatcroft 2012) and if a relatively small number of European Jews chose to settle there on land bought, at a good price, from local Arab landlords, this could only be a benefit to the local economy not unwelcome to the Turkish administration.

In any case Palestine had been lost to the Jews for thousands of years: indeed, following the final defeat of Christian Europe in the third crusade in 1192 (Sebag-Montefiore 2011: 263), the rulers of Palestine, whoever they might be, professed Islam, for which Jerusalem was one of the three holiest cities (ibid.: 170). None the less, some Christians remained, with the Church of the Holy Sepulchre as the centre of their religious life. This was extraordinarily embittered and complex, since different branches of Christianity, Catholic, Orthodox, Armenian, Coptic – to name the most important – each had their own rights in the church, with the actual legal guardian not a Christian at all, but an official of the local Turkish administration. The strong Orthodox presence meant that Imperial Russia had a stake in Jerusalem – so much so that in the mid-nineteenth century a dispute about rights in the Church of Holy Sepulchre led to war with France and Britain, whose concern was to defend western Catholic interests. The war was fought in the Russian Crimea, not in Palestine. Turkey, which had lost all its lands along the north coast of the Black Sea to Russia in the eighteenth century, joined as an ally of the western powers, to see Russia defeated after two years of combat. What is significant in the background to the Crimean War is that the eighteenth century expansion of Imperial Russia – already described in Chapter 1 – came at the cost of local Muslim populations, not only in Europe but in Asia. If, then, in the twentieth century, any European country counted, historically, as inimical to Islam, this was Imperial Russia (Gromyko 1989: 299). Even so, in the years before World War I, Russian pilgrims to Jerusalem out-numbered those of any other nation. The Soviet Union, at least until the end of the 1940s, was little concerned to change the historical record, and indeed within its own frontiers consistently treated Muslim minority populations as troublesome – as indeed they often were, and, for that matter, still are. Of these populations none, however, were Arabic-speaking.

After World War I everything changed following the defeat of Turkey. All the Arabic-speaking provinces were lost, with their future entrusted to France and Britain according to a treaty agreed between the two allies in 1916.[17] The most important result was that France became responsible for Syria and Lebanon, and Britain for Iraq and Palestine, with Jerusalem internationalized under France, Britain and Russia. In 1917, just at the time that the October revolution brought Lenin and the Bolsheviks to power in Russia, a letter from the British Foreign Secretary, Arthur Balfour, to Lord Rothschild (whose family had financed much of immigration of western Jews to Palestine before the war) declared that the British government viewed 'with favour the establishment in Palestine of a national home for the Jewish people . . . it being clearly understood that nothing shall be done which may prejudice the civil and religious rights of existing non-Jewish populations' (quoted Sebag-Montefiore 2011: 415). Although Balfour's own motives were largely idealistic, his declaration, politically, was a response to pressure from western Jewish communities – and more particular, that in the United States. The actual timing was chosen, somewhat precipitously, to open the doors to Russian Jews escaping from the Bolsheviks. At the same time the fall of Imperial Russia put an end to any prospect of the new Soviet state being involved in the government of Jerusalem.

In the interwar years the results of the Balfour declaration became, in increasing measure, disastrous for the British administration of Palestine. In the 1930s Jewish immigration increased very substantially as the result of persecution in Nazi Germany. With escalating Arab resentment – by no means confined to Palestine – at the presence of the new immigrants the British government tried hard to reduce their numbers. Even so tens of thousands arrived every year, while at the same time the rapidly expanding oil resources of the Arab Middle East made it essential for the British not to antagonize the local Arab populations. Needless to say, the level of Arab resentment was highest in Palestine itself, leading all too often to violence directed against both the British and Jews (ibid.: 438). The latter in turn mobilized their own militia, the Haganah, to fight back.[18]

World War II put a brake on the escalation of conflict in Palestine. After the German annexation of Austria in 1938, its occupation of Czechoslovakia and Poland in 1939, and of France – together with Belgium, Holland, Denmark and Norway – in 1940, the road to Palestine was closed to their Jewish populations; instead, the great majority (as related in Chapter 3) were to be victims of the holocaust, as were also hundreds of their brethren in the parts of the Soviet Union overrun by the Germans in 1941–1943. For those already settled in Palestine, the defeat of Germany became a cause more important than ending the British mandate. Although among Palestinian Arabs there was some support for Germany, the much strengthened British military presence made it ineffective.

For both Arabs and Jews in Palestine, the end of World War II in 1945 brought an end to any restraint on the use of violence for political ends on both sides of the line. The death of millions of Jews in the holocaust provided for those who survived an unanswerable case for establishing not just a Jewish home in Palestine, but an independent Jewish state capable of defending itself against any adversary. By the end of the 1940s this goal had been reached with the establishment of the state of Israel in the face of massive and violent resistance not only by Palestinian Arabs, but by Arabs throughout the Middle East.

For the Jews in Palestine the first step was to establish de facto control over an area sufficient to form the basis of the new state: demographic factors, as they had evolved in the process of Jewish settlement before 1939, defined, in broad terms, what this area would be. The Jewish position was then strengthened by new immigration by holocaust survivors, who were among the millions of displaced persons who found a temporary home, after 1945, in parts of Europe liberated – mainly by Soviet forces – from German occupation. In countries such as Poland, Hungary and Romania, returning holocaust survivors were far from welcome among populations that had also suffered the horrors of German occupation. For any number of such survivors a Jewish home in Palestine offered a much better future. What is more, with outside support, mainly from the United States, more than sufficient to pay for their transport to the promised land, ships were found to bring them to ports, such as Haifa, in Jewish Palestine. To the British this new scenario brought nothing but trouble: every Jew arriving in Palestine increased local Arab armed resistance, and support for it throughout the Arabic world. On the other hand the British policy of denying entrance to Jewish immigrants only increased the level of violence orchestrated by militant settlers, such as those who belonged to Haganah, or the smaller, but much more extreme Irgun Zvai Leumi;[19] with their policy inevitably failing to stem the flood of new immigration, the British lost both ways.

The only way out was to transfer the whole Palestine issue to the United Nations. This step, taken by London in February 1947, immediately gave the Soviet Union a voice in the future of Palestine (Rucker 2011: 16). On 14 May it was heard in the United Nations, with the Soviet delegate, Andrei Gromyko, as the spokesman. In his own words: 'Past experience . . . shows that no Western European state was able to provide adequate assistance for the Jewish people in defending its rights and its very existence from the violence of the Hitlerites . . . [This] explains the aspirations of the Jews to establish their own state. It would be unjust . . . to deny the right of the Jewish people to realize this aspiration' (ibid.: 17). With a democratic Arab–Jewish state unacceptable to both sides, this could only mean the partition of Palestine. To Zionist leaders it was an incredible opportunity, so long as the Soviet Union stood by them (ibid.: 18). On 29 November it was one of the 33 UN member states to vote in favour of the General Assembly Resolution 181 providing for partition and the creation of both a Jewish and an Arab state (ibid.: 20). With only 13 states voting against, and ten abstentions, this was sufficient for the required two thirds majority. It was also a remarkable instance of the United States voting the same way as the Soviet bloc. At this stage also, Israeli politicians willingly expressed their gratitude to the Soviet Union, for all it did to save Jews from the holocaust (Gromyko 1989: 354). The question is, what lay behind all this.

The answer is that supporting the Jewish cause brought the Soviet Union two short-term advantages: first there would be no restraint on European Jews, unwelcome in their own countries, emigrating to an independent Jewish state – something for which Poland, whose goodwill was important to the Soviet Union, would be extremely grateful (Gromyko 1989: 12); second, the emergence of an independent Jewish state in Palestine, would be a critical strategic setback to the British empire (which explains the British abstention in the UN voting), while at the same time sowing discord between London and Washington (Heikal 1978: 49). At this stage the destabilization of the Arab world was also welcome to the Soviet Union – with the prospect of fishing in troubled waters.

Following UN Resolution 181 the state of Israel was proclaimed on 14 May 1948; this opened the door to more than 300,000 European Jews, a number greater than that of the immigrants who had already entered illegally in the previous three years. With the Arab population of Palestine fighting hard, but unsuccessfully, to push back the frontiers of the new state, these new immigrants soon played a crucial role in defending it – so much so that when peace finally came in 1949 Israel had successfully incorporated valuable additional land. One result of this was that its residual Arab population also increased, to become, at the end of the day, Israeli citizens, with their own party in parliament. The status of those outside Israel (of whom many were refugees who had fled their homes in the war) was resolved in 1950, with Arab Palestine being incorporated into the Jordan – a kingdom firmly allied to Britain and the US (as it remains to the present day).

If, in all this, the Soviet Union played no more than a marginal role, by 1950 its support of Israel was steadily deteriorating. For this Stalin was largely responsible. For one thing, while he had encouraged states within the Soviet orbit to allow their Jewish citizens – such as they were after the holocaust – to emigrate to Israel, he refused categorically to allow Soviet Jews this right. This was critical, since the majority, with their homes in territory never overrun by the Germans, had avoided the holocaust. They therefore, as part of the European Jewish population, counted for much more than they had before World War II. What is more, their desire to emigrate to Israel never flagged, as Brezhnev knew only too well after he became *vozhd* in 1964. What this meant for Soviet politics, both domestic and international, is a story told in Chapter 6. As for Stalin, his paranoia regarding the role played by Jews, both in Soviet politics and as doctors in his own domestic circle, hardly helped Soviet relations with Israel (ibid.: 55).

On 23 July 1952 the Arab world changed radically when a group of young middle-ranking officers staged a coup that toppled the government of Egypt under King Farouk. Their leader was Gamal Nasser, but their spokesman, who broke the news to the world was Anwar Sadat, whose radio announcement told how the traitors who commanded the army had been arrested, while the army, under the new command would operate 'in the national interest under the constitution' (Cook 2012: 11). It was also determined to see the last of the British in Egypt (ibid.: 39). Although Nasser died in 1970, the government he established remained in power until 2011, when it fell in face of popular demonstrations in Cairo's Tahrir Square – and many other places in Egypt. After 1952, the Soviet Union saw an unprecedented opportunity for involvement in the Arab world, however displeasing this might be to Israel, which by this time had been brought firmly into the American camp by one of its best friends, US President Harry Truman. Given the way Egyptian forces had been engaged against Israel in the late 1940s, there was – seen from Moscow – every reason for an alliance between the new revolutionary government and the Soviet Union. Initially Soviet support for Israel in the UN in 1947 meant that Nasser was identified by Moscow as being opposed to Soviet interests (Heikal 1978: 53), the more so given the way he was ready, on occasion, to try individual Egyptian Communists for political offences (ibid.: 63).[20] When the tide changed, Dimitry Shepilov, the Soviet representative in Cairo, was instructed to assure Nasser that Soviet policy would not involve local communists; at the same time the Legation in Cairo was upgraded to Embassy (ibid.: 60).

Moscow's real chance in Egypt came in 1956 as a result of Nasser's ambition to build a high dam across the Nile at Aswan, both for generating electricity and controlling irrigation on an unprecedented scale. This project would be impossible without foreign finance, and for this Nasser turned first to the US, to be favourably received by Dulles, President Eisenhower's Secretary of State (Heikal 1978: 64), having assured him that there was no prospect of Egypt suffering the fate of eastern Europe and being incorporated into the Soviet bloc. Even so, two acts by Nasser forfeited such trust as he had built up with Dulles; the first was a large armaments purchase agreed with Czechoslovakia in August 1955 (Little 2010: 307), and the second, diplomatic recognition of Communist China in July 1956 (Cook 2012: 69).

On 19 July 1956 Nasser was informed that the US would not finance the Aswan high dam (Heikal 1978: 67). In June, however, the Soviet Union had offered a loan of $1,120,000,000 at 2 per cent, which Nasser, following the American refusal, was now eager to accept. To meet the prospective financial commitment to the Soviet Union, he went on to proclaim the nationalization of the Suez Canal on 26 July (ibid.: 64), a plan almost immediately supported by Soviet Ambassador Shepilov. Israel, convinced by Britain and France, the owners of the canal, that this meant renewed conflict with Egypt, itself took the initiative with a preemptive strike on 29 October (Cook 2012: 69). A week later, Britain and France, intervening as 'peacemakers', sent their own forces to occupy the banks of the canal in face of considerable resistance by the Egyptian Army. Moscow, anxious about being too deeply involved, refused military support, but the whole question became academic after Britain and France, under strong American pressure, halted their operation (Cook 2012: 71). The result was peace on the condition of total withdrawal of the British and French forces, and – to satisfy Israel – demilitarization of the east bank of the canal and the whole Sinai peninsula under supervision of a new ten-country UN Emergency Force (UNEF) (Little 2010: 310; Cook 2012: 70). The fighting along the canal had left it blocked by sunken shipping, but it was cleared within a year, leaving Egypt with what Nasser wanted, ownership of the canal. Moscow lost little time in profiting from the turn of events. Nasser, invited to Moscow as principal foreign guest at the annual celebration of the October Revolution (Heikal 1978: 73), was offered, as a gift, Soviet military aircraft to replace those lost by Egypt at Suez, and the replacement of the other arms lost at half price. More was to come: not only Soviet finance, but technical and material support, would be provided for the construction of the high dam. This was all due to Khrushchev, acting on impulse, and against the advice given by Molotov, his Foreign Secretary, not to engage in 'adventurism' in the nonaligned world. Khrushchev, however, insisted that the Soviet Union 'must aid national liberation movements' (ibid.: 91). This was critical for providing the *leitmotiv* of Soviet foreign policy, up to and even beyond the end (in 1982) of Brezhnev's days as *vozhd*. The first part of this chapter tells of the price paid by Africa south of the Sahara, and derivatively by Cuba. But what happened in 1956 was only the beginning of the story of what happened in Egypt, and much of the rest of the Middle East, on Brezhnev's watch.

Inevitably the new dam became a Soviet flagship project: with the funding agreement signed in 1958, construction started on 9 January 1960, with the first stage – which allowed the reservoir to start filling – completed in May 1964. This, the greatest engineering project in twentieth century Africa, provided the occasion for massive popular celebration at the dam site, with Khrushchev – already welcomed by jubilant crowds in Cairo (Heikal 1978: 135) – as the star guest. At Aswan he was joined by the heads of Arab states, such as Algeria, Iraq and Yemen, favourable to Nasser's Egypt. Following the public ceremony they all joined Nasser on his official yacht, *Hurriyeh*, for a cruise on the Red Sea. Khrushchev, the last to arrive, was greeted by the Arab leaders: when it was the turn of President Aref of Iraq, Khrushchev refused a hand '. . . stained with the blood of communists' (ibid.: 21). True enough, a number of Iraqi Communists conspiring, with others, to overthrow Aref, had been executed; this, he insisted, was not a move directed against the Soviet Union. Even so, the incident was only part of a long process by which Soviet power and influence throughout the Arab world steadily declined, to the point that when Brezhnev died in 1982 the Egyptian government was firmly in the American camp – so much so that when the turbines at Aswan, installed by Soviet engineers in the 1960s, were due for replacement in 1983, the US Ambassador, Nicholas Veliotes, easily ensured that the order went to the US (Cook 2012: 215).

What then had happened during the 18 years of Brezhnev's watch? The answer is that Egypt was twice at war with Israel. The first occasion was the Six-Day War from 5 to 11 June 1967, which started with Israel attacking not only Egypt, but its two Arab allies, Syria and Jordan. This followed considerable provocation by Nasser, who, ever since the Suez crisis of 1956, had resented the presence of the UNEF in Sinai, to the exclusion of Egyptian forces. Reports of Israeli attempts to establish settlements in Sinai confirmed Nasser in his view that the UNEF supported Israel. In the end, Nasser, having insisted on its departure, sent Egyptian forces to take its place (Cook 2012: 97). With Israel seeing this as a *casus belli*, King Hussein of Jordan, concerned about Arab solidarity, went to Cairo to seal his support for Egypt and Syria in the event of war with Israel (ibid.: 98). Nasser – relying on misleading Soviet intelligence (Kissinger 1982: 197) – then raised the tension by closing the Straits of Tiran, so that shipping could no longer reach Eilat, Israel's only Red Sea port. Israel reacted by invading Egypt, Syria and Jordan, to defeat all three in the so-called 'Six-Day War'. Victorious Israeli forces went on to occupy Syria's Golan Heights,[21] Gaza and the whole Sinai peninsula, and all Jordan west of the River Jordan – the so-called 'West Bank' (Little 2010: 315).

Even before the Six-Day War, there were signs that Egypt was turning its back to the Soviet Union; on 26 April 1965, in the first year of Brezhnev's watch, the small Egyptian Communist Party dissolved itself, at the same time directing its members join Nasser's own party, the Arab Socialist Union (Heikal 1978: 140). Then, the fourth Conference of Non-Aligned States was also planned for 1965,[22] to take place in Algiers, in March. The Soviet Union decided to attend with a high-level delegation including Brezhnev, Kosygin and Podgorny – the triumvirate that had toppled Khrushchev the previous year. With the Soviet presence strongly opposed by Zhou Enlai, (who had represented China at the three preceding conferences), Asian and African states were forced to choose between the two. With the conference postponed indefinitely on the advice of Nasser and India's Prime Minister Nehru, it was clear to Moscow that it did not have Egypt on its side. To rectify the position, Nasser, was invited to Moscow, where the same triumvirate met him at the airport, and escorted him to the Kremlin through streets lined with cheering crowds (ibid.143). Nasser, basking in a climate of approval after three days of top level Soviet hospitality, asked Brezhnev to cancel a debt of $500,000,000 owed by Egypt for arms purchased from the Soviet Union. His request was granted, and the path to war with Israel was clear. When the war came, with the disastrous results for Egypt related on page 180, Nasser once more turned to the Soviet Union to help make good the losses suffered in arms and equipment, and he was again rescued by Brezhnev (Cook 2012: 108). There was, however, still no sign of peace being agreed, and Nasser, with his own country decisively weakened by defeat in war, saw no alternative but to leave the Soviet

Union to negotiate on behalf of Egypt – not so much with Israel,[23] but with the United States (Heikal 1978: 191). But in the climate of détente this meant that Moscow, represented by Soviet Foreign Minister Gromyko, took much the same position as Washington, that nothing would be achieved without direct negotiations between the Arab states and Israel (ibid.: 195). To Nasser and other key Arab leaders this was out of the question. The only way forward was to rebuild Egyptian forces with the new arms supplied from the Soviet Union, so that sooner or later, war would be resumed and Israel defeated –no matter how much this policy was disapproved of by Moscow. Here Nasser could claim that the UN was on his side, for on 22 November 1967, Security Council Resolution 242 called for the 'withdrawal of Israel's armed forces from territories occupied in the recent conflict [and] the termination of all claims or states of belligerency and respect for and acknowledgement of the sovereignty, territorial integrity and political independence of every State in the area'.[24] To this day nothing positive has ever come from Resolution 242; implementation was always a lost cause, if only because Israel – even before the end of 1967 – allowed its citizens to establish new settlements in all the territories (including the eastern part of Jerusalem) occupied in the course of the Six-Day War.

On 28 September 1970 Nasser died. His successor, Anwar Sadat, taking office only ten days later, promised to follow his path, safeguard fully the rights of the Palestinian people, work toward Arab unity, continue the struggle against Israel, international Zionism and world imperialism, while at the same time affirming Egypt's policy of non-alignment (Cook 2012: 118). Leaving aside the rhetoric, Egypt, as left to Sadat by Nasser, was deeply committed to the Soviet Union, which, together with 20,000 military advisers, had the use of two ports and six airbases (Golan 1977: 6). This, effectively, was the price Egypt paid for defeat in the Six-Day War. To Moscow all this was a considerable hostage to fortune, quite apart from the costs involved. As Sadat, once firmly established as Nasser's successor, clearly set his sights on renewed conflict with Israel, the stakes became even higher for the Soviet Union. In the late 1960s the Soviet military build-up in Egypt was justified as a response to increased US military involvement in the Indian Ocean, as could be seen from the deployment of US Navy submarines equipped to launch Polaris and Poseidon nuclear missiles. By the early 1970s, Brezhnev saw that this could well be counterproductive: with the Suez Canal still blocked after the Six-Day War, a strong naval presence in the Mediterranean was little help in counteracting the US Navy presence in the Indian Ocean, while at the same time, the military presence in Egypt only made sense if its purpose was to support Egyptian forces being trained for renewed war with Israel. As seen from Cairo, the Nixon–Brezhnev summit in Moscow in May 1972 was a clear sign that Moscow was not intent on military action in the Middle East (Eban 1977: 480); on the contrary Soviet interests would best be served by a resolution of the conflict between Egypt and Israel (Golan 1977: 19,66). By this time, also, Sadat complained constantly about the lag in Soviet arms supply (Kissinger 1982: 204). In early July 1972 Brezhnev made clear his opposition to a military solution in the Middle East, and on 18 July Sadat ordered the Soviet advisers to depart within ten days (Little 2010: 319). There then followed a joint statement, agreed in Moscow by Brezhnev and the Egyptian Prime Minister, Aziz Sedki: 'Arab states have every reason to use all the means at their disposal for the liberation of Arab territories seized by Israel in 1967 and ensuring the legitimate rights of Arab countries and peoples, including the Arab people of Palestine' (Tass 14 July 1972; see also Kissinger 1982: 209). As for renewed hostilities with Israel, Sadat was on his own, which given the lack of Soviet cooperation, was the best place to be. Moreover, it opened the way to 'diplomatic overtures to the United States', leaving the Soviet leaders 'at a loss as to how to recapture their waning influence' (Kissinger 1982: 205). Sadat had already decided on a second war with Israel in the summer of 1972; his intent was to break out of the stalemate that followed Israel's decisive victory in the Six-Day War. His plan was to orchestrate a joint Egyptian–Syrian attack on Israel. With the armed forces of both countries strengthened by modern Soviet armaments (Golan 1977: 57), and their soldiers much better trained, there was even a good chance of victory, which would have solved all Egypt's problems. And if Golda Meir, Israel's Prime Minister was right in her conviction that Israel was 'militarily impregnable' (Kissinger 1982: 221), Egypt, even if defeated a second time, would be in a position to force the negotiation of a new peace-settlement (ibid.: 98). Given the status quo, as established after the Six-Day War, Egypt, with little further to lose, could only profit from such a scenario. To do so, however, the support of the US was essential, while that of the Soviet Union could only be counterproductive. The reason was simple: nothing could be achieved without Israeli consent, and here, while the US had considerable leverage, the Soviet Union had none.

Golda Meir and Anwar Sadat were both proved right. With a coordinated attack on Israel by both Egypt and Syria, the war opened on 6 October 1973. Since this was the Day of Atonement, Yom Kippur, the most solemn day in the Jewish religious calendar, the Arab generals counted on the Israeli forces being off their guard.[25] If so, they soon rallied, and although in the first week Egypt and Syria made considerable gains, the tide then turned, and Brezhnev, who had seemed little concerned about what was happening in the Middle East when meeting with Nixon earlier in the year (Eban 1977: 486), realized that he faced a crisis. Kissinger, urgently invited to Moscow, was finally able to persuade Brezhnev to sponsor a new Security Council Resolution (No. 338), calling for a ceasefire, within 12 hours, with the forces on both sides occupying the positions as they were at the time (ibid.: 531; Little 2010: 338). Brezhnev's ambassador in Cairo, Vladimir Vinogradov, having told Sadat, in advance, of the terms of the resolution, persuaded him to accept it; Israel, although resenting US failure to hold any prior consultation, still accepted that the resolution would leave it in an extremely strong position. Its forces had advanced further into Egypt and Syria than they ever did in the Six-Day War (Eban 1977: 529). However, the price paid for victory, in terms of lost men and material, was much higher,[26] and it was little consolation to Israel that Egyptian and Syrian losses were much greater. At the same time, if hostilities were to be resumed, Israel saw every reason to fear that the Soviet Union would supply the beleaguered Egyptian forces by air (ibid.: 557) – which, if it ever happened, would mean escalation of the conflict beyond all bounds. With hindsight Israeli concern was certainly exaggerated; Brezhnev's commitment to détente was unlikely to be jeopardized so recklessly. Indeed, at the UN conference held in Geneva in December 1974 to negotiate the final disengagement of the opposing forces in Egypt, Soviet Foreign Minister Gromyko made it clear that there was 'in principle' no bar to diplomatic relations with Israel (ibid.: 554). In the meantime there was no way the Soviet Union could avoid being eclipsed by US Middle East diplomacy, for as Kissinger himself said, 'the Soviet Union could make war but only the US could make peace' (Golan 1977: 131). When it suited him – as it did during a state visit to India in November 1973, Brezhnev could speak of 'firm peaceful co-existence and good neighbourliness between the Arab States and the State of Israel' (ibid.: 143), but the hidden message was then that the US called the shots. The disengagement negotiated at the end of 1973 left the way open to clear the Suez Canal of mines, and open it for traffic for the first time since 1967, but Gromyko had to work hard to ensure that the Soviet Union also played a role, albeit one subsidiary to that of the US and the UK: even so the Soviet contribution – six months of mine-sweeping – was gratis (ibid.: 212). With a prospective Nixon visit to Egypt in June 1974, this had to be accepted by Moscow as a price worth paying for a legitimate Soviet navy presence in Egypt (ibid.: 213). The game was already lost, as Gromyko was beginning to realize (Gromyko 1989: 350). Worse was to come: in March 1976 Sadat, noting that 'the Russians had nothing to offer', abrogated the five-year-old Soviet–Egyptian friendship treaty (Hosmer and Wolfe 1982: 61), and in October 1977 he was received by Israel's Prime Minister Menachem Begin in Jerusalem; the two of them then met again at Camp David, the US Presidents' country retreat, in September 1978, to join President Carter in working out final peace terms between Egypt and Israel – an achievement that earned them the Nobel Peace Prize for that year.[27] The final peace treaty, signed in March 1979, effectively returned the Sinai peninsula to Egypt (subject to restrictions on the forces that could be deployed there), guaranteed Israel freedom of passage in the Suez Canal and the Straits of Tiran, and provided for normal diplomatic relations between Egypt and Israel (Little 2010: 324). By failing to make any provision relating to Jerusalem, the West Bank or the Golan Heights, the Treaty was certain to be unacceptable to Syria and Arab Palestine; indeed by agreeing its terms Egypt effectively accepted alienation from the other Arab countries in the Middle East.[28] On the other hand, for some 20 years Egypt was to receive American aid worth billions of dollars – a sum that the Soviet Union could not afford to match.

With little to be gained from negotiating with Egypt in the years following the Yom Kippur war, the Soviet Union did its best to help the Syrians and Palestinian Arabs to retrieve lost ground. As to the former, it was a question of dealing with a recognized state, with at its head a formidable dictator, Hafez Assad; as to the latter, there was no such state, since all the territory that might belong to it was under Israeli military occupation – as were also, the Golan Heights, a substantial and fertile part of Syria adjacent to Israel. There was, however, the Palestine Liberation Organization, headed by Yasser Arafat, who in 1959 – that is eight years before the Six-Day War – had founded the Fatah Party, with one essential aim, Palestinian self-determination in what was then part of the Kingdom of Jordan. Since Fatah, in contrast to other Palestinian parties, had no history of outside support from any Arab state, the defeat of Jordan, Egypt and Syria at the end of the Six-Day War, in 1967, opened the way for Arafat to organize massive underground popular support in the Israeli-occupied West Bank. Within the year Nasser had recognized Arafat as the 'leader of the Palestinians', and in the summer of 1968 he was invited to accompany Nasser on an official visit to Moscow, travelling on an Egyptian passport. There, on 4 July, he met Kosygin, Brezhnev and Podgorny (Heikal 1978: 65), to establish an uncertain relationship with Moscow that would continue until well after the end of the Brezhnev era.

The problem facing Soviet diplomacy in the Arab world from 1974 onwards was essentially that it could do nothing to help retrieve the land lost to Israel in the Six-Day War. In Syria and Palestine there was no prospect equivalent to that of Egypt in relation to Sinai: with any number of Israeli settlements established in the Golan Heights and the West Bank in the years following the Six-Day War, there was no chance of Israel abandoning them, whatever government might be in power. Moreover, Washington left no doubts about its unequivocal support for Israel. None the less, in the early months of 1974, Kissinger, playing a cat and mouse game with Gromyko in the Middle East, did succeed in persuading Assad that there was something to be gained by negotiating with Israel (Kissinger 1982: 939), while at the same time Gromyko did his best to persuade him that Soviet support could still be useful to Syria. But as Zhou Enlai had said in Egypt in January 1973, 'What has happened to the first Socialist country in the world? It's become nothing but an armaments dealer, mopping up your produce to pay the interest on the arms you had to buy' (Heikal 1978: 14). That was more or less the truth, and Kissinger had said much the same.

Gromyko reassured Assad that the armaments, imported from the Soviet Union and lost in the Yom Kippur war, could be replaced – but then for what purpose? Was Syria contemplating a third war against Israel, to be fought without Egypt as an ally? Disengagement between Syria and Israel was finally negotiated in May 1974 – a result of the Geneva summit (where Palestine was not represented). Moscow, in dealing with Damascus, exaggerated both its own contribution to the settlement (Golan 1977: 231) and what had been achieved for Syria. Brezhnev himself, in a letter to Assad, presented Geneva as laying 'the foundation for the liberation of Syrian territory occupied by the Israeli invaders' (ibid.: 232). This was no more than a pipe-dream of a man who had been side-lined, but for the time being it suited Assad not to disillusion Brezhnev.

Occurring parallel to the events surrounding the Yom Kippur war (as related above), and adventitiously connected to them, an unprecedented crisis in the supply of oil disrupted national economies worldwide. The crisis developed within the framework of the Organization of Petrol Exporting Countries (OPEC), a cartel formed in 1960 by a number of the major oil-producing states. Because most of these states were in the Arab world, any confrontation with Israel, such as the Yom Kippur war, concerned them, even though neither Egypt nor Syria – the only two actual Arab combatants – belonged to OPEC. At the same time (1973), the US – which had long been self-sufficient – had reached a point where more than a third of its oil was imported. Western Europe, although almost wholly dependent upon imported oil,[29] none the less relied upon oil for some 60 per cent of its energy needs (Kissinger 1982: 859) – and the greater part of the imported oil came from the Arab world. As Kissinger later noted (ibid.: 860),'the balance of power on energy was shifting from the Texas Gulf to the Persian Gulf'.

By the 1970s it was only a matter of time before this would lead to a convulsion in world oil. One man set the ball rolling: Muammar Qaddafi, who had seized power in Libya in September 1969, soon realized the immense power that the country's oil wealth bestowed upon him. Even at current world-market prices he could afford to order 100 Mirage fighter aircraft from France, which, given his declared intent to eliminate Israel, might well be deployed – say, by being lent to the Syrian air force – in the process of achieving this end. For the time being, however, Qaddafi turned to another strategy: in the course of 1970 he imposed drastic cutbacks, coupled with increased prices, on an independent producer, Occidental Petroleum, operating in Libya (Kissinger 1982: 860–861). Occidental, with no other choice, yielded to the Libyan embargo, which Qaddafi then extended, with equal success, to cover all the oil companies operating in Libya. Although there was an immediate and unwelcome economic impact in western Europe, where 25 per cent of oil imports came from Libya, the national governments decided not to intervene (ibid.: 862).

The oil-states of the Persian Gulf, operating through OPEC, followed the Libyan precedent. Much more was at stake: production – on a much larger scale – was mainly in the hands of the world's seven major oil companies, and of these five were not only American, but key suppliers to the US market. As with Libya and western Europe, the 'gulf' oil-states were assured that there would be no US government intervention (Kissinger 1982: 864). The 'majors', left to look after themselves, had to accept the transfer – to be completed in the leading case of Saudi Arabia by 1982 – of 51 per cent of their shares to the states where they operated (ibid.: 868). At the same time drastic quotas were imposed, while in the course of 1973, the gulf states increased the price of oil from $3.01 (ibid.: 872) to $11.65 (ibid.: 885, 889) a barrel. Worse still, in the November, the Arab oil ministers made it clear that lifting the embargo would be linked to Middle East diplomacy (ibid.: 879) and more specifically to the withdrawal of Israeli forces from 'occupied Arab territories' (ibid.: 878; Little 2010: 320). At the same time, the embargo was relaxed in favour of the West European states not specifically tied to US policy on Israel.[30] By early in 1974 it became clear that Syria, not an OPEC member, was alone in holding out indefinitely against the US: this was natural enough, because no progress had been made toward disengagement from Israel. In the end President Huari Boumedienne of Algeria, Syria's closest Arab ally, persuaded President Assad to agree to end the embargo, which was lifted unconditionally on 18 March (ibid.: 978). The long-term result was then that the world economy had to adjust to a four-fold increase in oil-prices, a process that led inevitably to inflation and a critical brake on economic development.

Because all this happened during Brezhnev's watch, the question arises as to what effect the oil crisis had on the Soviet Union. As is clear from a number of instances already noted, Brezhnev himself, Gromyko, his foreign minister, and Soviet diplomats throughout the Arab world, worked hard to be involved. It was, however, as clear to Moscow as it was to Washington that government intervention would be counterproductive, if not dangerous.

All that Brezhnev could do was deal with the consequences of the oil crisis and its aftermath, such as they were for the Soviet economy. In principle these should have been relatively favourable. The Soviet Union was self-sufficient in oil, and with vast sums earned by Arab oil-states had a much improved market for its arms exports. Libya, in particular, not only bought Soviet arms, but had no difficulty in paying the full market price in dollars (Hosmer and Wolfe 1982: 70). Moreover the lesson from the 1970s was that money invested in developing oil resources was well-spent. If, at the same time, the harsh impact of the oil crisis on western industrial economies should have given the Soviet Union some competitive advantage, the inherent inefficiencies of its command economy hardly allowed it to be exploited.

Notes

1 In the words of the poet, Hilaire Belloc (1870–1953): 'Whatever happens, we have got/ The Maxim gun and they have not.'
2 The anthropological literature is voluminous, but see van Velsen (1964).
3 In the late nineteenth century and early twentieth century, in the vast Congo territory, run as a private venture of the Belgian King Leopold II (1835–1909), the appalling working conditions on the rubber plantations, where thousands died from abuse by their overseers, became an international scandal (Crump 2010: 305).
4 Even as late as 1960, only five people worked in the Africa directorate of the KGB (Haslam 2011: 183).
5 Although according to Point 3 of the Atlantic Charter, agreed between Churchill and Roosevelt in August 1941 to provide a basis for a post-war settlement, 'all peoples had a right to self-determination', Churchill made it clear from the start that this was not to be read as a blue-print for dissolving the British Empire; this was also the position of Clement Attlee, who succeeded him as Prime-Minister in 1945.
6 The consequences of this for the Soviet Union are examined on page 187.
7 The words first occurred in a speech made in Ghana on 10 January 1960, but they only caught world-wide attention when repeated in South Africa on 3 February.
8 This justified the claim, later made by Andropov, that 'the Soviet Union is not merely talking about world revolution, but is actually helping to bring it about' (Haslam 2011: 295).
9 Between November 1977 and April 1978 the Soviet Union also sent 2,671 air shipments of arms to Ethiopia (Haslam 2011: 315).
10 Much of what happened was orchestrated by Castro during his 1977 visit to East Africa, which decided him that Mengistu was much to be preferred to Siad Barre as a member of the socialist bloc (Haslam 2011: 314).
11 In the judgment of Marshal Sergei Akhromeev, the chief of the Soviet General Staff, Ethiopia 'was a serious mistake' (cited Mitchell 2010: 80).
12 The figures come from Tareke (2000).
13 Until the nineteenth century the export of Africans as slaves, mainly to Brazil, dominated the Angolan economy.

14 A major factor here was the return of up to a million Portuguese citizens from their homes in the former African colonies.

15 The amendment – to the Arms Export Control Act – was introduced by Senator Dick Clark of Iowa, at a time when the Democratic Party had a majority in both Houses of Congress. The Republican President, Gerald Ford, accepted the amendment, even though he had allowed covert arms sales to UNITA.

16 The leading figure in developing and enforcing this policy in Africa was Lord Lugard (1858–1945) who after five years (1914–1919) as governor-general of Nigeria spent 14 years (1922–1936) on the Permanent Mandates Commission of the League of Nations.

17 Known to history as the Sykes-Picot Treaty after the representatives of the two governments (Sebag-Montefiore 2011: 205).

18 The word itself means 'defence', and was adopted as early as 1920 by rural settlements concerned for their own security (Sebag-Montefiore 2011: 430).

19 From 1944 this was commanded by Menachem Begin (Sebag-Montefiore 2011: 461) – a prisoner of the Soviet Union in the first two years of the war (1939–1941) – who later, in the Brezhnev era, would become prime-minister of Israel (1977–1983) and be awarded the Nobel Peace Prize (1978).

20 This reassured local Muslims, who decried the Communist anti-religious stance (Heikal 1978: 63, Cook 2012: 52), while at the same time many members of the Party were identified as foreign or Jewish.

21 At this stage little prevented the Israeli forces advancing further to capture the Syrian capital, Damascus; that they did not do so may have been the result of Kosygin using the hot line to the White House, to warn of possible Soviet military intervention (Aid 2009: 139).

22 The first was at Bandung in 1955 (see page 69), the second at Belgrade in 1959 and the third in Cairo in 1961.

23 Following the Six-Day War the Soviet Union broke off diplomatic relations with Israel (Eban 1977: 552).

24 Clause 1(i) and (ii).

25 Moscow, having only learnt of the Egyptian plans on 3 October, recommended Soviet Nationals to leave Egypt on the following day; if this was a sign to Israel that war imminent, few reckoned that it would come only two days later (Golan 1977: 66, 69).

26 As the Israel Foreign Minister noted 'After all, the Jewish people does not have much blood left to lose' (Eban 1977: 530)'.

27 This was something of a relief to Brezhnev, who had feared that the prize might be awarded to the Soviet dissident, Yuri Orlov.

28 As Gromyko was pleased to note (Gromyko 1989: 352), not a single prominent Arab head of state attended Sadat's funeral, after he was assassinated on 6 October 1981.

29 At this stage North Sea oil was not yet on stream.

30 The Netherlands was the only exception.

11 South and Central Asia: challenges that Brezhnev could not ignore

The Indian Ocean and South Asia

On 8 June 1969, Brezhnev, in the course of a typical lengthy address to the World Conference of Communist Parties in Moscow, proclaimed his belief that 'the course of events is also placing on the agenda the task of creating a system of collective security in Asia' (*Pravda*, 9 June 1969). That in later years this principle was never developed effectively in Soviet foreign policy, leaves open the question as to what Brezhnev had in mind? The only effective Soviet intervention, the invasion of Afghanistan in 1979, came at a very late stage on Brezhnev's watch. For the rest, little can be done beyond relating Asian history from 1964 to 1979 from the perspective of Moscow. This takes up the first part of this chapter; the second part then deals with Afghanistan.

In September 1965, Brezhnev's first year as *vozhd*, the Soviet Union was one of the great powers whose intervention, through the UN, in the Second Kashmir War between India and Pakistan, led to a ceasefire after seventeen days of fighting had cost both sides thousands of casualties. Then, in January 1966, at a meeting at Tashkent, presided over by Soviet Prime Minister Kosygin, the Prime Minister of India and the President of Pakistan signed a declaration providing for the restoration of the pre-war status quo and 'good' relations between the two countries.

Whatever it achieved for the Soviet image internationally (Haslam 2011: 229), Foreign Minister Gromyko, who orchestrated the Tashkent declaration, was not pleased with its results. Relations between India and Pakistan remained bad; the fault, as Gromyko saw it, lay with Pakistan, which throughout its whole existence as an independent state, had been trapped in an 'insidious web' (Gromyko 1989: 316) spun by the West to serve its own 'political, economic and military' purposes.

There can be little doubt about which side Moscow supported. Both before and after the 1965 war the Soviet Union supplied India with economic and military aid on a massive scale, so much so that in the critical period, 1961–1964, it was together with Indonesia, the second largest recipient after Egypt. The reason for Soviet generosity was simple enough: government policy in both India and Indonesia demanded a high profile in the Non-Aligned Movement emerging from the Bandung conference in 1955. The conference itself had been convened by the Indonesian President Sukarno, with Indian Prime Minster Nehru also playing a prominent part. Critically, Chinese Foreign Minister Zhou Enlai was welcome, while the Soviet Union, as a European power, was excluded. Moreover, the conference's unanimous condemnation of 'colonialism in all its forms' also covered Soviet policies in eastern Europe and Central Asia (*Bandung Conference*, Encyclopaedia Britannica MOBILE, 2012). Although all five organizing states, Indonesia, Burma, Pakistan, Ceylon and India, would receive Soviet aid in the years after Bandung, in the Brezhnev era that granted to India far exceeded the total amount received by the other four states. (Indonesia might have benefitted on the same scale, had it not acquired a new government closely tied to the US following the deposition of President Sukarno after a *coup d'état* on 30 September 1965 (Crump 2007a: 239)). Looking once again, from the perspective of Moscow, at the five states listed above, Burma and Ceylon, were not only too small to count but also much too involved in domestic conflict.

At this stage, also, a cursory survey of the rest of South Asia from the perspective of Moscow will complete the picture. Because of the need to protect its own interests – particularly in the context of the war in Vietnam – the US maintained a rock-solid military presence in Thailand and the Philippines, supported by large-scale military and economic aid. Singapore and Malaysia, both members of the British Commonwealth, were firmly on the same side. Moreover the US presence had been immensely strengthened by the fall of Sukarno in Indonesia. Australia, on its way to becoming a major Asia–Pacific power, although also a Commonwealth member, was committed to Washington much more than to London – not that this meant any profound change in policy: quite simply, after 1967, the UK no longer had any defence commitment in the region (Crump 2007a: 319).

This was not all: the Soviet Union, if it was to achieve anything, also had to contend with China, and Chapter 12 shows all the problems which this involved – including war and peace in Vietnam. No wonder then that in Brezhnev's day, Soviet Asian diplomacy focussed on India. There Moscow had the advantage of dealing with a state that was not only resolutely *non-aligned*, but hostile to China (Hosmer and Wolfe 1982: 24). In New Delhi, the Soviet case, whatever it related to, was dealt with on its merits – at least in principle.

If it helped that for Moscow Pakistan was as much an enemy as a friend, the whole question of relations with India and Pakistan was put to the test – as it was for many other states – by the outbreak of the third Indo-Pakistani war in 1971. The background to the war was simple enough. Pakistan, which had been an independent state since 1947, was divided into two parts, East and West. East Pakistan comprised the eastern, and predominantly Muslim, part of the old Indian province of Bengal – with the western, predominantly Hindu part becoming a province of independent India. West Pakistan, at the other side of the Indian sub-continent, comprised the old North-West Frontier province of India, together with Sindh, Baluchistan and the predominantly Muslim part of the rich central province of Punjab (with the rest of this province going to India). West Pakistan also occupied and controlled about half of the former state of Kashmir, where in 1947 the ruling prince, the Maharajah of Kashmir and Jammu, by signing an Instrument of Accession with the Viceroy of India, had in principle agreed that it should be part of India. This was almost certainly against the wishes of the majority of the population, which being Muslim, would have much preferred accession to Pakistan. Pakistan, almost from the day of independence, claimed Kashmir, and to make good this claim sent in troops to occupy the principality. India, claiming its rights under the formal accession agreed by the Maharajah, responded by sending in its own troops, and inevitably the two sides met in armed conflict. This, the first Indo-Pakistan war, lasted until the 1 January 1949, when, as a result of UN intervention, a ceasefire was agreed along a line which still divides Kashmir, with Pakistan on the west and India on the east. Neither side was content with this solution, with the whole situation becoming even more contentious after China also claimed and occupied a substantial, but remote and mountainous part of Kashmir. In 1965, intermittent clashes between India and Pakistan led to full-scale war, which was finally settled by the Tashkent agreement of January 1966, which essentially restored the ceasefire line of 1949.

During all this time Kashmir represented a continuous burden on the resources of the government of Pakistan; in particular the continuing Kashmir crisis determined the size, composition and deployment of Pakistan's armed forces.[1] Although the same was true of India (which eventually developed its own nuclear weapons to meet the military threat from Pakistan) the burden on Pakistan, with only a fraction of the Indian population, was much heavier. What is more, it had to be shared with the Bengalis in the eastern part of Pakistan, who at the same time constituted a majority of its population. This was a source of considerable resentment: East Pakistan, on the other side of the Indian sub-continent, had little interest in Kashmir, but still had to contribute massively to the costs of Pakistan's military presence there. Worse still, the government of Pakistan, with the capital city – Karachi until the 1960s and then Islamabad – located in the West was little concerned with the problems of the East. Instead, the East, with an economy quite different to that of the West, was simply there to be exploited in the interests of the West. With the whole of Pakistan ruled by a military dictator, Ayub Khan, from 1958 to 1969, there was little prospect of the East exercising its democratic rights to put an end to its exploitation by the West. There was, none the less, considerable political activity, with the locally based Awami League, which had no concern for the interests of West Pakistan (including the stand-off in Kashmir), enjoying massive public support. At the same time, following the partition of India in 1947, a substantial part of the Hindu population of East Bengal, not only chose to remain there but were able to play an active part in public life – including local politics. What is more the Indian Communist Party had always been strong in Bengal, both East and West. With Ayub Khan firmly committed to the US[2] – a key source of aid to Pakistan – Soviet foreign policy, in relation to Pakistan, was geared to supporting the East against the West, in any conflict between the two. This was equally true of India. The question was, would there ever be cause for intervention?

There was not long to wait. In 1969, Ayub Khan – no longer in control of events, in spite of having declared martial law – was succeeded by General Yahya Khan, a strong man renowned for his military successes in the 1965 war. Yahya Khan, having first ensured that the election law would favour his own party – which would in any case control the entire state apparatus – declared a general election to be held at the end of 1970. The results were disastrous. In East Pakistan the Awami League, led by Sheikh Mujibur Rahman, won 167 out of 169 seats, while in the West, 85 seats – a much smaller majority – were won by the Pakistan People's Party led by Zulfikar Bhutto. From the West, with the seat of government in Islamabad, it soon became clear that the Awami League, which had not won a single western constituency, would not be allowed to form a new administration. Denied the fruits of victory at the polls, Sheikh Rahman, set up a civil disobedience movement, with overwhelming popular support in the East. The Pakistani Army, as always under western command, staged a brutal crackdown under the name of 'Operation Searchlight', arresting Sheikh Rahman and other top men in the Awami League. The result was civil war, with East Pakistan declaring independence as the new nation of Bangladesh on 27 March 1971. India's prime minister, Indira Gandhi, announced her support and pledged military aid. In the following months there were hundreds of thousands of casualties, mainly civilian, while millions – including almost all the Hindus from East Bengal – fled to India as refugees from what had become a reign of terror carried out by soldiers from West Pakistan. Although the Indian army had intervened at an early stage, open hostilities broke out on 3 December, leading to the third Indo-Pakistani war, which, as opposed to the first two (in 1947–1948 and 1965), was absolutely decisive. The Pakistani forces in Bengal surrendered on 16 December, leaving Yahya Khan in Islamabad without any hold at all on half the country he claimed to govern. He had no alternative but to resign, opening the way for Bhutto, long a bitter rival, to become the democratically elected president of what was left of Pakistan. By this time the country consisted only of the four western provinces; in the east the new state of Bangladesh was on its own, to be admitted a member both of the British Commonwealth and the UN in 1974.

Where then did all this leave Brezhnev and the Soviet Union? Support for Bangladesh was plainly indicated, for there was nothing to be gained in Pakistan – and nothing to be lost vis-à-vis India. There was, however, little that Moscow could do to profit from the emergence of the new state. With a vast population combined with a low level of development and relatively few natural resources, there was a crying need for economic aid – not, however, in sectors where the Soviet Union has anything useful to offer. Bangladesh certainly did not need the sort of arms package supplied to the Arab world; it was not going to fight another war. On the other hand investment in agriculture and flood control was sorely needed, but here the achievements of the Soviet Union relating to its own domestic economy had produced little that could be of any practical use in a country such as Bangladesh. The most valuable Soviet contribution came almost immediately after the end of the war in 1971, when the Soviet Navy helped clear two harbours, Chittagong and Chalna, of mines laid by Pakistan, but from the very beginning Soviet economic assistance was hardly more than 5 per cent of that provided by the US, to say nothing of aid, on a comparable scale, from Japan, the World Bank and the Asia Development Bank. Even so, the Soviet Union, with its considerable experience in generating electricity, did help in the construction of power plants. In spite of a low level of

Soviet economic aid to Bangladesh, relations between Moscow and Dhaka were extremely cordial, particular in the early years, with an official visit to Moscow by Sheikh Mujibur Rahman in 1972 being followed by numerous reciprocal visits at a lower level. All such displays of goodwill, however, cost little and achieved little: neither on Brezhnev's watch, nor later, was there ever a significant Soviet presence in Bangladesh.

Afghanistan

If for Soviet policy in South Asia only India was counted as important, then, almost at the end of Brezhnev's watch – when his own powers were clearly diminishing – Soviet armed intervention in Afghanistan turned this world upside down. In the history of the Soviet Union after the death of Stalin the invasion of Afghanistan in December 1979 proved to be as disastrous for its future as were the invasion of Hungary (under Khrushchev) in 1956 and that of Czechoslovakia (under Brezhnev) in 1968.[3]

As in these two cases, Soviet armed intervention in Afghanistan was planned as a rescue operation. From the perspective of Moscow, Afghanistan, like all the Warsaw Pact states, had a common frontier with the Soviet Union, and, after April 1978, a government which, although of doubtful legitimacy, was regarded as a useful potential ally in a part of the world where, as already related, there were few others that could be counted on. This new government seized power in a *coup d'état* orchestrated by Hafizullah Amin, a major figure in the *Khalq* ('masses') faction of the Afghanistan People's Democratic Party (APDP) (Collins 1986: 47). The party, founded in 1965, to 'build a socialist society in Afghanistan based on . . . adapting Marxist-Leninist revolutionary principles to conditions in Afghanistan' (ibid.: 28), was, needless to say, favoured by Moscow. Even so, there is little evidence of a Soviet hidden hand behind the so-called *Saur* ('April') revolution (ibid.: 51). However that may be, after the APDP, under the *Khalq* leader, Nur Mohammed Taraki, had proclaimed the new Peoples Democratic Republic of Afghanistan (PDRA) on 30 April, Brezhnev sent his congratulations to Kabul on 2 May. A few days later Amin (who had been appointed Taraki's deputy and foreign minister) was meeting Gromyko in Moscow (ibid.: 53): the result was a massive increase in Soviet aid, and in the number of Soviet 'advisers' in Afghanistan (ibid.: 52). The Taraki government then went on to introduce radical land and credit reforms, to the point that Brezhnev, speaking in Baku in September, could tell his audience that 'a people's revolution took place; the semi-feudal regime was toppled and the Democratic Republic of Afghanistan was proclaimed' (*Pravda*, 23 September 1978).

Brezhnev's trust in the new regime was ill-founded. The Taraki government's hold on Afghanistan was extremely precarious (Girardet 1985: 22). To begin with *Khalq* confronted a rival faction *Parcham* ('banner') within the People's Democratic Party of Afghanistan (PDPA), and although they joined in a coalition directly after the success of the *Saur* revolution, this broke up within a very short time, leaving the two sides at loggerheads. In July Taraki and Amin purged

Parcham, sending its leader, Babrak Karmal to Czechoslovakia as Afghan ambassador (Haslam 2011: 320). Two surviving *Parcham* members of the coalition were sentenced to death, the likely fate of Karmal, if he returned home. This was the beginning of a massive purge in which, on Amin's own admission, 12,000 political prisoners – not by any means confined to members of *Parcham* – were executed (Girardet 1985: 55). If *Khalq* was following the same path as the *Derg* in Ethiopia (as described in Chapter 10), Brezhnev appeared not to mind. On 5 December the Soviet Union and Afghanistan signed a Treaty of Friend-ship, Good-Neighbourliness and Cooperation, cementing, in Brezhnev's words, a 'durable friendship, permeated by a spirit of comradeship and revolutionary solidarity' (ibid.: 56). For Moscow this only made sense as a desperate measure to prop up a failing regime. It is doubtful whether as much as half the military supported the Saur revolution, but in any case thousands deserted and continued to do so under the PDRA. The Taraki government was insecure in Kabul, while large parts of the country were controlled by forces hostile to it. *Pravda* (1 August 1978) accused, specifically, the US, China and Saudi Arabia, and implicitly Pakistan and Iran, of supporting Islamic extremists.

Washington, having recognized the PDRA in May 1978 – only four days after Moscow – continued its aid programmes; the motive, as stated by US Secretary of State, Cyrus Vance, was to avoid losing 'the prospect of any influence in Kabul' (Vance 1983: 385). There, in February 1979, the US was overtaken by events: its ambassador, Adolph Dubs, was kidnapped and then killed by the local police in an ill-judged rescue operation (Collins 1986: 59). The kidnappers could have been simple bandits, Afghan dissidents, KGB, CIA or *Parcham* members: no-one ever knew. No matter, on 22 February the US cancelled the remainder of its 1979 aid programme, withdrew the Peace Corps (after 20 years in Afghanistan), and replaced the ambassador with a chargé d'affaires.

A month later, the eastern city of Herat, where there was a strong Soviet presence, was overtaken by violence: insurgents, helped by Afghan mutineers, captured the city and murdered any Russians they could get hold of (Girardet 1985: 23). In retaliation Afghan forces, supported by Soviet 'advisers', sacked the rebel-held town of Kerala, killing 640 of its male inhabitants (ibid.: 60). *Pravda* (19 March 1979) blamed Iran, Pakistan and China, with their western 'supporters' for the unrest. The Soviet response was to send seven generals to survey the situation on the ground: their advice was to increase greatly both arms aid and the number of military advisers. This did not quench the unrest, which was largely the result of Amin taking over the leadership of *Khalq*, and, by so doing, the PDPA government of Afghanistan. The results were catastrophic: Amin's unpopularity in his own faction led to a strong internal dissident movement, while, at the same time *Parcham* was still active behind the scenes. The PDRA was falling apart; clearly the 'People's Democracy' was neither popular nor democratic. Amin himself admitted that without '. . . vast economic and military aid from the Soviet Union, we could not resist the aggression and conspiracies of imperialism' (Collins 1986: 67). On 17 September Brezhnev and Kosygin sent a personal message to Amin stating their confidence 'that fraternal relations . . . will continue to develop' (ibid.: 68), but with every day that passed Amin (whose henchmen had murdered the more popular Taraki on 16 September (Girardet 1985: 24))[4] became more exasperating to the Soviet Embassy (where he even failed to attend the annual celebration of the Great October Revolution). At the same time there was large-scale mutiny and rebellion, with whole provinces lost to Amin, hundreds of thousands seeking refuge in Pakistan (Collins 1986: 69) and, inevitably, a collapsing economy. Even the Soviet Embassy had to report to Moscow that 'violent instability will probably remain a fact of life for years to come' (ibid.: 70). Moscow's reaction was to increase, very substantially, the Soviet military presence in Afghanistan; this process – denied by *Pravda* on 23 December as 'pure fabrication' – ominously included a visit by a MVD general, Victor Paputin.

December 24 – the day after *Pravda's* denial – witnessed the beginning of a massive three-day airlift of Soviet forces to the Bagram Airbase, outside Kabul. On 27 December special units were deployed to the Darulaman Palace, where they killed Amin (Girardet 1985: 12); the next day the whole city was in Soviet hands. The strongest resistance came from the Ministry of Interior, a *Khalq* stronghold. This was finally subdued by a Soviet detachment commanded by Paputin, who died in a final shoot-out with the Afghan defenders (Girardet 1985: 14). The *Parcham* leader, Babrak Karmal, emerged from the shadows, to be proclaimed by the Soviet media as President of the Revolutionary Council, General Secretary of the PDPA and Prime Minister (ibid.: 78). In his first radio address to the Afghan people (now known to have been broadcast from inside the Soviet Union) he promised 'a holy war against the enemies of the revolution'; telling his listeners that he was calling for Soviet military support (ibid.: 15) he did not mention that Soviet forces were already present in considerable numbers; without them the war would have been impossible. In fact, by the end of March 1980 there were some 85,000 Soviet troops in Afghanistan, most of whom were already there in the first week of the year. As for the civil government of Afghanistan, this was in principle a *Khalq–Parcham* coalition, but the Soviet military administration allowed Karmal little freedom of action. *Parcham* was a weaker political base than *Khalq*, largely because of the latter's strength in the armed forces, which by the end of 1980 had seen many desert to fight alongside the mujahidin freedom-fighters. The decline in manpower in the course of 1980 from 100,000 to 30,000 left the maintenance of law and order almost entirely to the Soviet forces – a task that in the course of the 1980s became increasingly hazardous and expensive. At the same time 140,000 tons of Soviet wheat had to be sent to make good the losses to Afghan agriculture as a result of the war (Collins 1986: 85), while the number of refugees in Pakistan and Iran exceeded 700,000 – a number that would increase to more than 2,000,000 before Brezhnev died in 1982 (ibid.: 143).

If inside Afghanistan the war had brought the Soviet Union nothing but trouble, internationally the cost was even higher. Not only did the UN General Assembly vote 104 to 18 (with 30 absences or abstentions) to 'deplore the recent [Soviet] armed intervention in Afghanistan', but among the votes in favour of the resolution were those of two thirds of the non-aligned states (including Yugoslavia); Islamic states, in two separate conferences, also voted to condemn the Soviet invasion

(Collins 1986: 86). China, in turn, saw it as part of a Soviet encirclement plan, which would include opening a land route from Afghanistan to the Indian Ocean (ibid.) – a replay of the nineteenth century 'Great Game'. If necessary, therefore, China could well have been ready to co-operate with Pakistan in supporting the mujahidin.

The strongest reaction came from the US; President Carter (who faced an election later in the year) cancelling, inter alia, the export of 17 million tons of grain and hi-tech equipment and know-how, also instigated a boycott of the Olympic Games scheduled for Moscow in August 1980 – leading some 55 other countries to do the same. Worse still – particularly for Brezhnev – was Carter's decision to withdraw the SALT II treaty from ratification by the US Senate. Not much was left of détente, the keystone of Brezhnev's American policy, to which he had given so much attention during the Nixon years.

Essentially, the Soviet invasion of Afghanistan leaves only one question to be answered: why was the decision to embark on such a disastrous enterprise ever taken? If, however, there is only one question, there are any number of different answers; far from their being mutually exclusive, two or more of them could well combine to provide one, more comprehensive answer. Which these must then be is almost impossible to know in the absence of any adequate record of what was happening behind the scenes in the Kremlin around the new year of 1979–1980 (Collins 1986: 103). A statement made by Brezhnev on 13 January 1980 was a strong affirmation of the Soviet intervention, echoed by Kosygin, Suslov, Andropov and Gromyko (ibid.: 101).[5] This in no way contradicts Kissinger's view (expressed before the Afghan invasion) that Soviet policy was more often than not the result of improvisation rather than the implementation of any grand design (Kissinger 1979: 107). Given the way Afghan history unfolded in 1979, Moscow, overtaken by events, was bound to be reactive rather than proactive. Deciding how to react involved, however, a series of critical misjudgements both of the true situation in Afghanistan and of the success of Soviet interventions, in other parts of the world during the Brezhnev years. As to the former, Moscow's favourable assessment of the PDPA's capacity to govern Afghanistan was little justified by the party's track record – as earlier recorded in this chapter. The political impera-tive to assassinate its leader, Amin, hardly justified the assumption that without him, the party would be fit to govern: events soon proved that it was not.

If the Politburo was blind to such adverse factors, then it was because it was reassured by Soviet successes (as related in Chapter 10) in Ethiopia, Angola in the 1970s, and above all, in Czechoslovakia in 1968 (Girardet 1985: 26; Latham 2010: 278). The lesson in every case was the US and its allies might well condemn the action, but having done so, would react no further. The Afghan intervention – on a much smaller scale than that in Czechoslovakia – was essentially a 'low risk' operation (Collins 1986: 134). (Significantly two of the Soviet 'advisers' sent to Afghanistan in 1979 were generals who had taken part in the invasion of Czechoslovakia (ibid.: 99)). Seen, once again, from the perspective of Moscow, adverse US reaction, in 1980, was even less likely, given the steady build-up of Soviet military power throughout the 1970s (ibid.: 111). It also counted that

Afghanistan bordered on the Soviet Union (ibid.: 124). Ideally, then, the Afghan intervention should have been exemplary for the Brezhnev doctrine, which was indeed applied to justify it post hoc (ibid.: 107). In the words of Brezhnev himself 'a hotbed of serious danger to the security of the Soviet state was created on our southern borders' (ibid.: 124) while for Marshal Grechko intervention was necessary for 'defending the entire socialist community and the worldwide historical values of socialism' (ibid.: 115). Here the threat from China also played a part. After nearly 30 years the Sino-Soviet Friendship Treaty of 1950 – following border clashes along the Soviet frontier with China (ibid.: 131) – had not been renewed in 1979; the fact that China also bordered on both Afghanistan and Pakistan was also seen as threatening the Soviet position in South Asia (ibid.: 130) – the more so as relations between Washington and Beijing became steadily closer.

Not only, therefore, were there for Moscow good reasons for defending the Soviet position in Afghanistan – even to the point of military occupation of the whole country – but a number of adventitious factors also reinforced this policy. Turkey's Cyprus policy meant it lost favour with the US; the fall of the Shah in Iran, and the Teheran hostage crisis, greatly weakened the US position in South Asia (Haslam 2011: 323; Mitchell 2010: 66); Pakistan's nuclear weapons programme following the war with India in 1971, to say nothing of its poor human rights record, had grievously alienated the US. With little prospect of the SALT II Treaty reaching the US Senate, détente, for which Brezhnev had worked so hard with Nixon, had run aground (ibid.: 70). What then was to be lost by intervening in Afghanistan? Did events justify Soviet complacency?

Today there can be no doubt about the answers to such questions. The Soviet Union gained no lasting benefit from its successful invasion of Afghanistan in 1980. Gorbachev, recognizing not only that this was the case, but also that the costs of remaining in Afghanistan were prohibitive, withdrew the Soviet forces in 1989. Brezhnev's whole Afghan adventure was based on a series of miscalculations; from such past events as are related in this chapter – and indeed from many others – he, and the other Soviet leaders of his day, consistently drew the wrong conclusions. It may be that left to himself, Brezhnev might have decided against the invasion, but this counted for little at a time when his chronic poor state of health meant that he was no longer an effective leader. As to Afghanistan, the main protagonists Andropov, Ustinov, Gromyko and Suslov – having alleged that Amin was a CIA agent[6] – pressured Brezhnev to accept the necessity for the invasion (Haslam 2011: 325) – which led to Amin's murder on almost the first day. The actual decision had been taken, two weeks earlier, at a meeting of the Politburo chaired by Brezhnev (ibid.: 326).

Afghanistan may be seen as the last of a series of critical Soviet miscalculations following the end of World War II; Stalin's role in the Korean War, Khrushchev's in the Cuban missile crisis, Brezhnev's in the invasion of Czechoslovakia, his intervention in Israel's two wars (1967 and 1973) with neighbouring Arab states, his support for Mengistu in Ethiopia or Neto in Angola, were earlier instances of the same essential failure of the 'entire Soviet conceptual apparatus' (Collins 1986: 118). If it possible to recover from one false step, or even from a succession of false steps, there always comes a point after which further recovery is impossible: in Afghanistan, in 1980, the Soviet Union reached that point. The US and its allies did not realize this at the time, for as Edward Crankshaw had already pointed out:

> One of the most serious mistakes of the West . . . has been to overrate, often to an absurd degree, the knowledge and understanding of the world enjoyed by the Soviet leadership . . . The mistake is serious because it has led us again and again to attribute great subtlety and exactitude of calculation to manifestations of Soviet government behaviour which often arise from ignorance and muddle
>
> (foreword to Khrushchev 1974: vii-viii).

Notes

1 This included the Navy, even though Kashmir was entirely landlocked (Admiral T. K. Khan, personal information).
2 At this stage Pakistan, for Kissinger, was critically important to Washington for providing the only diplomatic access to Beijing (Kissinger 1979: 913–914). In fact the US State Department was also in contact with the Chinese ambassadors to both France and the UN (Hanhimäki 2004: 156).
3 As related in Chapter 10.
4 Described by one western diplomat 'as the respectable element in the Kabul regime' (Girardet 1985: 23).
5 Girardet (1985: 25) suggests – without citing any authority – that Brehznev would have been content with a more limited intervention, sufficient to uphold an 'amenably pro-Soviet Afghanistan'; the actual invasion followed a policy proposed by Andropov, who then carried the day in the Politburo.
6 The seeds of suspicion were planted by Brzezinski, US President Carter's National Security Adviser, or so he claimed; delighted when the invasion actually took place, he noted 'We now have the opportunity to give the USSR its Vietnam war' (Haslam 2011: 326).

12 Brezhnev's confrontation with China

When, on 1 October 1949, Mao Zedong, in Beijing, proclaimed the People's Republic of China, the way this event, and its consequences, were judged in the outside world depended on two propositions. First, without material support from the Soviet Union, Mao's victory over the Nationalist forces of Chiang Kai-shek, would have been impossible; second, once Mao was established in power, the People's Republic and the Soviet Union, would be close allies for the indefinite future. Although both propositions were largely mistaken, there were good intuitive grounds for accepting their truth. As for the first, because Chiang Kai-shek, was always strongly supported – both materially and politically – by Washington, the logic of history required that Mao must have had comparable support from Moscow.[1] Second, once Mao had achieved power in China, the fact that his principles of government derived from Marxist-Leninism, reflected wide common ground between the People's Republic and the Soviet Union. Once again by the logic of history the People's Republic and the Soviet Union were born to be allies.[2]

To understand the relationship between these two large and powerful communist states during the Brezhnev years, 1964–1982, it must be accepted that the two propositions stated in the previous paragraph were false – at least as seen from Beijing, which is what counted most. As seen by Mao, the People's Republic owed little to the Soviet Union. What is more, as had already become clear while Khrushchev was in power in Moscow, the Soviet Union, rather than being an ally, was an adversary – and a potentially dangerous adversary at that. Now, with the benefit of hindsight, it is clear that the alliance was always under stress, simply because Mao could never accept any prospect of China being subordinate to any other power (Kissinger 2011: 276).

To a degree conflict with the Soviet Union was a self-fulfilling prophecy on the part of Mao: from the beginning of the 1960s,[3] if not earlier, his own policies vis-à-vis Moscow were calculated to create enmity between the People's Republic and the Soviet Union, and at least so long as the critical threshold of armed conflict with the Soviet Union was not breached, this state of affairs suited Mao's book very well. Although, following the fall of Khrushchev in October 1964, Mao conveyed to Moscow his 'utmost wish' to have a better relationship (Kissinger 2011: 489), the incident (related on page 90) involving Chinese Premier Zhou Enlai at a Kremlin reception on 7 November made this impossible to realize.

On the contrary, Mao, became almost paranoid about the possibility that senior colleagues, supported by Moscow, were plotting against him. Following criticisms of his policies at the Beijing 'Conference of the Seven Thousand' in January 1962 Mao already had reason enough for mistrusting many of his subordinates. With one thing leading to another, the result was the great purge, known as the 'Cultural Revolution' launched by Mao in the summer of 1966, in which those suspected of disloyalty often paid with their lives at the hands of 'Red Guards' – young people mobilized by Mao to further his cause at grass-roots level (Chang and Halliday 2005: 515). Critically for the future of China, Zhou Enlai was spared; Mao knew that he was indispensable.

The Soviet government was terrified by the outbreak of the Cultural Revolution (Schwartz 2003: 136), but there was still nothing that Moscow could do about it. The result, at least until the end of the 1960s, was simply a stand-off between the Soviet Union and the People's Republic. However unwelcome this may have been in Moscow, it certainly suited Beijing's purposes. With the Soviet Union, insisting – even after the fall of Khrushchev – in claiming primacy among all communist countries (Heikal 1978: 151), including China, there was little prospect of the position changing.

Critically, the US was also a player in this game. Brezhnev came to power at almost the same time as the Gulf of Tonkin resolution passed by the US Congress led – as related on page 91 – to a massive escalation of the war in Vietnam, which in the end led to US President Lyndon Johnson deciding not to stand for re-election in 1968. At this stage Brezhnev had no interest in involving the US in Soviet concerns about what was happening in China; indeed any attempt to do so would be futile since Washington still insisted that the only legitimate government of China was that of the Nationalists in Taiwan. What counted for Brezhnev at this stage was the possibility of negotiations with President Johnson relating to nuclear disarmament, a matter in which China was not involved. In the event Soviet involvement in Vietnam proved to be little hindrance to such a prospect.

If little happened during the 1960s to change the frigid relationship between China and the Soviet Union, with the 1970s, and a new US president, Richard Nixon, the position would change radically. This was the result of two foreign policy achievements of Nixon: first, he became the first US president to negotiate directly, and indeed fruitfully, with Mao Zedong and Zhou Enlai, and second, he ended the war in Vietnam. Although, in both cases, the consequences for the Soviet Union would be far-reaching, in neither of them had Brezhnev, or anyone else in Moscow, any say at all.

The position, for Moscow, did not change after Gerald Ford succeeded Nixon as US President in 1974, nor when Jimmy Carter succeeded Ford in 1977. The same was true when the People's Republic acquired new leaders following the deaths of first Zhou, and then Mao, in 1976. Throughout the 1970s China and the US were constantly in contact at the highest level, and for China's interests were best served, at least in the judgment of its leaders, by discouraging Washington from pursuing a similar close relationship with Moscow. When, therefore, President Ford, in November 1974, extended a trip – planned while Nixon was still in office – to Japan and Korea to include Vladivostok, where he would meet Brezhnev for the first time as President, it soon became clear that Mao was displeased. The Soviet presence in the Far East was always a sensitive issue for Beijing, as can be seen from the military clashes that even on Brezhnev's watch had taken place along the long frontier between the Soviet Union and the People's Republic. Vladivostok, in particular had only been lost to Russia in 1860, as a result of a treaty which imperial China – weakened by defeat in the second Opium War with Britain – was powerless to reject. Establishing the People's Republic as a power equal to that of the 'middle kingdom' – the official name of imperial China – during its best days, was always Mao's ambition. Although *realpolitik* meant that the lands lost to Russia in the nineteenth century could not be recovered as easily as the People's Republic had incorporated Tibet in 1950, their loss was still painful to Mao. In the context, therefore, of diplomatic relations between China and the US, the Vladivostok meeting between Ford and Brezhnev, 'technical convenience had been allowed to override common sense' (Kissinger 2011: 305). This, at least, was the perspective of the US Secretary of State. Seen from Moscow the meeting could be regarded as a diplomatic success, but even so it did not bring any useful gain to the Soviet Union. The reason was simple enough: throughout the 1970s Washington's achievements in its negotiations with Beijing were far too important to allow them to be jeopardized by a single 'clumsy American agreement' with the Soviet Union (ibid.: 304). Kissinger, following the Vladivostok meeting, immediately deployed all his diplomatic skills in damage control – and in any case Mao was 'desperately ill' (ibid.: 306).

The critical point for Brezhnev was that Moscow had to come to terms with the fact that Washington, for whatever reason, was giving unprecedented priority to its relationship with Beijing. Once again, in terms of *realpolitik*, there was every reason for doing so. First, it is worth noting a critical insight on the part of Nixon: quite simply, American politics had evolved to the point that it was broadly acceptable, both to the American people and the US Congress, that the Chinese nationalists, confined to Taiwan, should no longer be recognized as the legitimate government of China. Nixon, in 1971, accepted that the People's Republic was entitled to China's place in the UN, including permanent membership of the Security Council. This was the key move, and it mattered less that the US Embassy in Beijing only opened in 1979, when Carter was President. Even so, in Carter's view this was the step which 'drove the Soviets up the wall' (cited Mitchell 2010: 81).

For Washington there was more to it than just accepting the course of history. The new China policy had a number of specific advantages. First it affirmed the vast importance (stressed recently by President Obama) of the Asia-Pacific region. Beijing, by joining the Soviet Union, in supporting North Korea in the Korean war (1950–1953) – at the cost of hundreds of thousands of casualties – had ensured that the United States, for domestic political reasons, could be relied upon to block – into the indefinite future – the People's Republic taking over China's seat in the UN.

Fifteen years later the war in Vietnam was a different case. Although it was some time before it became clear to Washington, the People's Republic did not support Ho Chi Minh's aim to establish a unitary communist state including the whole of Vietnam, both North and South, and ideally, according to his book, not only Laos and Cambodia, but also Thailand (Kissinger 2011: 364). On the contrary this was a most unwelcome prospect to Beijing, as can be seen from the second-level delegation sent to Hanoi for Ho's funeral in 1969 (Chang and Halliday 205: 491).[4] Fortunately for Washington, Henry Kissinger, Nixon's National Security Adviser, was able to read the signs of a new order correctly, and persuade both the President and the US Congress that the time had come for drastic revision of America's China policy. Even more important, Kissinger was able to convince Beijing of the change of heart in Washington.

If the impact of all this on Moscow was left to one side, Washington was bound to discover, sooner or later, what this meant to Brezhnev. The denouement came in June 1973, at Nixon's own California home in San Clemente, at the end of a US–Soviet summit that had started in Washington. At a midday meeting between Brezhnev on one side, and Nixon and Kissinger on the other, Brezhnev made clear his hatred for the Chinese, who were perfidious, sly and – as witness the Cultural Revolution – capable of cruelty on a massive scale. Mao himself was 'treacherous' no doubt the result of his mental condition (Kissinger 1982: 294). Brezhnev warned that within ten years the Chinese nuclear programme would run level with that of the Soviet Union. Gromyko, also present at San Clemente if not at the midday meeting, repeated a warning already given, that any military agreement between the US and the People's Republic would lead to war. Kissinger re-affirmed that there had been no military discussions with China, but added that the US was certain to react to any Soviet attack on China (ibid.: 295). Brezhnev, however, reported that Soviet arms deliveries to North Vietnam had been suspended, following the Paris accords related in Chapter 00. Soviet sabre-rattling did not lead to any change of course in Washington's dealings with Beijing, for, as Nixon had always insisted, these had no military dimension. In the event, the US–Chinese rapprochement led Moscow to compete for Washington's favour, leading to a significant increase in contacts between the two nuclear super-powers (Kissinger 2011: 28).

From the perspective of Moscow, Brezhnev and Gromyko's misgivings, as stated at San Clemente, were still well-founded. Throughout the whole period, starting with the outbreak of the Korean War in 1950, the US maintained a very strong military presence in the western Pacific, with the Seventh Fleet constantly present in the East and South China seas, and a strong military and air force presence in Japan, South Korea and the Philippines, and equally strong – and also effective – diplomatic representation in Thailand and Indonesia. For Washington in all this wide area there was, so far as the Soviet Union was concerned no contest, and the same was largely true of China.

At the same time the People's Republic, for Washington, had two specific advantages over the Soviet Union. First it had no comparable history of empire-building outside its own frontiers, while the Soviet Union, as related in Chapter 10, was constantly fishing in troubled waters, whether in Africa, the Middle East or even Latin America. Second, although the People's Republic (with help from the Soviet Union in the 1950s) had developed its own nuclear weapons programme, it was – with its main operational bases deep inside China – on such a small scale as to constitute little threat to the outside world; the position could of course change as Brezhnev had warned at San Clemente. While for Brezhnev nuclear disarmament, which dominated negotiations between Moscow and Washington throughout his time, was a constant preoccupation, it counted for little in Beijing's foreign policy, whether in relation to Moscow or Washington.

In terms of international goodwill Moscow paid a far higher price for its treatment of dissidents than Beijing had to pay for the Cultural Revolution, even though the suffering of the Chinese people as it ran its course was incomparably greater than anything in the post-Stalin era in the Soviet Union. For one thing, in October 1970 Mao declared an end to the Cultural Revolution (Kissinger 2011: 207), so that Nixon, in dealing with Mao at an unprecedentedly high level during the early 1970s, could not convincingly be accused of condoning it. What is more, even the most prominent Chinese victims of the Cultural Revolution never had an internationally recognized profile equivalent to that of the leading Soviet dissidents, such as are named in Chapter 6. Indeed, in the mid-1970s – when (as related in Chapter 9) the Helsinki Human Rights Watch was active – the Soviet treatment of Jewish *refuseniks*, such as, notably, Shcharansky, was a major factor in inhibiting progress in US–Soviet negotiations relating to nuclear disarmament. Beijing, in dealing with Washington, faced no such problem.

Soviet policy in relation to the developing world (as described in Chapter 10) was another hostage to fortune not shared by the People's Republic. Soviet diplomatic failure allowed Beijing, in one country after another, to claim the moral high ground, and use it as the base for its own diplomatic initiatives. In this field the foreign policies of the two communist great powers reflected fundamentally different approaches to the world outside their own frontiers. Going back to the days of Lenin, and the founding of the Comintern, Moscow assumed the role of leading a revolution destined, according to orthodox Marxist-Leninism, for victory worldwide. When Zhou Enlai, having escaped from Shanghai in 1927 (Crump 2007a: 5), reached Moscow to represent the Chinese Communist Party in the Comintern, this was the objective that he, together with the delegates representing other national parties, was asked to accept.

Forty-odd years later, Zhou, as Mao's foreign secretary and right-hand man, ensured that the People's Republic followed a quite different course, which was traditionally Chinese. Essentially China – unlike the Soviet Union – was not concerned to become a 'super-power', but was intent only on securing its own territorial integrity (Kissinger 2011: 247). As to military confrontation with the outside world this would never go further than armed intervention in neighbouring states perceived as potentially endangering the security of China itself. While this principle explains two cases of such intervention: Korea in 1950 and Vietnam in 1979, it also explains a series of border conflicts with the Soviet Union, which, in 1969, culminated in Soviet and Chinese forces clashing on Zhenbao Island in the Ussuri River, part of the frontier between the two sides. This was a deterrent operation – named 'Retribution' by Mao (Haslam 2011: 257) – by the People's Republic, but it had the opposite effect: Soviet Forces, much increased in number, stepped up their operations along the whole frontier, to the point that the world became conscious of the possibility of outright war (ibid.: 258). The effect on US policy was crucial. Nixon, in his first year as President, regarded the Soviet Union as 'the more dangerous party', and while emphasizing US neutrality, accepted that if need be, the US 'should tilt to the greatest extent possible towards China' (Kissinger 2011: 218). This was the first, and most far-reaching, of the succession of events related in this chapter. Considering the way these unfolded in the interests of the People's Republic, the *casus belli* orchestrated by its forces along the Ussuri River in 1969 must be considered as a diplomatic master stroke. It was particularly successful because Washington, disregarding a report from Soviet Ambassador Dobrynin, preferred to believe that Soviet forces were the aggressor on Zhenbao island (ibid.: 216).[5]

In the final years of the 1970s the Soviet Union – as indeed the rest of the world – had to come to terms with new leaders in Beijing, following the death of both Zhou and Mao in 1976. Although for a year or two it was uncertain where power would finally rest, by the end of 1978 the matter was decided: in the course of 1978, Deng Xiaoping, a master politician banished by Mao, but allowed to return from exile in 1977, outplayed all rivals; in December 1978 at the third plenum of the eleventh Central Committee meeting of the Chinese Communist Party, he plainly dominated the party – a position confirmed by the fifth plenum two years later (Kissinger 2011: 339).[6] A pragmatist who shunned publicity and never held any major office, Deng was the supreme mandarin operating behind the scenes (ibid.: 334). This was the man whom Brehznev, already in the state of advanced ill health that would lead to his death in 1982, had to deal with in Beijing. Inevitably this meant that decisions were left to the Politburo, but this also was unable to stand up to Deng. Although Deng is now known mainly for his spectacular revival of the Chinese economy, he spent the years 1978–1979 travelling abroad. He missed no opportunity to portray the People's Republic as the victim of aggression by the Soviet Union and Vietnam (ibid.: 357), stressing at the same time its economic backwardness (ibid.: 358). In 1978, some 33 years after the end of the Pacific War, peace was agreed with Japan, and a year later, the first US Ambassador arrived in Beijing. By arranging to visit Washington just before his planned invasion of Vietnam in 1979, Deng succeeded in creating the impression that he had silent American consent to this operation (ibid.: 360).[7]

In all this the object was to intimidate the Soviet Union. For this purpose Deng also tried to mobilize the support of the considerable Chinese communities in Thailand, Malaysia, the Philippines and Indonesia, and although he learnt consistently that these countries feared the Chinese dragon more than the Russian bear, there was no doubt about the intent behind his mission, for as he told President Carter 'wherever the Soviet Union sticks its fingers, there we must cut them off'. (Kissinger 2011: 557, note 39). The threat may well explain Moscow's relative passivity in the 1979 war between the People's Republic and Vietnam, which, as suggested by Kissinger (ibid.: 374), 'in retrospect . . . can be seen as the first symptom of the decline of the Soviet Union'. For Deng even a tacit understanding with Washington counted for more than anything that could be achieved in Moscow (ibid.: 363). By the time Brezhnev died in 1982, the Soviet Union, as a major actor on the world stage, had been conspicuously degraded by Beijing. For the pragmatic Deng this was no more than a question of *realpolitik*.

Notes

1 Mao was actually in Moscow from December 1949 to February 1950 (Gromyko 1989: 318).
2 This was the advice consistently given to the US State Department throughout the 1950s (Haslam 2011: 192).
3 A key event in this process was a meeting of the World Federation of Trade Unions in June 1960, where the Chinese delegates, instructed by Mao, were lobbying hard against Moscow. European delegates, close to Khrushchev, were labelled 'servants of imperialism', to the point that Khrushchev, himself, noted how the Chinese were 'spitting in our face' (Chang and Halliday 2005: 463).
4 Zhou did go to Hanoi just before the funeral, but deliberately left early so as to avoid encountering any top Soviet leader attending it.
5 Somewhat oddly Zhenbao is not mentioned at all in Dobrynin (1995).
6 A Central Committee meeting took place intermittently over a period of five years, within each year a 'plenum' of all authorized delegates. Although these were staged events, the proceedings made clear the current line-up within the party, which meant that they were studied very closely at many different levels outside government, both at home and abroad.
7 Mao Zedong used the same strategy in 1957, when a long planned bombardment on the Nationalist held island of Quemoy took place shortly after Khrushchev's ill-fated visit to Beijing.

Part IV

Brezhnev and the fall of the Soviet state

13 Downhill all the way

Implicit in the title of this book, *Brezhnev and the Decline of the Soviet Union*, is the proposition that the final collapse of the Soviet Union in 1991 was at least in part the result of events occurring in the eighteen year period from 1964 to 1982, for which Brezhnev, as *vozhd*, must answer to history. It could hardly be otherwise: Brezhnev was at the helm of the ship of state for nearly half of the 38 years from the death of Stalin in 1953 to the eclipse of Gorbachev in 1991.

Even accepting that in 1964 Khrushchev left to his successors a ship already on the wrong course, domestically and internationally, economically and politically, the hard truth is that Brezhnev did little or nothing to change direction. Worse still, he must answer for any number of events which made it next to impossible for the Soviet Union to reinvent itself as a viable state: the most significant of these – placed in their historical context – are related in Parts II and III of this book. What they have in common is that while adding little or nothing to the well-being of the populations that comprised the Soviet Union they became a charge on its economy, which in the long run was unaffordable.

Consider first the vast and ambitious armaments programmes of the military industrial complex described in Chapter 5: although these undoubtedly provided well-remunerated employment for scientists and engineers, and to a lesser degree the technologists and skilled labour that supported them, this could only come at the cost of the millions who were not involved – at least not at this level.[1] So also, the stimulus to basic research, such as was brilliantly carried out by Sakharov – among many others – did little for the millions who were failed by Soviet state education. The same is true in sport and the arts: only a very small minority ever played football in the Moscow Dynamo Stadium or performed in the Bolshoi Theatre.[2] The result was that the great Soviet masses were continually being fed on the signal achievements of a very small minority – a diet of bread and circuses that would prove very thin in the long run.[3] At the same time, those recognized as top achievers belonged – much more that in the west – to another world, that of the *nomenklatura* (as described in Chapter 4). Here, it is significant how many of these top achievers (almost all recognized with the appropriate medals) were still ready to criticize the regime in public, not only within the Soviet Union but to the world at large. The dissidents named in Chapters 6 and 9, representing the whole spectrum of the arts and sciences, were far from being alone in revealing to the world truths about life in the Soviet Union which Brezhnev and his fellow members of the Politburo would rather have concealed – and consistently denied. Even so, punitive treatment of dissidents, rather than silencing them, only spread their message more widely,[4] particularly outside the Soviet Union.

Notwithstanding the adverse publicity, it is difficult to assess how far the whole process significantly hastened the decline of the Soviet Union, even after the Helsinki Final Act notably increased its momentum. Gromyko's complete ignorance of the whole Shcharansky affair (as recounted in Chapter 9) speaks volumes, for if the Politburo took it as a serious threat he would surely have been briefed about it. But then the Politburo could have been mistaken, as it certainly was on many other items on Brezhnev's agenda. In any case, the price paid by Brezhnev was a critical loss of credibility in negotiating questions, such as nuclear disarmament, which were extremely important to him: to appreciate this point it is only necessary to compare the record of his dealings with Washington during the time of Nixon's presidency with that of Reagan's. The failure on Brezhnev's part at the end of the day was doubly critical, because without the agreement he looked for the Soviet Union was committed to unprecedented expenditure on nuclear weapons as a result of new American advances in both production and technology (Skidelsky 1995: 96); although Brezhnev's appalling state of health during Reagan's presidency doubtless prevented him from appreciating this, this was yet another unaffordable charge on the Soviet economy.

The costs of maintaining the Warsaw Pact, particularly during the 1970s – Brezhnev's decade par excellence – were at a comparable level. The economic planning behind the Pact required industrial production in the NSWP states to be focussed on satisfying the demands of a command economy – that of the Soviet Union – which was disproportionately committed to the military industrial complex. This required the Soviet Union, in turn, to supply the NSWP states with energy and raw materials at below world-market prices: during the 1970s the average annual cost of this hidden subsidy was at the phenomenal level of $10,000,000,000 (Skidelsky 1995: 144) – equivalent to about $100 for every individual citizen of a NSWP state. While there was little direct benefit to the populations of the NSWP states, they were, from the beginning of the 1970s, allowed to borrow from the western world and so acquire the technology and capital goods required for increased industrial production (ibid.: 143). One result, in the short term, was an increased supply of consumer goods, leading to a welcome improvement in the standard of living – particularly in Poland. Since, however, the NSWP economies were still geared to that of the Soviet Union under a regional planning system known as the Council for Mutual Economic Assistance (CMEA) in which they were all represented (ibid.: 143) the economic gains from the new freedom of action were by the end of the 1970s unsustainable. The only way to service the indebtedness to the western world was by exporting to it, which the CMEA regime made very difficult. This was the economic background to the Polish crisis described on pages 130–2. All this was in effect a double whammy: the Soviet Union lost exports of energy and raw materials at world-market prices (which, under the OPEC-led economic crisis of the late

1970s, were higher than ever)[5] while at the same time the NSWP states lost exports of manufactures.

Quite apart from the costs of subsidizing the economies of the NSWP states, that of the Soviet Union was burdened, on a comparable scale, as a result of its political commitments to Third World nations. While three, the communist states of Vietnam, North Korea and Cuba were a charge on the Soviet economy throughout the Brezhnev era, new Soviet adventures in Africa, as related in Chapter 10 for Ethiopia and Somalia, Angola and Mozambique, involved vast expenditure with next to nothing in return (Pleshakov 2000: 234)[6] – to say nothing of the massive devastation of local populations. Almost everything gained in Africa was lost even before the end of the 1980s, as was also the credibility of Soviet foreign policy – if it still had any. Needless to say, the same was true of Afghanistan, the scene of the most disastrous of Brezhnev's foreign interventions.

Although this chapter – and indeed much of the rest of this book – leads almost inescapably to the conclusion that the decline of the Soviet Union, under Brezhnev, was the result of an armaments race in which the Soviet commitment to the production of devastating weapons of mass destruction was more than the economy could afford – at least in the long run – combined with commitments to other communist states, both within the Warsaw Pact and in the world at large, which were just as great a burden, this study would be incomplete without some notice of the public face of Soviet economic achievement as seen by the man in the street.

Here, the Marxist-Leninist mind-cast of Brezhnev and the Politburo – which was shared by almost all *apparatchiki* lower down in the hierarchy – inevitably meant an overwhelming bias in favour of large-scale projects (of which many under Stalin depended on Gulag labour). Even before World War II such achievements as the Moscow Metro and the world's largest hydroelectric station at Zaporozhye demonstrated to Soviet citizens the priorities of the state in providing for their welfare. Kolkhozes in the countryside (particularly in land reclaimed in the virgin territories) and vast blocks of flats in the cities proclaimed the same preference for mega-projects.

Of these, the complex of nuclear power stations at Chernobyl in the Ukraine, which on 26 April 1986 became part of world history as a result of a devastating nuclear catastrophe, was one of the largest civil engineering projects planned – and in part completed – under Brezhnev. The first two units, Nos. 1 and 2, were constructed in the period, 1970–1977, with units, Nos. 3 and 4, following on to be completed in 1983. The Soviet nuclear programme, launched by Stalin in the late 1940s, continued to expand up to the final days of the Soviet Union. Chernobyl, although only one part of a programme involving nuclear power generation in any number of sites throughout the Soviet Union, was exceptionally large in scale.[7] Even so, the units comprised in it were of standard design, and the actual catastrophe could have equally occurred elsewhere. With nuclear power being the responsibility of the Ministry of Medium Machine Building (Gorbachev 1997: 243) – just one of the many comprising the vast centralized Soviet bureaucracy – it can hardly be contended that the General Secretary of the CPSU, or, for that matter, the Politburo, were directly answerable for any local installation such as Chernobyl.

On the other hand, the nuclear power bureaucracy, as it related to Chernobyl, had all the shortcomings inherent in Soviet government – short-term expedients adopted to meet inflexible time-tables, poor security procedures, diffusion of responsibility; in any number of ways regulatory agencies in the west would have disallowed Chernobyl procedures, as in principle they should have done in the Soviet Union. All this was part and parcel of a system that Brezhnev – who never questioned Marxism-Leninism – was committed to maintain.[8] With this background Chernobyl was an accident waiting to happen, and that in a sector of the economy – electricity generation – which, from the 1920s onwards, always enjoyed priority. It should also be noted that the whole Chernobyl enterprise was supported by a new town, Pripyat, with nearly 50,000 inhabitants, built almost in the middle of nowhere during Brezhnev's watch. Even though Gorbachev was at the helm in the Soviet Union throughout 1986, the silent witness of Pripyat, completely and permanently abandoned after the disaster of April 1986, tells as much about the character of Brezhnev's regime as any other enterprise that it promoted.[9]

Leaving aside Chernobyl, prestigious public works had the further advantage for a man such as Brezhnev of providing the opportunity for a spectacular opening ceremony and, thereafter, carrying the name of a public figure appropriate to the scale of the enterprise. (Any number of completed projects had the words *imeni Brezhneva* – 'in the name of Brezhnev' (Zemtsov 1989: 121f) – engraved somewhere on the façade: the more imposing the construction, the more it pandered to the vanity of whoever it was named after.[10]) All too often the facade was on a scale far beyond the importance of the building in relation to its economic function. The train station at Dnepropetrovsk – the city where Brezhnev's political career was launched in the late 1930s – is one example from his time at the top. Behind an imposing façade on Petrovsky Square, the train station consists mainly of a vast empty concourse, with no commercial aspect – the ticket offices and cloakrooms are in a somewhat claustrophobic basement. Beyond the imposing station building there are twelve platforms, accessed down a flight of steps leading to a pedestrian tunnel, but there are remarkably few trains – and little sign of jostling crowds. Economically this makes sense: in Brezhnev's day Soviet railroads were mainly for transporting freight; passengers over short distances travelled by bus, and increasingly, over long distances, by air. While small retail outlets along the two short sides of Petrovsky Square make up somewhat for the animation lacking in the train station, the heart of the city's consumer micro-economy is to be found in the near-chaotic bus-station, a ten minute walk away. Even in Brezhnev's day this bustling rabbit-warren of small shops and ticket-windows, with crowded buses leaving every minute of the day for destinations both near and far, is still one of the best places to observe a true cross-section of the local population. While the train station reflects the stagnation (*zastoi*) long associated with Brezhnev's name, the bus-station much more reflects the local informal micro-economies essential for making good the shortcomings of state planning in meeting the needs of Soviet consumers. If Brezhnev deserves little credit for the success of the informal economy, the contacts within his own family with some of its most successful entrepreneurs can have left him in little doubt, not only about the scale on which it operated, but also about its importance in helping sustain the formal economy (Kenez 1999: 222) – to say nothing of the lifestyle (as described on page 82) of those at the top. There are no two ways about it: the top operators in the shadow economy were an indispensable part of Brezhnev's power base – and some indeed were close family friends.[11] Who else were the oligarchs who took over in the 1990s other than men whose business empires were already being built up before the fall of the Soviet Union? Freed from the constraints of the Soviet planned economy, these men had little problem operating in the full light of day.[12]

One is left asking not only what sort of man Brezhnev was, but also how much it really mattered? Was he anything more than a 'sleazy mediocrity' (Gellner 1994: 42) brought to the top by a gift for intrigue (Haslam 2011: 215) enabling him to profit from '. . . the law of self-selection of the unfit which governed promotion in the nomenklatura' (Skidelsky 1995: 148)? Once at the top Brezhnev constantly promoted second rate *apparatchiki*, chosen from acquaintances made at every stage of his career (Arbatov 1992: 127). If his success can be explained in terms of stock phrases, 'the right man in the right place at the right time', 'friends in the right places', 'more by good luck than good management', 'swimming with the tide', 'a safe pair of hands' and so on, it also counted that already as a young man he embraced not only the principles of Marxism-Leninism,[13] upon which the government of the Soviet Union was based, but knew how to adapt to the way they were interpreted and enforced by Stalin – which inevitably led to him becoming something of a control freak (Brown 2010: 37). In the Soviet Union of the 1930s all this was a hazardous course, for which Stalin saw no alternative.[14] Brezhnev's relative youth no doubt helped him survive: after all there had to be men of his generation to replace the thousands of senior *apparatchiki* purged by Stalin.

Brezhnev had a good war: with his whole family safe after being evacuated from Ukraine in face of the advancing German armies, he was able to concentrate on his career as a political commissar to the point that once the war was over he was able vastly to exaggerate the importance of his achievements,[15] which were crowned by his being a guest at the victory dinner in Moscow presided over by Stalin.

At this stage in his life Brezhnev was easy-going, dynamic, gregarious, loyal to his subordinates – at the same time being left in little doubt about the horrors of war (experienced at first hand during the Soviet advance into Central Europe in the last year of the Great Patriotic War). By this time it must have been clear to him that intrigue, in which side-lining possible rivals was an essential component, was the key to advancement (Arbatov 1992: 122). This also took for granted the rigid bureaucracy of the Soviet state, which Brezhnev was never minded to change. *Perestroika* had to wait for Gorbachev, when it was too late to save the system.

Although Brezhnev was not well-versed in Russian history and literature, he still believed that he one day would make his own significant contribution. This reflected the vanity which, particularly in the last years of his life, not only assumed absurd proportions but was pandered to by his subordinates, who – as recorded earlier in this book – bestowed upon him one honorary title after another, and awarded him every possible medal. This inordinate vanity was not without political consequences: Brezhnev's willingness to accommodate Washington in relation to the SALT treaties, or the other powers represented at Helsinki in relation to the Final Accord, was calculated to present the right image both to the Soviet Union and to the world at large. Here opportunism rather than long-term strategy guided Brezhnev, even though as an orthodox Marxist-Leninist he never entirely repudiated Lenin's principle that ends justified 'every means of struggle, including terror' (quoted Brown 2010: 33).[16] That he later might be held accountable – as notably in the field of human rights after Helsinki (Westad 2000: 333) – was never on the agenda of a man so blind to events and so lacking in vision, whose main concern, as often as not, was to preserve the privileges and comforts of his office. At the end of the day *nomenklatura* counted for more than political orthodoxy (Brown 2010: 55) – so that Marxism-Leninism was best left to the speech-writers, as was his own three-volume autobiography, published in the mid 1970s.[17] According to Gellner (1994: 3), writing just after the fall of the Soviet empire, '. . . strangely enough the sleazy but at least relatively mild squalor of the Brezhnev years proved far more corrosive for the image of the faith than the total, pervasive, random and massively destructive terrorism of Stalin'. Where Nero 'fiddled while Rome burned', Brezhnev – ideally in the company of eminent foreign guests such as Nixon – preferred to hunt game from his favourite *dacha* while Moscow smouldered. He never noticed.

One final question to be asked about the Brezhnev years: was there ever a point of no return? Looking first at the Nixon presidency and then that of Reagan, one is struck by the fundamental differences in perception of the world scene, and in particular the relative strengths – ideological, political and economic – of the United States and the Soviet Union; where the perception, in the former case, was that the Soviet Union was drawing level with the United States, in the latter, there was little doubt that the United States had regained a decisive lead – if, indeed, it had ever lost it. To a degree this was a matter of temperament, particularly on the American side: Nixon was a born loser, Reagan, a born winner. The year, 1975, was the turning point: Nixon pulled American forces out of Vietnam, while Brezhnev signed the Helsinki accords. If, at the time Nixon was seen as conceding defeat in an operation that had begun in the 1950s, and Brezhnev, by achieving definitive recognition of the frontiers in Eastern Europe, was able to claim a significant victory, the truth was that in 1975 the United States was freed from a critical hostage to fortune, while the Soviet Union had to come to terms with its oppressive human rights record. (In Czechoslovakia, with the remarkably effective Charter 77 movement of 1977, the 1968 Soviet invasion came to haunt the government). Worse still, Brezhnev, misreading the signs of the times (Mitchell 2010: 67) – in particular by seeing the American defeat in Vietnam as 'a Soviet opportunity to assert its power on a global scale' (Hanhimäki 2004: 338) – proceeded with the disastrous Soviet involvement in Africa related in Chapter 10, and then with the invasion of Afghanistan in 1979 – the only intervention by

Soviet troops outside Eastern Europe during the Cold War (ibid.: 84). And if there was one lesson, for both sides in the Cold War, it was that pursuing it, not in Europe, but on the periphery, was not a winning strategy (ibid.: 75). In all this, the unmistakable decline in Brezhnev's health in the late 1970s meant that Soviet policy was no longer shaped by his 'personal impulse' (Dobrynin 1995: 476): how much then were the disastrous events related above beyond his control? If he had remained the man who, in the early 1970s, was rightly seen by the western world in a 'relatively favourable light' (ibid.: 475), would history have taken a different course? Avoiding the hazards of counter-factual history, the fundamental truth about Brezhnev is that he stayed the course after he had played a minor part in bringing Khrushchev, his predecessor, to power in 1955, and then, a major part in deposing Khrushchev in 1962. Brezhnev must always have known that this could not be taken for granted, and what is more, that no-one at the top in the Soviet Union ever resigned of his own accord. Successful power-play inside the party – as evidenced by the side-lining of Kosygin and Podgorny – brought Brezhnev to such a position of strength that few thought of deposing him. News of his death in 1982 must have been a relief to many in the Politburo, particularly after the much more focussed Andropov succeeded him. By this time the Soviet Union was past saving, even by the redoubtable Mikhail Gorbachev (Suri 2006: 158), who was at the helm before it was finally dissolved in 1991 – less than ten years after Brezhnev's death.[18]

Notes

1 Note here the millions of prisoners or conscripted labourers employed on remote construction sites, or in winning the raw materials (such as notably uranium) required by the [nuclear] armaments industry. (For the Gulag contribution under Stalin see page 26).
2 Moscow Dynamo, if best known as the name of a leading football team, was only one manifestation of the All-Union Dynamo Sports Club, whose activities also extended far beyond football.
3 Accepting that supporters' clubs are a significant part of popular culture worldwide, it is still significant how much they are encouraged by authoritarian regimes such as that of Spain under Franco.
4 See the discussion of *samizdat* on Chapter 6, pages 105–110.
5 See page 99, note 13.
6 In Angola alone this had reached nearly $2,000,000,000 by Brezhnev's death in 1982 (see page 169).
7 Geographically the site was almost ideal: located in sparsely populated countryside, with the wide Pripyat River available to supply water on the scale required by nuclear reactors, it was still close to major industrial centres of Ukraine and Belarus, to say nothing of large cities such as Kiev and Minsk.
8 '. . . peaceful coexistence means neither the preservation of the social and political status quo nor the weakening of the ideological struggle and activity of Communist Parties' (*Pravda*, 16 September 1974).
9 The website, [URL]http://www.chernobylwel.com[/URL], shows how Chernobyl looks now, at the same time offering tourists the 'experience of the unique 1986 communist atmosphere in Pripyat.' The tour includes the Bridge of Death and the Cemetery of Technique. It is not a good advertisement for Marxism-Leninism.

10 The Dnepr power station was named after Lenin.
11 The dealing of Brezhnev's son, Yuri, and his daughter, Galina, as reported by his niece, Luba, leave no room for doubt here (Brezhneva 1995: 354, 355).
12 See Chapter 4, note 11 on page 87.
13 Although later in his life Brezhnev once observed 'who's going to believe I ever read Marx' (Arbatov 1992: 123).
14 'When the *nomenklatura* killed each other and accompanied the murderous rampage with blatantly mendacious political theatre, belief survived; but when the *nomenklatura* [under Brehznev] switched from shooting each other to bribing each other, faith evaporated' (Gellner 19934: 41).
15 This became only too clear in the mid-1970s, with the publication of the first volume, 'Little Russia', of Brezhnev's biographical trilogy. The title refers to a small corner of Russia on the Black Sea coast where Brezhnev first confronted the Germans: significantly the local campaign is hardly mentioned in any of the voluminous histories of the war.
16 See also Pleshakov (2000: 234–235), noting that Brezhnev also '. . . wanted to see the worldwide victory of communism and its embodiment – the Soviet empire. Nothing could be more erroneous than to suggest that the Kremlin after Stalin was satisfied with the status quo in international affairs. If it had been so, why would [Brezhnev] have actively interfered . . . in Indochina, Ethiopia and, finally, Afghanistan . . . in the core ideas that went into decision-making as a system, there was a very considerable continuity between 1945 and 1975, and perhaps even later.'
17 One of the jokes told about Brezhnev was his reported comment to an aide: 'Our press has so much praise for my latest book, I am becoming curious. I think maybe one day I'll read some of it myself'. The preface relates how one informant, at school in the Soviet Union in the 1970s, described the autobiography.
18 Andropov died less that a year after Brezhnev, to be succeeded by the much less effective Chernenko, who in turn died in 1985.

Glossary

apparatchik	Soviet bureaucrat (generally a Party member) appointed on recommendation from Moscow. See also *nomenklatura*.
bidniak	poor peasant, often lazy hard drinker, surviving mainly as hired hand
Central Committee	Party forum of CPSU directed by secretariat.
Cheka	The secret police organised by Lenin directly after the October revolution
CPSU	Communist Party of the Soviet Union
CSCE	Conference on Security and Cooperation in Europe (Helsinki)
Council of Ministers	(Formerly Council of People's Commissars) directs the bureaucracy (as opposed to the party) with the Chairman ranking, for protocol, as No. 2 to the President of the Supreme Soviet.
Curzon Line	A line proposed by the British foreign secretary Lord Curzon as the eastern frontier of the new state of Poland after the defeat of Germany in World War I. Although not then adopted, after 1945 it defined, more or less, the western boundary of the part of Poland claimed by Stalin for the Soviet Union.
Donbas	A large economically important region of south central Russia defined by the flood-plain of the Don river.
dvorianstvo	Traditional Russian landowning nobility
izba	typical Russian small wooden house
gimnaziya	secondary school providing a classical education
GULAG	*Glavnoye Upravleniye inspravitelno-trudovykh Lagerei i koloniy*, lit. 'head directorate of correctional labour camps and colonies': initiated by OGPU in 1930 it effectively provided large scale slave labour for the Soviet economy.

Kahal	Jewish institution of local self-government
KGB	*Komitet Gosudarstvennoi Bezopastnosti*, lit 'committee of state security', but for a period in Soviet Russia the principal organ of state security (cf. MVD, NKVD).
kolkhoz	*Kollektivny Khozyaistvo* (Collective Farm)
Konsomol	*Kommunistichsky Soyuz Molodyozh'* (Communist Youth Union) with indoctrination as its main function nation-wide.
krysha	(lit. 'roof') refers to a senior who can be relied on for protection, if not advancement – typically within the CPSU.
kulak	(lit. 'fist') richer self-made peasants, exploiting others, but with basically same social origins
MBFR	*Mutual and Balanced Force Reductions* followed Nixon-Brezhnev meeting with US-Soviet talks in Vienna continuing on and off until 1989.
MVD	*Ministerstvo Vnutrennykh Del*, lit 'ministry of internal affairs', but for a period in Soviet Russia the principal organ of state security (cf. KGB, NKVD)
NKVD	*Narodny Komitet Vnutrennykh Del*, lit 'national committee for internal affairs', but for a period in Soviet Russia the principal organ of state security (cf. KGB, MVD).
NSDD	National Security Decision Directive (US)
nomenklatura	privileged hierarchy of party/state officials in the Communist Party, Armed Forces, Arts and Science, and government ministries, with entrenched rights according to seniority. Subdivides into different categories, e.g. 'management nomenklatura'. See also *apparatchik*.
NSWP	Non-Soviet Warsaw Pact
oblast	region (aka *krai* in special cases)
obshchina	peasant village commune with common land
OGPU	*Obyedinonnoye Gosudarstvennoye Politicheskoye Upravleniye*, lit 'joint state political directorate' functioned as Stalin's secret police until 1934, when it merged with the NKVD.
Pale of Settlement	The part of imperial Russia to which Jews were confined.
party congress	infrequent forum of grass-roots CPSU members allowing for top party policy to be announced and reported in the media. Officially elects Central Committee, which in turn elects General Secretary.

pogrom	Yiddish adaptation of Russian 'by thunder' to refer to violent persecution of an ethnic group (in Russia pre-eminently Jewish).
politburo	highest decision making organ of CPSU, and in practice a self-perpetuating body, and as such top Soviet executive
Pölnische Wirtschaft	German for 'Polish economy', connoting 'chaos'
President (Soviet)	Chairman of the Central Committee
Prime-Minister (Soviet)	Chairman of the Council of Ministers
propinacja	monopoly of distilling and distribution of alcohol (Poland)
proteksia	patronage
pyatiletka	'five year plan'
rada	Ukrainian equivalent of *soviet*
SALT	Strategic Arms Limitation Talks
secretariat	controller of party bureaucracy
seredniak	middle-class peasant, owning horses and livestock, but seldom machinery
sejm	Polish legislature (at both national and local levels)
shtetl	Jewish self-contained community
starshyna	traditional Ukrainian land-owning aristocracy
soviet	lit. 'council', in Soviet Russia, the key political unit at every level of government.
START	Strategic Arms Reduction Talks
shtetl	a small town with its character defined by a substantial Jewish population
Supreme Soviet	USSR bicameral legislature, with one house elected from population at large, and other from national republics. The latter each had in turn their own supreme soviet.
svyazi	connections
szlachta	polish landowning elite
vedomost'	record
vydvizhentsy	someone tipped for advancement
vozhd	leader (cf German *Führer*, Italian *Duce*)
WP	Warsaw Pact
yeshiva	a Jewish educational institution for the study of sacred texts

Bibliography

Abramovitch, R.R. (1962) *The Soviet Revolution*, London: George Allen & Unwin.

Aid, M.M. (2009) *The Secret Sentry: The Untold History of the National Security Agency*, New York: Bloomsbury Press.

Alexander, M. (1998) British Diplomatic Oral History Programme, interview 34, [URL] http://www.chu.cam.ac.uk/archives/collections/BDOHP/Alexander.pdf[/URL].

Alexandrov, I. (1968) 'Ataka protiv sotsialistichheskikh ustoev Chekoslovakii' ('The attack against the socialist foundations of Czechoslovakia'), Moscow: *Pravda*, 11 July, p. 4.

Alexandrov-Agentov, A.M. (1994) *Ot Kollontai do Gorbachova: Bospominaniya Diplomata (From Kollontai to Gorbachev; Memoirs of a Diplomat)*, Moscow: Mezhdunarodniye Otnosheniya.

Alliluyeva, S. (1967) *Dvadtsat' Picem k Drugu (Twenty letters to a friend)*, London: Hutchinson.

Amalrik, A. (1970) *Will the Soviet Union Survive until 1984?* London: Penguin.

Anderson, J.L. (2011) *King of Kings: The last sayings of Muammar Qaddafi*, New York City: New Yorker (November 7: 44–57).

Arbatov, G.A. (1992) *The System: An Insider's Life in Soviet Politics*, New York: Random House.

Barberini, G. (2006) 'L'avvio del Ostpolitik vaticana', in A. Melloni (ed.) *Il Filo Sottile: l'Ostpolitik Vaticana di Agostino Casaroli*, Bologna: Società editrice il Mulino, pp. 49–106.

Kornbluh, P. (ed.) (1998) *Bay of Pigs Declassified*, New York: The New Press.

Bourne, P.G. (1997) *Jimmy Carter: A Comprehensive Biography from Plains to Postpresidency*, New York: Scribner.

Brezhnev, L.I. (1965) 'Velikaya Pobeda Sovyetschovo Naroda' ('The great victory of the Soviet Nation'), Moscow: *Pravda*, 9 May, pp. 1–2.

Brezhnev, L.I. (1968) 'Suberenitet i Mezhdunarodnaya Otvestvennost' Sotsialisticheskikh Narodov' ('Sovereignty and the international responsibility of Socialist countries'), Moscow: *Pravda*, 26 September, pp. 1–2.

Brezhnev, L. I. (1977) *A Short Biography*, Institute of Marxism-Leninism, CPSU Central Committee, Oxford, Pergamon Press.

Brezhnev, L.I. (1979) *Peace, Détente and Soviet-American Relations: A Collection of Public Statements*, New York: Harcourt, Brace, Jovanovich.

Brezhneva, L. (1995) *The World I Left Behind: Pieces of a Past*, New York: Random House.

Brintlinger, A. and Vinistky, I. (eds.) (2007) *Madness and the Mad in Russian Culture*, Toronto: University of Toronto Press.

Brown, A. (2010) *The Rise and Fall of Communism*, London: Vintage.

Bullock, A. (1991) *Hitler and Stalin: Parallel Lives*, London: Harper Collins.

Byrne, M. (1998) New Evidence on the Polish Crisis 1980–82, *Cold War International History Project, Bulletin No.11*, Washington: Woodrow Wilson Center.

Chadwick, O. (1992) *The Christian Church in the Cold War*, London: Penguin.

Chang, J. and Halliday, J. (2005) *Mao: the Unknown Story*, New York: Alfred A. Knopf.

Churchill, W.S. (1951) *The Grand Alliance*, Boston: Houghton Mifflin.

Coleman, F. (1997) *The Decline and Fall of the Soviet Empire: Forty Years that Shook the World from Stalin to Yeltsin*, New York: St Martin's Griffin.

Collins, J.J. (1986) *The Soviet Invasion of Afghanistan: A Study of the Use of Force in Soviet Foreign Policy*, Lexington MA: D.C. Heath and Company.

Cook, S.A. (2012) *The Struggle for Egypt: From Nasser to Tahrir Square*, New York NY, Council on Foreign Relations (Kindle Edition).

Corley, F. (1994) 'Soviet Reaction to the Election of Pope John Paul II', *Religion, State and Society*, 22: 37–66.

Cousins, N. (1972) *The Improbable Triumvirate: John F. Kennedy, Pope John, Nikita Khrushchev*, New York: W.W. Norton.

Crump, L. (2011) Closing Ranks or Drifting Apart? The Warsaw Pact on Thin Ice (1961–1969), PHP.

Crump, T. (2001) *A Brief History of Science*, London: Constable.

Crump, T. (2007a) *Asia-Pacific: A History of Empire and Conflict*, London: Hambledon-Constable.

Crump, T. (2007b) *The Age of Steam: The Power that drove the Industrial Revolution*, London: Constable-Robinson.

Crump, T. (2010) *A Brief History of how the Industrial Revolution Changed the World*, London: Constable-Robinson.

Davy, R. (2009) 'Helsinki myths: setting the record straight on the Final Act of the CSCE, 1975', *Cold War History*, 9: 1, 1–22.

Dear, I.C.B (ed.) (1995) *Oxford Companion to the Second World War*, Oxford: Oxford University Press.

de Klerk, F.W. (1998) *The Autobiography: The Last Trek – A New Beginning*, London: Macmillan.

de Meeus, A. (undated) *White Book on the Internment of Dissidents in Soviet Mental Hospitals*, Brussels: International Committee for the Defence of Human Rights in the U.R.S.S.

Deutscher, I. (1967) *Stalin: A Political Biography*, Oxford: Oxford University Press.

Djilas, M. (1957) *The New Class: An Analysis of the Communist System*, London: Thames and Hudson.

Djilas, M. (1969) *Conversations with Stalin*, London: Pelican.

Dobrynin, A. (1995) *In Confidence*, New York: Random House.

Eban, A. (1977) *An Autobiography*, London: Weidenfeld and Nicolson.

Ellsberg, D. (2002) *Secrets: a Memoir of Vietnam and the Pentagon Papers*, New York: Viking.

Ferguson, N. (2006) *The War of the World: History's Age of Hatred*, London: Penguin.

Figes, O. (2007) T*he Whisperers: Private Life in Stalin's Russia*, New York: Henry Holt and Company.

Fleming, P. (1963) *The Fate of Admiral Kolchak*, New York: Harcourt, Brace and World Inc.

Forstmeier, F. (1964) *Die Räumung des Kuban-Brückenkopfes im Herbst 1943*, Darmstadt.

Gaiduk, I.V. (1996) *The Soviet Union and the Vietnam War*, Chicago: Ivan R. Dee.

Garthoff, R.L. (2001) *A Journey through the Cold War: A Memoir of Containment and Coexistence*, Washington DC: Brookings Institution Press.

Gates, R.M. (1996) *From the Shadows: The Ultimate Insider's Story of Five Presidents and How They Won the Cold War*, New York: Simon & Shuster.

Gellner, E. (1994) *Conditions of Liberty: Civil Society and its Rivals*, London: Hamish Hamilton.

Gessen, M. (2005) *Ester and Ruzya: How my Grandmothers Survived Hitler's War and Stalin's Peace*, New York: Random House.

Girardet, E. (1985) *Afghanistan: The Soviet War*, London: Croom Helm.

Golan, G. (1977) *Yom Kippur and After: The Soviet Union and the Middle East Crisis*, Cambridge: Cambridge University Press.

Gorbachev, M.S. (1997) *Memoirs*, London: Bantam.

Gromyko, A. (1989) *Memoirs: From Stalin to Gorbachev*, London: Arrow Books.

Haldeman, H.R. (1994) *The Haldeman Diaries: Inside the Nixon White House*, New York: G.P. Putnam's Sons.

Hanhimäki, J.M. (2004) *The Flawed Architect: Henry Kissinger and American Foreign Policy*, Oxford: Oxford University Press.

Hanson, E.O. (1987) *The Catholic Church in World Politics*, Princeton NJ: Princeton University Press.

Harrison, M. (1985) *Soviet Planning in Peace and War 1938–1945*, Cambridge: Cambridge University Press.

Haslam, J. (2011) *Russia's Cold War: From the October Revolution to the Fall of the Wall*, New Haven CT: Yale University Press.

Hayter, W. (1966) *The Kremlin and the Embassy*, London: Hodder and Stoughton.

Hayter, W. (1970) *Russia and the World: A Study of Soviet Foreign Policy*, London: Secker & Warburg.

Heikal, M. (1978) *The Sphinx and the Commissar*, New York: Harper & Row.

Hill, F. and Gaddy, C. (2003) *The Siberian Curse: How Communist Planners Left Russia out in the Cold*, Washington DC: Brookings Institution Press.

Holloway, D. (1983) *The Soviet Union and the arms race*, New Haven: Yale University Press.

Holloway, D. (1994) *Stalin and the Bomb: The Soviet Union and Atomic Energy 1939–1956*, New Haven: Yale University Press.

Hosmer, S.T. and Wolfe, T.W. (1982) *Soviet Policy and Practice toward Third World Conflicts*, Lexington, MA: Lexington Books.

Israelyan, V. (2003) *On the Battlefields of the Cold War: A Soviet Ambassador's Confession*, University Park PA: Pennsylvania State University Press.

Josephson, P.R. (2000) *Red Atom: Russia's Nuclear Power Program from Stalin to Today*, New York: W.H. Freeman and Company.

Judt, T. (2010) *Postwar: A History of Europe since 1945*, London: Vintage.

Kemp-Welch, A. (2010) 'Eastern Europe: Stalinism to solidarity', in M.P. Leffler and O.-A. Westad (eds), *The Cambridge History of the Cold War*, Vol. 2: *Crises and Détente*, Cambridge: Cambridge University Press, pp. 219–237.

Kenez, P. (1999) *A History of the Soviet Union from the Beginning to the End*, Cambridge: Cambridge University Press.

Khrushchev, N.S. (1974) *Khrushchev Remembers: The Last Testament*, Boston: Little, Brown & Co.

Kissinger, H. (1979) *White House Years*, Boston: Little, Brown and Company.

Kissinger, H. (1982) *Years of Upheaval*, Boston: Little, Brown and Company.

Kissinger, H. (2003) *Ending the Vietnam War: A History of America's Involvement in and Extrication from the Vietnam War*, New York: Simon & Shuster.

Kissinger, H. (2011) *On China*, New York: Penguin Press.

Klier, J.D. (1992) 'The pogrom paradigm in Russian history', in J.D. Klier and S. Lambroza (eds.) *Pogroms: Anti-Jewish Violence in Modern Russian History*, Cambridge: Cambridge University Press, pp. 13–38.

Kramer, M. (1998) 'The Soviet Union and the 1956 crises in Hungary and Poland: Reassessments and New Findings', *Journal of Contemporary History*, Vol. 33, No. 2, pp. 163–214.

Kramer, M. (2010) 'The Kremlin, the Prague Spring and the Brezhnev Doctrine', in V. Tismaneanu (ed.) *Promises of 1968: Crisis, Illusion, Utopia*, Budapest: Central European Press, pp. 285–370.

Kravchenko, V. (1946) *I Chose Freedom: The Personal and Political Life of a Soviet Official*, New York: Garden City.

Kulchitsky, S. (1996) *Komunizm v Ukraini: Pershe Desyatirycchya (1919–1928) (Communism in Ukraine: First Decade (1919–1928))*, Kiev: Osnovi.

Latham, M.E. (2010) *The Cold War in the Third World, 1963–1975*, Cambridge: Cambridge University Press, pp. 258–280.

Levine, H. (1991) 'Alcohol monopoly to protect the commercial sector of eighteenth-century Poland', in M. Douglas (ed.), *Constructive Drinking*, Cambridge: Cambridge University Press, pp. 250–269.

Little, D. (2010) 'The Cold War in the Middle East: Suez Crisis to Camp David Accords', in M.P. Leffler and O.-A. Westad (eds) *Cambridge History of the Cold War*, Vol. 2: *Crisis and Détente*, Cambridge: Cambridge University Press, pp. 305–326.

Löwe, H.-D. (1993) *The Tsars and the Jews: Reform, Reaction and Anti-Semitism in Imperial Russia 1772–1917*, Chur: Harwood Academic Publishers.

Lukowski, J. (1999) T*he Partitions of Poland: 1772,1793, 1795*, London: Longman.

Lukowski, J. and Zawadzki, H. (2001) *A Concise History of Poland*, Cambridge: Cambridge University Press.

McNamara, R. (1995) *Retrospect: The Tragedy and Lessons of Vietnam*, New York: Random House.

Mandelstam, N. (1976) *Hope Abandoned*, London: Penguin Books.

Mastny, V. (2005) 'The Warsaw Pact as History', in V. Mastny and M. Byrne (eds.) *A Cardboard Castle? An Inside History of the Warsaw Pact 1955–91*, Budapest: Central European University Press, pp. 1–74.

Matthews, O. (2009) S*talin's Children: The Generations of Love and War*, London: Bloomsbury.

Maximov, L. (1976) 'The Helsinki Understandings Must Be Fulfilled', Moscow: *International Affairs* (No. 6).

Medvedev, Z.A. and Medvedev, R.A. (1971) *A Question of Madness*, London: Macmillan.

Melloni, A. (2006) 'La politica internazionale della Santa Sede negli anni Sessanta', in A. Melloni (ed.) *Il Filo Sottile: l'Ostpolitik Vaticana di Agostino Casaroli*, Bologna: Società editrice il Mulino, pp. 3–48.

Mićunović, V. (1980) *Moscow Diary*, London: Chatto & Windus.

Mitchell, N. (2010) 'The Cold War and Jimmy Carter', in M.P. Leffler and O.-A. Westad (eds) *The Cambridge History of the Cold War*, Vol. 3: *Endings*, Cambridge: Cambridge University Press, pp. 66–88.

Müller, R.-D. and Ueberschär, G.R. (1997) *Hitler's War in the East 1941–1945: A Critical Assessment*, Providence RI: Berghahn Books.

Navrátil, J. et al. (eds.) (1998) *The Prague Spring 1968: A National Security Archive Documents Reader*, Budapest: Central European University Press.

Neier, A. (2012) *The International Human Rights Movement: A History*, Princeton NJ: Princeton University Press.

Newman, B. (1952) S*oviet Atomic Spies*, London: Robert Hale.

Ouimet, M.J. (2003) *The Rise and Fall of the Brezhnev Doctrine in Soviet Foreign Policy*, Chapel Hill NC: University of North Carolina Press.

Parrott, B. (1983) *Politics and Technology in the Soviet Union*, Cambridge MA:MIT Press.

Pleshakov, C. (2000) 'Studying Soviet Strategies and Decisionmaking in the Cold War Years', in O.A. Westad, *Reviewing the Cold War: Approaches, Interpretations, Theory*, London: Frank Cass, pp. 232–241.

Reshetar, J.S. (1952) *The Ukrainian Revolution, 1917–1920: A Study in Nationalism*, Princeton NJ: Princeton University Press.

Rhodes, R. (1988) *The Making of the Atomic Bomb*, London: Penguin.

Rhodes, R. (1995) *Dark Sun: The Making of the Hydrogen Bomb*, New York: Simon & Schuster.

Reagan, R. (1990) *An American Life*, London: Hutchinson.

Rubenstein, J. (1980) *Soviet Dissidents: Their Struggle for Human Rights*, Boston: Beacon Press.

Rucker, L. (2011) *Moscow's Surprise: The Soviet-Israeli Alliance of 1947–49*, Cold War International History Project, Working Paper No. 46, Washington DC: Woodrow Wilson International Center for Scholars.

Rusk, D. (1991) *As I Saw It: A Secretary of State's Memoirs*, New York: I.B. Tauris.

Sakharov, A., *Memoirs*, London, Hutchinson, 1990.

Saltoun-Ebin, J. (2012) *The Reagan Files: The Untold Story of Reagan's Top Secret Efforts to Win the Cold War*, Kindle Edition.

Schulzinger, R.D. (2010), 'Détente in the Nixon-Ford years, 1969–1976', in M.P. Leffler and O.-A. Westad (eds) *The Cambridge History of the Cold War*, Vol. 2, *Crises and Détente*, Cambridge: Cambridge University Press, pp. 373–394.

Schwartz, T.A. (2003) *Lyndon Johnson and Europe in the Shadow of Vietnam*, Cambridge MA: Harvard University Press.

Seaton, A. (1972) *The Russo-German War 1941–45*, New York: Praeger.

Sebag-Montefiore, S. (2011) *Jerusalem: The Biography*, London: Weidenfeld & Nicolson.

Sharansky, N. (1988) *Fear No Evil: The Classic Memoir of One Man's Triumph over a Police State*, New York: Public Affairs.

Skidelsky, R. (1995) *The World after Communism*, London: Macmillan.

Snyder, T. (2010) *Bloodlands: Europe between Hitler and Stalin*, London: Bodley Head.

Spechler, D.R. (1982) *Permitted Dissent in the USSR: Novy Mir and the Soviet Regime*, New York: Praeger.

Stalin, J.V. (1947) *Problems of Leninism*, Moscow: Foreign Languages Publishing House.

Subtelny, O. (1988) *Ukraine: A History*, Toronto: University of Toronto Press.

Suri, J. (2006) 'The promise and failure of "Developed Socialism": The Soviet "Thaw" and the Crucible of the Prague Spring 1964–1972', *Contemporary European History*, Vol.15, No. 2., pp. 133–158.

Tareke, G. (2000) The Ethiopia-Somali War of 1977 Revisited, *International Journal of African Historical Studies*, pp. 640–665.

Tarsis, V. (1965) *Ward No. 7*, London: Collins and Harvill Press.

Taubman, W. (2003) *Khrushchev: The Man and his Era*, London and New York, Simon & Shuster.

Thomas, D.C. (2001) *The Helsinki Effect: International Norms, Human Rights, and the Demise of Communism*, Princeton NJ: Princeton University Press.

van Velsen, J. (1964) *The Politics of Kinship*, Manchester: Manchester University Press.

Vance, C. (1983) *Hard Choices: Critical Years in America's Foreign Policy*, New York: Simon and Schuster.

Volkov, S. (1979) *Testimony: The Memoirs of Dmitri Shostakovich*, New York: Harper and Rowe.

Walker, M. (1996) *The Cold War: A History*, New York: Henry Holt.

Wandycz, P. (1994) 'Adam Rapacki and the Search for European Security', in G.A. Craig and F.L. Loewenheim (eds.) *The Diplomats, 1939–1979*, Princeton NJ: Princeton University Press, pp. 289–347.

Weinberg, G.L. (1994) *A World at Arms: A Global History of World War II*, Cambridge: Cambridge University Press.

Westad, O.A. (2000) *Reviewing the Cold War: Approaches, Interpretations, Theory*, London: Frank Cass.

Wheatcroft, G. (2012) *Can They Ever Make a Deal*, New York Review of Books, 5 April.

Yekelchyk, S. (2007) *Ukraine: Birth of a Modern Nation*, Oxford: Oxford University Press.

Zaloga, S.J. (2002) *The Kremlin's Nuclear Sword: The Rise and Fall of Russia's Strategic Nuclear Forces 1945–2000*, Washington: Smithsonian Institution Press.

Zemtsov, I. (1989) *Chernenko: the Last Bolshevik: the Soviet Union on the Eve of Perestroika*, New Brunswick (NJ) and Oxford: Transaction Publishers.

Zubok, V.M. (2009) *A Failed Empire: the Soviet Union in the Cold War from Stalin to Gorbachev*, Chapel Hill: University of North Carolina Press.

Index

Adenauer, Konrad 62–3, 126, 150, 157
Addis Abeba 163, 165: Soviet Embassy 163, 166
Afghanistan: Peace Corps withdrawn 191; Peoples Democratic Republic of Afghanistan (PDRA) 190; point of no return 195; refugees 192; Soviet aid 190; Soviet invasion 127, 142, 144, 154, 186, 190, 192, 207, 210; Soviet withdrawal 194; Treaty of Friendship, Good-Neighbourliness and Cooperation 191; *see also* mujahidin; *Saur* ('April') revolution
Afghanistan People's Democratic Party (APDP) 190–2: *Khalq* faction 190–2; *Parcham* faction 190–2
Africa 159–70: World War II 161
African National Congress 169
aggiornamento 129
agriculture 35–6: collectivization 27; *see also* kolkhoz
Akhmatova, Anna 107
Albania 19, 43, 62, 121; China alliance 122
alcohol 13
Alexander I, Tsar 9
Alexander II, Tsar 9, 13, 14: assassination 14
Alexander III Tsar 14
Alexeyev, Alexander 73
Algeria 92, 162, 170–1, 177, 183
Algiers 178
All-Russia Constituent Assembly 16
Allen, Richard 145
aluminium 45
Alves, Nito 169
Amalrik, Andrei 111
American Relief Administration 23

Amin, Hafizullah 190–1: KGB agent 194; murder 192, 194
ancien regime 6
Andropov, Yuri 84–5, 110, 113, 117, 123, 132, 193–4: CPSU First Secretary 84, 211
Andrusovo: Treaty 17
Angola 92, 127, 157, 159–60, 166–7, 193, 207: Cuban intervention 164–9
Anschluss (1938) 43
anti-ballistic missiles (ABM) 110, 137–8; treaty 140–1
Apollo Space Programme 93, 95: Apollo 8; Apollo 11 (first on moon 95, 138)
apparat 79–81
apparatchik 29, 79–80, 207, 209
Arab League 164
Arab Socialist Union 178
Arab world 48, 133, 164, 170–84: destabilization 175
Arabia 170
Arafat, Yasser 181–2: Moscow welcome 182
Arbatov, Georgy 24
Arbenz, Jacobo 157
Arctic Sea 26
armaments 11, 14, 35: export 90, 92, 133, 184, 199; parity 133
Armenia 20
armistice, *see* Brest-Litovsk
'arms race' 64, 207
Asia Development Bank 189
Assad, Hafez 181–3
Aswan dam 176–7
atomic bomb 45: Chinese 90; Soviet 47
'atoms for peace program' (US) 96
Australia 187
Austria 4, 6, 17, 18, 19, 41, 43, 62
Awami League 188–9

232   *Index*